Living Like a Tudor

Living Like a Tudor

a Tudor

WOODSMOKE & SAGE:
A SENSORY JOURNEY THROUGH
TUDOR ENGLAND

Amy Licence

PEGASUS BOOKS
NEW YORK LONDON

LIVING LIKE A TUDOR

Pegasus Books, Ltd.
148 West 37th Street, 13th Floor
New York, NY 10018

ISBN: 978-1-64313-815-2

10 9 8 7 6 5 4 3 2 1

Printed in the United States of America
Distributed by Simon & Schuster
www.pegasusbooks.com

Living Like a Tudor

CONTENTS

PART II: SMELL

PART III: SOUND

PART IV: TASTE

PART V: TOUCH

INTRODUCTION

Woodsmoke and sage, peacocks and cinnamon, falcons and linen.

These were the textures of the Tudor world, woven through gowns, served up at feasts, lingering in the air. Life is always a tactile experience and no matter what 'higher' ideologies of politics, religion or science were occupying the minds of our ancestors, daily life was sustained by the physical fabric of environment, both immediate and distant. The Tudors reached towards abstract concepts standing on the solid foundations of empiricism, and the world they created both reflected and informed their understanding of self.

As a 12-year-old girl devouring an illustrated history of the past, I had something of an epiphany. Here was a book that gave serious attention to cooking in the Tudor kitchen, the games children played, what herbs were used to make perfume, what underwear they wore: all the things I assumed were unworthy of being a proper subject of study. It was a revelation. History was suddenly a tactile experience, relatable to mine. I could see my own morning – breakfast, dressing, my walk to school, friends in the playground, queuing at the KitKat machine – in a new light. These were points on a graph that might have shifted slightly, but they were consistent with the journey of human experience, just as a 12-year-old girl in 1485, or 1585, would have woken, eaten, dressed, interacted, sought a treat.

Only in recent years has the history of material culture been taken seriously. What people ate, or wore, or how they decorated their houses, was too often dismissed as a frippery, mere window dressing or, even worse, vulgar, while the 'proper' academic study continued elsewhere. Domestic, daily and 'trivial' aspects of life were frequently the sphere of marginalised figures such as women, children, servants and minorities. It was almost inconceivable that kings might eat and use the toilet, too. Then, a number of factors created a shift in the popular imagination: interest in archaeology and regular local digs; the rise of re-enactment and reconstruction, with the resulting hands-on experience which has created a new body of knowledge; the publication of books dealing with everyday life and the proliferation of accessible TV programmes bringing dead people's secrets into our homes.

Thankfully, a considerable reassessment of what constitutes history has resulted in a shift in perspective to encompass all aspects of life in the past. No details are off the table, from sexuality and intimate health, to dirty linen and toilet habits. The human experience cannot be understood in its entirety while the daily and mundane are excluded: the shoe that pinches on our walk, the rumbling tummy that prevents us from concentrating, the accidental downpour that soaks us on the way home. This is life. If we understand this, we understand that, like us, the Tudors were also continually experiencing their own physicality, as the basal rate from which every other aspect of life stemmed.

If nothing else, the study of the material world was a study of the human condition, but, more than this, it was literally and metaphorically the building bricks the Tudors used to decode the meaning of existence. It was by cutting up fruit, or human organs, or peering at flasks of urine that doctors formulated theories about the workings of the body. Through the style of a gown or the ornamentation upon a cap a man's social standing was identified, and he might be rejected, or advanced, accordingly. As many Tudor thinkers admitted, there was much in their world that lay beyond the scope of their understanding and the five senses were essential to deconstructing meaning and self-fashioning.

This book is not just a study in material culture, it is a celebration of the experience of being alive in Tudor times. Although significantly more evidence survives for the lives of the upper classes, I have sought out material relating to the lower and middle classes as much as possible, and the lives of 'ordinary' Tudors to contrast with the elite. The Tudors were a very visually oriented culture, so this book's section on Sight is, of necessity, the largest, although it is nowhere near as large as it could have been, while the delicate traces of lost smells and sounds have been more elusive to track down. Above all, this book hopes to capture a different aspect of the enduring appeal of the Tudors and explore the physicality of life in the past. It is a time-travel experience on the page, a celebration of what material culture can offer and a box of delights for lovers of the Tudor years.

Amy Licence
Canterbury

PART I

SIGHT

PEN AND BRUSH

⚜ *THE AMBASSADORS* ⚜

In 1533, the German artist Hans Holbein completed a new work, painted in oil and tempera, upon oak boards cut from English woods. In rich tones of green and red, black and gold, he portrayed two young men, both foreigners in London like himself. They were the 29-year-old Jean de Dinteville, ambassador of Francis I of France, and the 25-year-old Georges de Selve, soon to be Bishop of Lavaur, whose ages are inscribed upon the ambassador's dagger and on the page end of the bishop's book respectively. They gaze directly back at the viewer with a mixture of pride and patience, meeting our eyes at a time when the sitters of most court portraits, even members of the royal family, including the king and queen, are portrayed in demure semi-profile. These men are bold. They are cultured and fashionable. They have money. They want you to know it.

Dinteville, who commissioned the work, stands on the left, dressed in the most elegant outfit for an ambassador: a black velvet doublet and pink silk shirt, slashed with white at the chest and wrists. Over it, he wears a heavy coat with puffed sleeves, lined with lynx fur, and the fashionable round-toed shoes of the Tudor court. De Selve's colouring is more modest, his long brown gown with fur lining covering a plain black garment and white collar beneath, more suitable to his religious calling. He wields his gloves in his right hand and wears the trademark soft, black Canterbury cap of Catholicism, with its square corners.

Together, these two young men have come to be known to history as *The Ambassadors*. For years, they hung in Dinteville's chateau in the village of Polisy, about 125 miles south of Paris, but now they are seen daily by thousands of visitors to London's National Gallery. And they offer the modern viewer a glimpse into the crucial theme of sight and perception in the Tudor world.

Dinteville and de Selve are the main dishes in a Tudor visual feast. As part of a carefully composed still life, they lean upon a two-shelved unit, over which is draped an expensive oriental tapestry, a status symbol more commonly found over tables than underfoot. Although the centres of the European tapestry market were in the Netherlands and Arras, this piece appears to have come from a more exotic Turkish location. Items on the top shelf represent man's study of the heavens: a celestial globe painted with the constellations; a sundial and other astrological instruments used to measure time and space; a quadrant, a shepherd's dial and a torquetum, which was a sort of prototype analogue computer.

The shelf below displays a collection of earthly pleasures: a terrestrial globe, a pair of flutes, lute, compass, a book of arithmetic and a Lutheran psalm book, representing the new religious influences that the Catholic de Selve continued to resist. Further subtle references are made to the Reformation through the prominence of the Latin word *dividirt*, or 'let division be made', and the broken lute string of ecclesiastical disharmony.

The top left-hand corner contains a crucifix, partially concealed behind the heavy green backdrop, and scholarly analysis of the various instruments indicates a date of 11 April, or Good Friday, 1533.[1] The ensemble stands upon a polished marble floor, taken from the Cosmati design in the sanctuary at Westminster Abbey, of inlaid coloured stones in geometric shapes. One of the floor's original inscriptions, created in the year 1268, stated that the 'spherical globe here shows the archetypal macrocosm' with the four elements of the world represented in the design, which were believed to also govern the human body, or world, in microcosm. The ambassadors want us to know they are standing at the cutting edge of technology, in a rapidly changing world.

But the picture's 'trick' is hidden. To the casual observer, even one standing in awe before the work, the most famous detail of *The Ambassadors* might pass completely unnoticed. Nestled in the centre at the bottom, between the two men's feet, sits an anamorphic skull, distorted in paint so that it leaps into perspective only when the viewer looks at the canvas from a certain angle. Visitors to the National Gallery are directed to a vantage spot marked on the floor, where the image suddenly jumps into life. This morbid shock was quite deliberate, and continues to surprise twenty-first-century observers, but it was somewhat unusual for Holbein, who is likely to have been acting on the instructions of the sitters.

Dinteville chose the term 'memento mori' as his personal motto, a reminder of human mortality, which was a frequent motif in medieval and Tudor culture. This theme is also represented in the brooch he wears upon his cap, featuring a grey skull on a gold surround. The skull on the floor symbolises the inevitability of death and the spiritual life, in contrast with the material and temporal luxuries on display. Its deceptive perspective reminds us that death is always present, waiting to claim us, even when we cannot see it, but the element of surprise is paradoxically playful and macabre.

More sinister, perhaps, is the implied limitation of human perception, a sobering and humbling observation despite all the science and learning displayed in the picture. Not even the sophisticated instruments of measurement, of which the ambassadors appear so proud, can predict the approach of death. Seen and unseen, the memento mori is, both of the picture and external to it, a *trompe l'oeil* whose very skill exposes the complex message of mortal strength and weakness. And yet, perhaps, it is the act of painting, art itself, or artifice, which has the final word. For while the two young men are dead and buried, claimed by the Grim Reaper almost five centuries ago, they still stand staring out at us today – colourful, larger than life, in the pink of health.

The Ambassadors also contains a number of contrasts: macrocosm and microcosm, heaven and earth, world and man. And thus, it helps establish a sense of scale in the Tudor aesthetic – the individual as a cog in the wheel of God's plan. By surrounding Dinteville and de Selve with the accoutrements of Humanist and Reformation learning, the artist identifies them, by association, as being contextual with global exploration, science and the arts, social hierarchies and the unfolding crisis in the English Church. In commissioning the details of this work, the ambassadors have selected favoured objects as a cultural shorthand, a cherry-picked collage of their specific, Humanist world. Posing amid these symbols, they offer their carefully crafted identities, in microcosm, to the transformative process of paint. Their chosen moment is given a permanence by the artist's brush, which had the ability to outlive old age, changing fortunes and death, so long as the work survived. The act of painting, and the physical existence of the work itself, gives them an empirical position within an aspirational social framework.

Holbein's masterpiece was an intellectual exercise as well as an aesthetic one. The image is crammed full of visual clues for his cultured contemporaries to decode, a complex and detailed message that requires sufficient learning to unpack. It was designed to appeal to an elite, but its majestic impact would not have been lost on any strata of society, should they have had access to view it.

A parallel experience for those lower down the social scale, the majority of whom were illiterate, could have been the walls and windows of colourful pre-Reformation ecclesiastical art. Depicting saints and sinners, the performance of miracles and damnation in hell, these were plastered above their heads on an immense scale whenever they went to pray, reinforced by the deliberate contrast made of light and darkness, of flickering candles in the gloom.

The Tudors were a highly visual culture and the 'look' of things mattered to them. This was true right through the social spectrum, from the poor woman's pleasure in receiving the bequest of a new gown in a friend's will, to Elizabeth I's cloak embroidered all over with eyes and ears, implying that she saw and heard everything. That large percentage of society who could not read were far from being visually illiterate.

The Tudor elite used heraldic devices, badges and liveries as indicative of their lands and lineage: animals and flowers, symbols that were instantly recognisable. However, a rise in mercantilism and an increased social mobility by meritocracy allowed the middle classes to adopt their own series of visual codes. Everything that could be seen, from the rings upon a finger to the shape of a shoe, were coded references to social hierarchy.

In such an aspirational culture, clothing increasingly replaced birth as the first indicator of personal identity, allowing for acts of sartorial stealth and deception like never before. The Tudor man or woman would attempt to wear and display the accoutrements of a higher social stratum, as a means to achieving it. Size and quantity mattered. Location mattered. Subject to strict hierarchies, you would judge, and be judged, by the material self you projected.

The Ambassadors offers a useful entry point to the complicated material culture of the sixteenth-century world. The deliberate way in which it was planned, composed and executed reveals the centrality of personal status to the Tudors. Holbein demonstrates this through his presentation of the complex identities of Dinteville and de Selve, in terms of clothing and appearance, posture and positioning, and the careful, deliberate arrangement of symbolic items in location. Perhaps the portrait itself is the only answer to the memento mori it contains. It was Holbein's artistic vision which conferred immortality upon its subjects, whose names and faces could otherwise have been footnotes in history.

⚜ STRUTTING KINGS ⚜

In 1537, Henry VIII commissioned the first full-length portrait of an English ruler. Himself. Yet the Whitehall mural, probably painted onto the wall of the king's privy chamber, shows not just one but four monarchs, summoned to reflect Henry's new purpose and validate his dynasty. Henry's parents, Henry VII and Elizabeth of York, are resurrected to stand on a step at the back, while Henry and his third wife, Jane Seymour, pose in front of them, either side of a plinth draped with carpets, inside an ornately decorated room in the Renaissance style.

The two women stand demurely with clasped hands, looking off into the distance, but the contrasting men's positions echo the plinth's inscription that while Henry VII was a great king, Henry VIII was an even greater one. Nowhere is this clearer than in Holbein's depiction of his employer. The stance he chose has become iconic, reproduced worldwide, and is instantly recognisable. Feet wide apart, Henry VIII faces the viewer squarely, one fist on his hip, with padded shoulders and puffed sleeves, prominent calves and codpiece, dagger pointing towards the Latin text. The image presents the exaggerated masculinity of a king anticipating fatherhood and has become the most enduring and recognisable visual shorthand for Tudor majesty, just as it was intended to. In contrast, a tired-looking Henry VII rests upon the plinth, swathed in loose clothing, with sloping shoulders, although his direct gaze speaks of his quiet authority.

The Whitehall mural is the most recognisable piece of propaganda surviving from the Tudor era. It conveys the aspirations of a man who was only the dynasty's second king and had yet to sire a legitimate son. Depicting himself as the apogee of Renaissance masculinity, Henry created a larger-than-life idealised doppelgänger, whose virility was so demonstrable that it obviated any doubt. In the wake of the Anne Boleyn scandal of 1536, in which the king's sexual performance was questioned, and following the miscarriages and stillbirths of his former wives Catherine and Anne, the painted Henry shook off any responsibility for the reproductive shortcomings of his real-life counterpart.

In 1546, Henry commissioned two portraits to commemorate the investiture of his only surviving son and heir, Edward, as Prince of Wales. The first was finished that same year by the newly employed Flemish artist, William Scrots. It depicts the 9-year-old boy as a royal icon, his outline instantly recognisable, as is the work's debt to Holbein's Whitehall mural.

Edward echoes his father's stance but in reverse, a mirror image, facing the left where Henry faced the right, with all the connotations of succession this suggests. The boy stands with feet wide apart, his right hand clasping a dagger, his left tucked into his belt. His clothing exaggerates his silhouette, literally taking up more space than he needs, as a show of importance. The puffed doublet has gold embroidery, with a high collar, and the red coat is lined with lynx or ermine, richly decorated with gold, through which his slashed sleeves show. He wears white hose, displaying his calves, garters, white square-toed shoes and the gold chain of the Great George, as a Knight of the Order of the Garter. Upon his head sits a jaunty black cap with gold ties and a white feather, the type of cap likely to have inspired the 1565 *Pleasant Dialogue*. The effect is that of a mini Henry.

Where Henry used an exaggerated body shape to emphasise his virility, the same technique serves a dual purpose for a boy making the transition to kingship. By echoing the 1537 mural, the pose reminds its viewers of his father's reputation, reinforcing Edward as the true heir of the Tudor legacy.

In addition, though, the distorted shoulders, padding and stance send a message of health and strength in a child who had frequently suffered periods of illness. The Italian physician Girolamo Cardano mentioned Edward's small stature and pale face, while the Imperial ambassador commented on his posture, remarking that his right shoulder was higher than his left.[1]

With Henry in rapid decline, and Edward's succession imminent, the boy-king needed to inspire confidence in his ability to rule. For the Tudors, this was correlative with physical well-being. Dressing Edward up and painting him in rude health was one way of demonstrating his fitness to rule, but it was also an act of enshrining an idealised version, a simulacrum, of the frail boy.

First identified in the sixteenth century, the concept of simulacra sprang from perfected artistic representations of individuals, particularly classical gods, concurrent with the developing cult of semi-deifying monarchs in portraiture. The portraits were designed to compel awe and allegiance to the son of the all-powerful Henry VIII and convince Edward's subjects to obedience.

The contrasting settings of the two portraits capture a crucial moment of transition. The Scrots painting places Edward in, or near, Hunsdon House, in Hertfordshire, where he was resident between May and July 1546. The entire house is visible at a distance outside the window, viewed from the interior in which Edward stands. Perhaps he is in a related property on the Hunsdon estate or a hunting lodge. Or else the portrait contains a conceit, simultaneously depicting both the interior and exterior of the house. His room is decorated with carved Renaissance figures and a marble pillar which bears an inscription alluding to the Roman emperor, Mark Antony.

It is unclear where the second portrait of Edward is set. Deriving from the workshop of Master John, and probably intended as a copy of Scrots, it was not completed at the time of Henry's death in January 1547. Its subject started out as a prince, then became a king, and these changes are visible in the work. The new Edward VI stands inside an even more lavish room – a room fit for a king. It contains a large chair of estate with gold claw feet clasping gold balls, dressed in blue velvet, with fringe and tassels. Behind it, the bright golden cloth of estate rises up, framing the young king.

Modern X-ray analysis of the panel indicates that originally two windows were planned to feature on either side of the chair, but only one appears in the finished work. There is no view, though, no vista of a distant palace: kingship has come to Edward, rather than him looking upon it from afar. Instead, the window is a simple blue-grey lattice panel, which brings to mind the outside world but is devoid of detail. It is a blank canvas upon which Edward might paint his life and reign, the *tabula rasa* known to the Tudors from Avicenna, Aquinas and the late-fifteenth-century Sir John Fortescue. Over the place originally intended for the left-hand window, a classical pillar has been inserted, decorated with the royal coat of arms. Edward's inheritance has been realised.

✳

Who, exactly, were these paintings intended to impress? If, as it is believed, the Whitehall mural was painted on the wall of Henry's privy chamber, its audience was a favoured elite of rich and powerful courtiers. Servants, chamberers and grooms would have passed before it, but the majority of Henry's subjects would never have seen it, nor were they intended to. The people outside the palace weren't the kingmakers. Power rested in the hands of a small percentage of leading nobles, whose support could make or break a monarch, particularly at moments of transition.

Such was the importance of loyalty and respect in the privy chamber that it had been reformed by the Eltham Ordinances of 1526, which insisted upon the discretion of those granted access. It was precisely in such close proximity to the king that the most dangerous plots could be hatched, and Henry, in dressing, sleeping and washing, was at his most vulnerable. His privileged circle saw these works because they were its target audience; they served as both memorial and warning, glorification and instruction. The painted eyes of Henry VIII and his son would watch over their court, as rulers of the earthly realm, and from the afterlife.

There was something superstitious, almost magical, about the king's portrait. It was intended to stand in for his presence, and be revered, just as the king would be. Thus, it became a secular icon. The Ordinances stated that 'the King being absent ... they shall ... give their continual and diligent attendance in the said chamber',[2] as if the image was of near equivalent worth to the actual flesh and blood of the king himself.

By dictating this response, Henry added a symbolic value to his portrait, by equating reality with the depiction of reality. Through a mimetic process, the painting was charged with royal power, just as pre-Reformation saints' icons were venerated as a conduit to the Divine.

It was no coincidence either that this royal deification in paint was developing concurrently with the closure of the monasteries and destruction of saints' shrines. The religious sanctum centred upon the holy statue or relic was being replaced by that in the king's inner rooms. In addition, this careful placement of royal imagery served to reinforce the hierarchy, by defining who was considered worthy of access to the image, whose rank allowed them to see the king in paint. The general public, who flocked to pre-Reformation pilgrimage sites, were excluded from viewing these new icons. The manipulation of sight, through the placement of royal images and the control of their audience, was another means by which the Tudor dynasty promoted their power.

Ultimately, though, such images were too powerful to not be utilised elsewhere. Copies were made and displayed by those seeking royal favour, as if they might absorb some of their iconic power. This was made possible due to new templates of the king's image being circulated among members of the Worshipful Company of Painters and Stainers, who regulated artists' workshops and apprenticeships.

John Bettes, an English-born disciple of Holbein, was a member of this guild and was first recorded working at Henry's court in 1531, so it is likely that he was the 'Master John' traditionally ascribed to the second portrait of Edward. Yet Bettes was a rarity, as in the same year, Sir Thomas Elyot commented upon the paucity of good artists England produced, as 'if we will have anything painted, carved or embroidered', we must 'abandon our own countrymen and resort unto strangers'.

Many of the most famous artists working in England during the Tudor dynasty were Flemish: Hans Holbein, William Scrots, Marcus Gheeraerts, Lucas and Susannah Horenbout, Levina Teerlinc, Hans Eworth, Anthonis Mor and Steven van der Meulen. As early as 1491, the 'wardens and other good men of the Art or occupation of payntours' came before the Mayor of London 'complaining of the members of the crafts becoming impoverished by the influx of foreyns' and asked that no freeman 'henceforth employ a foreigner when he can get a freeman equally capable and as good cheap'.[3] The monarch was above the rules, though. It is an irony that the archetypal images of Tudor monarchy, of the ruling English elite, were fashioned by foreigners.

❦ PORTRAITS IN COURTSHIP ❧

Shakespeare's Sonnet 24 claims that love enters through the eyes. In this case, they record an internal image of the beloved, for which the lover's body acts as the frame:

> Mine eye hath played the painter and hath steeled,
> Thy beauty's form in table of my heart;
> My body is the frame wherein 'tis held,
> And perspective that is best painter's art.
> For through the painter must you see his skill,
> To find where your true image pictured lies.

For those hoping to marry in the sixteenth century, first appearances mattered.

Love and courtship were undertaken in the Tudor world for a host of reasons, from the mercenary to the romantic. Advantageous marriage was the ultimate goal, but romance could derail even the most lucrative negotiations, as the precedent set by Edward IV established. When it came to the wooing of kings and queens, who frequently sought spouses outside their realms, the exchange of portraits might be the only opportunity to see one's bride or groom before the ceremony. For all the value they placed on breeding, diplomacy and fortunes, the Tudors still valued a pretty face. The appearance of good health and regular features also suggested the ability to bear healthy sons.

In 1505, when he was seeking a new wife, Henry VII set out a list of twenty-four intimate questions for his ambassadors visiting Joanna of Aragon, dowager Queen of Naples, enquiring about her complexion, the colour of her hair, the size and shape of her features, whether hair grew on her top lip, the sweetness of her breath, her stature and bodily features and her bodily smell.[1] This was no mere match of diplomatic advantage to Henry. What Joanna looked like really mattered to him. He wanted a woman he would find physically attractive and whose appearance would complement his dignity and position. To be certain, he also requested that a painting be made of her, surreptitiously, so as to be as accurate as possible and avoid the need for diplomatic flattery, but if this portrait was created, it no longer survives:

I humbly entreat you, if it be possible, and if it should not be considered an improper thing, that you would please to send me, as quickly as may be, a picture of the said Queen, portraying her figure and the features of her face, painted on canvas, and put in a case. Let this, moreover, be done very secretly, and the picture sent to me by your Highnesses, without the Queen of Naples, or her Serene Highness, the Queen her mother, knowing or suspecting anything about it. I say and ask this because the King greatly desires it, if I may judge by the very particular questions he asked respecting the Queen.[2]

By the late 1530s, Henry VIII was seeking a fourth wife after the death of Jane Seymour in childbirth. First, he dispatched Jean Mewtas to France to paint Mary of Guise, but upon being told she was unavailable, sought permission instead to paint Louise and Renée of Guise and Anne of Lorraine. Unwilling to trust the evidence of paint, Henry suggested meeting the women in Calais, but this was ridiculed by Francis I, who joked that Henry wanted them to trot before him in display, like horses.

Early in 1538, Hans Holbein was sent to Brussels to obtain a likeness of Christina, the young, widowed Duchess of Milan, reputed to be one of the most beautiful women in the world. Holbein produced a sketch of Christina in her mourning clothes in the space of three hours, between one and four on the afternoon of 12 March. He then turned this into one of the most stunning of all sixteenth-century portraits. Wearing a long black robe with puffed sleeves, lined with brown fur, a black dress with hints of white at collar and sleeves, and a black cap, not even the simplicity of her clothing or the plain blue background can detract from the duchess's charms.

Henry was so impressed that he was 'in better humour than ever ... making musicians play on their instruments all day long'.[3] However, Christina was not keen to be the English king's next bride, commenting sharply that if she had two heads, she would not mind putting one of them at Henry's disposal.

In the summer of 1539, undaunted by these rejections, Henry was considering a match with a German princess. Holbein travelled with the English ambassadors to Duren in June for an audience with the Duke and Duchess of Cleves, to create a likeness of their two unmarried daughters, Anna and Amalia. A sketch of Amalia shows a young woman with dark hair and eyes, regular facial features, strong cheekbones and firm chin, but it was the elder, Anne, whose image was worked into a full painting, begun on parchment and later mounted on canvas.

Henry's negative reaction to Anne's appearance on meeting her is so well documented that analysing the portrait out of context is difficult. Yet the notion that Holbein deliberately flattered Anne, so often used to explain Henry's disappointment, is belied by the universal praise of her person by other contemporaries. Henry never blamed Holbein's representation, nor questioned the truthfulness of his ambassadors who described her as attractive, or the painting itself, which was considered a 'very lively', or realistic, depiction.

Seen in three-quarter length, Anne wears the Germanic fashions of the 1530s, a red and gold dress decorated with pearls, with a nipped-in waist and long, trailing sleeves. Her features are even, her eyes hooded and her hair scraped back under a gold headdress. She wears two gold chains, several rings and a cross in black and gold. No doubt she chose her clothes carefully to represent the latest fashions at her parents' court and to demonstrate their good taste and wealth. It just wasn't English taste.

The portrait arrived in England in August 1540, followed by the Duke of Cleves' ambassadors in September, with the marriage contract concluded early in October. Soon afterwards, she began the journey to Henry's side.

Henry's dislike of Anne was a visceral, personal reaction, but it was as much a cultural construct as a response to her face and body. Unfortunately for Anne, beauty resided in the eye of a king with a very specific Anglo-French aesthetic. French ambassador Marillac commented that the German entourage's clothing was sufficient for them to be labelled as ugly, but this was not an unsurmountable object and the new queen's clothing was quickly exchanged for something considered more attractive in a tent at Greenwich. When she appeared in English clothes with a French hood, contemporary chronicler Hall commented that it 'so set forth her beauty and good visage that every creature rejoiced to behold her'.[4] But not Henry.

Fashionable presentation had influence, and could be transformative, but Anne's anglicising makeover came a few days too late. She was already doomed, because she had failed to recognise Henry when he surprised her unannounced, and in disguise, at Rochester Castle.

Anne had pulled away when the king broke etiquette by trying to take
her in his arms and kiss her, without knowing who he was. Hoping
she would understand the sophisticated rules of the game of disguise,
Henry's plan had been scuppered by Anne's surface reading of his costume. She had taken his external appearance literally. Clothes made
the man, and the bride's rejection of a man in a hooded gown as beneath
her in status dealt an irrevocable blow to Henry's masculine pride.

When Mary I sat for her portrait by Antonis Mor in 1554, she was
putting her best side forward in a last-ditch attempt at marriage. Mor
was sent to England to capture her likeness on the orders of Emperor
Charles V, the father of her intended husband, Philip of Spain. At 37 to
Philip's 26, Mary had waited a long time for queenship and marriage
and was past the age at which some of her contemporaries had reached
the menopause or even become grandparents. By sixteenth-century
terms she was not attractive, but what she had to offer, and what she
needed to represent, was England. And England was attractive.

Sitting for her portrait, Mary strove to represent the best embodi-
ment of her country that she could manage, and it was on those terms
that she succeeded. Seated in an embroidered, red velvet chair within
a shadowy interior in which only a classical pillar is discernible, Mary
presents a muted, understated contrast to the vision of royalty offered
by her brother and father. The message conveyed is one of refine-
ment and quality, rather than the gaudy display and colours of the
men's attire. Mary's plain, dark purple gown reveals just enough of her
embroidered silver kirtle and sleeves to be suggestive of riches within
and, apart from the central pendant, a gift from Philip, her jewellery
is understated.

The portrait conforms to betrothal conventions with the inclusion
of a single flower, held by Mary between finger and thumb of her right
hand, while gloves rest in her left. Traditionally, this was a red carnation, but the detail suggests it may have been substituted, in this case,
for a rose, her national symbol.

Philip agreed to marry Mary, meeting her in person a few days
before their Winchester-based ceremony in July 1554, but it was not
for her personal charms. As a Spanish aide confessed, 'The marriage
was concluded for no fleshly consideration, but in order to remedy

the disorders of this kingdom and preserve the Low Countries.'[5]
Philip had accepted England's queen rather than Mary for her
own merits.

Tudors from the middle ranks of society also commissioned courtship
portraits. In the later 1530s, Simon George, a young nobleman from
Quocoute in Cornwall, posed for Holbein with explicitly romantic
iconography. Dressed in extravagant fabrics with his shirt collar open,
he holds up a red carnation and a badge upon his beret features Leda
and the swan, a seduction scene that points to his motivation.

As a fashionable youth and a minor official at court, George chose
to be depicted in the Italian-style Tondo, a round portrait 30cm in
diameter, too large for jewellery and too small to make an impact
when hung upon a wall. It was just the right size, though, for a woman
to carry about with her like a personal icon and constant reminder
of her betrothed's ardour. George married Thomasine, daughter of
Richard Lanyon, from another old Cornish family.

The stunning 1540 miniature of Jane Small, née Pemberton, the
wife of a London merchant, represents a rare face from outside the
world of the court. Born to a Northamptonshire gentleman, Jane
married into the cloth trade in her early twenties, an event which the
painting may have been commissioned to celebrate. Her simplicity
of dress reflects her status, being barred by the sumptuary laws
from wearing certain fabrics and colours, even though her future
husband may have traded in them. The black and white dress boasts
a fashionable blackwork collar and the obligatory red carnation is
tucked into her bosom. Her eyes are cast down and her expression
sits midway between demureness and concern. Yet she also has a few
flourishes of luxury, a fine linen hood, frilled cuffs and gold rings. In
all, it is a human, touching image of a young woman outside royal
circles on the verge of a new life in London.

❦ THE PORTRAIT ELITE ❦

Every Tudor Tom, Dick and Harry wanted their portrait painted, but not many of them could afford it. Holbein, Scrots and Gheeraerts were well out of most people's price range but the middle classes might pay an apprentice artist from one of the London workshops to recreate their likeness. Hung in hallways and parlours or over the dining table, they would impress friends, relatives and visitors, but also conferred a fleeting permanence upon their subjects in a world where fortune, success, health, even life, were changeable factors. A portrait was a way of saying, 'I have arrived, if only for today'.

Few of these portraits have survived. Fire, flood, damp, carelessness and changing fortune made them only as durable as the paper, wood or canvas upon which they were painted. Holbein's sketchbook shows many more images than the total number of completed works known today. The features of men and women from the Tudor court gaze back from his pages, part formed, their eyes and headwear picked out in sharp detail, concealing a smile or a knowing expression, while their limbs and extremities fade into sketchy nothing.

There was also a direct correlation between the fickleness of power, and the survival of portraits. Perhaps the most obvious case is that of Anne Boleyn, who was sketched by Holbein and must have been the subject of many paintings during her decade at Henry's side. However, the lack of any completed works in existence today, and the hurried erasure of the initials H and A, carved into the stone of royal architecture with an intended permanence in the late 1520s, suggests a wide-scale process of destruction of her image in the wake of her fall. As Henry snuffed out Anne's life, so he removed any reminders of her.

Painting in Henry VIII's reign was dominated by Hans Holbein the Younger, a German who came to England on the recommendation of the Humanist scholar, Erasmus. During his first visit in 1526–27, a number of Henry VIII's courtiers sat for him against vivid blue-green backgrounds, often framed by a green curtain, pillar or natural elements like leafy branches. This highly stylised, Mannerist form of posing, blends elements from the indoor and outdoor, with bright, almost jewel-like colours, producing works that place a realistic portrait over an almost stained-glass or iconic backdrop.

Sir Henry Guildford, one of the king's closest friends, looks off to the right-hand side in a patterned gold doublet under a brown furred coat and wearing the Great George of the Order of the Garter. Facing to the left, in anticipation of her image being hung beside that of her husband, is Henry's wife, the voluptuous Lady Mary Guildford, who stares directly at the viewer while holding a book beside an ornate Renaissance pillar. Her finished portrait gives her the air of being somewhat formidable, but another of Holbein's preparatory sketches captures her laughing, showing a different side to her entirely.

Assuming the same position as Henry Guildford, with the green leaves behind, Anne Lovell was painted in a work known as *The Lady with a Squirrel and Starling*. Her black and white dress is simple and modest, without adornment, and her white headdress and shawl speak of modesty. These early works combine a formal, stylised approach with the sense of humanity that set Holbein above his peers.

On his second visit to England from 1532, Holbein was still using the dark turquoise background with vines and leaves. The king's usher and gentleman, Thomas Reskimmer, appears in simple black, with a trail of white from his collar and brown fur lining. His long beard touches the tips of his upturned fingers as his hands rest together before him in a pose of contemplation.

The artist also made sketches of husband and wife, Sir Thomas and Lady Margaret Elyot, whose completed portraits have since been lost. These half-finished images were executed with a delicate, intimate touch in pen and coloured chalks. Like the Guildfords, the couple look towards each other in two separate works designed to hang together, dressed in dark clothes that have some elements of decoration and status, like Margaret's gold headdress and Thomas's fur collar and gold chain. Thomas, in particular, represents a man resistant to a changing world, wearing his hair in a long, old-fashioned style and his chain suggestive of a crucifix and adherence to the old faith. Holbein may have been aware that diplomat Thomas had recently returned to England after a fruitless visit to Emperor Charles V in an attempt to resolve Henry's divorce.

During this period, Holbein produced many more court portraits, including the elegant but stern-looking Margaret Lee, sister of the poet Thomas Wyatt, in a dark red gown with gold ties, pearl headdress, gold chain, rings, gold pendant and red rose. Formerly Mistress of the Wardrobe to Anne Boleyn, and once her close friend, Margaret looks askance at the artist with an air of worldly cynicism. Thought to have sat for her portrait in around 1540, just four years after having accompanied Anne on her final journey to the Tower (and possibly even standing beside her on the scaffold), Margaret bore nine children and died in 1543, but in her portrait, her social standing and survival are recorded in colour by the master artist, speaking a powerful mimetic truth that outlasts the fluctuations of her fortunes.

Another engaging pair of Holbein's are those of Sir Thomas Godsalve and his son John, lawyers from Norwich. Thomas was a friend of Thomas Cromwell and used his influence at court to establish a career for John. In their joint portrait, executed in 1528, John was aged 23 and newly admitted to Gray's Inn. He is standing immediately behind his father, paper in hand as if assisting him in business. Thomas faces the same way, perhaps towards an unseen client, his quill poised over a sheet of paper, interrupted in the act of writing. The picture is sombre and dark, with both figures dressed in the brown and black appropriate to their class and profession, with white shirts visible beneath; the father wears a black hat while the son is bare headed. The family resemblance is clear in the prominent eyes, heavy brows, long noses, the shape of their mouths and the cleft chin.

John Godsalve was also depicted alone in a second work, dating from around 1532, when four more years had allowed him to grow into a confident young businessman, able to operate independently. Still recognisable as the youth of the first work, his changed appearance echoes that of his father, with his broad brown collar and black cap, but he now looks towards the viewer with an expression of subtle awareness and understated mastery. Unfinished, the work has a thin, sketchy blue background, suggesting that Holbein intended to paint in his usual intense turquoise, but the subject's eyes provide the image with a compelling fulcrum. This painting was created at a time when John was acting as Clerk of the Signet, which required him to purchase gold and steel laces from the German merchants at the Steelyard, while Holbein was known to be living and working there, allowing for easy sittings.

Another painting of John, by an anonymous sixteenth-century imitator of Holbein, is darker in palette, presents the sitter facing forward, eyes averted, and has nothing of the charm of the original. It is clumsy where the first had finesse, blunt where it was bright, and pedestrian where Holbein's image sparkles.

John also commissioned a portrait of his first wife, Agnes, by the German master, but neither this nor any identified preparatory sketch of her survives. Thomas Godsalve died in 1542 and his son John became MP for Norwich and was knighted on the succession of Edward VI, dying in 1556. Yet, as was intended in the commissioning of their portraits, the material measure of their successes lives on.

⚜ FAMILY GROUPS ⚜

Some of the most fascinating Tudor portraits are family groupings. Perhaps the most famous of these depicts Thomas More, with the residents and guests of his Chelsea home in 1527. Although Holbein's original painting was destroyed in a fire of 1752, his preliminary sketch survives, as does a copy made by Rowland Lockey in the 1590s, allowing a glimpse into the dynamics of a wealthy Tudor family.

On the extreme left stands Elizabeth Dauncey, More's daughter, wearing a dress with huge bag sleeves turned back at the elbow and the tied sleeve beneath with frilled cuff. Her waist is circled by a girdle that falls to two tassels, from which a chain is suspended. Aged 21 at the time of this work, Elizabeth had married William Dauncey in September 1525 and the slight swelling above her girdle might suggest the first or second of her seven pregnancies. Holbein produced a close-up sketch of her face for the final work, with her eyes cast down, her eyebrows and lips pale, in an expression of quiet patience. Beside Elizabeth stands More's adopted daughter, Margaret Giggs, who is similarly clothed and leaning forward to point out something in a book to old John More. The aged father sits in the foreground with his hands in his lap, staring solidly forward as she speaks in his ear. Thomas sits to the right of his father, staring off to the right, both feet placed squarely on the floor. He appears to be the solid fulcrum around which the family turns.

Beside Thomas is his son John, who wears the puffed sleeves and the pageboy haircut made fashionable by the young Henry VIII. John's face is a study of seriousness and concentration, his lips set firm as he reads from the book he holds in front of him in both hands. A little detached from the group, John's fiancée, the 15-year-old Anne Cresacre, looks on from between the two patriarchs, head held high, alert and focused on the scene outside the group. A separate sketch gives her light brown hair, pale blue eyes, a sensitive mouth and rounded chin, but her expression and her positioning places her a little on the outside of the family group.

Beside John stands the family's fool, Henry Patenson, a bearded figure, perhaps middle-aged, with badges on his cap. He breaks the pattern adopted by the others by staring directly at the artist, in an almost challenging way. In this, he may show a lack of guile, a lack of willingness to enter into the social disingenuity of posing and the performance of pretending not to be aware of the artist's presence. The status of the fool allowed him to stand outside conventions, to make eye contact, to disturb and unsettle and to delineate and cross boundaries. His gaze gives an immediacy and naturalness to his portrait, which contrasts with the sophistication of the other figures, a deliberate choice that reminds the viewer of the 'staged' nature of the work.

Three women seated on the floor before Patenson make up the final portion of the group: More's daughters, Margaret and Cecily, and their stepmother, Alice. All three women hold books, but Alice More, kneeling behind them at a small desk, is the only one reading hers. While their dress is very similar, their faces differ, capturing the artist's close observation. Where Alice is devout and concentrating, Margaret's gaze is alert and sensitive, while Cecily's pose is reminiscent of da Vinci's *Lady with an Ermine*. Having married Giles Heron in 1525, Cecily's pregnancy is visible in the detail of her bodice being loosened and laced over her yellow kirtle to accommodate her increasing girth.

Such family groups were visual records of domestic and material success, important social markers, both in the act of sitting and the subsequent display of the work. For a family like More's, it would come to be a reminder of former happiness, following Thomas's execution just eight years later.

Receiving a copy of the picture, the More family's friend, Erasmus, wrote to Margaret Roper from Freiburg:

Cannot express the delight which he felt on receiving Holbein's picture of the More family. Recognised everyone in it, none more than herself. Methought I saw a soul shining through this most beautiful household even more beautiful. Sends her a letter from a chaplain to Mary, formerly queen of Hungary. Begs his letter may be shown to her sisters, and his compliments to her mother Louise. I have kissed her picture, as I could not kiss herself. My best wishes to your brother John More, and your husband Roper.[1]

An increasing number of family portraits were produced as the Elizabethan era advanced. Around 1567, William Brooke, Lord Cobham, sat with his wife, sister and six small children around the dinner table with their pets, with a Latin inscription reading, 'God grant that the line of Cobham beget many offspring such as Joseph'. The many fruits displayed on the table – apples, grapes, pears and walnuts – testify to his success as a progenitor as much as the six children poised to eat them. The picture also suggests a source of their wealth. Their monkey and parrot are imported from the New World and Lady Cobham's diamond pendant takes the shape of a ship, echoing her husband's role as Lord Warden of the Cinque Ports.

Connections with foreign riches were often included in such works, like the portrait of three unidentified children of the 1580s, by another unknown painter. A girl aged 7 stands flanked by her brothers, who are 6 and 5, all beautifully dressed in their best fashionable clothes, with ruffs, lace collars, slashed doublets, rings, feather caps, bows, chains and pendants. She cradles in her arms the first guinea pig ever to be depicted in English art; the animals were brought across the Atlantic to Spain from South America in the 1530s. It is painted in realistic detail, clearly from life, in profile with a black beady eye, white, brown and black fur and one little white foot braced against the girl's dress.

In 1568, Edward, Baron Windsor, and his wife Katherine sat for a family portrait which included their four children and an older woman, whose age is given as 61, possibly a nurse, or perhaps the representation of either Edward or Katherine's mother, both of whom had predeceased the portrait. Her clothes are plain and modest, and she faces away from the Windsors, who both look to the left.

All the family follow the style set by Queen Elizabeth in wearing black and white with gold trimmings. Edward's ruff is a small line of folds above the high collar of his doublet, which is picked out in gold lines, with matching buttons, but his cloak, or coat, is so dark as to blend in with the background. Like Cobham, Windsor is a man of 40, with a high forehead and receding ginger hair disappearing under a beret, his features slightly reminiscent of those of Henry VIII, with the small eyes and mouth, and the beard and moustache of the period. Standing to his left, his wife, Katherine, wears the typical costume of Elizabeth's early reign. Her tight, high ruff sits close under the chin, up to her ears; the cuffs on her dress match the ruff in miniature. A simple headdress is placed further back on the middle of her head, her sleeves are slashed and pulled through with the fabric below and she is adorned with jewels. Their four children, all boys, stand before them around a table, in the middle of a game of cards and chess. Dressed identically, the artist has not given them all the same facial features, as the children in the guinea pig portrait have. These boys each have a distinct character of their own. Unusually for the time, every individual included in this work, even the children and old woman, make direct eye contact with the viewer.

Pregnancy portraits became a fashionable genre during the late Elizabethan period. They were not necessarily inspired by fears for an expectant mother before she underwent the dangerous ordeal of childbirth but were a record of fertility. One of the earliest such portraits depicts Catherine Carey, Lady Knollys, cousin of Elizabeth I, probably by Steven van der Meulen.

Painted with her lap dog, she wears a black, high-collared coat trimmed with white fur, buttoned over her chest, then open to reveal her large white belly and the ties that are holding it together. Directly in front of it, she holds up the long chain of a pomander, bringing its sweet wholesomeness level with her unborn child.

Many of these pictures reveal the mechanics of pregnancy dressing: the ties, extra fabric and additional stomachers used to accommodate a woman's growing child. Here, clothing acts as both sign and metaphor for the concealed state of pregnancy. The audience is alerted to the pregnancy by the alteration in attire and sees that pregnancy stretches the confines of the 'usual' or prescribed, propelling a woman into a state of 'otherness' for the duration of nine months. This conferred a 'specialness' upon an expectant mother as a conduit, which finds echoes in the choices of colour and ornamentation in many of these works.

The most popular colour for the women to be portrayed in is a virginal or chaste white or pale silver, with the purity represented by strings of pearls. This underlines their imminent fulfilment of the most precious of contemporary aspirations: the delivery of a live heir. Thus, these portraits are unusual in revealing Tudor women at the moment of success and on the verge of danger, but often represent the only likeness or reference to them.

In 1578, George Gower painted an unknown pregnant woman, wearing a small ruff and with tight, red curls arranged around her face. Her dress is grey and black, but is stretched to the limit, and the addition of a stomacher allows for her expansion.

Another unidentified sitter, depicted by William Segar between 1585 and 1590, appears very large in her silver gown. Heavily pregnant, her gaping dress is held together by a belt and she looks back at the sitter with an expression that could be something touching trepidation. The dimensions of her body are exaggerated, with her head sitting in the centre of a wide ruff, her sleeves stuffed almost to the point of tautness and the voluminous skirts filling the whole frame. The gold chains she wears rest across the top of her belly.

Two works of 1595, both by Marcus Gheeraerts, show expectant mothers in silver grey, with pearls and embroidery. The first, unnamed and swathed in white decorative detail like a bride, smiles directly out at the viewer with a mixture of pride and display, while the second, often identified as Elizabeth or 'Bess' Throckmorton, wears a special pregnancy dress, with a huge roll of fabric lying across her belly and midway over her hips. Her expression is ambiguous, almost frozen, and in contrast to the other, may express something uncomfortable in the mood of this depiction. If it is Bess Throckmorton, her controversial pregnancies angered Elizabeth, to the extent that Bess was jailed in the Tower, but no successful delivery is recorded for her in 1595, as her sons arrived in 1592, 1593 and then, after a gap, in 1605. Of course, it is possible that the painting is dated incorrectly, or that this pregnancy resulted in miscarriage or stillbirth.

Barbara Sidney, Countess of Leicester, and her six daughters posed for an unknown artist in 1596. Standing inside a plain, dark interior, their pearly white dresses are the focus, rather than any external ornate details: they are the jewels of the family, rather than any ornamentation. Barbara wears a wheeled farthingale above the waistline to accommodate her pregnancy but which otherwise conceals her condition.

All the portraits of pregnant Elizabethan women, and their children, are notable for the direct gazes of their sitters, who stare out straight at the viewer. This suggests a need for recognition of what they have achieved – conception and pregnancy – and what they are about to endure. There's also a brutal honesty about this exchange of looks, of the realities of life and death which transcend the formal posturing of the image. The proximity of imminent danger, at a time when some women did die in childbed, and many infants were lost, adds a directness to the works, almost an admission of dynastic dependence upon women. The combination of palette and symbolism creates an odd juxtaposition of purity and pregnancy, with these mothers-to-be epitomising both the earthly imperative of procreation and the chaste state of an icon, similar to that of the Virgin Queen. These works are not only reflective and celebratory, but aspirational, as constant visual reminders of the Tudor wife's duty.

⚜ ORDINARY TUDOR FACES ⚜

If we were to judge by surviving Tudor portraiture alone, our impression of the sixteenth century might be of a world populated by stately, if somewhat stuffy, colourful figures adorned with jewels. This would be as misleading as a future generation interpreting the modern world through the pages of *Tatler* magazine alone. Only a small percentage of Tudors achieved the immortality of their face on a canvas that was considered important enough to be protected during the intervening centuries. The faces of 'ordinary' Tudors are far more difficult to uncover, but some do exist.

Anonymous faces appear in the background of illustrative works, as the servants and officials pictured in images of coronations and processions. The black and white woodcut of Henry VIII and Catherine of Aragon's joint coronation in June 1509 shows a sea of faces behind the two thrones, but none of these are distinguishable. They represent the mass of 'others', the dispensable supporting cast outside the central narrative of the king and queen, a rule which generally holds true for much of the art produced in the Tudor era.

However, the corresponding parliamentary roll for the coronation is more personal, showing a few specific officials accompanying the king, dressed in livery, and four small, tonsured figures bearing his canopy. But they are present because they have to be. The canopy could not hold itself up, nor could the king be central in a procession if no one processes with him. These anonymous faces are the foils that establish the king's identity.

Likewise, contemporary drawings of Elizabeth I's coronation in January 1559 include her gentlemen pensioners and footmen, dressed similarly with only the slightest variation, as mere representations of people – or of their role – rather than as individuals. Again, they are present because officers had to be present, to ensure the smooth running of the event, as the props upon which royal majesty rested.

A source like the 1511 Westminster Roll, depicting Henry's arrival at Warwick Castle, features a number of the royal guard, with similar faces but with small variations and with a range of different hair colours. It is impossible to know, here, whether the artist had any knowledge of the subjects he depicted; whether they had names or specific faces, for him, or even if that was a question that mattered to him. They represent generic Tudor servants, as many of these sources do, but in doing so, they are also representative of an anonymous Everyman figure, the 'everyman' or 'everywoman' of Tudor life.

Undeniably, though, the one demonstrable exception was when the artist depicted Henry VIII's black trumpeter, John Blanke, whose face appears among the ranks of the musicians in this roll. Distinguishable by his skin colour alone, Blanke's ethnic difference in Tudor England has conferred upon him an identity far more lasting than the majority of his English-born peers.

Human faces appeared on church walls frequently in the pre-Reformation decades of the Tudor era. Unlike the figures on tombs, which were often carved from life or recent memory, those featured in murals might represent anonymous, abstract or historical figures. An embracing couple at Llancarfan Church are mere symbols, depicted with crude, simplistic features, as the message of their sin overrides the need for realism. Similarly, the figures rising from their coffins in the Doom painting at St Mary's in North Leigh, Oxfordshire, wearing Tudor clothing, are symbols of resurrection, not individuals.

The church at Tilbury-by-Clare in Suffolk contains an image of a Tudor man with a horse, standing before a house in a more specific context, which might portray a patron or local figure, now unknown. A very distinctive gentleman was painted on the wall at St Swithin's Church, Launcells, wearing a black, brimmed hat, with long fair curls, a red coat and wide belt and luxurious heeled yellow shoes. He may have been based on a local character, but his facial features are fairly crudely painted – merely symbolic, rather than indicative, of identity.

Simple representations of Tudor men and women also appear in domestic interiors. The walls of a row of cottages at Piccotts End, Hemel Hempstead, were adorned with religious images soon after their completion in 1527. Although they depict a number of individuals in biblical scenes, which identifies them as specific figures, their faces are either very plain or entirely blank. Perhaps the artist made a deliberate choice not to personalise them, or maybe the arrival of the Reformation, hot upon the heels of the builders, led to their disfigurement. Parallel moves inside churches saw the mutilation of the faces of icons and the whitewashing over of the images of saints on the walls.

Domestic painted cloths on display in Owlpen Manor, in Gloucestershire, show Joseph and his brothers with generic faces and no distinguishing features. For the purposes of the work, the biblical figures did not need to look like anyone specific; in fact, the association of Joseph with a recognisable individual may have been considered to detract from its religious message, perhaps even to be blasphemous. And yet, certain contemporary carved bosses and statues can be pointed out in many churches as representing known craftsmen, patrons and local dignitaries, so at five centuries' remove, we can only speculate as to whether painters based their work upon the likenesses of their friends and foes.

The Black and White House in Hereford contains the picture of another Everyman-style labourer in profile, while an old Dunstable shop has a Tudor huntsman smoking a pipe, in cartoonesque sketchy form, with a long, loose beard. These appear to focus more on an occupation than a resemblance: if the faces had any personal significance to the artist or owner of the house, it has been lost with history.

Some residents did choose to be depicted, in a fairly lifelike way, on the walls of their homes. Two women in a Shropshire house were painted in 1580, with their prim faces and respectable costumes, surrounded by animals, flowers and musical instruments – permanent, ageless doppelgängers to watch over their real-life counterparts.

Occasionally, an artist might seek inspiration from a more well-known face. At Shandy Hall, in Coxwold, a Tudor soldier painted on the wall bears an uncanny likeness to Henry VIII. He is dressed in a suspiciously royal costume of red, slashed to reveal the pull-through white lining, and a red cap with feathers, just like the surviving Bristow hat, known to have been worn by the king.

Other domestic works can be identified in relation to the property's owners. A little ochre bride, painted on the wall of Whitehouse Cottage in Barry and dated to 1580, is likely to be commemorative of an actual wedding. The couple pictured together on the panelled wall of Althrey Hall in Flintshire represent the builder Elis ap Richard, who died in 1558, and his wife, Jane Hanmer, dressed in their best clothes. Another married pair, painted together at The Star at Hoddesdon, could well be the individuals who owned the property, or else were commissioned after it came into the possession of Elizabeth's chief minister, William Cecil, Lord Burghley, in 1580. The hunting scenes at West Stow Hall, built around 1520, are likely to have been created for the hall's owner, Sir John Crofts, Master of the Horse to Mary Tudor, Duchess of Suffolk.

In painting and writing, the correlation between personal depiction and inspiration is highly subjective. Unless painted figures are specifically identified for the purposes of portraiture, they cannot be stated with certainty to represent certain individuals, especially after the passage of time. Some Tudor murals certainly contain people with more carefully crafted identities, but these could have been intended as representatives of biblical or cultural figures or professions, or simply as representative Everymen or -women.

Symbolic and abstract figures conveyed messages as well as fulfilling decorative functions or could be memorials or statements of identity. As a general rule, though, the faces of 'other' or 'ordinary' Tudors were not personalised in their features and were far less likely to survive, unless they featured as the supporting cast members to a high-status figure.

❧ PEN PORTRAITS ❧

Occasionally, Tudor letters contain pen portraits of individuals, shedding light upon contemporary ideals of beauty and what were considered to be distinguishing features. One unusual little description survives of two brothers from 1571, who were implicated in the Ridolfi plot:

Codberd Red is a young man of the age of 23, black coloured, low
of stature, having no beard or very little, black-headed, and is Lord
Ross's fifth son, and can speak Latin. John Codberd is of the age of
28, as I judge, pale-faced, low of stature, a thin yellowish beard, a
yellowish head, without any hair of his cheek, both steward and
secretary to the Bishop of Ross.[1]

The medieval belief that a person's character was visible in their
appearance still lingered into the Tudor era. Kings and queens should be
beautiful and villains should be ugly or malformed. In 1533, Anthonie
Brusset was Captain of Gravelines, in the territory of the emperor but
close to the border with English-held Calais, which was then governed
by Arthur Plantagenet, Lord Lisle. Although Anglo-Imperial relations
were less than friendly at the time, on account of Henry VIII's divorce
from the emperor's aunt, Catherine of Aragon, officials of the two
towns were able to co-operate for the sake of justice.

Brusset wrote to Lisle that November, asking him to apprehend a
fugitive murderer who had taken refuge in Calais, a Spaniard by the
name of Ylayre, an unpleasant-looking villain 'that has the nose on
his face very red and thick with pimples like a leper'.[2]

The appearance of the Duke of Alençon, to whom Elizabeth was
considering marriage in 1572, was described in a letter by Dr Valentine
Dale to Cecil, which does not shy away from frank commentary about
the pox scars that disfigured his features. Dr Dale also observed that a
recent painting of the duke was a good likeness:

> For his personage, me thinketh the portrature doth expresse hym very
> well, and when I sawe hym at my last audience, he seemed to me to
> grow dayly more hansom than other. The treat of hys visage may be
> gathered likewyse by hys picture but not hys colour, which ys not
> naturally red ... the pock holes are no greate disfigurement in the rest
> of hys face bycause they are rather thick than deepe or greate. They
> upon the blunt end of hys nose are greate and diepe, how much to be
> disliked may be as it pleaseth God to move the heart of the beholder.[3]

What is noticeable about both these examples is the writers' awareness
of subjectivity in beauty. The phrase 'as I judge' allows for a margin of
error, while Dr Dale commits the duke's deformities to the eye of the
beholder. Clothing and the external manifestations of identity could

be easily quantifiable in terms of their desirability – cost, material, cut, colour, design, ornamentation – but the attractions of the person were far more difficult to pinpoint.

The faces of royalty were not above public commentary. Often this was formulaic and flattering, such as the coronation verses for Henry VIII in 1509 which describe him as being as beautiful as a young God, and the Venetian ambassador Giustinian's comments that Henry was:

> the handsomest potentate I ever set eyes on; above the usual height, with an extremely fine calf to his leg, his complexion very fair and bright with auburn hair combed straight and short in the French fashion, and a round face so very beautiful that it would become a pretty woman, his throat being rather long and thick.[4]

Thomas More's coronation verses for Catherine of Aragon state how 'in her expression, in her countenance, there is a remarkable beauty uniquely appropriate for one so great and good'. These also focus upon qualities that conform to convention, such as hair colour. In 1501, Thomas More described Catherine as having 'hair hanging down abowt her shulders, which is faire auburn', and in 1509, her hair was 'hangyng donne to her backe, of a very great length, bewtefull and goodly to behold'.[5]

Great contrast was made later between the Spanish queen's red hair, inherited from her Lancastrian descent, and Anne Boleyn's black eyes and hair, with the moral implications of darkness and temptation being exploited by Anne's enemies. The Venetian diplomat Sanuto described Anne as 'not one of the handsomest women in the world; she is of middling stature, swarthy complexion, long neck, wide mouth, a bosom not much raised and eyes which are black and beautiful'.[6] The Catholic Nicholas Sanders, a source hostile to Anne, writing half a century after her death, used contemporary Tudor beliefs to paint a physical caricature which implied her moral degeneracy:

> Anne Boleyn was rather tall of stature, with black hair and an oval face of sallow complexion, as if troubled with jaundice. She had a projecting tooth under the upper lip, and on her right hand, six fingers. There was a large wen under her chin, and therefore to hide its ugliness, she wore a high dress covering her throat.[7]

It was also understood that appearance could be altered by emotions such as intense grief. In 1584, ambassador to France Edward Stafford wrote home from the court of Henri III and his mother, Catherine de Medici, who had recently suffered the loss of the king's younger brother, Hercules:

> Since his brother's death he is a marvellously altered man in face, and men think that he thinketh more of it than he maketh show. The Queen-Mother also is never out of great dumps and studies, which nobody hath seen her subject to afore. She told my wife the last day, that time might wear this grief away to the show of the world, but out of her heart never.[8]

A rare glimpse of Mary, Queen of Scots was given by an N. White in a letter to William Cecil in 1559:

> For besides that she is a goodly personage, she hath without an alluring grace, a pretty Scottish speech, and a searching wit, clouded with mildness. His own affection by seeing the Queen our Sovereign is doubled, and thereby he guesses what sight might work in others. Her hair of itself is black, and yet Mr. Knollys told him that she wears hair of sundry colours.[9]

When discussing the potential marriage of Elizabeth I to the Duke of Anjou in 1579, William Cecil considered the pros and cons of undertaking such a risk at her age. Elizabeth was then 45. He cited the example of the last Duchess of Savoy, who was older when she married and was a 'woman of sallow and melancholy complexion and in all respects inferior' to Elizabeth, but who went on to bear a son. In comparison, the queen was:

> a person of most pure complexion, of the largest and goodliest stature of well-shaped women, with all limbs set and proportioned in the best sort, and one whom in the sight of all men, nature cannot amend her shape in any part to make her more likely to conceive and bear children without peril.[10]

⚜ THE ICONIC VIRGIN ⚜

Perhaps the ultimate Tudor icon is Elizabeth I, the 'Virgin Queen'. The process of deifying a royal subject in paint, which was begun by Henry VIII, came to fruition under his daughter, with her painted face, gauzy wings and pearls. As she aged and the chances of her marrying decreased, the queen maintained careful control over her own image, both in person and in portraiture. She was painted most frequently in her favourite colours, typically black and white or silver, which accentuated her colouring to greater dramatic effect, echoing the chiaroscuro techniques of late-Renaissance art.

As the Renaissance gave way to Mannerism, increasing numbers of symbolic items and motifs appeared with her, such as the pearls for virginity and purity, fans representing wealth, the English symbols of the rose and greyhound, the pelican and phoenix of motherly love for her nation, the white gloves of aristocracy, the globe representing the world over which she reigned, and the intricate ruffs and lace cuffs of a woman who was not required to do manual work.

Elizabeth was particular about who portrayed her likeness, too. Court painters had been licensed since 1563 but, between 1581 and 1596, artist George Gower was given responsibility for approving all representations of Elizabeth, to ensure they conformed to her standards. Anyone found spreading an image by Isaac Oliver, who the queen disliked, had their work confiscated and burned, while an alternative 'mask of youth' image made by Nicholas Hilliard was replicated at least sixteen times in the final decade of the queen's life.

The visual cult that Elizabeth nurtured around her person found a new outlet in paint, where she was afforded a quasi-divine status – a virgin worthy of veneration, in the style of the old Catholic iconography of Mary and the saints. As she aged, representations of her face became fixed and the ever-widening ruffs echoed the saints' traditional halo, combined with the more secular fairy wings suggested by poets such as Edmund Spenser and John Davies. By the end of her life, bald, wrinkled and toothless, Elizabeth had successfully crafted her own self, her simulacrum of queenship, into an enduring legend.

Elizabeth is possibly the most painted English monarch, from demure portraits of the princess in the 1540s through to the 1600 copy of a lost coronation portrait of the young queen in gold robes, with long flowing hair. The narrative of her image tells the miraculous tale of an imperial virgin, able to control the ravages of the weather and the onslaught of time.

Painted in 1575, the Phoenix portrait by Nicholas Hilliard indicates a step midway towards the deification of the queen. Elizabeth wears her favourite colours, a black dress with puffed sleeves, embroidered with gold leaves and pearls, slashed and pulled with white sarcenet, her narrow waist encircled by pearls. The dress is open at the breast but closed at the throat by two pieces of blackwork lace, and her skirts open to reveal a white forepart. A pearl headdress sits upon her neatly arranged curls, from which hangs a delicate gauzy train. One spotless, unadorned white hand holds a red rose, while in the other a white fan is visible. Around her neck hang two gold chains of pearls and enamelled flowers, and from the lower of the two is suspended the phoenix pendant that gives the work its name.

The pure white mask of Elizabeth's face, with its dark eyes and small mouth, is not confronting for the viewer in the way her father's or brother's images are. Her gaze does not challenge or need to assert her authority. She looks serenely past the viewer as if she is above them. She represents a real, temporal authority and an abstract concept of the Divine, standing out like an icon against a plain, dark red background. The Phoenix's partner, the Pelican portrait, dating from the same period, appears like its mirror image, with Elizabeth's clothing taking a similar shape, but differing in colour and pattern. Also created by Nicholas Hilliard, or his workshop, modern infrared analysis has revealed that the exact same facial template was used in the second work as in the first.

A decade later, Elizabeth's image had furthered its own complex iconography. The Ermine portrait of 1585, usually attributed to Hilliard, has the queen in black again, with her dress decorated in gold beads and pairs of gold slashes or cuts. The outfit makes a feature of a central seam, heavily embroidered in gold work and gems, matching a thick gold chain of more precious stones and pearls. A barely visible cloak cascades about her shoulders and arms in see-through ripples. The queen wears a delicate cartwheel ruff, matching her cuffs, pearl bracelets and a tall, heart-shaped headdress, studded with pearls and gems.

Set against a black background, the bright gold of her dress is striking and finds an echo in the gold of the sword of state resting on the table before her. Behind her right shoulder, the grey daylight behind the latticed panes of a narrow window intensifies the chiaroscuro effect and offers the only suggestion of reality and context to what could otherwise be an almost abstract icon. The window grounds Elizabeth in a room, inside a building, connecting her with the earthly realm, where otherwise the dramatic colouring gives her a sense of 'otherness' as the muse of artists, ephemeral and inspiring in her abstraction. The painting derives its name from the ermine sitting upon her left arm, an animal associated with royalty, which wears a small gold crown about its neck.

Three years later, the Armada portrait of 1588 places the queen-as-icon figure against an unfolding landscape or narrative. Reproduced in three near-identical versions, and with the original formerly attributed to George Gower, the image is now thought to have been created by unknown artists, again using the mask template. In each, Elizabeth's black cloak, bodice and skirt are trimmed with bows, jewels and pearls and her creamy white sleeves shimmer through their embroidery of gold.

The theme is her mastery of the seas, with the failure of the Spanish Armada portrayed through two windows behind her. Elizabeth stands facing left, where a bright vista shows the English fire ships moving towards the enemy vessels. Also on this side stand the state crown and a globe upon which the queen rests her hands, fingers pointing towards America, where the first English colony has just been established. Behind her back, the Spanish fleet is shown in chaos, in dark colours, tossed by storms and driven onto the rocks. A mermaid carving upon a chair to the right is armless and in profile, like a ship's figurehead, and, with her naked breasts, represents sexual temptation and betrayal.

In contrast, Elizabeth's pearls associate her with the pure prod-ucts of the sea, the tamed and cultivated sea-gems, a large example of which hangs from her bodice, level with her crotch, are equal to the male display of a codpiece but representative of her chastity. Her sleeves feature what might be golden starfish and her ostrich-feather fan suggests her responsibility for whipping up the 'Protestant wind' that wrecked the Spaniards. The cartwheel ruff locates her face at the centre of the universe, sun-like in its rays, while her chosen palette of black and white alludes to Cynthia, goddess of the moon, with her pull over the tides. Four years later, Walter Raleigh, her adventurer in the New World, wrote the poem 'The Ocean to Cynthia', full of melancholic symbolism, lamenting his loss of the queen's favour.

By the end of her life, Elizabeth's manipulation of her image in paint, her self-deification, had created a visual cult that defined her era. To the outside world, she remained Gloriana, Cynthia, Diana and the Faerie Queen, yet it was a flawed aesthetic, unable to halt the advance of old age, as the gap widened between art and the physical reality of her deteriorating body, creating a diegesis of which she lost control. When the impulsive Earl of Essex burst into her dressing room at Nonsuch Palace early on a September morning in 1599, he found the Faerie Queen without her wig, make-up or gown, a breach of etiquette neither of them ever forgot, and which Elizabeth never forgave. It was only after her death that an artist dared to depict the queen in old age, sitting slumped and wrinkled with her head in her hand, while the figures of death and time approach from behind. Upon her demise in March 1603, the artistic fiction with which her court had colluded was finally over.

Portraits made a significant but niche contribution to the visual culture of the Tudor world. Their influence and purpose varied with class, as did the location where they were displayed and the audience to which they were accessible. For the royal family, portraiture could be a tool of control and authority, with a larger-than-life depiction of a king or queen exuding status and watching over their subjects. Increasingly, their image was manipulated to create a recognisable visual identity for a monarch which almost superseded the reality; they were bigger, brighter, stronger and more permanent in paint than their flesh-and-blood counterpart, whom they also frequently outlived. This two-dimensional deification developed from Henry VIII's Whitehall silhouette into the iconography of Elizabeth's image. Formal individual and family portraits commissioned by the upper-middle classes and nobility were intended as records of success, prosperity, culture and fertility.

For the Tudors, commissioning a portrait created a permanent record in an impermanent world. Painted images consciously located sixteenth-century men and women in their social and cultural context, but even without the overt memento mori of *The Ambassadors*, they exposed the Tudor preoccupation with the paradoxes of heaven and earth, cerebral and material, local and global.

The tactile realities of sixteenth-century life were used by artists to depict a microcosm within a frame of the wider Tudor experience. Portraiture was a deliberate act of fabrication, or crafting a vision of success, even if the robes or the props then had to be returned or were lost. In some ways, parallels can be drawn with the carefully edited and posed 'selfies' of the twenty-first century, in their fleeting depiction of an evoked perfection which may be far from the truth.

The Tudors recognised the element of suspended disbelief inherent in the act of portrait painting. This allowed for the depiction of states of hyperreality, where symbolic or mythical figures appear, along with allegories, metaphors, exaggeration and simulacra, unnatural or non-sequential juxtapositioning and the depiction of the dead as in life. This acknowledgement of conscious artifice was less about a painting deceiving a viewer and more about convincing the viewer of wider, more significant truths than the presentation of mere humanity could convey. It was a conscious striving towards a stylised ideal.

Royal portraits from Henry VIII's Whitehall mural onwards express the truth that the king or queen's power and influence was embodied in, and greater than, the physical body of that monarch. In the twenty-first century, we must read the Tudors' visual culture as they intended it; although we have, no doubt, lost many of their coded references over time. They painted themselves as they wanted the world to see them.

CLOTH AND THREAD

❦ EARLY TUDOR PEACOCKS ❦

In 1565, a satirical pamphlet rolled off the London printing presses. In *A Pleasant Dialogue or Disputation between the Cap and the Head*, the disgruntled cap accuses the head of being a slave to fashion by making numerous embellishments to it, adding ribbons, brooches, laces and more. As a result, the poor cap complains that it has been transformed into something ridiculous, a sartorial laughing stock:

> Thou art not contented with making me to wear red, yellow, green and blue laces, but besides that, thou encumbrest me with birds' feathers, thou betrickst me with brooches, Valentines, rings, keys, purses, gloves, yea, fingers of gloves; thou wrappest me in chains, thou settest me with buttons and aglets, thou lardest me with ribbons and bands, thou cuttest me, borest me and slashest me, both above and beneath without any compassion or pity, and so by this disfigure me, impairing my dignity.[1]

Indeed, portraits of the 1560s do contain some very ornate headwear. From Elizabeth I's jaunty, encrusted scarlet cap in the Gripsholm portrait, to Mary, Queen of Scots' confection of pearls and flamboyant white feather, they appear as ornate statements of art and beauty.

Even men layered on the decoration, with Robert Dudley's little black number strung about by a gold chain and gems and set with a carved cameo brooch and red feather. One of the items owned by Lady Jane Grey in her imprisonment in the Tower in 1553–54 was 'a cap of black velvet, having a fair brooch with a little square table ruby, and divers pictures enamelled with red, black, and green, with eighteen buttons, with small rock rubies, and eighteen buttons also of gold with three small pearls the piece'.[2]

The English idiom to 'wear a feather in your cap' survives into the twenty-first century as a signifier of achievement. Although it no longer represents the literal reading of the sixteenth century, when a courtier might sport an expensive soft white plume in order to join the fashionable elite, the signifier of the feather as aspirational remains a constant. While the Tudors would have been amused by the *Pleasant Dialogue's* sartorial conceit, they valued the message contained in every coloured ribbon, feather or ornate brooch. All these were elements in what Mary E. Hazard has identified as an 'Elizabethan silent language', a complex visual code of signifiers relating to the material world.[3] By these subtle means, personal identity was established and individuals were located within the social framework.

On 10 June 1520, Henry VIII dined with the court of Francis I of France at Ardres, during the festivities for the Field of Cloth of Gold. Determined to impress and to outdo his rival, Henry chose to epitomise the gold theme, adorning himself with gold fabrics and jewels and blazing bright in the summer sunshine, as a Renaissance prince of dazzling wealth. His double mantle of cloth of gold was 'embroidered with jewels and goldsmith's work, a "seion" of cloth of gold frieze also embroidered with jewels', and he wore a 'beautiful head-dress of fine gold cloth'.[4] When the king of England set out to make his mark with clothes, he had the resources to ensure he shone like the sun.

The first Tudor king and queen knew how to use clothing, colour and jewels as essential tools of majesty and their example established a practice which their children and grandchildren brought to fruition. In October 1485, the planning documents for the coronation of Henry VII suggested he might wear a doublet of green or white cloth of gold and a long gown of purple velvet, furred with powdered ermine. When she became Henry's wife the following January, Elizabeth of York wore a circlet of gold set with pearls and stones, a kirtle of white damask and cloth of gold, furred with pure miniver, a mantle and train with damask cloth of gold and great lace, buttons and tassels of white silk and gold.

At the start of the new dynasty, when their survival seemed precarious, the Tudors quickly established a cycle of visual affirmation. To express their new-found status, they dressed according to an elite code, and their clothing projected an authority which simultaneously reflected and increased their power. During the Tudor period, royalty looked the part, and looking the part helped convey the ideal of royalty.

For the wealthy Tudors, clothes were a statement of belonging. The colours, styles and fabrics they chose were not an expression of their individuality but represented what was available to them in their

social sphere, as dictated by law and cost. Sumptuary laws were reinforced throughout the dynasty, restricting the use of certain items
to people of rank, as if the price of cloth of gold or Venice lace were
not already prohibitive enough. Yards of fabric to make a new gown
or cloak were costly, often requiring as much as a quarter or half of
a working man's income, or greater than the largest investments he
might make, such as rent for his house, a bed or a horse. With the odd
exception, brand new custom-made clothes were a luxury reserved for
the upper classes, or wealthy merchants and bankers, to display their
upward social mobility.

Rich patrons might also give away items of clothing to demonstrate
how much they had: Henry VIII frequently gifted his clothes to his
friends, like the cloak admired by Seigneur de Bonnivet, Admiral of
France, in 1520, which the Frenchman then received. The wardrobe
accounts kept by Thomas Wolsey reveal just how much of his clothing
Henry regularly gave away as a mark of his favour. His cousin, Edward
Stafford, received a purple gown with matching doublet, jacket and
hose in March 1518 and an outfit of crimson and white velvet and
cloth of gold in December 1520; his brother-in-law, Charles Brandon,
was given a doublet and hose of black damask gold in March 1517, a
gown of white damask silver and a white doublet in July, a crimson
velvet coat in 1518, and a gown of russet cloth of gold in 1519.[5]

Until 2015, St Faith's Church in Bacton, Herefordshire, possessed
an unusual altar cloth – a T-shaped silver chamblet embroidered with
botanical, hunting and marine motifs and detailed with daffodils, roses,
foxgloves, strawberries, mistletoe, acorns and oak leaves. Analysis
suggests it could be a piece of Elizabeth I's Rainbow portrait gown,
completed in around 1600. If so, it is the only surviving item from the
2,000 items listed in the queen's wardrobe at the time of her death.

Clothing was ephemeral and likely to perish through use, loss or
accident. Later figures were less inclined to preserve and respect significant items. In 1649, Oliver Cromwell sold what remained of the
royal wardrobe and all other items were destroyed in the Great Fire of
1666. To understand what the Tudors wore, modern historians have
to rely upon surviving fragments, descriptions from eyewitnesses,
letters, accounts and portraits. Many middle- and lower-class men,
women and children received hand-me-down clothes, bequests in
wills, or made or adapted clothing from other pieces of material. Items
were reused until their condition deteriorated, often through two or

three generations, or they were cut down into cushions or household rags. It is little surprise, therefore, that more information exists on the clothing of the upper classes.

A timeline of 'milestones' in Tudor fashion is, therefore, represent-ative of a small, privileged coterie, which set the artistic and cultural tone. In colourful displays, at feasts, jousts, court ceremonies, diplo-matic meetings and even in observing and dispensing justice, great magnates established precedence through the length of their coats and shoes, the number of their gold chains and the yards of fabric used for their sleeves. The element of the fantastic in daily dress blurred the lines between non-occasion clothing and the elaborate costumes of masques and jousts, which could be symbolic and carry coded messages. Elizabeth I's cloak of 1600, embroidered with eyes and ears to show she saw and heard everything, has its origins in the mottos and motifs embroidered in her father's jousting outfits. Like portraiture to this visually oriented culture, dress became another facet of Tudor performance.

Costume needed an audience. For their coronation in June 1509, Henry VIII and Catherine of Aragon fully utilised the visual impact of their persons upon the watching crowds. Henry chose symbolic and striking colours, wearing a crimson velvet robe furred with ermine, a jacket of raised gold, the placard of which was embroidered with diamonds, rubies, emeralds and pearls, and a string of great rubies about his neck. His horse was trapped in damask gold, edged with ermine and his entourage wore crimson velvet or scarlet. By contrast, Catherine opted for an absence of colour, representative of purity and simplicity. She chose white embroidered satin, with her hair long and loose down her back and a coronet of many rich 'orient stones'. Carried through the streets in a litter pulled by two white palfreys trapped in white cloth of gold, she was accompanied by attendants wearing cloth of gold, silver and tinsel.

Henry's love of formal costumes was notable early in his reign. The 1512 Parliament Roll showing his procession to Parliament depicts him under a canopy of blue and gold checks, with a central Tudor rose, fringed with the dynastic colours of white and green, held aloft on gold poles. The king wore a long robe with wide sleeves of deep pink velvet, bordered and lined with ermine, a mantle of blue velvet with ermine border, a gold and jewelled collar, a black bonnet with a jewel and round-toed black shoes.

A visiting Venetian in 1515 described Henry dressed as a Knight of the Garter in a 'very costly doublet, over which was a mantle of violet-coloured velvet, with an extremely long train, lined with white satin'. On his head was a 'richly jewelled cap of crimson velvet of immense value, and round his neck he wore a collar, studded with many precious stones'.[6] Later that year, he was spotted by the same Venetian, wearing a French-style crimson velvet cap, the brim looped about with lacets and gold-enamelled *aiglettes*, a Swiss doublet striped alternately with white and crimson satin, scarlet hose, a purple velvet mantle lined with white satin and open sleeves trailing for at least four Venetian yards. His mantle was tied with gold cords, over which he wore a gold collar with a diamond pendant of St George. A crimson velvet hood hung over his right shoulder, a pouch of gold contained a dagger and his fingers were 'one mass of jewelled rings'.

Undoubtedly, Henry was the greatest peacock of the era. An inventory of his wardrobe, made in 1516, reveals that he had 134 doublets made from twenty-nine different fabrics and, soon after, the Venetian ambassador Sebastian Giustinian declared Henry VIII to be the best-dressed sovereign in the world. A second inventory, compiled in 1521, reveals Henry's wardrobe to have been valued at around £10,380, the equivalent of £4 million today.

Increasingly, the king's body shape dictated fashion, with shorter cloaks worn to reveal the calves, and a stockier figure established the correlative of power and physical space, driving thinner men to wear padding. The broad shoulders, legs and codpiece were designed to enhance male virility, while women kept their bodies and hair covered. This male silhouette became increasingly exaggerated until it found fruition in the Whitehall mural of 1537.

For the privileged, the desire for display was combined with a personal preference for colour, influence and style. Through the latter half of 1519 and into 1520, Henry VIII frequently chose the colour russet, an autumnal reddish brown similar to the 'murrey' of the old York dynasty. In October 1519, to celebrate the marriage of the Earl of Devon, the king jousted in russet velvet with cloth of silver, cross-lozenged with gold, and every lozenge embroidered with 'trueloves' of gold.

That December, a mummery held at Greenwich for fourteen performers required coats with puffed sleeves of russet satin tufted with white sarcenet, matching bonnets and hoods, russet cloaks and Turkish bonnets. The following February, Henry jousted in russet and white damask, and at the Field of Cloth of Gold that June, Henry, his wife and his horse all wore russet velvet or satin.

Even when it came to fighting in a tournament, the king wore silver tissue and russet velvet featuring the motif of a lady appearing from a cloud and striking a knight with a deadly blow, and the legend 'In love, whoso mounteth, passeth in peril'. Embroidery was used to identify allegiance and convey secret messages in the tradition of courtly love. Jousting against the French, one English side wore blue velvet embroidered with a lady's hand pouring water upon a man's burning heart, while another wore white satin embroidered with gold letters, while Edmund Howard led a company of eleven dressed in crimson satin sewn with gold flames. Clothing reinforced the subtext of passion that lay beneath the ceremony and procedures of chivalry.

The young king's playful side allowed for the game of dressing up to incorporate international, even fantastical, elements. In 1516, Henry staged a masque for himself, the Duke of Suffolk and two other gentlemen, who wore mantles of cloth of silver lined with blue velvet, 'the silver pounsed in letters so the velvet might be seen through', with great Portuguese capes, and matching doublets, coats and hose. Four ladies with them wore Savoy-style dresses in blue velvet lined with cloth of gold, silver mantles and bonnets of burnished gold, accompanied by torch bearers in white and blue satin. According to the contemporary chronicler Edward Hall, this ensemble 'pleased much every person and in especial, the queen', who invited them into her chamber for a torchlit dance. In August 1519, an order for the revels at New Hall, in Essex, included twelve coats, six green with gold dragon scales and six yellow with silver scales.

In particular, though, the young king loved to dress up as the character Robin Hood, or a similar outlaw huntsman figure, riding to Shooter's Hill in 1515, with Catherine, and a cast including Lady May, Maid Marion, Friar Tuck and Little John. The serious business of Tudor clothing could easily spiral into the fantastic, even the dreamlike, fusing the person of the king with the characters he played, and giving him a touch of godlike magic to adopt a range of real, historical and fictional identities. In this sense, Henry began the process of using clothing to transcend the limits of his mortality which his daughter, Elizabeth I, would use to preserve an image of eternal youth as the 'Faerie Queen'.

※

The king was not the only peacock at court. One leading Tudor courtier used his wealth and position to display the dangerous aspirations that adorned his path to the executioner's block. Henry's closest male relative, Edward Stafford, Duke of Buckingham, was renowned for his flamboyant dress.

In 1509, he was singled out by chronicler Edward Hall for his choice of clothing at Henry's coronation, wearing a 'gown all of goldsmith's work, very costly', and in 1514–15, he spent £226 5s on textiles, £125 on cloth, £62 13s on 'precious things and jewels' and £25 2s on furs, at a time when a labourer might earn between £5 and £10 a year.[7] Stafford continued to vie with the king's appearance, but however annoying this proved to Henry it was his cousin's open speculation about the succession that ultimately ended his aspirations.

Other noblemen also dressed to impress, with Nicholas, Lord Vaux, attending the wedding of Prince Arthur in 1501 wearing a 'gown of purple velvet adorned with pieces of gold so thick and massy that besides the silk and fur, it was valued at a thousand pounds, and also a collar of "S"s, weighing 800lb in nobles'.[8]

At his death in 1513, the inventoried clothes of John de Vere, Earl of Oxford, included a black velvet gown at £6, a crimson velvet gown lined with marten at £10, a gown of crimson velvet upon velvet, lined and edged with marten at £12 and a black gown of tinsel satin furred with sable, costing £20. The shopping list of another royal cousin, Henry Courtenay, Earl of Devon, in 1519, contained a velvet partlet, a black satin doublet, an arming doublet, a Spanish cloak, 26 yards of black velvet for a gown and frock at 10s per yard, new shoes, buskins, gloves, points and garter ribbons, and the repair of two shirts and a black velvet gown.

Queen Catherine of Aragon's clothing equalled her husband's for majesty. In spring 1520, her wardrobe department was preparing for the sumptuous trip to France, sourcing fabrics to make her new dresses. One merchant was paid £150 for providing her with two pieces of white satin at over 86 yards long, 58 yards of green velvet, 73 yards of green Bruges satin, yellow and russet velvet, black velvet, crimson velvet and green cloth of gold. Another vendor, Barker 'of Chepe' (Cheapside, London), supplied the queen with more white satin and his neighbour, Barton, also 'of Chepe', sold her black sarcenet and green and russet velvet.

An agent named George Bryggus purchased 14s 4d worth of crimson velvet for Catherine from 'Colier of Chepe', who also received an order for yellow damask from the Lord Chamberlain for the queen's use.[9] A John Norris in Friday Street supplied linen cloth; Master Smith of Watling Street gave red kersey; and broad grey cloth was bought from an unspecified seller at Blackwell Hall.[10]

Catherine's wardrobe would also have been supplied by the luxury foreign imports arriving at the London docks from all over Europe and beyond: cloths of silk, damasks, satins, violet and black camlet from Venice; double-twisted wimple silk and seed pearls from the Persian Gulf; lamb skins from Puglia in Italy; dyed silks in yellow, blue and green from Turkey, Sicily and Greece; and gold from the New World.[11]

The use of colour sent overt messages about social status and personal preferences. Luxury dyes, such as purple and gold, were limited by sumptuary laws, while others, like white and green, or red, were adopted as dynastic symbols. Henry VIII appears to have favoured the earthy russet, Mary wore Spanish black and Elizabeth tempered her black with the white of her virgin state.

In the early sixteenth century, developments in dyeing introduced a greater range of red and orange shades, using kermes and madder. Henry's wardrobe shows the popularity of these in the 1540s, but the most frequent colour he ordered was the expensive black, with blue and green being relatively little used outside the creation of hunting clothes. An inventory of the clothes of Henry's illegitimate son, the Duke of Richmond and Somerset, made in 1531 when he was 12, shows that most of his wardrobe was black and white with the occasional splash of colour, such as a yellow doublet, or embroidery of roses.[12] Some of the brightest colours were found on the king's jousting costumes and arming doublets, where combinations of opposites such as purple and yellow or blue and tawny were popular.

As the sixteenth century progressed, the dyer's palette expanded. Increased trade during Elizabeth's reign brought purple from seashells in Lebanon, dark blue from the Indian indigo plant and crimson from the Aztecs' cochineal beetle. Colours were associated with certain emotions, with red for courage appearing on the condemned as they mounted the scaffold, most famously Mary, Queen of Scots, and white for purity being worn by Catherine of Aragon, Anne Boleyn and Elizabeth I on the way to their coronations.

Brown and grey, for humility and simplicity, were the colours of monastic orders, and appeared frequently in association with the lower classes, as their dyes were much cheaper to produce. Paler, unfixed vegetable dyes indicated social status, just as the intense colours of fixed dyes spoke of their wearer's wealth. Harrison lists some of the newly invented shades 'to please fantastical heads' as 'goose-turd green, peas-porridge tawny, popinjay blue, lusty gallant and the devil-in-the-head', although the colour of the last two is only to be guessed at! In the 1530s, a John Williamson wrote to Thomas Cromwell about the pattern of new coats or the privy chamber and that he had a 'new colour sad' to be made up for the minister.[13]

Two accounts of women's clothing payments in 1533 highlight the contrast between those in power and those aspiring to it. Honor, Lady Lisle, entrusted her shopping list to a servant to take to market for her, which included 20 ells of black velvet at 11s per ell, 2 ells of cloth of gold costing 34s per ell, 7 ells of white damask at 6s, 1 ell of white satin costing 9s, and 11 ells of black satin at 7s.[14] Honor hoped to place her two daughters in the household of the new queen, Anne Boleyn, who was crowned on 1 June that year.

The royal wardrobe accounts list the materials for Anne's complicated coronation robes as requiring 1 yard of crimson satin, 3 yards of crimson taffeta to line her gown, 2 yards of black satin, 2 yards of black buckram to line her bodice, 3 yards of frieze to line the pleats of her gown, 1 yard of white satin 'to make habiliments for her head', 5 yards of white satin for a kirtle, 2 yards of red cloth to line her kirtle, and 'seventeen pieces of goldsmith's work'.

For the journey through the London streets, Anne followed the example of Catherine of Aragon by wearing 'filmy white with a coronet of gold' and travelling in a white satin litter lined with white cloth of gold. On the day of her coronation, though, she took a litter of crimson velvet, lined with crimson damask, bordered with black velvet and gold and silk fringe. She wore a violet velvet gown, furred with ermine, a kirtle of crimson velvet, a cap of pearls and stones under her coronet and her ladies dressed in matching crimson.[15]

Records for the privy purse expenses of Lady Mary, eldest daughter of Henry VIII, aged 21 in 1537, reveal the wardrobe of a young, Catholic royal who had been through a period of hardship. She paid for two sleeves to be embroidered and a border to be lengthened, while 10s rented her a room at Greenwich in which to store her robes when she visited court. New clothes were made from 2 ells of linen, 7 yards of white satin, 4 yards of worsted for a kirtle, which was lined with fur costing 3s, and taffeta costing 2s.

Mary was conscious of the need to maintain her royal appearance, paying John of Antwerp £4 17s 7d for goldsmith's work, 2s to Francis for making a brooch, £66 13s 4d to Farnando for 100 pearls and £16 to another goldsmith named Orton for 'certain pieces' of work. She also took part in the traditional gift giving at New Year 1538, presenting her newborn brother with a cap, and looked after her servants, giving the male staff satin doublets and paying 20s for new hose and shoes for her fool, Jane.[16]

Painted in her childhood in a miniature by Lucas Horenbout, Mary wore the badge of her fiancé, Emperor Charles V, and strings of pearls around a central cross pendant. Sitting for Master John in her mid-twenties, she chose a gold-embroidered dress with large red turn-back sleeves, lined with white, the cuffs slashed and adorned with gold *aiglettes*. Pearls are used on her headdress, throat, bodice and waist. She wore a few rings and two pendants hang one above the other around her neck and at her breast, one featuring a red rose and the other with black and red stones, both of which have a pearl drop suspended below.

Later portraits of Mary show her far more sombrely, although she is just as majestic in her attire. Her betrothal portrait, painted by Anthonis Mor and featuring the symbolic red carnation, gives her similar jewellery in the pearls and brooch, with a gold girdle and pomander, which are also replicated in her joint picture with Philip, by Hans Eworth.

Jewels were an essential ingredient of a Tudor monarch's majesty and the inventory of Mary's collection, dating from 1542–46 when she was an unmarried 'illegitimate' daughter of the king, included rubies, emeralds, diamonds and pendants featuring biblical tales, crosses, flowers and dolphins from her engagement to the Dauphin of France. Mary owned gold girdles, like the one in her picture, enamelled with white and black, diamond and gold rings, gold bracelets, beads of garnet, coral, agate and lapis lazuli, and symbolic items that had been gifts from her parents, stepmothers and fiancés. Even the most modest and sombre of Tudor monarchs understood the need for visual display as a signifier of power.

⚜ CLOTHING AS BATTLEGROUND ⚜

Clothing could become a battleground, or diplomatic tool, for individual Tudors or specific groups. This might indicate particular religious or diplomatic allegiances, or national or cultural identities. In 1545, ambassador Thomas Vaughan wrote home from Antwerp about an individual who had aroused suspicion due to his appearance:

> Lately received their letter describing two men, an Italian and a Norman, but could not get knowledge of any such here, till he remembered the being in the English house of a man 'clothed in a cloak, girded abouts him, of sad russet mantle frieze which had a square cape sewed behind to the same of yellow buckram, or some other thing that was yellow. This yellow was patched on behind the cloak poorly, as the cloak also was very poor. He had a black beard growing the breadth of iij. fingers beneath his chin; his face somewhat broad and lean; a pair of black hose worn asunder above his shoes; a black cap, double turffed, worn threadbare and greasy'.[1]

The man claimed to be English, and spoke like an Englishman, but admitted he had left Venice after getting into trouble there and intended to return to England and become a gunner. The bearer of the letter was warned to follow him closely, to 'dog' him, if she should come across him, and then have him arrested.[2] What had revealed him was the fact that his clothing was shabby and did not match his expected status.

At the English court, the rivalry that developed between Catherine of Aragon and Anne Boleyn in the late 1520s was reflected in their respective use of Spanish and French fashions as metonymic for their opposing European sympathies. The London crowds of 1501 were bemused by the 'straunge fashion of the Spanyshe nacion' of hooped farthingale skirts and the young Catherine's red cap that resembled that of a cardinal. However, Catherine quickly read the mood and

changed into an English hood and English-style skirts to please her
subjects, even wearing the fashionable French hood for a while. When
in 1520, Catherine was reluctant to attend Henry's meeting with
Francis I, her deliberate choice of a Spanish headdress, with 'a tress of
hair over her shoulders and gown, a dress of cloth of gold and jewels
around her neck', signalled her disapproval.

However, the French fashions, which were considered somewhat
inappropriate, appealed to some of the ladies in her retinue. The
chronicler Polydore Vergil observed that 'the women of England
adopted a new manner of dress from the more wanton ladies of France,
not very fitting for their modesty', abandoning 'the very honourable
style of their ancestors'[3] and continuing to wear it after their return
home. If French fashions were associated with loose morality, their
embodiment in Anne Boleyn would make them even more dangerous
in the following decade.

After six years at the sophisticated French court, Anne returned to
England in early 1522, 'unrivalled in the gracefulness of her attire',
and became 'the model and mirror of those who were at court, for
she was always well-dressed, and every day made some change in the
fashion of her garments'.[4] By 1527, she had captured Henry's heart.

Anne's Francophile influence contrasted with the Spanish and English
styles worn by the queen and Princess Mary. In public, Catherine
reacted by increasing her authority through display, adopting even more
jewels and sumptuous clothing, in a clear, material demonstration that
her status superseded Anne's. Behind the scenes, Catherine retained
her habit of sewing Henry's shirts by hand and ordered her embroiderers to continue to link the royal initials together in their designs. In the
late 1520s, she used both the production of clothing and her personal
appearance as material tools to fight for her marriage. When Anne discovered this in 1530, she employed a seamstress.

However, none of this manipulation of the fabric of rank could
decrease Henry's desire for a son. In 1532, a year after Catherine had
been banished from court and when Henry was on the verge of marrying Anne, the former queen was ordered to relinquish her jewels
to her rival. To have one's visual indicators of status removed by
force, just as Thomas Cromwell was stripped of his badges of office
at court in 1540, was a particularly cruel degradation to the Tudors.
The Duke of Norfolk was dispatched to Hatfield to retrieve the items,
but Catherine refused to 'give up my jewels for such a wicked purpose

as that of ornamenting a person who is the scandal of Christendom'.[5] In the end, she was not given a choice and was only permitted to retain a small gold crucifix containing a shard of the true cross.

Henry was already lavishing gifts of jewellery upon Anne, including a gold wheel set with diamonds costing £4 and a golden girdle costing £18, while Holbein designed a pendant with interconnecting initials H and A. Between May 1531 and May 1532, over £100 was spent on jewels for the queen-in-waiting, including the resetting of stones that had formerly been owned by Catherine.

Just as Anne had defined herself in visual opposition to Catherine, Anne's own replacement, Jane Seymour, favoured a more modest English style and motifs in her dress. Where Anne had been dark, French and elegant in her attire, Jane was fair and demure. When Honor Lisle's daughter, Anne Bassett, was granted a position in Jane's household in 1537, she was swiftly disabused of the misconception that she could wear her French-style clothes but needed to replace them with gowns of black satin and velvet, and simple bonnets with frontlets and a pearl edging. An early biographer of Henry VIII, Edward Herbert, compared the two queens, saying, 'The richer Queen Jane was in clothes, the fairer she appeared, but that the other [Anne], the richer she was apparelled, the worse she looked', and Sir John Russell wrote that Jane was 'discreetest, fairest and humblest of the king's wives'. Clouded as these comments were by subsequent events, they reveal just how far clothing was a gendered weapon, a construct of attraction, identity and status, and a tool of self-definition which could backfire.

Choosing to associate with the clothing of a particular nationality was a statement of identity and intention. Naturally, Princess Mary favoured the Spanish fashions associated with her mother. In 1544, her cousin, Maria of Aragon, sent her a gift with a note which read that she 'had heard from the bearer of this letter, Captain F, that she is very fond of Spanish gloves, and takes the liberty of sending some, which she hopes will suit her Highness'.[6] When Mary was pursuing her marriage with Philip of Spain in 1553–54, she frequently wore black, a colour associated with the Hapsburg Empire, her heritage on her mother's side, and displaying affiliation with her future husband. Wearing black almost had a symbolic or sympathetic force, as if she could will the union to succeed and bring her husband to her side.

When Philip arrived on English soil in the rainy summer of 1554, dressed in a splendid coat embroidered with gold, he was asked to abandon his Spanish clothing and wear instead a French gold coat set with precious stones, to echo Mary's own costume. This was indicative of the atypical balance of power in the marriage, just as the usual rules of the bride standing on the left were inverted during the ceremony to present Mary as more powerful. At Mary's insistence, Philip adopted the coat and rules of his new kingdom, but his advisor, Ruy Gomez, believed Mary would have been better to wear Spanish fashions, which would have made her look less 'old and flabby'. However, Philip's influence led to the English adopting the high-standing collar, the shorter Spanish cloak, sleeveless jerkin, soft leather and sombre colours. Coupled with the case of Anne of Cleves, this indicates just how far ideals of beauty were equated with national dress and clothing which offended the aesthetic of a bride's adoptive country could contribute to their downfall.

Clothes could also represent areas of social conflict. Sumptuary laws, or Statutes of Apparel, had historically been used as a means of keeping people in their place and allowing for an accurate reflection of rank when it came to expenditure on visual display. They were not only restricted to apparel, but included spending on all areas, including food and drink.

Henry VIII's maternal grandfather Edward IV had introduced rules restricting the use of cloth of gold, purple silk and certain furs to the ranks of knight and above, while shoes or boots with pointed toes above 2in long were forbidden to those below the status of lord. Henry VII limited the quantities of material used in gowns, measured according to rank, with dukes, marquises and archbishops permitted 16 yards, earls 14, viscounts 12, barons 8 and knights 6 yards. Still, however, aspirational Tudors sought to dress for success.

Sumptuary laws were reissued by Henry VIII in 1509, 1514, 1515 and 1533, once by Mary I in 1554, and nine times more by Elizabeth. Henry reserved the colour purple and certain fabrics for the use of the royal family alone, while furs, silks, cloth of gold and silver were to be used only by the elite, in response to the rising number of wealthy townsfolk and merchants who were dressing up to increase their social standing.

The justification for this implementation was given as the correlative lawlessness, as 'the great and costly array and apparel used within this realm ... hath been the occasion of great impoverishing of divers of the King's subjects and provoked many of them to rob and to do extortion and other unlawful deeds to maintain thereby their costly array'.[7] Women were not included in these laws, in the expectation that their attire would be subject to the status and regulation of their husbands. It was intended that the laws were enforced by Justices of the Peace, aldermen, mayors and sheriffs, but many considered this a rule worth breaking, with the result that fines were introduced in 1515 for repeat offenders.

Yet these rules and fines were repeatedly ignored. Tudors of all ranks judged that they were worth flouting in order to reap the benefits of aspirational display. By 1533, it was necessary to reissue them due to the 'utter impoverishment and undoing of many inexpert and light persons inclined to pride, mother of all vices', which, 'not good laws notwithstanding', had increased 'either by the occasion of the perverse and froward [sic] manners and usage of people, or for that errors and abuses rooted and taken into long custom'.[8]

Anyone under the estate of a duke, marquis or earl, save for Knights of the Garter, was forbidden from wearing blue, crimson or scarlet velvet, or the fur of civet or lynx, or any kind of embroidery. In an attempt to revive the flagging wool industry, individuals were also confined to only wearing woollen items made within the realm and no foreign imports. No man under the rank of baron's son or knight was allowed to wear a gold chain, or any gold jewellery, except for rings, which weighed above 1oz, or to decorate their horse likewise. Nor could they wear velvet, lynx fur or pinking embroidery, created by making a pattern out of fine holes pricked into fabric. Cloth of gold tissue and purple silk were reserved, again, for royalty, although a little gold tissue might be used on the doublets and sleeveless coats of dukes and marquises. Gentlemen whose incomes were less than £20 a year were forbidden from wearing silk or the furs of black rabbits and lambs.

However, even clergymen tried to flout the laws, as a letter from William, Archbishop of York, exposes:

The injunctions given by the Archbishop, forbidding dissimilarity of habit, as some use worsted and others precious vests, to the great scandal of their religion; and others again ordinary vests. All are to dress alike. The Abbot shall take once a year a general consultation with the convent on the state of his house. He shall not allow wine to be sold within the precincts. He shall not wear in his hood or his sleeve, internally or externally, silk of velvet or any other silk, nor gilt spurs; nor, in the saddle or trappings of his horses, silk or gold.[9]

In 1535, Thomas Legh, one of Henry's visitors investigating the monasteries, was accused of conducting himself in an arrogant manner. This related to his clothing as well as his behaviour. In his defence against 'enormities and abuses unjustly laid to my charge', Legh responded firstly to comments that his velvet gown was 'not fit for me to wear' as probably above his station. He accepted this, saying he was 'content to leave it' but he knew 'right well, in some things I can wear no worse'. He had worn no other since arriving from London 'but one that Richmond's wife bought for me of Garter's son immediately after his death, fur and all for £4', and because it was 'light and warm', he took it with him.[10] Legh's gown is a powerful metaphor for the antagonism his role raised when judging monastic lifestyles. Although he purchased the gown, he is being accused of wearing 'borrowed robes' in the sense that he was displaying a 'sensual appetite' deemed inappropriate for a man accusing the monks and nuns of comparable vices.

In 1578, William Harrison was so outspoken in his mockery of his countrymen's penchant for flamboyant dress that he was clearly addressing a familiar trope:

We do seem to imitate all nations round about us, wherein we be like to the polypus or chameleon; and thereunto bestow most cost upon our arses, and much more than upon all the rest of our bodies, as women do likewise upon their heads and shoulders. In women also, it is most to be lamented, that they do now far exceed the lightness of our men (who nevertheless are transformed from the cap even to the very shoe), and such staring attire as in time past was supposed meet for none but light housewives only is now become a habit for chaste and sober matrons. What should I say of their doublets with pendant codpieces on the breast full of jags and cuts, and sleeves of sundry colours? Their galligascons to bear out their bums and make their attire to fit plum round (as they term it) about them. Their fardingals, and diversely coloured nether stocks of silk, jersey, and such like, whereby their bodies are rather deformed than commended? I have met with some of these trulls in London so disguised that it hath passed my skill to discern whether they were men or women.[11]

If the Tudors were keen to commission portraits to mark their social successes, they were also determined to use their own bodies as living canvases and wear their wealth for all to see. Visiting London in 1592, the Duke of Württemberg observed that in some cases clothing was even prioritised over food in the constant dance of display of the Tudor streets: 'They go dressed out in exceedingly fine clothe [sic], and give all their attention to their ruffs and stuffs, to such a degree that ... many a one does not hesitate to wear velvet in the streets ... whilst at home perhaps they have not a piece of dry bread.'[12]

A year later, Thomas Nashe commented that 'the rich disdain the poor' and women 'disdain to wear that everyone wears'.[13] If ordinary Englishmen and women came dangerously close to bankrupting themselves for the sake of their wardrobe, it was in the attempt to emulate the upper classes, and the example set by the king.

Lower down the social spectrum, individuals had less disposable income to spend on clothing, but they were still subject to legislation. Serving men must ensure the material in their hose cost less than 2s the yard, and their overgarments not more than 3s the yard, unless they were wearing their masters' livery. The sergeants and yeomen of London's mayor had got into the habit by 1486 of making their gowns too long, so it was ordained that the hems of their gowns must be 1ft above the sole of their shoe, upon penalty of losing their office.[14]

Those of the lower ranks might only wear grey rabbit fur but not black, English lamb, English-produced wool, or any decoration anywhere and they could not even wear a silk ribbon on their bonnet. No journeyman, or those taking wages in handicrafts, might wear clothes costing more than 2s 4d the yard, and hose of only 16d.[15]

At court, and in the streets, the subtleties of coloured fur mattered a great deal, and such small details were constantly observed with a rigidity that created a visual, social vigilance that none could evade.

Thomas Harte, a master gunner of the king's ordnance, dwelt in a 'mansion place' in Rotherhithe and died in December 1526. His

wardrobe contained two long gowns, a marten fur, two doublets, one of
taffeta and one of velvet, a riding hood and three velvet jerkins. He also
still had a collection of clothing belonging to his wives: gowns, furred
and lined with velvet, buckram and taffeta, two kirtles of tawny camlet,
a velvet bonnet, two pairs of silk sleeves and a velvet stomacher.[16]

A Robert Whethill was described in a letter by Thomas Warley,
written on 2 May 1535, strutting about court in his finery:

> Whethill brags freshly in the court in a coat of crimson taffeta, cut
> and lined with yellow sarcenet, a shirt wrought with gold, his hosen
> scarlet, the breeches crimson velvet, cut and edged and lined with
> yellow sarcenet, his shoes crimson velvet and likewise his sword
> girdle and scabbard, a cloak of red frisado, a scarlet cap with feathers
> red and yellow. He hath many lookers-over.[17]

One of Mary I's first actions was the reintroduction of the sumptuary laws. Those earning less than £20 a year were prohibited from
wearing silk, under the threat of three months' imprisonment and
the hefty fine of £10 a day and for every subsequent day the offending item was worn. If any servant broke this law, their master was
liable for a fine of £100, ensuring that private households were carefully regulated from the top down. This was a huge amount when
servants were accustomed to punishments such as one penny for
cursing, or not making their bed. And yet the errant Tudor peacocks
were not deterred.

Upon Elizabeth's succession in 1558, a proclamation was issued
reminding her subjects to dress according to their status, in line with
former guidance. When this failed, she appointed officers to arrest
anyone coming to court incorrectly dressed and ordered that four men
of good standing be chosen in each town to ensure the rules were followed. Hosiers and tailors were forbidden from making any pair of
hose out of more than a yard and three-quarters of material, on pain of
being barred from their profession. This amount was further limited
three years later, and a table was drawn up to clarify which rank was
permitted to wear which material, as a simpler, visual shorthand for
the people.

By 1575, it was necessary to reissue the law as a result of the 'daily
increasing excess', particularly 'the wasting and undoing of a great
number of young gentlemen, otherwise serviceable ... seeking by

apparel to be esteemed as gentlemen'. Courtiers were bankrupting themselves. Fixated on the 'vain show of these things', they were consuming themselves, 'their goods and lands, which their parents left unto them, but also run into such debts and shifts, as they cannot live out of danger of laws, without attempting of unlawful acts'.

As the playwright Ben Jonson had one of his characters quip in 1590, 'T'were good you turned four or five hundred acres of your best land into two or three trunks of apparel.'[18] This must have been a difficult tendency to curb, as trendsetters like Elizabeth's favourite, Robert Dudley, were spending sums like £563 on seven doublets and two cloaks.

In another observation, William Harrison commented upon the fickleness and expense involved in following English fashions:

> The fantastical folly of our nation ... is such that no form of apparel liketh us longer than the first garment is in the wearing ... if it be not laid aside to receive some other trinket newly devised by the fickle-headed tailors ... Today there is none to the Spanish guise, tomorrow the French toys are the most fine and delectable, ere long ... the high Almain [German] fashion, by and by the Turkish manner ... it is a world to see the costliness and the curiosity, the excess and the vanity, the pomp and the bravery, the change and the variety, and finally the fickleness and the folly ... Oh, how much cost is bestowd nowdays upon our bodies, and how little upon our souls.[19]

The development of that Elizabethan icon, the ruff, provoked particularly strong reactions. Originating from the small ruffle at the drawstring collar of a shirt or chemise, it was initially fairly modest, with Elizabeth being content in 1565 with 10 yards of cambric for use at her throat and wrists. Later, though, it was discovered that the ruff could be stiffened with starch from the Netherlands and heated goffering irons were used to mould them into elaborate folds. Occasionally they were tinted pink or yellow, as a result of the vegetable dyes used, but Elizabeth forbade the existence of pale blue ruffs, which had become symbols of Scottish nationalism. By the end of the 1570s, ruffs had increased in width to a quarter of a yard wide, requiring 18 or 19 yards of fine lawn (linen or cotton), starched and supported by wiring or rods, but could only be worn once before they needed to be reset.

An act of the Privy Council singled out excessively long cloaks and the 'outrageous, monstrous and abominable ruffs', which were 'super-fluous, wasteful and unwieldy'. Philip Stubbes' 1583 *The Anatomy of Abuses* referred to the 'devilruff' as being soaked in the 'devil's liquour'.[20] The sense of high fashion being a cultural costume, unsuit-able for work and daily life, underlined the status of those fortunate enough to afford it, and furthered the cult of royalty and the elite.

At Easter 1580, a dispute arose when the Lord Mayor attempted to act upon the queen's commands 'for the reforming of monstrous ruffs'. Having spotted a Mr Hewson, son-in-law of the Lord Chief Baron, wearing such a confection 'in the open street', the Mayor 'admon-ished him' in a 'friendly' way, only for Hewson to reply 'in a very contemptuous speech'. For the 'credit of his office', the Mayor had been 'compelled to take further steps to enforce the royal commands' but, as a result, had 'given great offence to the Lord Chief Baron'. Fearing 'his displeasure for the rest of his life', the Mayor wrote to the Lord Treasurer, asking him to help smooth the matter over.[21]

While Elizabeth reissued new restrictions, her own ruffs grew wider and more exaggerated. A new element of the fantastic developed, with gauzy fairy wings and cartwheel ruffs being complimented by embroi-dery. This featured elements of the natural world, including flowers and plants, often taken from the printed herbals of the day, animals, birds, insects, fish, astronomy and mythical creatures. As the embodi-ment of England, Elizabeth's clothing reflected her role as Mother Nature, an alternative figure of fertility to the role of motherhood she had rejected. In nurturing her country, enabling it to flourish, Elizabeth was identified as the Empress of Flowers, as early as Lucas de Heere's 1572 allegory of the Tudor family, with Elizabeth followed by the god-dess of Plenty, carrying her horn filled with fruits and flowers. She was simultaneously a symbol of earthiness and the ethereality of her Faerie Queen status, echoed in Edmund Spenser's fantastical allegory.

By the end of Elizabeth's reign, the increasingly widespread use of luxury fabrics was noted by foreign visitors to court, with Breuning von Buchenbach writing home to Württemberg in 1596 of the many 'earls, lords and knights [who] wore gold and silver dress and their raiment embroidered with precious stones and pearls'. He had never seen 'so much splendour and such fine clothes' at any other court.[22] It was this message of opulent dress that conveyed a sense of national identity and strength, with the glittering queen metonymic for a powerful England.

❧ CLOTHING, GENDER AND SEXUALITY ❧

The patriarchal Tudors used clothing as signifiers of gender identity. This required firstly dressing according to one's social status,
as dictated by the sumptuary laws, but also conforming to gendered
expectations when it came to items of apparel, headgear and hair-
styles. Women dressing as men, or the less common case of men
dressing as women, compromised visual codes and rigid behavioural
expectations. By doing so, men emasculated themselves and women
rejected their subordinate position. For both, it implied a dissolution
of the self, as argued by Philip Stubbes in 1583: 'Our apparel was given
as a sign distinctive to discern betwixt sex and sex, and therefore one
to wear the apparel of the other sex, is to participate with the same,
and to adulterate the veritie of his own kind.'[1]

The Tudor correlation between cross-dressing and sexual identity
was complex, and lines between transvestitism and homosexuality could be blurred in the eyes of authority figures, transgressing a
swathe of cultural codes and resulting in punishment. Sometimes
cross-dressing may have been a statement of sexual preference or
even an erotic act, but it could also have occurred for practical reasons, such as for disguise, necessity or if a woman attempted to ensure
equality of treatment.

For men, the adoption of female attire led to accusations ranging from
effeminisation to homosexuality, and censure from the 1533 Buggery
Act, although this act was aimed at cases of sodomy, whether of men,
women or animals, not only confined to sexual acts between males.
Tudor popular culture reacted with horror to men whom it perceived
had compromised their masculinity and offended the eye of God, as the
late-Elizabethan Protestant critics were quick to assert. Thomas Beard,
in his *Theatre of God's Judgements*, described cross-dressing men
as 'lascivious and effeminate ... dishonest and ignominious',[2] while
William Harrison was increasingly unable to differentiate between
men and women, so that 'women are become men and men transformed into monsters'.[3] Most critics were in agreement that the greater
affront to nature was committed by transgressive men than women.

Changes in the masculine silhouette indicate a less exaggerated
sartorial virility as the sixteenth century advanced. As early as the
1490s, the tight hose, beardless face and crimped hair of fashionable

courtiers attracted commentary, such as that by the poet Sebastian
Brandt, author of *The Ship of Fools*:

> An honour t'was to grow a beard
> Effeminate dandies now say no!
> Smear apish grease on face and hair
> And leave the neck entirely bare ...
> Vile sulphur, resin curl their hair
> An egg white's added too, with care ...
> Their number (of lice) would now wax untold
> Since modern clothes have many a fold
> Coat, bodice, slipper, also skirts
> Boots, hose and shoes, and even shirts.[4]

The new fashions led to an indecent exposure of anatomy, which was
easily correlated with immodesty, loose morality and sexual disgrace.
Brandt continues:

> What nature would conceal and hide,
> You bare it, make a public show.
> 'Twill lead to evil, lead to woe,
> And then grow worse and harm your name.[5]

Sometimes fashion forced the Tudors into very strange shapes. By the
reign of Henry VIII, codpieces and swords grew larger and more prominent, with broad shoulders and the lower leg revealed by a shorter coat.
From the middle of the century, sleeves became wider, puffed with
wired support, and the Spanish farthingale's conical skirts were replaced
by a French wheel or drum, made from whalebone, coupled with the
cartwheel ruff which set the head on a separate plate above the rest.

For men, the doublet became rounded and protruding with stuffing,
creating a peascod belly, and while the hose also underwent a period
of exaggerated padding, they later shrunk to be close fitting. Then, the
elongated legs, disappearing codpieces and minimised weaponry of
portraits in the last decades of Elizabeth's life created a wider fluidity
of identity, as observed by a Dutch visitor to England, who described
how the people 'dress in elegant, light and costly garments, but are
very inconsistent and desirous of novelties, changing their costumes
every year, both men and women'.

This type of slavishness to fashion was also associated with loose morality and inconsistency, and was considered an inappropriate preoccupation for a man. As one Elizabethan woodcut read:

Many men are become so effeminate that they care not what they spend in disguising themselves, ever desiring new toys and inventing new fashions. Therefore a certain man that would picture every countryman in his accustomed apparel ... he pictured the Englishman all naked, unto whom he gave a pair of shears in the one hand, and a piece of cloth in the other, to the end he could shape his apparel after such fashion as he himself liked.[6]

The one place where cross-dressing was acceptable, and even then, it was not always acceptable, was on the Elizabethan stage. There, it commanded laughs and created plot confusion with boy actors taking the female roles. With no women permitted to act, the romantic and comedy potential of clothing was exploited in characters ranging from *Twelfth Night*'s Viola, who woos and is wooed as a man, while concealing her femininity, to Francis Flute playing the role of Thisbe in *A Midsummer Night's Dream*, despite sporting a full beard.

It has been debated by some literary critics whether this was less an Elizabethan dramatic convention than a charged, homoerotic expression of attraction, which indicated undercurrents of social and cultural subversion.[7] Recently, Laura Levine has added that male characters who compromised their sartorial identities experienced a parallel loss of virility and became powerless, as if their masculinity was a changeable factor.[8]

However, it may be that this was more reflective of their inability to enact their masculine qualities while dressed in female clothing. As 'women' they were temporarily sharing the experience of women under a patriarchal regime, required to modify their behaviour as actors and individuals, and eliciting the correlative masculine responses. Such plays usually highlight exactly what women were not permitted to do in society, with female characters reacting to restrictions but often gaining a brief taste of freedom. Yet they always conclude with the female cross-dresser happily casting off her masculine attire and returning to a position of subservience.

An unusual case of February 1566 involved the cross-dressing of Mary, Queen of Scots, in court theatricals. A masque was held to invest Mary's young, troublesome husband, Lord Darnley, with the French Order of St Michael. One of the bones of contention between the couple had been her refusal to allow him to be crowned king, and her parallel refusal on this occasion, not permitting him to use the royal arms, was an indicator that he would not achieve his wish in the forthcoming Parliament.

Lately, their relationship had deteriorated and, with Mary five months pregnant, Darnley was merely referred to as 'the queen's husband'. Where his name had formerly taken precedence on documents, he was now placed after her.

When Mary and her ladies danced in a masque before Darnley, they were 'all cled in men's apperrell', an unsubtle show of literally who was wearing the trousers in the marriage. Darnley was unable to tolerate such a display. Within weeks, his plans to rebel came to fruition and Mary's favourite, and reputed lover, David Rizzio, was murdered.

Nor was this the first time that cross-dressing had played a role in Scottish court entertainments. In November 1561, two teams of six men had been pitted against each other to run at the ring, one team dressed in the usual costumes and masks, while the others were disguised as women. Interestingly, it was the 'women' who won, subverting the usual conventions about superior male abilities.[9]

Another powerful example of cross-dressing could be found across the Channel. Henri III of France, whose fifteen-year reign ended in assassination in 1589, often dressed as a woman as an aspect of the homosexuality he openly displayed at court. Henri and his favourites appeared at masques, tournaments and parties wearing women's dresses, make-up, earrings and jewellery.

Contemporary French diarist, Pierre d'Estoile, recorded that the king's *mignons* wore their hair the way whores in a bordello did – pomaded, artificially curled, recurled and flowing back over small velvet bonnets.[10] The attacks by Henri's critics focused upon him reducing, or feminising, his masculinity, with the implication of ineffectuality and, by extension, inability to govern.

He and his favourites were not criticised for looking like women, but for looking like whores, which in this case were depicted as caricatures of female sexuality. It has been suggested that his mother, Catherine de Medici, encouraged this form of display, inviting guests to attend masques in cross-dress, either to indulge her son or to contribute to his effeminisation, which allowed her to retain power.

One of Henri's favourite outfits was a combination of male and female elements: breeches with a doublet which had an open throat to expose the lace collar and strings of pearls that were fashionable among the ladies of the court. Such occasions provided fuel for his enemies, and a plethora of pamphlets attacking him for transvestitism and sodomy were produced, contributing to his unpopularity.[11] Wearing overly ornate women's clothing was thought to make a man 'weak, tender and infirm, not able to abide such sharp conflicts and blustering storms', an abhorrence to nature, a true 'monster', by the Tudor definition.[12]

Examples of cross-dressing outside the theatre were comparatively rare, especially when it came to men dressing as women. The second half of the sixteenth century gave women increasing licence to adopt more masculine styles, following the fashion of a queen whose doublets were cut along the male line, and who declared herself equal to the abilities and qualities of her male peers.

Examples also survive of urban prostitutes wearing mannish clothing or with short haircuts, although how this affected their business is unclear. In July 1575, Dorothy Clayton, spinster, was brought before the Alderman's Court as, 'contrary to all honesty and womanhood', she 'commonly goes about the city apparelled in man's attire. She has abused her body with sundry persons and lives an incontinent life.' Dorothy was sentenced to 'stand on the pillory for two hours in men's apparel and then to be sent to Bridewell until further order'.[13]

In 1601, Margaret Wakeley was recorded as 'having a bastard child' and wearing man's apparel.[14] The dangerous androgyny and patriarchal challenge implicit in Tudor women wearing men's clothes was not just a case of sending out misleading signals, but indicative of a wider fear of social disorder and subversion that could lead to greater lawlessness. It would not be until 1620 that the pamphlet *Hic Mulier*, or *This Manlike Woman*, was published, condemning the practice of women cutting their hair, wearing doublets and wide hats, stating that 'to switch coats is to undo the work of heaven', but the seeds of its sentiments had been sown decades before.

❈

Yet, beyond the vocal reformist critics of the Elizabethan era, cross-dressing does not appear to have upset patriarchal values in England as much as it might. This may have been because it found some acceptance as part of the carnival nature of misrule, play and dressing up. Recent research in London court cases has identified only a small number of women who were punished for dressing as men, just thirteen between 1450 and 1553, and none outside the capital.[15] These cases range from the full adoption of male attire to the wearing of a hat or the cutting of hair. Some were representative of women furthering their cause or for self-protection, while only a few cases equated the change in clothing to an expression of sexuality.

In 1493, two women were lodging together, one of whom wore male clothing and was described as a concubine living under the roof of one Thomasina, suggestive of a same-sex relationship. A servant from Littlebury, in Essex, was accused in 1585 of wearing 'men's apparel disorderly in her master's house'.[16]

Where the wearing of men's clothes had been a sexual act, the subsequent punishment might include elements of sexuality and display, in order to reassign gender identity. In 1554, John Mordaunt's unnamed female partner, whom he induced to shear her hair and wear men's clothes, was tied naked to the Standard in Chepe for three hours, shamed and sexualised in her punishment and having her gender publicly reaffirmed. In 1576, Alice Young, who was 'brought like a rogue in a man's apparel', was set to labour for two weeks, while the suspicions in 1601 that Elizabeth Griffin lived an 'ill and lewd life' were 'evidently proved to the court' as she 'has used to go in man's apparel'. Both underwent 'correction' at Bridewell Prison.[17]

In comparison with the rule-breaking thespians, very few real-life cases of men cross-dressing are identified in the records or were prosecuted, and usually these received lenient punishment. Penalties in the London cases appear harsher for female transgressors than for men, such as the 1556 case of Robert Chetwyn and Robert Miles, who went out in women's clothes and in a scarf, respectively, and were merely 'pardoned their folly'.[18]

The numbers of individuals who may have cross-dressed in private cannot possibly be estimated, but their motivations, whether for erotic pleasure, personal comfort, refashioning their own identities or other, were functions of their existing relationship with clothing. An individual needed to have more than a simple utilitarian conception of clothing in order to indulge in dressing up, and either access to items worn by the other gender or the finances to afford them.

Individuals wore unusual clothing for a range of reasons. In November 1535, an unidentified woman visited Imperial ambassador Chapuys in London in disguise, to deliver controversial news, as Chapuys wrote to Charles V:

> The personage who informed ... me that the King meant to have the [Queen and Princess] dispatched at this next Parliament, came yesterday into this city in disguise to confirm what she had sent to me to say, and conjure me to warn your Majesty, and beg you most urgently to see to a remedy.[19]

To speak of Henry VIII's supposed murderous intentions towards his wife and daughter might well necessitate a disguise to prevent the individual from being condemned for treason.

In 1569, Johanna Goodman was whipped and sent for correction at Bridewell for dressing as a male servant in order to accompany her soldier husband to war.[20] Such acts, with their clear motivation of self-preservation, still attracted sexual slurs. During the Ridolfi plot of 1571, it was discussed that Mary, Queen of Scots should 'disguise herself and so have stolen away by laid horses', but the 'manner was not determined'.[21] When a Master Holland planned to assassinate the Earl of Leicester early in 1587, he was to approach him 'disfigured and shaven', and therefore unlike himself, so as to be unrecognised and to buy a few necessary moments in which to commit the act.[22]

To a society used to decoding identity according to clothing, cross-dressing sent troublesome mixed signals. In effect, for the Tudors, it was a trick of the eye, a deception that distracted from biological gender and challenged perceptions of appropriate behaviour. Cross-dressing juxtaposed the realities of personal life with the crafted image projected by clothing.

In 1595, the Lord Mayor sent the details of an examination of Jonathan Best, who had been apprehended for being 'supposed to be a woman in the habit of a man'.[23] The investigation, though, which presumably was invasive and undignified for Best, revealed that he was not crossdressing, but was intersex. His clothing was neither disguise nor costume, but something about his appearance alerted the authorities to invade his person for not neatly fitting into the defined boxes.

Best was likely to have been an exception. He was picked up because his appearance exposed a gap between public and private identities which, it was feared, would allow people to transgress boundaries that legislation like the Buggery Act and sumptuary laws were designed to enforce.

Cross-dressing was seen as indicative of unruly behaviour and role reversal on a wider scale, so those accused might be suspected of unorthodoxy and rebellion in other aspects of life, in morality, religion or general lawlessness. The very act of unruly dress was unruly in itself. It was even thought to be a manifestation of madness, for to depart from the norm was a form of madness, as the appearance of a déshabillé Ophelia signifies in *Hamlet*. Philip Stubbes' *Anatomy of Abuses* cites unruly dress as a method of breaking down social structures.

And yet, despite this, the men and women of the sixteenth century were attuned to the subtleties of costume and performance with a sophisticated ability to read visual clues and unveil deceptions, as evidenced by the numerous appearances of cross-dressing in Elizabethan drama and their constant play with signs and symbols. Often, they could see exactly what lay behind a costume choice, they just didn't like it.

⚘ ORDINARY PEOPLE'S CLOTHING ⚘

At the time of her death, Queen Elizabeth's colourful wardrobe contained around 2,000 items. In contrast, the inventory made of the clothing of a poor Oxfordshire widow, Agnes Soundie, comprised two woollen aprons, one worsted apron, one linen apron, two linen neck rails, three petticoats, one white cap, one neckerchief and two bands. No gowns were listed. Agnes may have already given these away, or else she was wearing her sole gown when she died. Poor women didn't have the luxury of owning many clothes.

Tudor wills reveal the patterns of bequeathing clothes between men and women outside the aristocracy. With new garments being expensive and time-consuming to make, durable items were passed down by men and women, with a clear sense of hierarchy in the worth these represented. Someone else's clothing, presumably the newer and cleaner the better, was worth having to the Tudors. Even the upper-middle classes engaged in this practice.

Dame Katherine Hastings, dying in 1507, left scarlet laces adorned with pearls, and sets of coral and white jasper beads. The following year, Dorothy Clopton of Kentwell Hall, who died in her twenties, left three black velvet bonnets, one of which, her 'best', was garnished with crimson velvet, and other items of brightly coloured velvet.

Sometimes garments were left to religious establishments, to ensure the continuity of worship. In 1519, Dame Joyce Perry left a cope of tawny damask, embroidered with lily flowers, to the Friars Minor in Beverley, so they would continue to pray for their benefactors, and a black velvet, crimson and cloth of gold vestment to the Lady Chapel at Aldeburgh.

When Lady Anne Cobham died in October 1558, she left to her daughter, among other items, 'a gold ring, a taglet of gold for a lace to a kirtle and two of my best wrought handkerchiefs', to her daughter-in-law, 'a gown of wrought velvet furred with jennets, a kirtle of purple velvet, and 4l. in money to pay for the nursing of her child', but the only material items she left her son were two of her handkerchiefs. She did, however, leave an unusual bequest for her staff: 'All my yarn & hemp I give & bequeath amongst my laundry servants, and all the wool that I refined for myself to be likewise divided amongst them to make them frocks.'[1]

The possessions of the middle-class Alice Bates of Appleby were inventoried in 1578, with each garment assigned a monetary value, determined by the nature of the material and its condition. The most expensive piece in her collection was a 'middle' gown valued at 6s 8d, at a time when it cost 3s to hire a horse from Dover to London; 8d for a small book; 2d to lodge for a week in an inn; a loaf of bread cost 2d and a chicken 1d. Alice had an 'old pink gown' priced at 3s 4d, an 'old middle gown' at 2s 6d and a 'middle frock' at 2s. Three red petticoats, selected for red's supposed health-giving properties, were valued at 4s 6d, and 3 yards of unused red cloth at 6d. Three 'old flaxen' smocks were valued at 6d, two handkerchiefs were 10d, but one flaxen handkerchief was 12d and a plain kerchief was valued at 8d. Alice also owned two russet aprons worth 10d, two linen aprons at 6d and what must have been a fairly smart hat at 16d.[2]

Lower down the social scale, Margaret Chadwell of Kingham left her best black gown and her worsted gown to her daughter, Jane Hyll, and her black train gown and a worsted kirtle to Mary Hyll, the clear difference emphasised in the use of the word 'best' to distinguish between two very similar dresses and delineate the closer relationship Margaret had with her daughter.[3]

In 1581, Amy Busby of Sandford left her daughter Katherine, perhaps her eldest, 'my best russet gown' and 'my best apron'. Her daughter Alice received 'my best kerchief', while another daughter, Jane, was bequeathed 'one kerchief, one smock and my good petticoat'. Amy did not forget her son's wife, either; she was generous in giving her 'my second gown, one smock and one kerchief' but the lack of adjectives such as 'best' and 'good' show the clear preference given to blood relations.[4] When Elizabeth Wenham wrote her will in 1591, she gave 'the better part of my apparel, both linen and woollen, to my sister Margery and the worse sort to my servant Phyllis, but I give my gown that is making, or newly made, to Mistress Coffin'.[5]

Men also bequeathed clothing, giving preference to family members, but in fewer numbers than women. When Thomas Cromwell made a will in 1527, thirteen years before his death, he was already one of the most powerful men in the land and had a significant amount of clothing to bequeath. To his nephew, Richard Williams, he left his best gown doublet and jacket; to his other nephew, Christopher Wellyfed, he gave his fifth gown doublet and jacket. His brother-in-law, William Wellyfed, received his third gown, a jacket and doublet, while a John Williamson got a gown, doublet and jacket, and his servant Ralph Sadler received his second-best jacket and doublet.

William Busbe of Gaginwell left all his clothes to his son in 1573, while William Parish of Coton bequeathed his dead wife's clothes to his daughter at the time of his death in 1580, and Thomas Burgoyn left his wife 'all her own apparel, rings, jewels and ornaments' in 1546. Henry Farren of Kingham left his brother Edmund 'my best robe', while to Richard Eaton he left 'my russet coat and a pair of russet hose', and Thomas Manys received a pair of hose and a petticoat (then a waistcoat).

William Colcott, a Merchant of the Staple who died in 1593, passed on his second-best gown to an Anthonie Plant, relationship unknown, and his best ring to his cousin. John Gennyns of Mollyngton left his russet coat to John Knowles and a blue coat and a pair of hose 'to the herde', either to the herdsman of his cattle or to be sold to raise funds to maintain the animals.

As a rule, though, men identify fewer clothing items in their wills, focusing instead upon property, livestock, financial sums and household objects. Men had a greater range of such possessions in their ownership, as women were unable to bequeath more than personal artefacts during the lifetime of their husbands and tended to own less in their own right as widows or spinsters, due to the pattern of patriarchal bequeathing. Men's wills did include their clothes, but under the catch-all phrase 'all my other goods'.

※

Even wealthy people recycled and adapted clothing. In 1535, John Williamson wrote to Thomas Cromwell, then Henry VIII's chief minister and, after the king, the most powerful man in the land, 'I received your letter by a servant of Mr. Treasurer, and have had two coats made for you, one of a remnant of velvet in my custody, the other of green, taken of Mr. Hobylthorne.'

Just over a week later, Williamson wrote again, 'By your servant, Richard Swift, you will receive your gown of black damask and two coats', which had just been dispatched from London.[6] Necessary items of clothing were transported considerable distances, often rowed along the Thames between royal properties, when people of status required them. Jane Bassett, another daughter of Honor, Lady Lisle, had not been able to find the 'large piece of canvas' left behind at Subberton but made four pairs of sheets and a cupboard cloth out of a smaller piece of cloth instead. In the light of her sister disgracing herself by running off with a gentleman, Jane was keeping her clothes, which she had sent for, until hearing otherwise from their mother.[7]

Clothing, jewellery and items of dress were also exchanged. When Lady Lisle sent yards of violet frieze to Anne Rouard for use by her son, in November 1535, Anne prepared a night mantle of red cloth as a return gift for her daughter, Mary.[8] The same month, Paris-based Anthony Barker sent Lady Lisle a 'girdle of the best fashion' and the best enamel he could find, but promised, 'If you do not like it, return it, and it shall be changed.' He said he could 'find none that would less hurt your sleeves and the wreaths upon the enamel would keep it long'. Barker also wrote that Lady Lisle's son, James, was merry, and he had 'bought him a gown and made less his velvet bonnet'. In return, Barker received certain items of jewellery, 'a flower with four diamonds and one ruby, and three pearls hanging', a brooch of Our Lady, a brooch in the shape of a gillyflower, which was delicate because the branches were slender, and a cross of gold.[9]

Clothing was considered valuable and significant enough to feature regularly among the items taken during burglaries. Items belonging to both genders were stolen, with little apparent relationship to the gender of the thieves, suggesting that they were intended for resale rather than personal use. Spinster Maud Wade, of Moulsham in Essex, stole from Thomas Scott one coloured petticoat worth 4s and one worth 12d, a woman's gown of black material, a taffeta hat costing 12d and parcels of linen. Labourer John Baylie of Ardleigh took two hoods worth 20s, two pairs of breeches worth 2s, a woman's gown valued at 5s and two hats costing 2s.

In 1598, two spinsters from Colchester, Joan Anderson and Jane Spencer, broke into the home of John Willecombe and took a French tawny gown costing 5s, a leather doublet for 10d and a sackcloth doublet at 12d. Two labourers from Shellow Bowells, John Smyth and William Johnson, were indicted for taking a gown costing 30s, three sheets, a pair of stockings worth 4s and a parcel of linen, and baker Michael Kere of Stifford was charged with the theft of two pairs of sheets, a gown, a hat and two shirts worth 30s.[10] Clothing was often stolen along with other items, probably as it was relatively small and portable and easily sold on, making its theft an opportunistic crime.

❋

Tudors in service were issued with clothing by their employer. A shared badge or colour scheme was the swiftest way to indicate allegiance and power in numbers to a lord or monarch. Those working for a noble family were issued with plain jerkin and hose with a cognisance, or badge, worn upon the left sleeve, while members of guilds and civic officials were entitled to wear their colours or devices.

In 1519, the Mayor of Bristol's four servants were kitted out in gowns of 16 broad yards of cloth, costing 4s 4d; the city recorder received 10 yards of scarlet and fur; the town clerk also got fur and a gown of 6 broad yards; the steward, town attorney and chamberlain had gowns of 5 yards, while the clerk's clerk had a gown of 4 yards. The priest, water bailey, keeper of the market and the city waits all received a gown apiece. An apprentice's indenture usually specified that his master was responsible for providing necessary woollen and linen clothing.

Liveries were a mark of acceptance. In 1535, an individual named Moryson wrote to Thomas Starkey, expressing his gratitude for the charity he had been offered after a period of extreme poverty, which had literally provided the clothes on his back. The offer of a job and a livery gave Moryson more than the physical comforts they brought, but were symbolic of being accepted again, and offered a position of belonging:

> You have put me in great hope. You cannot imagine in what misery I have been; but that is past; and how great it would have been in winter if the kindness of Signor Polo had not rescued me from hunger, cold, and poverty. My books, good as they were … would have been worth twice as much if I could have sold them. My clothes are all gone. I am wearing Mr. Michael Throgmerton's breeches and doublet. I am his man, for I wear his livery. Philosophy can do much, but it is too great a trial to have nothing, and to be in debt besides. I am not so much ashamed of poverty as of being forgotten by my patron.[11]

Royal servants were issued with liveries decorated with decodable symbols, personal initials or devices, heraldic coats of arms, crests or colours. At his coronation in October 1485, Henry VII's newly formed bodyguard wore crimson satin doublets and gowns of white cloth of gold, changing into crimson satin and blue velvet gowns for his wedding the following January.

An order surviving from 1486, which requests that a Richard Doland receive the livery he was owed, shows the difference between the provision made for winter and summer:

> To the keeper of the Great Wardrobe for the time being. Order to grant Richard Doland the arrears of his livery, that is raiment of furs, and linens of tartarin each year such as Thomas Stratton received: and for winter the livery amounted to nine virgates of cloth, a cape and a bys [sic] fur: and for summer nine virgates of cloth in grain and a piece of tartarin.[12]

William Harrison commented upon the visual effect of servants gathered together in livery to wait upon Queen Elizabeth in the 1570s:

... with differences of cognisances on their sleeves, whereby it is known to whom they appertain. I could also set down what a goodly sight it is to see them muster in the court, which, being filled with them, doth yield the contemplation of a noble variety unto the beholder, much like to the shew of the peacock's tail in the full beauty, or of some meadow garnished with infinite kinds and diversities of pleasant flowers.[13]

Liveries created a group identity, demonstrated the wealth and power of the master and made a visual demonstration of the relationship between servant and lord.

The use of specific fabrics associated servants with the rank of their master, while the choice of colours made those in certain positions easily identifiable. The daily uniform of yeoman warders was 'blue undress', but on special occasions they wore state dress and the usual white and green of the Tudor livery was replaced in 1514 by scarlet.

In 1519, instructions were issued that 'no man should wear Prince's apparel, in order that the king's estate might be above all as to his pre-eminence' and the king's guard were each issued with two coats, the first of scarlet and gold with goldsmith's work and the king's device, and the other red with a rose and crown upon the breast. The queen's retinue had coats and doublets in the Tudor colours of white and green, and an embroiderer named Ebgrave sewed them with the motif of feathers. Milanese bonnets were bought for them from Gerard the capper, at 6s each, orange-coloured boots at 4s 3d a pair, spurs at 6d a pair, coifs of gold for Catherine of Aragon's ladies at 10s each and eighteen shirts, which cost 8s each to be made. The footmen received scarlet cloaks, grooms wore green satin from Bruges and the men carrying Catherine's litter were to be dressed in black and yellow, velvet and satin.[14]

Private, wealthy individuals would have their own liveries for staff, especially if they were important players at court. In 1553, Sir William Cecil reassessed his staff, making a list of the servants to whom liveries had been given. Cecil was then in his early thirties and, after having served as secretary to King Edward, had reluctantly signed the succession in favour of Jane Grey, before vehemently backtracking in favour of Mary. His change of staffing may represent a change in his fortunes after Mary's triumphant proclamation. Twelve of his staff were to receive liveries of the best cloth with badges, eleven others had one and a quarter yards of best cloth each with cognisances of the second sort and nine received coats of the second cloth.[15]

Symbolic items might also represent an allegiance or job, standing in for livery or as a sign of gratitude or friendship. In April 1553, Sir Philip Hoby was at the court of Charles V in Brussels when he was appointed ambassador to Flanders. After receiving his new instructions by letter from Cecil, he wrote a reply which contains a charming personal detail, resonant of the individuals involved. Hoby wrote that he had received Cecil's letter 'and the rose, which he has tied to a lace, and carries about his neck, in token of his office'. He offered his 'most humble thanks for it' to the king and council.[16]

For aspirational middle-class Tudors, there were a number of key items of clothing worth investing in. For men, the gown was most desirable, showing high status as it was cumbersome and ill-suited to manual labour. Many gowns appear in wills, as worthy of bequeathing, but they were also pawned by those in need, as the first unnecessary luxury to be converted into cash.

The second-hand market for elite clothing in London's Birchin Lane was a good source of pawned clothing and that of the recently deceased, as well as recycled fur trims and linings to add visible value. Other clothing markets could be found near St Bartholomew's and in Long Lane, Houndsditch. Yet there was a degree of snobbery attached to such purchases, so that tailors who specialised in reworking second-hand clothing were known as bodgers and the women who made a living selling such items on were derided.

Guild men and merchants represented a group who might have the money to afford – and the access to – clothes above their station. Although William Hamilton commented in the 1570s that the London merchants were modestly dressed, it was their wives who 'would be very loth to come behind the fashion in newfangledness of manner'.[17]

People of a certain standing were permitted to make purchases from abroad, such as Lady Lisle, who was informed by John Hussey in 1538 that she would have saved 'almost a third penny' if she had bought her silks from Flanders.[18] In November 1535, a Spanish merchant, Fernando de Ibarra, was imprisoned by the Mayor of Chester 'for the sale of certain cloths in the open market'. He had been married and settled in the city for fifteen years, but his practice of riding 'about the country and buying up cloths for foreign merchants', usually those in Chester, contravened the city charters. Whether or not Ibarra was aware he was acting illegally is not clear, but his case was considered serious enough to be brought to the attention of Cromwell.[19]

However, when some guilds suffered financial insecurity, the livery was one of the first expenses to go. This was a dereliction of their civic duty, as they were often called upon to attend public functions in appropriate dress. In 1495, the wardens of the art of 'Pastelers [*sic* – pastille-makers]' complained to the mayor that 'whereas in time past they had been of power to have a company of themselves in one clothing, and had been able to bear the City's charges, they had now fallen into such poverty' through competition with other guilds, 'that they could no longer appear in one clothing, nor were able to bear the City's charges unless speedy remedy be applied'.[20]

At the bottom end of the social scale, clothing had to be fit for work. Those labouring, working in the fields, in industry or undertaking manual tasks had to be clothed in fabrics that were strong and durable, often in all weathers. Leather and canvas, or cloth soaked in linseed were used by sailors and those frequently in contact with wet conditions. Basic underwear was made at home, from scraps of cloth, usually of linen, in the form of shifts and hose.

Sumptuary restrictions meant that the families of farmers and workers were not permitted fabric worth more than 2s a yard and were banned from wearing imported cloth, even if it was significantly cheaper.

One of the ways in which the poor could offend through their clothing was by manipulating it to beg for false alms. In 1565, Nicholas Jennings was apprehended in London, begging while dressed in a sleeveless jerkin, ragged leggings and a bloodstained coif, while also owning a black frieze coat, a Flanders linen shirt, new white hose and a fine felt hat, valued at 16s. Jennings claimed to be suffering from the 'falling sickness', or epilepsy, but was placed in the pillory, alternately in rags and then in his fine clothes.[21] This strange show of contrasts was intended to publicly expose the duality of his use of costume and his character.

✻

For the Tudors, clothing was a demonstration of allegiance and belonging. The body was a canvas for display as much as the home or the portrait in the detail, colour, fabric and style adopted by the wearer. For some, this was a simple, plain garment indicative of manual work, while for others it was a gown embroidered with symbols. Clothing was an assemblage of parts: colours, textures, layers and accessories, just as much as the props chosen for *The Ambassadors*. Brooches, feathers, sleeves, armour, hats, trims, furs, gloves, ruffs, hairpieces, caps, bonnets, headdresses, shoes, jewellery, buckles, bows and ties were added for display at social gatherings and in public arenas.

While new clothing was a luxury reserved for the few, it was the process of bequests, individual skill and recycling which was responsible for keeping the poor clothed. Between these extremes, the vast middle classes dressed according to their budget, their aspirations or their master's pocket.

To adopt a uniform, a livery of court, a noble household or a guild was a statement of identity; the visual indicator of a social network and conformity to cultural codes. Clothing might also indicate a political, religious or international affiliation and, for many Tudors, the advantages of being absorbed into a group's identity outweighed the desire for individuality in dress.

Where rebellion occurred, such as in cross-dressing, it was often in order to belong to a different group, or to confer anonymity or fairness of treatment, rather than to draw attention to an individual. The only correct Tudor arena for that was the stage.

For the Tudors, clothing was not so much an extension of the self but a direction of it, a declaration of the way the individual wished to travel. It was the quickest method of social classification, a construct of worth, used paradoxically to both transgress social boundaries and demonstrate conformity. Where adornment was a form of performance, the Tudors' use of clothing represented an extraordinary act of Renaissance self-fashioning.

BRICK AND FIELD

❧ HOW ENGLAND LOOKED ☙

Tudor England is best seen from the perspective of its visitors. Crossing the turbulent Channel and landing under the lea of Dover's white cliffs or in harbour at Portsmouth, Bristol or Hull, these foreign arrivals saw the country with fresh eyes. And, more than anything, it was green. Before them unfolded a fertile and pleasant land, spread across with fields of sheep, rolling hills and woodlands, rivers and valleys, villages and cities, markets and monasteries.

In 1500, a visiting Venetian left an account of 'the most beautiful, the best and most fertile part of the whole island', where everything was 'produced in abundance'. He was most impressed by the flora and fauna, delighting in the 'springs of hot water', the 'lands in cultivation', 'extensive meadows' and 'agreeable woods' and 'every description of tree'. There was an 'immense profusion of animals' to be found, including stags, deer, goats, pigs, oxen, sheep, rabbits, hares and game birds, and he thought it 'truly a beautiful thing to behold one or two thousand tame swans upon the river Thames'.[1]

In 1485, the population of England was around 2 million and there were at least two sheep filling the fields for every person. Less than a tenth of people were resident in towns or cities, while the others lived in villages or rural farmsteads. Three-quarters of Tudors were engaged in agriculture of some kind, but on a small scale, and large areas of land remained uncultivated in the form of forests, marshes and moors, or were used for grazing. Thus, it was a largely rural country, only lightly cultivated, with small, scattered urban pockets.

However, those urban centres were spreading, and by the end of the century, this expansion would be causing concern. London was the largest city, home to the monarch, the courts of law, foreign merchants, the main port and the centre of trade. Most noblemen and clergy also had a London base, as did medical and manufacturing professionals, and it was the most frequent location for Parliament to meet.

Historians have estimated that it took until around 1520 for England's population figures to recover from the impact of plague and famine from the previous two centuries. In that year, London boasted around 50,000 people and years of rapid expansion followed so that by 1600, it housed around 200,000!

After the capital, the largest cities, in order, were Norwich, Bristol, Newcastle, Coventry, Exeter, Salisbury, Ipswich, Bishop's Lynn (King's Lynn after 1537) and Canterbury. In 1520, the fifth-largest city, Coventry, experienced a dearth of corn and grain, resulting in an escalation in prices, and conducted a census to record the needs of its inhabitants. Spread across ten wards, ranging in size between 354 and 1,018, its total population that year was assessed at 5,909.

Tudor towns and cities looked far smaller, darker and more compact than their modern counterparts. In 1535, Thomas Cromwell was warned about the potential dangers of crowded urban living: 'I fear these great humidities will engender pestilence at the end of the year, rather after Bartholomew tide than before. If you lie near London you must avoid confluence of people.'[2]

London had its landmarks. Bounded by a wall and ditch that circled most of what is now referred to as the 'square mile' and flanked by the river in the south, it was marked by the Tower in the east, Blackfriars in the west, with Westminster beyond, and St Paul's Cathedral at its highest point, overlooking the city.

One of the most remarkable aspects of the city was its single bridge, London Bridge, built in the twelfth century and 8m wide, crammed full of buildings, including shops and a chapel, as if it was a normal street. The bridge accounts for 1537–38 highlight that, for rental purposes, it was divided into six sections: the principal east part comprised twenty-three rents between the values of £10 and 40s, the principal west had twenty rents between £13 4s and 60s, the middle-east part had fourteen rents, the middle-west part thirteen, the east end fourteen and the west end sixteen. This made a total of 100 properties.

The accounts reveal details of the bridge's day-to-day running, with John Woode being paid £20 for control of the passage of carts; £10 going to John Orgar, the chief mason, for supplying 'all manner of hard stones of Kent'; another £10 to Richard Ambrose, chief carpenter; while the labourers loading and unloading boats filled with chalk were rewarded with 6s 3d each.[3] The southern gatehouse was the location upon which the severed heads of traitors were displayed for those using the bridge or vessels daring to pass through the rapids below.

As the sixteenth century advanced, the appearance of the English countryside subtly changed. In the 1510s common land was being enclosed to be more intensively farmed or grazed, squeezing out the villagers who had been accustomed to its use:

> The growing attention to agriculture had caused the landholders of the villages of Islington, Hoxton, and Shoreditch, in the neighbour-hood of the city, to inclose their grounds: the citizens were hereby restrained in their field exercises and sports, which, if they pursued, they were indicted for trespasses. The populace were enraged, and excited to a riot, by a fellow disguised in a merry Andrew's coat, who ran up and down the streets calling for spades and shovels: with which implements they soon levelled the new banks and ditches. A commis-sion was granted by the king to inquire into this disorder, and the city magistrates were reprimanded for their inattention in suffering it.[4]

Two decades later, larger, more symbolic tracts of land were passing into private hands. In pre-Reformation England, the largest landowner after the Crown was the Church, which rented out its properties and fields and ran influential agribusinesses. Their towering edifices of Gothic spires and arches, buttresses and windows dominated the land-scape from Exeter in the west to Canterbury in the east, to Durham and Carlisle in the north, in around 900 establishments that housed one in fifty of the adult male population.[5]

After the seizure and sale of the monasteries in the 1530s, the nobil-ity dismantled or converted former religious properties, more pasture land was enclosed and tenants were ejected. From collective or rented use, they were given over to the more lucrative production of wool, to line the pocket of a single family. The number of decayed monas-teries was such that the young Edward VI commented upon them, asking what they had formerly been and wishing his father had merely punished the offending monks but 'suffer[ed] such goodly buildings to stand, being so great an ornament to this kingdom'.[6] The English coun-tryside of the 1540s onwards was full of ruins, adapted ruins and sheep.

Between 1538 and 1543, the Londoner John Leland travelled through England and Wales, recording his observations in his *Itineraries*, just as the Reformation and economic change were impacting. His bucolic details of rivers, crops, settlements, landmarks, land use and buildings paint a vivid picture of England outside the capital. Of Elmley in Worcestershire he wrote:

> There standeth now but one tower, and that partly broken. As I went by, I saw carts carrying stones thence to amend Persore bridge, about two miles off. It is set on the top of a hill full of wood, and a townlet hard by, and under the root of the hill is the Vale of Evesham.

He noted that in the Chiltern Hills, 'many will be well replenished with wood, and partly with corn, all the soil being a chalk clay'. At the village of Brougham, Leland found the old castle, which was 'set in a strange place by reason of rivers enclosing the country thereabouts' and the former site of pilgrimage to the Virgin Mary. Ploughmen in the fields found 'square stones, tokens of old buildings', as rural settlements were abandoned or shrank and larger properties became difficult to maintain.[7]

Strolling through the Dorset manor of Ewerne, or Iwerne, in September 1553, a traveller found the surrounding countryside to be 'very commodious and plentiful of wood, water, corn, pasture and meadow' and full of common fields that had recently been enclosed. The tenements were small and had little land attached. Without the benefit of the common land, about half the tenants had been unable to pay their rents and had migrated to the towns. Thus, the urban population was expanding as that in the countryside contracted.

A similar journey through Mudeford and Hinton, in Somerset, dating from 1554, lays out a picture of the division and use of land. Just like Ewerne, it was 'very commodious and plentiful of wood, water, meadow land, arable and pasture' and was divided into small hamlets, each of which had three common fields. These were connected by a river running through them, upon which the lord's mill sat. The soil was fruitful and bore plenty of straw, the ears of corn were 'fair to the sight', but not as productive as could be hoped, as it produced 'seldom three or four good kernels in an ear'.[8] The manor house stood near the mill, enclosed by a moat, previously stately but now in a ruined condition, and the family had moved away.

The increasing desertion of the countryside in favour of urban living is reflected in a petition to Queen Elizabeth in 1587, concerning the enclosure of common ground at Grindleton in Yorkshire. Lately, the town had 'greatly increased in buildings and dwelling houses and thereby much more populated than heretofore it hath been', so that the former grounds used for tillage and pasture could not meet demand and 'muche povertie doth daily increase amongst them'.[9] If the common land was enclosed and divided into portions, it could be put to more profitable use.

A decade later, the urban spread was even causing concern in London. The Privy Council acted to halt the influx into the capital by 'restraining and prohibiting ... new building of houses and tenements for habitation in and about the city' due to the 'access of multitudes of people to inhabit the same' and its 'over large increase due to the decay of other towns, boroughs and villages within the realm'.[10]

Although it had been the intention to punish those who built new houses, by 1590 there had been such 'slender effect' that building in the city had 'continued and greatly increased'.[11] Thus, the queen commanded that London's Justices of the Peace, stewards and bailiffs enquire as to which houses had been erected since the prohibition and send the builders and owners to appear before the Star Chamber.

At the end of the century, in 1597, German lawyer Paul Hentzner arrived in England on a ship that docked at Rye, in East Sussex. Now a silted-up river from which the sea has receded 1.5 miles, it had once been a thriving port, the starting point of Hentzner's journey through Kent to the capital. Sixteen years earlier, the mayor had expressed his concern about the impact of industry upon the surrounding area: 'By sundry iron works and glass houses now erected, the woods growing near unto the three towns of Hastings, Winchelsea and Rye, are marvellously wasted and decayed.' This was critical because, 'if speedy remedy be not had, the said woods will in short time be utterly consumed, in sort as there will not any timber be had for shipping, waterworks, housebuilding, nor wood for fuel'.[12]

Either 'speedy remedy' had been made by 1597 or Hentzner was oblivious to this. Seeing through the eyes of a foreigner, he described the east Kent countryside as full of surprising and abundant riches, its houses as 'elegantly built', its churches fine and its towns strong, but it was London that ultimately drew him. London was 'magnificently ornamented' and built upon 'the fruitfullest and wholesomest soil in

England'. The streets were 'very handsome and clean' and London was fed by the Thames, which 'wafted' the wealth of the world into the city, its banks 'beautified with fine country seats, woods and farms'. The account also mentions the swans, symbolic of something bucolic, observed by the Venetian of 1500, which 'swam in flocks' and were 'vastly agreeable to the fleets that meet them in their course'.[13]

The Tudor emphasis upon visual indicators of wealth is apparent in Hentzner's account of his visit to the Tower of London. He laid out the appearance and structure of the site, highlighting its whiteness and its 'very deep and broad ditch, as well as a double wall, very high', which enclose the 'very ancient and very strong tower' in the centre, and four other towers around the perimeter. Upon entering, he was shown the royal treasures, which he itemised and described according to their quantity and quality:

> Above a hundred pieces of arras ... made of gold, silver and silk ... an immense [number] of bed-furniture, such as canopies and the like, some of them most richly ornamented with pearl, some royal dresses, so extremely magnificent as to raise anyone's admiration at the sums they must have cost.[14]

He noted the Tower menagerie, which contained a lion and three lionesses, a wolf, a lynx, a porcupine and an eagle, all valuable and rare signifiers of status, kept at the queen's expense.

The Tower was also described by Elizabethan antiquarian John Stow as having turrets and walls rising from a deep foundation, a central White Tower, castellated walls and bulwarks, and mortar tempered with animal blood. In 1598, Stow compiled a survey of his perambulations around London. Observing the material fabric of the city and the lives and customs of its people, the account divides it into wards and describes their composition in terms that are appreciative of civic beauty.

In Tower Ward, the grounds had been 'greatly diminished' by the building of tenements and garden plots, but the north side was 'beautified' by 'certain fair alms houses, built of brick and timber, with slate roofs'. The ditch that ran along the city walls:

which of old time was used to be open, always from time to time
cleansed from filth and mud, as need required; of great breadth, and
so deep, that divers, watering horses where they thought it shal-
lowest, were drowned, both horse and man. But now of later time
the same ditch is enclosed, and the banks thereof let out for garden-
plots, carpenters' yards, bowling allies, and divers houses thereon
built, whereby the city wall is hidden, the ditch filled up, a small
channel left, and that very shallow.[15]

Stow described the districts that housed different traders, giving an
idea of how the city was carved up according to its guilds. The colourful signs and window displays of shops and workshops identified
which professions were resident in a certain area and boasted of the
luxury and wealth of a great city.

The Venetian visitor of 1500 noted the concentration of goldsmiths
in the Strand:

In one single street ... there are fifty-two goldsmith's shops, so rich and
full of silver vessels, great and small, that in all the shops in Milan,
Rome, Venice and Florence put together, I do not think there would
be found so many of the magnificence that are to be seen in London.[16]

By the time Stow was writing, though, ninety-eight years after the
Venetian had visited, the goldsmiths had abandoned the Strand and
set themselves up on the south side of West Chepe.

Certain areas were becoming overcrowded with market stalls, too.
In 1601, the council responded to complaints about the stalls of 'huck-
sters, hawkers and pedlars ... encumbering the streets' by inflicting
penalties of 20s upon any citizen who permitted a stall to be erected
before their house.[17]

Tower Ward, in the East End, afforded Londoners a means of escap-
ing out into the countryside that ringed the city:

Hog Lane stretcheth north toward St. Mary Spittle without
Bishopsgate, and within these forty years had on both sides fair
hedge rows of elm trees, with bridges and easy stiles to pass over
into the pleasant fields, very commodious for citizens therein to
walk, shoot, and otherwise to recreate and refresh their dull spirits
in the sweet and wholesome air, which is now within a few years

made a continual building throughout, of garden-houses and small cottages; and the fields on either sides be turned into garden-plots, yards, bowling alleys, and such like.

Alongside Houndsditch Field was a row of small stone cottages, two storeys high with back garden plots, set aside for 'poor bed-rid people', who used to place their bed close to the window and lie a linen cloth and beads over the sill. Devout Londoners would walk past, especially on Friday 'purposely … to bestow their charitable alms'.[18] Formerly a track, Stow notes that this road had been paved in 1503, and the nearby field was enclosed by a gunmaker and the cottages possessed for commercial use. His account highlights the changed city at the end of the century, from a greener, domestic and religious space to one that was increasingly urbanised and commercial.

The eighteenth-century historian, R. Baldwin, writing a history of London, concluded that the worsening crowding of the city in the 1580s was the result of people being drawn to the capital. 'Multitudes who were born in various parts of England end their days in London' and although the city appeared to be a 'gulf that continually requires filling', it also sent out inhabitants 'to various parts', especially abroad. He observed that deaths in the city appeared to eclipse births, due to migration, but also that many of the births had not been recorded or were recorded elsewhere.

The negative effects of London's architecture upon health could not be denied, though. 'The actual inconveniences of close dwellings crowded with inmates … the frequent contagious disorders were a fatal proof of them' and the 'dearness of provisions' was 'attributable to the enormous consumption of necessaries' but also because 'our markets are not sufficiently supplied'. He commented, too, that the nature of business and pleasure in the late Elizabethan era kept 'many of the inhabitants in a state of celibacy; labourers, servants, sailors and the three regiments of guards, are generally single men'. From the perspective of the enlightened eighteenth century, when the streets of central London had been cleared and rebuilt along neoclassical lines, the Elizabethan age appeared cramped and restrictive.[19]

To the environmental- and climate-aware twenty-first century, Tudor England may appear a hopelessly romantic and bucolic place, an Eden of green fields, cottage industries, small urban centres, organic farming and other ideals, with swans swimming along the

Thames. Yet the Tudors observed their changing world with alarm, concerned by the evolution of their cities, overpopulation and the changing ownership of the land.

The majority of people lived in close relation to the natural world, farming it, dependent upon its crops, experiencing its changes in seasons and weather and grounded at seaports in anticipation of favourable winds. By their own observation, towns and cities were becoming more crowded, with the population rising to 4 million by 1600 and more migrants arriving on market days. As the century advanced, and the aesthetic of the Renaissance took greater hold, the visual contrast between the rich man's table and the beggar at his gate became increasingly apparent.

❦ ROYAL BUILDINGS ❧

The sixteenth century proved to be a period of building. Great mansions, palaces and civic buildings were no longer fortified but represented the latest Renaissance styles of domestic luxury. The visual impact of royal architecture was twofold. Firstly, it was designed to impress through sheer size and scale; by the height of walls and towers, the size of rooms and windows, the number of acres it occupied. Secondly, the level of ornamentation, beyond the functional, was crafted to appeal to a cultured elite, but also to contain coded messages about the owners, their identities, wealth and allegiances, in portraits, names, heraldic symbols, colours and mottos. The Tudor monarchs wanted their building projects to scream their own names back to them, in a stylised and elegant form of tagging.

All this required a small army of workers. A hierarchy of craftsmen was employed to ensure that the royal palaces constantly reflected their owner's identity, keeping them present, especially during their absence. The king's painters created the designs to be executed by the lower-ranking serjeant painters who painted and gilded residences, coaches, tents, banners and anything associated with the royal family.

Some of these were homegrown talent, such as John Browne, a heraldic painter since 1502, who became the king's painter in 1511 and serjeant painter in 1527 until his death in 1532. On other occasions, the royal family recruited artists from abroad, like Anthony Toto, or Antonio di Nunziato d'Antonio, an Italian who came to England in

1519 to work with Pietro Torrigiano, the artist who had created the bronze tomb of Henry VII and Elizabeth of York a decade earlier.

They were also responsible for the rapid changes required to keep up with the king's complicated love life, so in the early 1530s, all associations with Catherine of Aragon were expunged, and in 1536, the 'HA' initials and falcon device celebrating the wedding of Henry VIII and Anne Boleyn were chiselled away to make way for the phoenix of wife number three, Jane Seymour.

The effacement could also be xenophobic. In 1535, it was reported by Sir William Fitzwilliam:

> Certain naughty persons have razed out the French king's arms from a table that stands upon the altar in the chapel built by M. de Vaux, late ambassador in England. I have pacified the French friar, who found himself aggrieved thereat, and am making search for the authors of the mischief.[1]

The Tudors inherited a number of royal properties from the Plantagenet regime, many concentrated in the environs of the capital, such as Windsor, Westminster, Greenwich, Eltham and Sheen, in addition to a host of castles and manors spread throughout the realm.

Greenwich had been a childhood home of Elizabeth of York, who redesigned the gardens as queen. Henry VII added a new brick frontage along the river-side, enlarged the site and made repairs.

In 1497, Henry was forced to completely rebuild the palace of Sheen as Richmond, after a fire destroyed most of the original medieval complex. Aping the style of new Renaissance architecture from Europe, a new palace rose from the ground from tessellated brick and white stone, with inner courtyards filled with fountains, a long gallery to display sculpture, octagonal turrets, gardens and orchards, chapel, great hall, brass weather vanes and gilded domed chimneys, covering 10 acres and filled with works of art gifted to the king by Italian bankers. Three storeys high, its walls were hung with tapestries, its ceilings and available surfaces painted and carved with portcullises and gilded roses.

Richmond was given to Anne of Cleves as part of her marriage settlement from Henry VIII in 1540, although she did not occupy it much. It became a favourite of Elizabeth I, who liked to hunt in the park and died there in 1603. All that remains of the building today is a gatehouse on Old Richmond Green, bearing the royal arms of the red dragon of Wales and the Richmond greyhound.

❇

The title of Tudor palace builder must go to Henry VIII. In the early 1530s, Henry developed two existing palaces that had been confiscated from Cardinal Wolsey after his fall: Hampton Court, on the Thames, west of the city, and Whitehall, formerly York Place, between Blackfriars and Westminster.

At Hampton Court, Henry found a geometrically planned palace influenced by Italian Renaissance architecture, which the poet John Skelton described as being unequalled in England. Thomas Wolsey had acquired a simple brick manor in 1514 and expanded it to include a huge hall with long, glazed windows, new courtyards and lodgings spread over three floors.

In 1535, Henry ordered work to begin on the blue and gold ceiling of the Chapel Royal, under a master carver, master carpenter, fifty other carpenters and more labourers based upriver. Trees were felled from Windsor Park and transported downriver, where nine months of work were required to install the timbers and pendants, which were painted and varnished with the royal arms, motto and angels. Henry also built a new tiltyard and tennis courts on the site for recreation.

The imposing architecture of Hampton Court was described by a German visitor at the end of the sixteenth century. It was 'magnificently built of brick', he explained, by Cardinal Wolsey, to 'display his wealth', with five 'very spacious courts' surrounded by 'very elegant buildings'.[2] The first court was covered with flagstones and decorated by twelve gilded terracotta roundels depicting Roman emperors, and in its centre stood a fountain topped with the figure of Justice on black and white marble columns, wearing a gold crown. The gate into the second court bore a large gold rose and the royal motto *Dieu et mon Droit*. Enormous in scale and intricate in detail, the architecture of Hampton Court echoed classical precedent, vied with the best palaces of the Renaissance and projected the heraldry and visual symbols of the Tudor dynasty.

Whitehall was developed by Henry from the existing York Place, a residence which had been formerly used by Plantagenet kings as an alternative to their main base of Westminster. Rebuilt by Thomas

Rotherham, Archbishop of York, between 1480 and 1500, it later passed to Thomas Wolsey who, between 1514 and 1516, reworked:

the hall, the chapel, the grete gate towards the strete, the grete bakery gate into the Gardyn, a breke wall from the brode gate ayenst the Grene unto the grete gatehouse of my lords place, the chapel garden, the counting-house, the bake-house, the kitchen, the buttery, the wine-cellar, the fish-house, the scullery and the wardrobe.[3]

He enlarged it significantly, taking over nearby properties in order to expand and using it to host banquets and masques for the king, who would attend by river. The inventory taken upon his fall in 1529 lists a gallery hung in cloth of gold and silver; a gilt chamber laid out with tables and cupboards filled with expensive plate, inlaid with pearls and jewels; and a council chamber furnished with white and gilt plate.

Acquiring the lease and much of the surrounding land, Henry built a huge palace complex straddling the road, with 'distinct, beautiful, costly and pleasant lodgings, buildings and mansions, for his Grace's singular pleasure, comfort and commodity, to the great honour of his highness and of his realm'.[4] In addition to the palace buildings, there was a tiltyard, tennis courts, bowling alley, cock pit and pheasant yard, orchards, gardens and viewing galleries.

The building records of the early 1530s suggest that Anne Boleyn had an input into the design of Whitehall, the place she was married in January 1533 and retired to after her coronation that June, where great jousts were held in her honour. It was also the place where Henry married her successor, Jane, days after Anne's execution in 1536.

Henry's last major building project was Nonsuch Palace, begun in 1538. Drawn by Georg Hoefnagel in 1568, it is a fantasia of blue-grey stucco work designs covering the frontage, over 2,000m^2 in length. It was built to rival the French Château de Chambord, with octagonal towers costing £24,000, or over £1 million in modern money. Included in John Speed's 1610 Map of Surrey, the level of ornamentation to the exterior is unsurpassed in a new royal project of the era.

Henry had admired the location of a manor house at Cuddington, near Cheam in Surrey, and transformed it into what the sixteenth-century antiquarian Camden described as a 'monument of art', upon which you would think 'the whole science of architecture' had been exhausted. 'It has such a profusion of aminated statues and finished pieces of art,' he wrote, 'rivalling the monuments of ancient Rome itself', so that it was a *nonpareil* of English architecture.[5]

Hentzner wrote of the grounds:

> The palace itself is so encompassed with parks full of deer, delicious gardens, groves ornamented with trellis work, cabinets of verdure, and walks so embrowned by trees, that it seems to be a place pitched upon by pleasure herself to dwell in along with health. In the pleasure and artificial gardens, are many columns and pyramids of marble; two fountains, that spout water one round the other like a pyramid, upon which are perched small birds, that stream water out of their bills: in the grove of Diana, is a very agreeable fountain, with Actæon turned into a stag, as he was sprinkled by the goddess and her nymphs, with inscriptions. There is besides another pyramid of marble full of concealed pipes, which spirt upon all who come within their reach.[6]

Incomplete at the time of Henry's death in 1547, it was sold by Mary I to the Earl of Arundel, who made the final touches.

An echo of Nonsuch Palace was built in 1578. The four-storey building, with gilded onion domes in each corner, named Nonsuch House, was unusual for being built in a precarious location upon London Bridge itself, from prefabricated pieces shipped from the Netherlands. Flanking the bridge on the Southwark side, it arrived in numbered pieces of timber and was reconstructed entirely using wooden pegs, without mortar or nails. Its imposing large windows, carving, columns and stepped gables were visible across London on account of its elevated position. It took two years to complete but survived for two centuries, being drawn by Canaletto shortly before it was demolished, along with all the other buildings, to allow for the bridge to be widened in 1757.

Nonsuch House was not the first Tudor prefabricated building. In 1520, a temporary pavilion was erected for the Field of Cloth of Gold at Guisnes, or Guînes, built speedily over the preceding weeks with the painted roses barely dry before the revellers arrived. Its foundations were made of stone, the walls built of brick and the rest wood, covered with cloth painted to look like more brick. Huge first-floor windows, with many panels, stretched right up to the crenellation that marked the roof line.

Captured in a painting of 1545, the dark, rectangular roof of painted oil cloth appears open in the centre above the inner courtyard, set with small casement windows, plain chimneys and heraldic beasts bearing flags. Even the French and Italians enthused about it, with French chronicler Florange describing 'half the house' being made of glass and the Mantuan ambassador Soardino saying it had a clarity, as if it were 'on display' and particularly praising the 'very large diamond-shaped panes of very white glass'. Contemporaries estimated that the external walls were around 50ft high, with a frieze midway up and a sloping roof, upon which 'a beautiful scale pattern' had been painted on brass.[7]

Entrance to the pavilion was through a tall, arched gateway, with red pillars on each side and battlements across the top. Along the roof-line, on top of the pillars, were figures depicting men of war, ready to cast down great defensive stones. Above the gate sat ancient princes such as Hercules, Alexander and others, richly painted in gold and the English colours. The 1545 painting also shows the space above the arch being painted with two Tudor roses, garlands, the English arms and topped with a scallop-shaped decoration.

A porter in royal livery stood guard at the lodge within the gate. Passing through, the visitor found themself in a beautiful courtyard, filled with glazed windows and clerestories, decorated with gold and resin figures, the outward parts 'illuminating' the eye of the beholder with 'sumptuous works'. Statues in silver armour with 'sore and terrible countenances' guarded the way, between the doors to the many palace chambers.[8]

The hall was lined with a gilt cornice from which hung magnificent tapestries. Above it was a line of windows and the floor was alternating checks of white and yellow taffeta intersected by red roses. The hall, and each of the other rooms, had a large lantern in the centre, in the form of a crown 'with octagonal windows, more for ornament than for light', which made the walls so 'luminous ... it is like being in the open air'.[9]

An Italian account describes the palace as being:

adorned with silk and red roses, and the emblems of the King of
England ... but marvellous were the tapestries with which the whole
palace was hung, all of gold and silk, some representing figures,
others foliage, which it would not be possible to paint more beautifully; the figures really seemed alive.[10]

Two weeks later, the whole edifice was torn down as the court
departed, and the pavilion and sea of golden tents surrounding it
became little more than an expensive memory.

As with many of the Tudor great entertainments, temporary buildings were erected for a single occasion, usually the visit of a special
guest. In 1551, a banqueting house was built in Hyde Park for the
entertainment of Jacques d'Albon, Marshal St André. It stood 62ft long
and 21ft wide, with stairs of 60ft in one direction and 30ft in the other.
Inside were three ranges for roasting and furnaces for boiling, a range
of tables, forms, trestles and rushes, surmounted by a turret. Together
with a second, but less imposing, construction in Marylebone Park,
this temporary show cost a significant £450.[11]

⚘ RICH AND POOR ⚘

The increased wealth of mercantile and commercial classes was visible
in building projects and interiors in and around London. One such house
was Crosby Hall, built in 1466 in Bishopsgate by Sir John Crosby, a rich
wool merchant, owned by Richard III in 1483 and described by Stow as
'of stone and timber, very large and beautiful, and the highest at that
time in London'.[1] In 1501, the Mayor of London, Bartholomew Reed,
hosted a banquet for 100 guests there and it provided lodgings for ambassadors sent from the emperor in 1503. Later, it was described as having
a great hall with a minstrel's gallery, a throne room and a council room,
as well as service rooms, bedchambers, solars, gardens and tenements.

Thomas More's London residence of The Barge at Bucklersbury was
formerly a public weigh house, which was divided into tenements,
then restored into one residence, a 'great mansion', by More. On the
ground floor, it had a great hall, kitchen, pantry, larder and service
rooms, with a summer parlour giving access to the garden. On the
first floor was a gallery, great chamber and parlour, and on the second,
bedchambers, More's study, a counting house and chapel.[2]

Thomas Cromwell lived in a house with three storeys and fourteen rooms, within the precincts of the Austin Friars. Through purchasing the neighbouring houses, forcibly evicting other tenants and benefitting from the Dissolution, he was able to build a new mansion on the site, around three courtyards, with fifty rooms at a cost of around £1,000. In August 1535, a Thomas Thacker, overseeing the building, wrote to his employer with updates about the progress of the work:

> At Friars Austins the wall of the kitchen towards the street, with the windows of freestone, with the scullery and other offices, is clearly finished. The carpenters are raising the roofs, and all is complete except the windows of the side of the hall towards the court. Your own lodging, with the chamber and gallery above, are finished and plastered, and want only the glazing. The pay there for 46 workmen, on Saturday last, was 20l. 14s. 7d.[3]

Cromwell was also simultaneously building at the Rolls, Ewhurst, Hackney and Stepney. Thacker reported that at Hackney, the brick work of the kitchen was finished to the roof, the roof was being framed and the main lodgings set with windows and glass. At Ewhurst, in Surrey, the hall floors and walls were finished, with a solar below, but carriage was 'scarce because of hay time and harvest'.[4]

Poor people were unlikely to own their own homes unless they built them with their own hands, or they were inherited. According to the sumptuary laws, it was actually illegal for a person of the lower class to purchase a plot of land or property above a certain value in particular areas, even if they could afford it. In 1559, former statutes were reissued, allowing 'no husbandman, yeoman or artifice to purchase above £5 the year of inheritance, no clothier, tanner or common butcher above £10 a year, save in cities, towns and boroughs for their better repair, one house only to be purchased over and above the said yearly value'.[5] Merchants were forbidden from purchasing plots above £50 a year, except if they were aldermen or sheriffs, who, 'because they approach to the degree of knighthood', were permitted to spend up to the value of £200. Labourers and servants were actively forbidden from leaving the 'hundred or place where they dwelled' at the end of their term of service.[6]

More often than not, the poor were tenants, renting from the Church, a guild or the local landowner, which might entail the farming

or cultivation of associated land. This was particularly true of the pre-
Reformation period, when monastic landlords oversaw the production
of crops or rearing of sheep. Before the Reformation, poorer people
also found shelter in monastic communities, while employed on
site, or on a temporary basis in hospitals, which could accommodate
travellers, or even by casually accessing the late-medieval hospitality
at the gates of the wealthy. There is a clear correlation between the
Dissolution and the rise in vagrancy, and the Poor Acts and Vagrancy
Acts of 1536, 1547, 1572, 1598 and 1601 attempted to shift charity
onto secular shoulders.

One result of the monastic closures was an increase in the building of almshouses by wealthy patrons, particularly to cater for guild
members and their families. In 1550–51, Lord Mayor Andrew Judd of
the Skinners' Company established six houses in Bishopsgate, where
the pensioners received 8d a week and a supply of coal. In 1567, mayor
and goldsmith Sir John Langley founded twelve more in Cripplegate
for 'poor and aged people', giving them 7d, five sacks of charcoal
and twenty-five bundles of firewood a week. The Merchant Tailors'
Company built fourteen brick and timber cottages on Tower Hill to
house single women, with a weekly allowance of 1s 4d and fuel.

Richard Carew, compiling a survey of Cornwall, described the
homes of husbandmen as simple 'walls of earth, low thatched roofs,
few partitions, no planchings or glass window, and scarcely any chimneys, other than a hole in the wall to let out the smoke'. The bed was
often a low, wooden frame, filled with straw and a blanket, lacking
in sheets. Carew noted that the poorest dwellings contained little
furniture or possessions: 'a mazer [drinking cup] and a pan or two,
comprised all their substance'. The Spaniards who arrived in the train
of King Philip in 1554 commented that the English people's houses
were made of 'sticks and dirt'.[7]

By the 1570s, there had been general improvement in living standards compared with two generations before. As Harrison commented,
many old dwellings now had a multitude of new chimneys, but also
'our fathers ... have lain full oft upon straw pallets, on rough mats
covered only with a sheet, under coverlets made of dogswain [rough
cloth] and a good round log under their heads instead of a bolster or
pillow'. They lived in 'great poverty' and ate from wooden platters,
which had since been replaced by pewter or tin.[8]

❧ INSIDE THE HOME ❧

In 1532, Gilbert Walker was a guest in a proud but modest household, welcomed with the speech:

> Come on, you shall go see my house the while. It is not like your large country houses; victuals be here at such high prices that much money is soon consumed; nevertheless, assure yourself that no man is welcome than you to such cheer as you find. And bringing me through divers well-trimmed chambers, the worst of them decorated with rich tapestries, some with rich cloth of arras, all with beds, chairs and cushions of silk and gold.[1]

If you were invited to visit a Tudor home, you would find that the interiors varied depending more upon class than personal taste. Every aspect was determined by social standing: the quantity of rooms, especially those for private use, their dimensions and decoration, the height of the ceiling, the number of hearths and windows, what was on the floor and walls. Just as with clothing, bigger was considered better, as the more space an individual could take up, the more powerful they appeared.

As a general rule, walls were first painted in a plain colour or white-washed, but on top of this, they were hung with tapestries by the rich, or painted panels or papers by the aspiring classes, or murals painted to represent patterns, people and stories. Surviving examples across the country show a variety of domestic decoration with geometric patterns, natural scenes, foliates, florals, coats of arms and black and white designs.

Bishop John Hooper's house in Gloucester, built in around 1500, has traces of dark red paint on its beams and paintings of Tudor roses and fleurs-de-lys on the ground floor, and white grotesques on a black background upstairs. Ellys Manor House, the home of a wool merchant in Lincolnshire, features tapestry-like paintings with trees, flowers and animals set in decorative borders, while the upstairs painted room in Ledbury Council's Offices has floral designs on a black surround, in imitation of Elizabethan knot gardens.

By 1578, Harrison could state:

The walls of our houses on the inner sides in like sort be either hanged with tapestry, arras work, or painted cloths, wherein either divers histories, or herbs, beasts, knots, and such like are stained, or else they are ceiled with oak of our own, or wainscot brought hither out of the east countries, whereby the rooms are not a little commended, made warm, and much more close than otherwise they would be.[2]

In addition to decoration on the walls themselves, friezes were added in wood or plaster. Surviving examples featured flowers and plants, mythical beasts and figures such as mermaids, with nods to antiquity in the shape of vases, similar to the kind of decoration painted on the walls or embroidered on expensive clothing. In 1510, Thomas Wolsey commissioned the Italian sculptor Giovanni de Majano to create eight terracotta roundels depicting Roman emperors for his new palace of Hampton Court.

Friezes might be attached to carved wooden panels covering all, or part, of a wall's surface. These might be plain with borders, or in the popular linenfold style, or feature heraldic devices or coats of arms. Ceilings were usually plain, sometimes smoke-blackened and crisscrossed by beams, but occasionally ornately decorated. The Tudor House at Worcester contains a recently restored original ceiling, featuring swirling patterns, roses and prancing horses in a cream-coloured wash. At the other end of the spectrum, the most elaborate blue and gold, star-studded Tudor ceiling survives in the chapel at Hampton Court.

The central point of a room was its hearth, with elaborate carved wood fireplace designs surviving by Holbein, but also in situ at places like Cheshire's Little Moreton Hall, where the plaster arms of Elizabeth I are supported by caryatids.

The huge portrait of Henry VIII and his family completed in around 1545 reflects a level of ornamentation almost exclusive to royalty. Set in the Great Garden at Whitehall, the king's heraldic beasts and green and white railed spaces can be glimpsed through archways to the right and left, while the family are arranged between four central pillars, with two further pillars on each side. These pillars, Corinthian in style, overlaid with gold fretwork of interlaced vines, reflect the pattern on the wooden panels behind, which are also overlaid with gold. The ceiling is divided into checks in a similar way, but each of these is filled with a red and white Tudor union rose. Beneath their feet, what appears to be a white marble floor has a bold red and blue design of circles and diamonds, where it is not covered by Turkey carpet or gold cushion.

Henry VIII's psalter of 1546 shows him sitting at a wooden table to play the harp in a room with grey stone walls, a fireplace set with green marble and a red-and-yellow-checked tiled floor. A second image places him reading in a blue 'x-shaped' royal chair, before a huge bed hung with blue curtains fringed in gold, with an elaborate dragon's foot. Behind the king, red marble pillars lead towards a door over which his arms are carved, and light filters down through a circular skylight onto a grey floor set with alternating red and green tiles.

The 1527 portrait of Thomas More and his family in their Chelsea home, by Hans Holbein, depicts the interior of a family of status and learning. The group is arranged around a central bench, behind which hangs a floor-to-ceiling curtain, at the top of which is set a rectangular clock with dangling pendulum. To the left stands a large, carved wooden cupboard, or sideboard, bearing plates and jugs. To the right, past an ornate doorway leading through to a window, a smaller windowsill is crowded with jug, candlestick and books. Holbein's original was lost in a fire, but Rowland Lockey's version of 1592 makes the back curtain a rich dark green, replaces the wooden back of the cupboard with a gold cloth and covers it with a carpet, upon which sit musical instruments, books and floral arrangements. The small footstool on the ground before them has been replaced by sleeping lapdogs.

In the late 1520s, Holbein depicted Thomas Cromwell sitting upon a wooden bench with a high back and leaning upon a table covered in a green cloth, probably literally the Board of the Green Cloth, at which the royal household accounts were arranged. A jewelled book with gold clasps, letters with broken seals, quill, scissors and purse upon it are suggestive of business. To his left, a more expensive tapestry, patterned in orange, black and green, covers another table and holds a scroll or account roll. Behind Cromwell, the wall is painted dark blue, and decorated with a darker blue or black foliate pattern.

Other possessions depicted in paintings were the visual clues as to a sitter's identity or profession. Holbein's 1532 painting of the German merchant of the Steelyard, George Giese, shows the young man's workshop with its wooden boards, shelves with carved brackets and carpeted table, as well as the pen, seal, inkpot, balance, boxes, scissors, keys and coins of his trade.

The Sieve portrait of Elizabeth I gives a glimpse of her sophisticated palace. Painted by Flemish artist Quentin Metsys in 1583, it depicts the queen in her favourite black and white, holding a sieve, which associates her with the Roman Virgin Tuccia, and with wisdom and judgement. The globe on her right is a measure of her influence and the cosmopolitan nature of her court, and shows ships sailing westward across the Atlantic to the New World. To the left, a decorative pillar in black and gold bears roundels depicting scenes from the life of Dido and Aeneas, taken from Virgil's *The Aeneid*, representing resistance to temptation and self-sacrifice in love. Behind the queen, drawn out in perspective which invites the eye, a row of terracotta columns line the wall of a hall or waiting chamber. Set between a black pedestal and capital, they rise towards stone archways, which may also have had windows inset. To the left, a slice of green floral decoration may be a mural, curtain or tapestry. The hall is peopled by the Queen's Guard, dressed fashionably in red and gold and bearing the halberds that were part of their job. At the very far end, the side of a grey stone archway can just be seen, probably leading through into another chamber. More than any of her other portraits, this image seems as if she has just walked away from her busy court and is offering us a more unguarded glimpse of her material surroundings.

The interiors of Tudor homes varied hugely between the classes. From the luxurious, showy rich displaying their gold and silver plate on a cupboard, with tables draped in carpets and walls hung with embroidered hangings, designed to impress their status upon any visitors, to the functional, plain rooms of the poor, they were a microcosm of their occupants' position in the world. Visitors knew how to read a room, and how to behave accordingly.

❧ POSSESSIONS ❧

The Tudors were proud of their possessions and liked to display them. In 1597, a London tailor named Leonard Smith brought out the surprising items of a 'hippocamp and eagle stone' to impress the visiting Paul Hentzner, and 'a most perfect looking-glass, ornamented with gold, pearl, silver and velvet'. It was the norm for middle and upperclass Tudors to fill their homes with luxury items:

In noblemen's houses it is not rare to see abundance of arras, rich hangings of tapestry, silver vessel, and so much other plate as may furnish sundry cupboards to the sum oftentimes of a thousand or two thousand pounds at the least, whereby the value of this and the rest of their stuff doth grow to be almost inestimable. Likewise in the houses of knights, gentlemen, merchantmen, and some other wealthy citizens, it is not rare to behold generally their great provision of tapestry, Turkey work, pewter, brass, fine linen, and thereto costly cupboards of plate, worth five or six hundred or a thousand pounds to be deemed by estimation.[1]

From the palaces of the monarchs, full of objects of beauty, to the tiny, remote cottages of farmers, hung with tools, a house's contents revealed its residents' social standing like no other material source.

Beds, chairs, tables, carpets, pots and pans have their own stories to tell, yet theirs is a complex, socially nuanced tale, and not necessarily representative of free choice. As expected, Mary Tudor, former queen of France, slept in a gold bed with hangings and sheets of gold, while the flock bed of the widow Agnes Soundie of Arley had a painted head cloth (tester) and a linen sheet. Such details confirm their comparative social differences, helping to create a material picture of their worlds, but tell us little about them as individuals.

Privacy and space were luxuries guarded by the upper class. The majority of Tudors had to live under someone else's roof, so only the wealthiest could commission tapestries to hang on their walls or carpets to drape over their tables. The concept of home ownership by a single individual or nuclear family is a relatively modern one and, five centuries ago, people related to their spaces differently.

Servants, apprentices, workers, tenants, protégés and relatives formed a more sprawling household, and could exert little control over the interior decoration of their environments. The rooms in which they ate and slept often doubled as a shared working or functional space in which the Tudor man or woman was permitted to coexist, rather than claim and define. Thus, as many contemporary wills reveal, rooms were used more as receptacles for possessions and for facilitating work and the functions of daily life.

So, the Tudors had different expectations of interior space, and were identified by it, rather than being able to control and shape it for themselves. Only those who had some degree of ownership over their rooms might use decoration or display as cultural, dynastic or personal signifiers. Nowhere is this more apparent than in the expensive show items, or Veblen goods, collected by the monarchy.

Paul Hentzner's account describes what he considered worth seeing in Whitehall Palace. The queen's bed was 'most artfully built of wood in various colours, with silk and velvet coverings most richly embroidered with gold and silver' and a pearl-encrusted chest, in which the queen kept her personal effects. Her library was full of books in Greek, Latin, Italian and French, bound in silk of varied colours 'but especially in red ... ornamented and decorated with plates and clasps of silver and gold, and also pearls and other precious gems'. Among the other royal possessions on display were a clock decorated with a rhinoceros carrying an Ethiopian on its back and servants who nodded their heads when it chimed, and the 'little home of a certain Hermit, most elegantly carved from wood and concealed, as it were, behind rocks', which reputedly stood in the privy chamber.[2]

There was something sacred about the queen's personal possessions, passed on by association with her anointed body. An inventory of Elizabeth's possessions made in 1574 includes all her gold, crowns and jewels, as well as orange strainers, spice boxes, perfume pans and the more prosaic snuffers, for the extinguishing of candles. She also possessed a gunpowder flask which had been taken from the body of James IV after the Battle of Flodden in 1513, a reminder of England's great victory.

Personal effects, for the care of Elizabeth's body and known as a woman's 'necessaries', had particular value through their physical connection to her. Two thieves discovered this in September 1564, when they were hanged for the theft of the queen's lye pot, comb, looking glass, gold bodkin to plait her hair 'and such other small ware out of her chamber in her progress'.[3]

Hentzner also visited Hampton Court, where tapestries depicted historical scenes and 'lifelike representations of the costumes of Turkey and America'. In the hall, the visitor found a 'very clear mirror' decorated with alabaster columns, an 'artfully constructed globe', various musical instruments, including one made almost entirely from glass, gold cushions and bed covers lined with ermine, gold and silver flooring and a room known as 'Paradise', in which the precious metals and gems shone so brightly as to be dazzling.[4]

Such objects typified not only wealth but education, sophistication and investment in the world's expanding geographical horizons. As curiosities beyond the reach of most of the queen's subjects, their presence made the palace a showpiece, a gallery, a full-size cabinet of curiosities for the visitor, which screamed of privilege.

The presence chambers were 'radiant with tapestries of gold, silver and variously coloured silk', where the royal canopy of state was sewn in pearls with the message 'Long Live King Henry VIII', who had by then been dead for fifty years.[5] There were also further reminders of Queen Elizabeth's parentage in her bedroom, in a canopy woven by Anne Boleyn as a gift for her husband. As well as the personal significance this had for Elizabeth, it was intended to make a powerful dynastic statement to reinstate the reputation of a woman who had been condemned, executed and her image erased in the 1530s.

A 1553 assessment of furniture and possessions by the keepers of the Palace of Westminster revealed some spectacular and unusual items. There was a bedstead made of walnut with valances of crimson cloth of gold and 'blue velvet cloudwise' striped with purple velvet, a tick feather bolster, three wool-filled quilts and a counterpane of crimson Turkey silk. Following that was a chess set with one half of white wood, the other of black, a wooden walking stick with a black cross on top, and two horse-tops of red and yellow feathers. A number of layers of coloured glass were listed, one of jasper colour, alongside a glass quarter full of civet, nine looking-glasses, a small box of toothpicks, five pipes of Venice gold, a cabinet covered with leather of Paris work, a Venetian lute and a crimson cradle cover.[6]

When Lady Jane Grey was committed to the Tower as a prisoner in the summer of 1553, after being ousted upon the succession of Queen Mary, a number of items were sent to her from Westminster, likely at her own request. Even an imprisoned royal and usurping queen was to languish in splendour:

One muffler of purple velvet, embroidered with purples of damask gold, garnished with small pearls and small stones of sundry sorts, and furred with sables.

One sable skin, with a head of gold, muffled, garnished and set with four emeralds, four turquoises, six rubies, two diamonds, and five pearls; four feet of gold, each set with a turquoise; the tongue being a ruby.

One hat of purple velvet, embroidered with pearls of damask gold, garnished with small pearls, and small stones of sundry sorts, and fringed with gold.

A brooch of gold, with a face and a helmet upon his head, and a white ostrich feather.

Three garters, having buckles and pendants of gold.

A shirt, the collar and ruffles of gold.

Three shirts; the one of red work; the other of gold and black; the third of gold, silver, and red silk.

Two little images of box, graven, representing the king's majesty, and the late king Henry his father.

A purse of sable skin perfumed.

Two dog collars, wrought with needlework, the iron gilt.

One Turkey bow, and a quiver of Turkey arrows, the quiver of crimson velvet, embroidered with leather, and a cover for the same of red cloth.

A coronet for a duke, set with five roses of diamonds, six small pointed diamonds, one table emerald, six great ballas rubies, seven blue sapphires, and thirty-eight great pearls, with a cap of crimson velvet, and a roll of powdered ermines about the same.[7]

Gifts were traditionally exchanged at court on New Year's Day. Courtiers vied to outdo each other in the quality, size and value of their gifts and equally watched closely to see who received particular marks of favour from the monarch. To his sister, Mary, Duchess of Suffolk, Henry gave a pair of gilt pots and a gilt cup with cover, and to his daughter, Princess Mary, he gave two gilt pots, three gilt bowls with covers and a gilt layer. In return, Henry received an impressive array of gifts. His sister Mary gave him a pair of writing tables with a gold whistle. There was also a flagon of gold for rose water, a St George on horseback, of gold, a doublet of embroidered purple satin and a pair of gold bracelets, enamelled blue.[8]

When Henry VIII deliberately made no gift to Catherine of Aragon on 1 January 1532, it reinforced his decisive move to leave her at Windsor the previous summer and never live with her again. Many of Catherine's possessions had already been confiscated by 1533, when she was replaced as queen by Anne Boleyn, including very specific, personal items: an enamelled Spanish collar, a gold cup with the image of St Catherine and a wreath of pomegranates, a salt cellar depicting dancing Moors, a Spanish cup and silver-gilt tabernacle, and heirlooms given to her by her mother.

Moving down the social scale exposes the correlation between rank and the material and quantity of possessions. The Trevelyan family acquired their family home, Nettlecombe Court, in Somersetshire, in 1452. Shortly before it was renovated and rebuilt for the first time in 1530, inventories were made of the rooms, affording a glimpse into the upper-class world of a Tudor knight.

The hall was the heart of the house, dark when its windows were boarded up, warm and smoky from the fire, and strewn with rushes. At Nettlecombe, the walls were hung with red saye cloth, a popular English form of woollen cloth, which was colourful and kept out the draughts. Three boards served as dining tables, with four forms (benches) to accommodate the diners, while a cupboard would have displayed the family's plate and silver. After feeding all guests and family, these would have been stacked away at night for the convenience of sleeping servants, who found their rest in the warm corners. The Trevelyan family retired into the chief chamber, hung with green saye and heated by two chimney pieces. It was dominated by a feather and flock bed, with a bolster, two pillows, taffeta sparver (canopy) and a cover of 'counterfeit Arras', imitative of the real, expensive tapestries found at court. The ten other bedchambers contained more hangings, carpets, cushions, a Spanish basin and a portrait of the king: a 'cloth of Henry VIII'.[9]

A second Trevelyan property, Whalesborough in Cornwall, was inventoried in March 1543 and reveals the activities of a remote, self-sufficient household. The hall contained the expected boards, benches, cupboard, chair and coffer, while the great chamber's three bedsteads and coffers were supplemented by pillows, blankets and keys, as well as a lantern, shears, arrow quivers, staffs, brushes and horseshoes. There were two other bedchambers with bedsteads, chairs and coffers, and a green room containing armour: helmets, chainmail, harnesses, splints, arrows, bows and jerkins. The kitchen was well stocked with dishes, saucers, knives, pots and pans, while the larder held baskets, boards, ladles, pots, tankards, dishes, butter pots, flesh buckets and mouse traps.

After this, the remaining rooms were dedicated to cottage-industry-style production. One chamber was described as being set aside for spinning, but held a bedstead, close stool, trestle and board, bows and bow case. The 'day house' had boards, hutches, cheese vats, butts, chains, wheels, an ox harrow and a brake for bread. The brewhouse had tubs and malt sacks, and the malthouse had boards, troughs, barrels, pieces of timber, cheese racks and an apple press.[10] Whalesborough's contents were an interesting mix of the heraldic and domestic.

In 1596, the possessions of Reginald Rawdon Hastings of the Manor House, Ashby-de-la-Zouch, reveal the material comfort enjoyed by a man of wealth and education. Accustomed to entertaining, his long gallery contained seven trestles, fourteen stools, a cupboard, a long green carpet and maps, including one of England. If guests were invited into Hastings' little chamber, they would have seen the walls hung with tapestry hangings with a floral lining, green, needlework and Turkey carpets, embroidered chairs and cushions, a curtain of gold lace, a range of different-sized tables and a black velvet close stool and pan. Hastings slept in a down bed with a matching bolster, with wool bed and mattress, and two Spanish blankets.[11]

Further down the social scale, farmer Christopher Porter of Radley, his wife Joan and their five children lived in a five-roomed house in the 1570s, comprising hall and parlour downstairs and three chambers above, one of which was occupied by a maid. Often, the desire to maintain or increase a family's social standing through the employment of servants was greater than the need for personal privacy and space.

Widower John Porter, likely to have been a relative of Christopher's, was living nearby in a property with three rooms. There was one large hall containing a cupboard, chest, two stools and a painted cloth, and two chambers above it, one containing a chest, wood, wool and hemp, and a bedchamber with 'all furniture thereunto belonging', another old bedstead, a table, coffer and the clothes of both John and his dead wife Alice.[12]

The small, rural home of the widow Helen Porter in Radley, Berkshire, comprised two rooms. In 1558, the hall contained two table boards, trestles and a bench, which could be erected and dismantled as the main surface where meals were prepared and eaten. To cook with, Helen had three brass pans, three kettles, three brass pots, a possinet, a frying pan, two basins, a pair of andirons, two pot hooks, a trivet and two broaches. Also in the kitchen, perhaps beside the fire, she had one chair and the tools of a hedging bill, a prong, a bucket and a basket.

Helen's bedchamber was dominated by its largest item, the feather bed with bolster, coverlet, bedstead and a white tester. For storage, she had a cupboard, two coffers, a chest and a casket of checker work. In them, she may have kept the twenty pieces of pewter, three candlesticks, 13lb of wool and yarn, three pairs of sheets, a kerchief and other 'napery' (cloth items). There was a single round table, two barrels, a tureen, a bushel and other 'lumber', probably fuel for her fire.

Outside in her barn, she had a cart and plough, six horses, seven hogs, three bullocks and quantities of wheat, barley, pulses and hay. Helen's life would have been closely tied to the land, passing long summer days in the fields and cooking over her fire on dark winter nights.[13]

The possession of personal items was not enough to guarantee ownership. As the decades passed, the Tudor coffers filled with the confiscated objects that had been owned by the fallen, whose splendid residences had been adorned by their personal symbolism.

Just as Anne Boleyn received Catherine's items, so they came to Jane Seymour after Anne's fall.

Servants and protégés also inherited from masters, as Thomas Cromwell did from Cardinal Wolsey in 1529. Such objects were the talismans of success and the first indicators of a fall, and fate turned full circle when the Earl of Southampton and Duke of Norfolk tore the badges of Cromwell's office from his body in 1540.

Minor diplomats could also be stripped of their goods as the first step in a disciplinary process. The property of Sir William Sharrington in Bristol was seized in 1549 when it became clear that he had been embezzling the newly established mint of which he had been appointed controller. Three of the king's officers reported that they had followed his instructions and hastened to Bristol, calling in on the way at Sharrington's house, where 'they collected all the writings, money, plate and jewels they could find, and sealed them up in chests, leaving four servants in charge thereof', while one Mr Paget 'took all Sir William's writings away with him'.[14] It transpired that Sharrington had been drawn into a plot by Sir Thomas Seymour, but as he posed no real threat he was pardoned, while Seymour went to the block.

Being entrusted with someone else's possessions was a matter of great importance and responsibility for the Tudors. It also required good character. In 1553, Ewelme Manor in Oxfordshire was in the possession of Lady (Princess) Elizabeth, given to her by her brother Edward after he became king, and to which she travelled intermittently. The management of the interior had been given to a Thomas Key, whose lack of care caused concern among the princess's household, who wrote to William Cecil about Key's 'lewd demeanour' in 'his management of the possessions of the house'.

A previous certificate of the property had been submitted without mention of 'the plate, ornaments, ready money or jewels of the said house, amounting to good round sums, nor yet the other lands belonging to the house' which were 'similarly wasted and spoiled and converted from the poor'. These needed to be 'speedily' considered, 'lest the foundation and almshouse come to perpetual ruin'. Elizabeth 'tenders much this matter at her heart' and asked for Cecil's advice as to how she may best 'remedy the evil'.[15]

The same year, the inventory of items at Westminster Palace included pieces that had been lent to certain individuals and not returned. Seven yards of black silver tinsel had been borrowed by

Mrs Jerningham for the wedding of her daughter, Mary; three kirtles, in white velvet, crimson taffeta and purple damask had been given for the use of Susan Clarencieux, close friend and servant of Mary I, who had also delivered two sheets to the Savoy Hospital for the use of the poor; eight napkins of diaper work had been lost by the Duke of Northumberland; and two wooden playing tables had been given to the Bishop of Winchester when he was ill at court, but had been lost after his subsequent death. A counterpane of ostrich feathers had been lent to the Duchess of Northumberland; a green velvet bag of chessmen had been sent out to St James's Palace and lost; and 'two little babies [dolls] in a box of wood, one of them having a gown of crimson satin and the other a gown of white velvet' had been taken by Sir Henry Jerningham.[16]

Ambassadors and diplomats were vulnerable to the control of their possessions as an exercise of power when serving abroad. In January 1545, Stephen Vaughan and William Damesell wrote to Henry VIII from their posting in Antwerp in indignation at the treatment they had received there. They were dining with their host on Twelfth Night 'in the English house at Antwerp', when a scout arrived to arrest them 'and commanded that no goods should be conveyed out of the house', having already been to Damesell's lodging and 'sealed up his counting house, chests, and other things' and had done 'the like to all other Englishmen'. With international relations souring between the two countries, it was a measure of distrust made manifest in the restrictions placed upon the foreigners' items of business.[17] Ten days later, John Sturgeon, governor of the English merchants at Antwerp, was arrested as he ate dinner, along with 'all the merchants of our nation' and 'their goods were arrested in the Emperor's name' because 'complaint was made by certain merchants and mariners of Zeeland that their ships and goods were strained and pilled by the King's subjects'.[18]

What items you inherited might depend upon your gender. This was most obvious when it came to clothing, as explored previously, but could hold true for bequests of necessary possessions, tools or gifts related to work. In 1602, widow Elizabeth Denzie of Great Bourton left her son, John, 'my quartern [sic] of a yard land in the fields of

Bourton, and all its lands, leys, meadows, pastures, common feedings etc', while her daughter, Alice, received 'nine pairs of sheets and a small sheet with an open seam, two tablecloths, two towels, four table napkins, three platters, two porringers, a saucer, the worse brass pan, a kettle, a loom, a cowl, a coverlet, a bolster, a winnow-sheet and a blanket'. Elizabeth's clothing was to be equally distributed among all three of her daughters, but John was to have all of the rest of her possessions. While it would benefit John less to have been left his mother's attire, the clear expectation of gender roles is typical of the times: the man would continue to run the family farm, while the women were responsible for maintaining a household.[19]

However, sons were not always so readily available. When sheep farmer Thomas French died in 1545, he was left with one daughter, then under the age of 21. His solution was to leave her to the care of his siblings: his married sister received twenty sheep, and his brother ten sheep, while the young Elizabeth was bequeathed five sheep, a team of horses and her father's best cart, as well as half his crop and half his household stuff. The remainder of his goods went to another brother, who was charged with the 'keeping' of his niece and the execution of Thomas' legacy. Elizabeth could have legitimately continued to run the farm after she had come of age, as a feme sole, but it would have been anticipated that she marry and the property and possessions pass into the hands of her husband.[20]

Essential work items were also bequeathed, with silkwoman Jane Geste leaving the contents of her workshop to her nieces, and many wills of manual labourers passing tools, ploughs and livestock on to their families and friends. In 1588, Simon Mery Senior, of Lower Heyford, passed on to his cousin one strike of wheat, to his daughter eight sheep and to his son, ten sheep.

A bequest might also be a means of protecting loved ones, such as Richard Macham's 1540 gift of 'goods' to Thomas Denton, his landlord, as 'I desire him to be good to my wife'.[21] As repositories of worth, possessions reflected different kinds of value: from those that conformed to the later description of Veblen goods – the expensive, luxury indicators of status – through to essentials which allowed a business, or a family, to continue their work, even to survive.

Occasionally, the purpose of 'things' receives further analysis in official Tudor sources. During the Privy Council's investigations in 1573 into Nonconformist priests, Edward Dering stated that he believed the poor should be either committed to the keeping of the rich, or supported out of 'the extravagance of many', asserting that he did not believe in 'a community of things' which only gave rise to 'a common confusion'. He was pushed on his beliefs about the poor and how they might be defined and helped:

> Then said Mr. Chaderton, 'Whom would you account poor?'
> He answered, 'Not such as were able to have plate at their table.'
> 'Why, Mr. Dering, I trust you do not think it unlawful to have plate?'
> 'No truly,' said Mr. Dering, 'for of late I had plate myself, I thank God, and good friends, till I sold it to buy me a house, which I now have sold again and lost but two shillings.' And more he said, if Mr. Hudson kept account of all that he gave to the poor at his door and abroad, he were better to keep two poor all the year long.[22]

Dering's definition of the poor as those who were unable to have plate at their table assumes individuals had a roof over their head and food to eat. In his example, the individuals are not homeless, hungry or lacking a fire on which to cook. Nothing prevents them from consuming the food they possess. Poverty, therefore, as he saw it, was the lack of items required to elevate the satisfaction of bodily requirements to a social ritual. Plate was a luxury, not a necessity, and its quantity and quality indicative of rank. Its absence, therefore, equated to no rank.[23]

There is no question that stuff mattered to the Tudors. Having your valuable items on display was part of that visual shorthand, that 'silent language' to which all classes were attuned. Those possessions that were non-perishable were recycled like clothing, but often in ways which suggested a profession or allegiance, prompted by a blood connection or one of sympathy. Servants could inherit from their masters as an indicator that they were stepping into their shoes, as Thomas Cromwell did upon the fall of Wolsey in 1529–30.

Symbolic items, often monogrammed, served as reminders of debts to the dead and even the rehabilitation of their reputation, with Elizabeth commissioning the Chequers Ring bearing her mother's portrait. The design for a table fountain, made by Holbein for Anne Boleyn in the 1530s, was also listed among her daughter's possessions in 1574. Objects were a physical talisman, representing continuity with the past and a sense of social, familial and personal identity.

❧ WORKING INTERIORS ☙

The 1596 book *The Pleasant History of Jack of Newbery* describes a busy weaving factory:

> Within one room being large and long
> There stood two hundred looms full strong
> Two hundred men the truth is so
> Wrought in these looms all in a row.
> And in another place hard by
> An hundred women merrily
> Were carding hard with joyful cheer
> And in a chamber close beside
> Two hundred maidens did abide
> In petticoats of stammell red
> And milk-white kerchers on their head.

It was typical of the era for a weaver to bequeath their looms and other specific tools to family members. In 1596, Francis Caster, a Dutchman living in Colchester, left 'one of my looms furnished and a pair of combs with the furniture likewise belonging to it'.

William Tyll, writing out his wishes in 1594, gifted 'to my son William my broad loom that stands in my shop, with my warping and all that belongs to it; to my son Thomas my broad loom that is at Rands with the narrow slays, the shotting boards and trestles'. In the same year, John Badcock of Halstead bequeathed 'all my looms, slays, reeds, shuttles, wheel and blades' to be divided equally among his two sons.[1] Their wills value these items not as symbols of status, or for their intrinsic monetary value, but for the continuation of business and the securing of livelihoods.

In contrast with the interior home decoration and display of personal items the Tudors used to express their wealth, working spaces were largely behind the scenes and functional. The use of this space varied, as storerooms and workshops for machinery, equipment, labour and production. The will of John Harte, a butcher of Thaxted, reveals that his premises contained 'one great scalding tub and one great cauldron and all such trestles ... iron pins and all other instruments'.[2]

The 1596 bequests of Robert Fellexe of Great Oakley – bellows, an anvil, hammers and shoeing tools – indicate that his profession was a smith.

The shelves of apothecaries would have been stacked with herbs, bottles, jars, astrological and measuring instruments and ingredients for cures. The display of items, in the window or inside the shop, was essential to attracting trade, but also a practical way to store works in progress or recently completed. Craftsmen might run a separate market stall at a different location, such as shoemaker John Rogers of Moulsham, who bequeathed 'all the lasts and working tools in the shop and my stall and tilt which I use in the market'.[3]

Manuscript illuminations depicting workshops from the late fifteenth century rarely include any interior adornment. Usually they feature a bench and stool, especially for those trades engaged in close, detailed work, a large window, shelving and occasionally a wooden shop front, sometimes covered in a coloured cloth.

German images from the Guild of St Thomas depict furniture makers carving, cutting wood and sharpening tools in bare rooms with plain walls and floors. A goldsmith's shop from the *Book of Simple Medicines* shows a tiled floor, wooden counter and shelves for display.

Varying trade interiors are shown in the 1568 German *Book of Trades*, with glass painters, silk embroiderers, gem cutters, illustrators, painters and similarly focused artists seated for close work at benches before windows. Their surroundings are often simple, even plain, although they might have a picture on the wall or a vase of flowers beside them.

The engraver has a highly decorated table, with carved feet, and the apothecary's crowded shelves and benches piled high with vessels are topped by decorative mirrors, baubles and what looks like a garland. The weavers sit in a plain room dominated by the large loom; the tailors are cross-legged before a huge window; and the furriers and shoemakers sit at a bench.

In most cases, the interior has no adornment save for completed or partially completed goods, displayed on hooks and beams. However, a notably different work interior is that of the kitchen, with its open fires, brick ovens, storehouses, larders, serving hatches, tables and storage items in sacks, barrels and baskets. This was one workspace that customers were not intended to see, awaiting the results on the private table or in the hall, so they are rarely decorated except for the great flutes of smoke up the walls and the ubiquitous shelves and hooks.

Basic shop fronts, like those illustrated in sixteenth-century editions of Froissart's *Chronicles* and Giles de Rome's *The Government of Princes*, show typical wooden fold-down shop fronts facing the street, over which customers might view and buy goods, but were not invited to enter the interior. Items are visible on the shelves behind, on the counter itself and hung from a pentice, or projecting pole above. One apothecary's shop awning bears the words '*Bon Ypocras* [Hippocras]', advertising the drink available for sale, with an expensive cone of sugar and spices on plates laid out on the counter. A barber's establishment has a number of shaving bowls hung up from the pentice and a towelled customer in the chair.

In 1486, right at the start of the Tudor era, a brewhouse and its contents in the parish of St Mary Somerset was bequeathed to William Robynson. It included a copper kettle, a mash vat, a tap trough of lead, a vegetable vat, two coolers for vegetables, three wicker baskets and three wooden rudders, three brass hand kettles, two lead cisterns for liquor, a firehook, a rake, an iron pike, twenty little tubs for yeast, a mesh tub, a water tub, a cleaning axe, a fan, a steeping cistern, a malt mill, a beer dray with two pairs of wheels and a 'black hair' for a kiln.[4] These details help create a behind-the-scenes picture of the brewhouse making its produce on site, and the hard manual work that went into the process. Robynson received these as a temporary measure, as the real heirs were underage, and he was expected to run the place until they came of age and could decide what they wished to do with their inheritance.

A few illustrations show workshops and shops which have been adorned for aesthetic purposes, perhaps intended to attract customers into a more 'elite' establishment. The *Livre de Bonnes Mœurs* of Jacques Legrand shows a mercer's shop with grey-green tiles on the floor, a carved trestle table with gold scales and weights, carved wooden wainscot and shelving with decorative panels flanking the window. If the space was one into which customers were invited, small improvements and welcoming decor made for a different shopping experience to the simple exchange of goods.

The *Tacuinum Sanitatis* shows a clothier's shop with a patterned floor, the walls painted red and the ceiling decorated with geometric designs. Another image of a Renaissance apothecary shop depicts a complex interior with three separate tiled floors, each with a two-colour design, blue walls and a brown arched ceiling with a decorative edge.

A rare glimpse inside the Tudor school room survives in the 1545 inventory of Wye College, Kent, a training institution for priests founded a century earlier. The parlour contained three tables, four other trestles and four benches, a pair of cushions and one long, padded seat. The hall also contained tables and trestles, benches and cupboards, as well as hangings of red and green saye and painted cloths. The buttery, where the students were likely to have eaten, was furnished with a board and trestles, candlesticks, cloths, basins and ewers as well as a hanging cage, the size and purpose of which were not clarified. The kitchen was well equipped to supply the trainees, with a collection of brass pots and pans, kettles, dishes, ladles, gridirons, forks, hooks, colanders, mortars, spits, plates, dishes and saucers, iron racks, kneading troughs, a moulding board and two great tuns for malt. Within the chapel, there was an alabaster table, two great chests and several oaken boards. Where the trainee priests slept is unclear, possibly on truckle beds or straw in the hall, as the only bedchamber mentioned contained one old feather bed, with bolster, mattress and blankets.[5]

Thomas Tusser's 1577 *Book of Husbandrie* contains a poem describing the necessary furniture for 'husbandry', or the running of a self-sufficient household. It runs to twenty-one verses, but the first four are sufficient to create the impression of the wealth of tools required:

Barne locked, gofe ladder, short pitchforke and long, flaile, strawforke and rake, with a fan that is strong: Wing, cartnaue and bushel, peck, strike readie hand, get casting shovle, broome, and a sack with a band.

Stable well planked, with key and a lock, walls stronglie well lined, to bear off a knock: A rack and a manger, good litter and haie, sweete chaff and some provender everie daie.

A pitchfork, a dungfork, sieve, skip and a bin, a broome and a paile to put water therein: A handbarow, wheelebarow, shovle and a spade, a currie combe, main combe, and whip.

A buttress and pincers, a hammer and naile, an aperne and siszers for head and for taile: Hole bridle and saddle, whit leather and nail, with collers and harness, for thiller and all.[6]

❋

The decoration of interior space was significant to companies such as the city guilds, or livery companies. By 1485, most had their own halls, usually adapted from large houses bequeathed or donated by wealthy members, to be used as meeting and organisational spaces. From feasts to investiture ceremonies, these houses frequently entertained guests, so were ceremonial as well as functional, and displayed items within that were designed to impress.

The London Merchant Taylors, who maintained their headquarters between Bishopsgate and Threadneedle Street, possessed a large amount of ceremonial plate for special occasions, such as when they entertained royalty, dignitaries or foreign ambassadors. Their hall had whitewashed walls and was carpeted with rushes, but the roof required replacing with fresh slate in 1584, and the windows were reglazed three years later.

One inventory of 1512 fills the hall with decoration and colour, with nine red saye hangings of the life of St John, which had hung there 'the more part of the year', a gilt image of the saint standing on a tabernacle, and a blue and green velvet cloth embroidered with a white rose and St John's head, fringed with gold Venice lace. They possessed a high table, a number of movable tables and benches, cushions, banners, streamers, diamond-patterned tablecloths, embroidered napkins and a cupboard 'with four feet' upon which plate from the cupboard room might be displayed. Guests arriving to dine, when all these items were in place, were treated to a display of silver and gilt basins, ewers and salt cellars topped with carved animals, spoons decorated with strawberries and acorns, pots, bowls and standing cups, most gifted by members and their families.[7]

The company's material display of wealth was a recognition of collective identity and purpose, and of the guild's history and prosperity. It was a measure of its success so far, gave thanks to its members and was a future promise of belonging and prosperity.

Records relating to the Guildhall muniment room in Bury St Edmunds suggest a range of items that were stored within it and some of the different functions to which it was put, as a repository of religious and necessary items and a centre of organisation. In 1520–21, payments were made to those collecting the pilgrims' staves; 4d to those who cleaned St Edmund's sword; and 5s for the shrine-keepers for 'carrying it through the year'. Sums were also paid for ginger for the prior in Lent, for Paradise-sops, or bread steeped in wine, cinnamon, cloves, rice, flour and wine. Minstrels were rewarded for playing in the hall and the 'Boy-bishop' of the festival of St Nicholas received 12*d*. Theological degrees were taken, offerings managed, monks rewarded, feasts held and mention was made of the Image of Pity.[8] In all, the records suggest a working interior that fulfilled a public, ceremonial role but was also the epicentre of the 'behind-the-scenes' management that kept the establishment running.

In contrast to the private spaces controlled by guilds, the markets where their goods were sold were public buildings. The Stocks Market, named after the stocks which stood alongside in which miscreants sat to be punished, stood beside the Church of St Mary Woolchurch to the east of Cheapside. Originally selling meat and fish, a new stone building was erected in 1462, which had two storeys. By 1543 it housed twenty-five fishmongers' stalls, eighteen butchers and had sixteen upper rooms. More fish was sold in the arcaded building on Billingsgate Wharf, while streets like Eastcheap were lined with shops on both sides.

The Royal Exchange was founded in late 1566 by Sir Thomas Gresham as a meeting place for merchants:

> The city accordingly purchased fourscore houses, which composed two alleys leading out of Cornhill into Threadneedle-street, called new St. Christopher's, and Swan alleys, for 3532*l*. They sold the materials of these houses for 478*l*. and Sir Thomas Gresham, with some of the aldermen, laid the first bricks of the new building, June 7, 1566, each alderman laying one, with a piece of gold for the workmen: and the work was pursued with such alacrity, as to be roofed in by the month of November, in the following year. The queen would not have it called, as in other countries, the Bourse; but, when it was finished, came and dined with the founder, and with the heralds at arms, by found of trumpets, proclaimed it by the name, of the Royal Exchange.[9]

Based on the Exchange in Antwerp, the London version was built along the lines of a Roman forum, with stone, slate, glass and wooden wainscoting from the Netherlands. A contemporary engraving by Wenceslaus Hollar shows a large courtyard with colonnades on all sides and two storeys above, with ornate windows and Renaissance decoration, and it must have proved a crowded, bustling space full of goods, vendors and customers. Just a decade later, though, in June 1581, the

Lords of the Council reported that 'some part of the building ... had lately fallen down' and put the cost at around £20, asking that 'this worthy monument might not be suffered to fall into ruin and decay'.[10]

⚜ RELIGIOUS INTERIORS ⚜

Before the Reformation, churches, chapels and monastic buildings had an interior design scheme of their own. Their painted walls and stained-glass windows featured brightly coloured images of saints and devils, intended to inspire the devout or to warn a congregation of terrible fates that awaited them in the afterlife. Worshippers were ushered through a set route, designed for maximum visual effect, with tombs, candles, icons and the display of symbolic items often recounting a journey, or story, specific to the location.

Many of the late-medieval Doom paintings survived, such as that in Waltham Abbey's Lady Chapel, with the damned being dragged down to hell. Some had local significance or were reflective of the congregation's location, lives and affiliations. A series of frescoes in St Swithin's at Launcells in Cornwall depict the story of Abraham sacrificing Isaac and agricultural images of a man leading an ass, while another pauses to drink. Llancarfan Church, in the Vale of Glamorgan, has newly uncovered paintings of St George as a Tudor knight in jousting armour and youths engaged in the seven deadly sins pursued by devils.

Parish churches would also be notable for their carved rood screens and reredos, often painted with depictions of saints, whose presence was also felt in statues, icons and stained glass. Original Tudor designs on glass were vivid, complex and often referenced individual patrons. In the private chapel at The Vyne in Hampshire, the Flemish glass-work features Henry VIII, Catherine of Aragon and Margaret Tudor, with their personal devices, and Christ upon the Cross. Seventy years after its foundation, King's College Chapel, Cambridge, was completed in 1515, with a fan-vaulted ceiling, a rood screen erected in honour of Anne Boleyn's marriage in 1533, and twelve large windows completed by Flemish glaziers in 1536.

Cathedrals, monasteries, abbeys and the larger churches contained some of the most important of all ecclesiastical architecture in the shape of shrines and tombs. The Venetian traveller of 1500 remarked that their decoration was 'more like baronial palaces than religious houses' and found nothing comparable to the tomb of Thomas Becket at Canterbury. His visit took place as the sun was setting and the weather cloudy, yet he was stunned by the dazzling radiance of the tomb, entirely covered over with carved plates of gold. The tomb's gold was 'scarcely visible from the variety of precious stones with which it was studded' – diamonds, sapphires and emeralds, including one rare ruby gifted by the king of France.[1]

This display was also witnessed by Dutch scholar Erasmus, who visited between 1512 and 1514, judging that the jewels were 'surpassingly large' and some were the size of goose eggs. His account satirises the shrine 'experience', designed to appeal to the senses of pilgrims through the theatrical use of music, incense, darkness and light, and pulley systems to raise and lower aspects of the tomb.[2] Coupled with the pre-Reformation bread and wine of Communion, which was then considered to be the actual body and blood of Christ, immersion in the Catholic Church was a full, sensory experience.

The building of new churches had always been indicative of a community's wealth, or that community's patron's wealth, and their adornment, inside and outside, was considered a function of their flock's devotion. It had knock-on effects for worshippers too, as even the poorest were considered to receive spiritual benefits from the investment of their lords and employers.

The most famous of the Tudor era was Henry VII's Lady Chapel at the eastern end of Westminster Abbey, begun in 1502 and completed in 1509 at a cost of £14,000. With its ambitious pendant fan-vaulted ceiling, the chapel contains the tombs of Henry and Elizabeth, designed by Florentine artist Pietro Torrigiano, as well as those of Edward VI; Mary I; Mary, Queen of Scots; and Elizabeth I, and was referred to by sixteenth-century historian John Leland as the 'wonder of the world'. It was still incomplete at the time of Henry's death seven years later, and in his will he set out instructions for the continuation of the project:

The said chapel be decked, and the windows ... be glazed with images, arms, badges and cognisants, as is by us readily devised, and in picture delivered to the Prior of St Bartholomew's ... Master of the Works ... and that the walls, doors, windows, arches and vaults, and images of the same within and without, by painted, garnished and adorned, with our arms, badges, cognisants and other convenient painting, in as goodly and rich a manner as such work requires, and as to a king's work appertains.[3]

In the pre-Reformation world, the overlap of material adornment and religious devotion was not considered contradictory, but rather as a means of worship, until the tides of reform started to question the Church's wealth. Back in the thirteenth century, Lucas, Bishop of Tuy in Spain, argued for the inclusion of beauty for its own sake, describing how:

> There are, in the church, painted forms of animals, birds and serpents, and other things, which are for adornment and beauty only … for the house of God must shine with varied worship, so that its outward beauty in itself will lead men to it … the outward beauty of the house of God soothes the eye.[4]

The Venetian visitor of 1500 wrote that there was 'not a parish church in the kingdom so mean as not to possess crucifixes, candlesticks, censers, patens and cups of silver', as well as many other ornaments.[5]

It was also in chantry and private chapels, with their limited congregations, that the wealth of founders was displayed. Lord Darcy's private chapel at Hirst contained cushions of cloth of gold and damask on which to lay the mass book, altar cloths of gold and velvet, chalices, candlesticks and silver cruets, bells, censers and paxes, linen cloths, towels and a hanging lamp of glass. It also had the necessary vestments for an officiating priest, one of sarcenet with a blue cross, one of embroidered tinsel satin and another of gold.[6]

By contrast, the lives of monks, nuns and others living within closed orders were intended to be abstemious and austere. When the property of Thomas Golwynne, a London monk, was inventoried in January 1520, it mostly comprised humble items of clothing and books. He owned three habits, three shirts, three collars and three hoods, a coat, a mantle, and a wide fur 'slop' to 'put over all my gear'. He had two caps, three pairs of hose, five pairs of socks, a pair of double-soled shoes and one pair of cork-soled ones, felt boots and lined slippers for Matins. His small domestic collection included pestle and mortar, pewter dishes, saucers, bottles, butter dish, saucepan, brass pan and chafing dish. His books included a journal, a primer, a psalter, mass books, prayer books and penance books, along with the *Ars Moriendi* (*The Art of Dying*), the *Golden Legend* compilation of saints' lives, and the more prosaic *Shepherd's Calendar* and *Aesop's Fables*.[7]

While monastic buildings were sold off during the Reformation, the interiors and contents of churches underwent huge changes. Former relics that had been venerated for centuries were confiscated by the Crown and absorbed into the Treasury, destroyed or sold. Henry VIII's investigator, Richard Layton, wrote from Bath in 1535:

> I send you vincula S. Petri, which women put about them at the time of their delivery. It is counted a great relic, because St. Peter is supposed to be the patron of the church. It is a very mockery and a great abuse that the prior should carry it on Lammas day in a basin of silver in procession, and every monk kiss it after the Gospel with great solemnity, though they have no writing to show how they came by it. I send you also a great comb called Mary Magdalene's comb, and St. Dorothy's, and St. Margaret's combs.[8]

Afterwards, Layton travelled to Glastonbury and Bristol, gathering more relics for the royal coffers:

> I send you relics, two flowers wrapped in white and black sarcenet, which on Christmas Even 'will spring and burgen [bud], and bear blossoms, quod expertum este [*sic*], saith the prior of Maden Bradeley'; also a bag of relics, strange things, as God's coat, Our Lady's smock, part of God's supper ... I send also Our Lady's girdle of Bruton, red silk, and Mary Magdalen's girdle, covered with white, sent to women 'travailing'; which last the empress Matilda, founder of Ferley, gave them, 'as saith the holy father of Ferley.' I have crosses of silver and gold, and more shall be delivered to me this night by the prior of Maden Bradeley.[9]

The following month, Henry himself visited Winchester, where he 'caused an inventory to be made of the treasures of the church' but took for his own use 'certain fine rich unicorn's horns, and a large silver cross adorned with rich jewels'.[10]

At Dover in October 1535, Layton made an inventory of the goods of the Priory of St Martin's, including items and clothing used in worship, relics and necessary objects for daily living. It appeared by this point that the buildings were dilapidated, and the monks were living in straightened circumstances. In the choir and vestry, there were silver crosses, chalices, censers, basins, cruets and spoons, 'an old relic partly covered with silver plate' and a 'pix of copper and gilt containing relics'. A number of embroidered copes, vestments and tabernacles were recovered, along with altar cloths, cushions and panels. In the prior's chamber were two beds, other furniture and half a Bible on parchment, while in the adjoining chapel were two mass books, alabaster images, a desk and a bell. The great chamber contained hangings and a chest of books, the prior's inner parlour held tables and chairs, in the 'vault where the monks do dine' was a table, a bench, a cushion and a Bible, and the buttery contained a silver salt cellar, six silver spoons and gilt cloths. In addition, there was a very basic schoolmaster's chamber with a feather bed, a bolster, a pair of sheets and a coverlet.[11]

However, the prior of St Martin's, John Folkestone, petitioned Cromwell to explain all the steps he had taken over the last four years to improve the place:

> The glass in the windows which was rusty and dark, was taken down and scoured, and new glass added, where necessary, at his expense. Paved the church; bought new vestments from John Antony for £16, and spent other sums. Has mended the bakehouse ... procured new brass and pewter at his own cost, 'and no marvel though it be simple and scarceness thereof, for the strangers resorting be so wasteful that it is not possible to keep any good stuff long in good order, and many times and specially strangers ambassadors have such hurtful fellows that have packed up table cloths, napkins, sheets, coverpanes, with other such thing as they could get'. Has been at great cost with English and foreign ambassadors. Begs him to consider deeds more than words which may not be true.[12]

The prior's appeal did nothing to stay the course of the Dissolution and St Martin's was closed in 1538. Almost at once, the people of Dover plundered the buildings for lead and stone, leaving little intact. Between them, the prior, archdeacon and commissary of the archbishop were given pensions totalling 37s 6d.[13]

The reforms continued into the reign of Edward VI. Stow records in September 1547 how the king's visitors arrived at St Paul's Cathedral, where 'alle images [were] pulled down' and the order given for the

same throughout England and 'alle churches new whytte-lymed' with
the Ten Commandments written on the walls. They also 'pulled up
alle the tomes, grett stones, alle the altars, with the stalls and walls
of the choir' and sold them. The rood, the cross standing on top of the
carved wooden screen before the nave, was dismantled, followed by
the removal of all the side altars and chapels. The visitors were on the
verge of destroying the tomb of John of Gaunt until a command came
from the royal council to spare it.[14]

The change was not rolled out with synchronicity, though. In
May 1553, all the plate and ecclesiastical garments were removed
from the London churches, so there were very few processions and
much grief among those who followed the old faith. Another source of
the same year, for an unknown church, outlines the expenses incurred
for garnishing staffs and crosses with gilt, and decorating books with
images of saints.[15]

Mary I's restoration of Catholicism later that year saw the return
of many devotional items and pieces of ecclesiastical furniture.
At St Mary Hill in London, 1s 8d was paid for 'putting out' the scripture
that had only been painted over the frescos as recently as 1547 at a cost
of £4. They also ordered two loads of lime to rebuild the altars and a
silver cross, two candlesticks and a censer were borrowed, in order that
the incumbent clergy might resume old patterns of worship. It was an
ideological struggle played out in paint, wood and silver.

Yet the Catholic Counter-Reformation in England was brief, ending
with the accession of the Protestant Elizabeth in 1558. The following
year, St Mary's reported that the 'great rood with its figures of Mary
and John', the sepulchre and altars were all taken down, and 12d was
paid to those who brought down the 'images to Rome land and other
things to be burned'. A payment of 16d went to the rakers for carrying
away the stone rubble from the destruction of the altar.

The rapidly changing church interiors across England, with their
whitewashing and iconoclasm, were the most visible face of the
emergence of a new national Church. The Tudors had a complex relationship with their interior spaces, depending upon the purpose to
which these spaces were put. The way they decorated their churches
was a direct statement of faith and the clearest visual code for the
congregation about the changing state of the national religion. Walls
and altars were decorated in line with the monarch's conscience, and
the flock reacted according to theirs.

CROWD AND RITUAL

❧ ENTRANCES AND EXITS ❧

The Tudors were masters of ceremony, understanding the impression that costume and ceremony, ritual and crowds could confer legitimacy and authority upon their regime. The christening of the first Tudor heir in September 1486, symbolically located at the 'Arthurian' city of Winchester, was attended by a host of royals and dignitaries, processing in order, with their gifts and symbolic items, through a specially erected passageway:

> First, my Lady Cecily bore my lord prince to church, my Lord Marquis and my Lord of Lincoln led my Lady Cecily, my Lady Marquess and, after, Cheyne as Chamberlain, bore the train of the mantle. My Lady Anne, the queen's sister, bore the chrism.
>
> The whole chapel met with my Lord Prince in the queen's great chamber. My Lord Laware [sic], my Lord Woodville, my Lord John of Arundel and Master Audley bore the cloth of estate. The torches, unlit, met him at the stairs' foot of the queen's great chamber, and so went before him unlit to the church. Many ladies and gentlemen followed him ... The sergeant of the pantry was ready with a rich salt, and my Lord of Essex bore the same salt before my Lord Prince ... the sergeant of the ewery was ready with a pair of covered basins and a fair towel lying there upon and my Lord Strange bore them to the church.
>
> Sir Richard Guildford ... had the keeping of the church doors with his men. Four gentlemen and yeomen of the crown had the keeping of the barriers about the font ... two gentlemen ushers had the keeping of the traverse by the font, where my Lord Prince was [undressed] ... and there, fire and fumigations and many royal things done ... My Lord Neville bore the taper before my Lord Prince, after the christening to the high altar. After all the observances was given spices and wine to the estates. My Lord Prince was had from the high altar to St Swithin's shrine, and there offered, and there was sung Te Deum

Laudamus. All the torches lit, brought my Lord Prince to his chamber. And the trumpets blew after.[1]

Even a brief audience with royalty had to be imposing, especially
when the impression would be carried away and relayed to inter-
ested parties. In 1488, when the Spanish ambassadors were brought
before Elizabeth of York 'at an unexpected hour', they found her
'with two and thirty companions of angelic appearance' and all they
saw was 'very magnificent, and in splendid style, as was suitable for
the occasion'.[2]

When Catherine of Aragon first entered London in November 1501,
the city was decorated to reflect her heritage and hopes for her future.
On London Bridge, the first pageant was a structure with two storeys,
painted blue and gold and decorated with the symbols of the Tudor
dynasty: red English lions, Beaufort portcullises, ostrich feathers of
the Prince of Wales and the Lancastrian rose. Catherine was met by
her own namesake, the figure of St Catherine, announcing her presence as 'Kateryn of the Court Celestyall' and claiming the princess's
long-standing devotion to her from the day of her christening.

Catherine was then conducted to the 'Castle of Policy', which contained a panel of characters, some historical, some biblical and others
as abstract virtues. The qualities of Virtue and Nobleness sat alongside
Job and Boethius, Catherine's ancestor Alphonse and the Archangel
Raphael, patron of marriage and procreation. Together, they combined
to offer the princess lessons on 'policy', or how to rule, as without
their 'help all they that think to reign, or long to prosper, labour all
in vain'.[3] A vision of Catherine and her future husband Arthur seated
side by side in the Court of Honour promised the rewards of their
efforts to employ the lessons offered by this political wisdom. Many
more pageants lined the route, with symbolic meaning, as a welcome.

The second pageant saw Catherine greeted by the union rose, the
combined symbol of the red rose of Lancaster and white rose of York,
a clever piece of propaganda on the part of the Tudor regime. The
pageant included two elaborate gateways, and in order to pass through
them, Catherine had to accept the terms offered by Policy, that 'this
sound castle is for virtue, not for nobility, but without me no entrance
lies open in this place'.

Next, third in the sequence, came a vision of Arthur's chariot, an
astrological feature set in a recreation of the heavens, the stars, zodiac

signs and information about the waning and waxing of the moon, all covered over by a cloth painted in Tudor white and green checks.[4]

The fourth pageant saw Prince Arthur presented as the Sun King, whose brightness illuminated the Earth and who dispensed wisdom and justice. The pageant itself was a tall construction with pillars supporting Welsh dragons and English lions, against a backdrop painted with stars, angels and clouds. A mechanised wheel carried more astrological symbols and was turned by three young boys, before the figure of Arthur appeared in a chariot.

The fifth was entitled 'The Temple of God', with the figure of the Lord adorned in gems and pearls, seated on a throne surrounded by burning candles, and singing angels. A huge red rose was borne aloft by heraldic beasts, reminding Catherine of the Tudor Lancastrian line. These were as much to impress the crowds with the dynasty's lineage and power as they did the young princess, whose English may not yet have been sufficient to allow her to follow all the words.[5]

In 1520, Henry VIII hosted a variety of spectacles in order to impress the French. Even travelling across fields and along rural roads had to be done in style.

Catherine was carried in a beautiful litter covered in crimson satin, embroidered in gold, followed by Mary, Duchess of Suffolk in a litter of cloth of gold, wrought with lilies. Three wagons followed, one gold, one crimson and one azure, filled with ladies, the rest of whom followed on palfreys, 'handsome and well-arrayed'.[6] The French Queen Claude rode in a litter of cloth of silver, covered with gold knots, dressed to match in cloth of silver, with her undergarments of gold and a necklace of precious stones. She was accompanied by twelve ladies in brocade and jewels, with three more wagons following, before the king's mother, Louise of Savoy, rode in a black velvet litter with her ladies in crimson velvet with sleeves lined in gold.

The two kings followed at the appointed hour. Francis rode a courser covered in purple velvet, broached with gold and embroidered with ravens' feathers in black, picked out in gold. Henry's horse was trapped in cloth of gold tissue, 'cut in waves of water work' and each wave 'rawe through and frised with damask gold' and laid loose over the top of russet velvet, knit together with gold points that symbolised the narrow waters, perhaps of the Channel. Henry's attendants were apparelled in royal livery, which was 'white on the right side and on the left side, gold and russet, both hose and garment'.

On foot, Henry was attended by six knights, twenty squires, 100 officers and twelve 'persons', of which all the knights and gentlemen had particoloured coats, half silver and half cloth of gold and russet, and the other officers were clothed similarly in satin. With 'honour and noble courage', the two kings and their companies entered the field and presented themselves to the queens, and 'did them reverence'.[7]

The Parisians also put on a comparable show of splendour to welcome James V, king of Scotland, when he came to marry Princess Madeleine of Valois at New Year 1537. James rode a 'goodly horse' with a 'canopy of gold borne above his head' through the streets in procession with fourteen bishops and three cardinals. The Dauphin and king of Navarre rode behind him 'with a great sort of gentlemen'.

The following day, he was received by the king at Notre-Dame 'upon a stage of great height', with instruments played before and after him, then the guard and ten gentlemen bearing pollaxes, eight heralds, cardinals, the dauphin, king and queen, Madeleine, with a 'precious close crown of gold upon her head' and a 'coif of gold set with stones very precious', followed by three 'goodly ladies in cloth of gold gorgeously decked following as waiters of the bride'.[8]

The banquet that followed proved overwhelming in its pomp and display, even for the Scottish king:

That night there was a banquet at the Palace and the ladies princes of France were never in so rich apparel; cloth of tissues was least set by by reason of brotheries, pearls, and precious stones. Thinks the king of Scots never saw such a sight, who has an honourable company of his countrymen apparelled in the French fashion, 'goodly gentlemen and very proper men'. Wrote of the king of Scots 'using himself with beckes and dewgardes after the Norden fashion'. Found him, however, very sober and discreet insomuch that the French King, the Great Master, Winchester, and the writer could not persuade him to some things when he had reasons to the contrary.[9]

❈

These examples of early sixteenth-century spectacle combine the key visual elements of majesty: colour, clothing, procession, hierarchy, wealth, display and co-ordination. They signal intensive organisation behind the scenes, household departments working day and night to ensure that all the various elements came together harmoniously, and the smooth running of such events was a critical aspect of visual success. However, these rituals were a continuation of the tradition of medieval pageantry. They were situated on the cusp of the emerging modern world, combining early Renaissance symbols and themes with the old-style pageantry of morality and mystery plays, and the Arthurian motifs adopted by the Plantagenet kings.

As England made its slow transition through the Reformation, with its destruction of old mores, the style of performance and the cast they figured, became increasingly sophisticated. The presence of the monarch, with all the accompanying ritual, remained a dazzling constant throughout the century.

Paul Hentzner describes visiting Greenwich on a Sunday in 1597 while Elizabeth was in residence, and being ushered into the presentation chamber, which was strewn with rushes and hung with tapestries. Entry into Elizabeth's inner rooms was controlled by the Lord Chamberlain, George Carey, wearing silk and a gold chain, who selected those to be admitted.

Hentzner witnessed the queen processing out to her chapel, with a retinue of officials holding the symbolic sceptre, sheathed sword and royal seal in a red silk purse. At 64, Elizabeth had perfected the art of appearing majestic, with her face 'oblong' and 'fair' but wrinkled, her eyes small yet 'black and pleasant', hooked nose and narrow lips, in spite of the blackened teeth from too much sugar. She had two drop pearls hanging from her ears, false red hair upon which sat a small gold crown, her bosom was uncovered according to the English tradition of unmarried women, and she wore a necklace of 'exceeding jewels'. Her air was 'stately' and her manner of speaking 'mild and obliging' as she swept past Hentzner, dressed in white silk bordered with pearls the size of beans, a collar of gold and jewels, and a mantle of black silk shot with silver threads, with the long train carried by a marchioness. When an ambassador wished to speak with her, he approached and knelt, whereupon she removed her glove, gave him her hand to kiss, and raised him to his feet. Behind her came her ladies, mostly dressed in white to match, guarded on each side by fifty gentlemen pensioners with axes, and all knelt as she passed by.[10]

Coronations were planned in lengthy detail for maximum effect, with iconography, jewels and ritual. Their intention was obvious: the symbolic start to a monarch's reign needed to be memorable and awe inspiring, establishing a lasting authority and allegiance. Displaying the new king or queen in public dripping with jewels, set to poetry and music, encouraged loyalty and established the paradox of their otherness and humanity. An actual sighting of royalty went a long way in the popular imagination, and the Tudors maximised this street theatre to their advantage.

In February 1547, Edward VI travelled to his coronation along the traditional route, from the Tower to Westminster. The streets were adorned with pageants and hung royally with fabric and flags, carpets and streamers, and all the guilds lined Chepe Street, 'presenting them as loving subjects unto their king'. At St Paul's Cathedral, a rope was tied from the steeple and anchored to the ground, with 'a man running down the said rope as swift as an arrow out of a bow, down with his hands and feet ... not touching the rope'.[11]

During the succession crisis of 1553, Lady Jane Grey's arrival at the Tower, the day after having been proclaimed queen, lacked decoration. It was her presence rather than her arrival that was significant and intended to convince onlookers of her legitimacy to rule. Arriving with a great company of lords and nobles, the reluctant Jane was followed by her mother and ladies bearing her train. Guns were fired to announce her presence, then trumpets sounded before a proclamation was read all through the streets that Mary Tudor was 'unlawfully begotten'. This did not deter one young man, who was arrested for 'speaking certain words of Queen Mary, that she had the right title'.[12]

In contrast, great public display was put on for Mary when she rode triumphantly into the capital in August 1553. She was received at Whitechapel by the mayor, who delivered to her the ceremonial sword and mace. Aldgate was 'goodly hanged with cloth, banner and streamers', where singers performed, and the same at Leadenhall, where the guilds turned out in their best clothes. Around the Tower, 'every house hanged' with decoration, with 'singers, organs and shawms'

and 'so glad did the people's hearts rejoice'. Between her arrival in
London and her coronation, the citizens worked to adorn the route.
They hung the streets with fabric and banners, and prepared pageants,
repaired conduits and standards, and erected wooden scaffolds to
house every guild.

Observer Henry Machyn recorded Mary's coronation procession
a month later, as she rode in a gorgeous chariot past pageants of
giants and streets hung with gold, to the blowing of trumpets, where
St Paul's was hung with streamers, the gates were painted, and people
cheered all the way to Westminster.[13]

In January 1559, the capital witnessed its third coronation in twelve
years as Elizabeth I rode out in a chariot from the Tower, with her
entourage and a procession of around 2,000 horses. A little snow had
fallen, so the streets had been laid with fresh sand and gravel. Wooden
railings kept back the anticipated crowds.

Elizabeth rode in a litter of white cloth of gold, lined with pink
satin, flanked by footmen in scarlet cloaks and pulled by two mules.
At Gracechurch Street, she was met by a pageant depicting her lineage, including her parents Henry VIII and Anne Boleyn, a pairing
which had not been celebrated in public for over two decades. In total
there were eleven pageants, depicting Edward VI, nature, Albion, the
Church, historical figures, religious messages and mythical beasts,
concluding with Elizabeth depicted as the biblical judge, Deborah.

In contrasting mood, royal funerals were sombre and lacking in
colour, but often created as powerful an impression. The unexpected
death in childbed of Elizabeth of York in February 1503 was marked
by a dramatic and symbolic ceremony, where colour and light were
carefully deployed to intensify her sacrifice. Two hundred paupers,
dressed in black at the king's expense, led her procession. Two sets of
virgins, dressed in white linen and Tudor wreaths of white and green,
lined the route to Westminster holding lighted candles, and the torch
bearers wore white, woollen gowns. Eight white palfreys draped in
black, bearing her ladies in waiting, were led along in single file by
men in black robes.

The coffin was borne in a black velvet chariot led by six horses, with
knights bearing shields of royal arms riding alongside. White banners

were draped across her black velvet pall, surmounted by a cross of white cloth of gold. It was embroidered with her motto 'humble and reverent', crowns and symbols of the Tudor dynasty. All the London churches were draped in black and as the entourage passed them, the bells pealed out, and the vicar appeared to cense the coffin. More than 1,000 candles burned on the hearse and the vaults and cross inside Westminster Abbey were hung with black cloth. A wax effigy of Elizabeth, her loose hair cascading around her robes of estate, decked with jewels, was placed on top of the coffin, but removed before its interment. As in keeping with royal funerals, her employees broke their white wands of office and cast them down into the tomb with her remains.

When Henry VII died in April 1509, the subsequent payments suggest the pomp of the occasion. Fifty-six merchants were required to supply the lengths of black cloth ordered to dress the dozens of women in attendance, from his daughter Princess Mary to Perott Doren and Jane Walter, chamberers to his mother. The king's wardober, Andrew Windsor, was paid £1,000 for livery garments for lords and others present, and for black cloth hanging in the chapel.

The payments made to goldsmiths and tailors suggest that the hearse coverings, palls, robes and the gowns for the nine 'henxmen' were richly embroidered, and decorative painted borders, banners and flags were supplied by a dozen men. There were 2,940 metal escutcheons transformed with bright colours, and twenty-six coats of arms, 118 escutcheons on sarcenet, 1,014 pencells, fifty-six banner rolls and two embroidered coats, one for the Garter King of Arms and the other for the dead king. On the hearse alone 1,557lb of beeswax was used with a further 3,606lb at Westminster. Alms were distributed from sixty country churches along the route, from Richmond to London, as well as to some poor people in the Clink Prison, while a few at Newgate were granted their liberty.[14]

Several accounts survive of the process of Henry's interment. The briefest of them, an anonymous record, provides a narrative overview while resisting giving exhaustive details about all the attendees:

> After the body had been embalmed, it was brought out of the privy chamber to the great chamber and rested there three days, on each day three masses and dirges being sung by a mitred prelate; then carried to the hall for three days with like services; then to the chapel

for three days. On Wednesday, 9 May, the corpse was brought in a chariot drawn by five great coursers from Richmond to St. George's in the Field (met there by clergy), London Bridge (met there by the mayor, &c.) and St. Paul's, where it was placed in the choir under a goodly hearse, and there was mass and a sermon by the Bishop of Rochester, during which time the King's household, with the mourners, reposed them in the bishop's palace. Next day the corpse was removed to Westminster, Sir Edward Howard, on a courser trapped with the arms of the defunct, bearing the King's banner. There it was set under a curious hearse made of 9 principalles full of lights which were all lighted. Next day, after three masses and the offerings, the choir sang Libera me, the body was put in the earth, the Lord Treasurer, Lord Steward, Lord Chamberlain, Lord Treasurer and Comptroller of the King's household brake their staves and cast them into the grave.[15]

In contrast, the quiet, simple funeral requested by the queen dowager, Elizabeth Woodville, has prompted much debate among historians. Having spent the last five years of her life in retirement at Bermondsey Abbey, she died there in 1492, two months after drawing up her will.

A short while after her death, Elizabeth's body was placed in a wooden coffin and taken by barge to Windsor, accompanied by a small retinue, while her children and other relatives travelled to Windsor to meet her body. A herald commented that 'ther was nothing doon solemnly for her saving a low hearse suche as they use for the common peple with iiii wooden candilsticks abowte hit' and 'never a new torche, but old torches, nor poore man in blacke gowne nor hoods, but upon a dozen divers olde men holding old torches'.[16]

She was buried in St George's Chapel, beside Edward IV, on 12 June. Her only surviving son, the Marquis of Dorset, paid the 40s in alms out of his own pocket. Elizabeth's burial was consistent with her final years in retirement and suggests that her desire for poverty and piety was genuine. She had chosen a humble wooden coffin, a marked contrast to the regal magnificence of her life as queen.

The funerals of important citizens also involved light, display items, clothing, decoration and the presence of significant people. In the years before the Reformation, these were even more flamboyant and visual, like the funeral of Sir William Roche, alderman of London, recorded by the Draper's Company in September 1523. At the head

of his procession came priests and clerks dressed in surplices, carrying branches of white wax and singing. Following this was borne the
standard of Roche's crest, the red roebuck's head, with gilt horns and
wings, with mourners following, before heralds carried various items
including his arms, target, helmet and coat of armour. Clerks and
assistants to the Drapers followed, dressed in their livery and hoods,
after which came the body, with Roche's son leading more mourners.
A sword bearer followed, and the Lord Mayor dressed in black, the
aldermen and sheriffs, the whole 'livery of this fellowship in order',
ladies and gentlemen, and the aldermen's wives.

In the church, the sword, target and helmet were offered to the
priest, followed by the banners, and Communion was taken, before
the body was interred. Afterwards, the guests returned to Roche's
house where they dined on brawn and mustard, boiled capon, roast
swan, pigeons, tarts, gallons of French wine and wafers.[17]

Funerals were less elaborate down the social ranks. Guild members
would be guaranteed a good number of mourners, though, especially
among the weavers who, in 1491, made it obligatory for all 'brothers'
to attend the funeral of a member, being fined 8d for non-attendance,
unless they had 'reasonable excuse'.[18]

In 1559, Sir John Baker of Kent was buried with a standard, a coat
of arms, banners, torches and mourners in black gowns, followed by a
'great dinner'. Mistress Matsun, wife of Captain Matsun, was buried the
same month, with two white wax branches, four great tapers and twelve
torches, two banners, twenty-four escutcheons or arms and a herald.

In 1560, the body of Lady Harper was borne from Blackfriars to
Ludgate with a pennon of arms and two dozen escutcheons, then
buried in a church hung with black drapes. That same year, Machyn
records the burial in St Mary Wolnorth, in Lumbard Street, of a man
whose name he does not know, who was laid to rest with two dozen
escutcheons of arms.

Sixteenth-century wills usually specify where the testator wished
to be buried, sometimes even whereabouts within the church, and
the style of mourners and decoration, even perhaps a memorial to be
erected, or a dinner or wine to be enjoyed afterwards. The general rule
was, though, that the poorer the individual, the less pomp and display.

The poorest members of society would have been buried simply,
with mourners dressed in whatever was suitable, without the accoutrements of status, with a minimum number of candles and tapers

and banners. The funeral of Elizabeth Woodville, ironic as it is that of a dowager queen, reveals the most about the way the poor were laid to rest – simply, in wooden caskets, without crowds or long processions – especially for the decades following the Reformation. As with other aspects of Tudor life, it was wealth and status that facilitated visual spectacle.

❦ REVELS ❦

At New Year 1511, a dazzling pageant was unveiled at Greenwich. There was not only a castle, but:

> gates, towers and dungeon, garnished with artillery and weapons after the most warlike fashion, and on the front of the fortress was written *La fortresse dangerus*, and within the castle were six ladies clothed in russet satin, laid all over with leaves of gold … knit with laces of blue silk and gold, on their heads, coifs and caps all of gold.[1]

Chronicler Edward Hall relates how the drama developed:

> After this castle had been carried about the hall, and the queen had beheld it, in came the king with five others, apparelled in coats, the one half of russet satin, spangled with spangles of fine gold, the other half rich cloth of gold, on their heads caps of russet satin, embroidered with works of fine gold bullion. These six assaulted the castle, the ladies seeing them so lusty and courageous, were content to solace with them, and upon further communication, to yield the castle.[2]

Richard Gibson's revels accounts give the costs of the production. He tells us that 13s worth of alder poles were used for the castle wainscot, 1lb of wax for setting the leaves, 18s 4d for silver paper to cover the battlements and gates, 8d for green foil to 'gravelling', and 1lb of verdigris for colouring moss and ivy leaves. The pageant also required scissors for cutting out roses and leaves, gold for the banners and sheaves of arrows, a bundle of ash hoops for lining the towers and a rope used for the 'traverse' (crossing of) the hall, although this had been stolen during the pageant.

The record also lists that the 95 yards of russet satin, 72 yards of yellow satin and lesser quantities of white and green had been purchased from mercer William Bottre, as well as a whole separate set of clothes for Henry and his friends to cover their secret apparel. White sarcenet, white fustian, black buckram and Venice gold and ribbon, and caul pipes of gold had been required for the ladies' costumes. Robert Amadas, the court goldsmith, was paid £8 for fine gold letters that were attached to Henry's jacket, which he gave away to lords and ladies of the court. It also cost 6s 8d to clean Sir Edward Borrow's 'place', where the pageant was made, and another 6s 8d to the painters 'for hire of old sails for covering the pageant'. Transporting it to Greenwich required two barges and ten rowers, at a cost of 36s.

Although Hall's version lists the drama of the event, he could not know that through exuberance that evening, the castle was destroyed and was listed by Gibson as 'the pageant, being broken, was sent to the Prince's wardrobe as broken store'.[3]

Hall's descriptive account of the festivities for Christmas 1517–18 can also be overlaid with Gibson's costs. On Twelfth Night at Greenwich, Henry and Catherine were entertained in the hall by 'a garden artificial, called the *Garden of Esperance* [hope]'. It was 'towered at every corner, and railed with rails gilt, and all the banks was set with flowers artificial of silk and gold, the leaves cut of green satin, so they seemed' real. In the middle was set 'a pillar of antique work, all gold set with pearls and stones', on top of which was a gold bower 'within which stood a bush of roses, red and white, all of silk and gold, and a bush of pomegranates, all of like stuff'. In the garden, six knights and six ladies danced, 'richly apparelled'.[4]

Gibson's account describes how the garden was filled with marigolds, rose campions, daffodils, columbines, roses, eglantines, holly oak 'and other plants', made from 36s 6d worth of green, gold and silver paper, and 2s 4d of 'party gold', and how it was constructed from 250 oaken boards costing 6s 8d. The carpenter's wages were £3 4s and the painters received £8.

Gibson also relates how the knights wore purple and the ladies wore purple and cut works on white sarcenet and green, embroidered with yellow satin, and with damask gold headwear. The fabric had been supplied by William Bottre again, who charged £24 10s for 196 yards of purple satin, 60 yards of yellow, and smaller amounts of black, blue, green and crimson.

Six black velvet bonnets from Milan were purchased from Sir John Baker for 18s each, and thirty-six ostrich feathers were bought from a shop called the 'Dagar' on London Bridge. The ladies' headwear required gold damask, after the style of Amsterdam, and the 108,000 gold spangles costing 45s 8d were sewn on by William Mortimer, the embroiderer, for £10 16s. The men's tailor was paid £3 4s 8d, but the women's tailor, a John Skatt, only got 40s.

Lord Buckingham's barge and eight rowers were required to transport the pageant downriver to Greenwich for 20s. Again, the frame of the pageant was broken and was stored in the prince's wardrobe.[5]

In May 1522, Henry received the Holy Roman Emperor Charles V, who was newly landed at Dover, and conducted him to Greenwich. He was lodged in the king's apartments, which were 'so richly hanged that the Spaniards wondered at it, and specially at the rich cloth of estate'. They were treated to a royal joust, in which the king and his company were dressed in cloth of gold, adorned with silver letters with great plumes on their heads, while the Duke of Suffolk's men wore russet velvet, and eight courses were run, with lances broken every time.

At supper that evening, members of the royal family took part in a spectacular masque, with colourful costumes including more caps and capes of gold. A tournament was also devised for their entertainment, with men on horseback clashing swords who 'fought bravely' before taking supper in a chamber where a cupboard of twelve shelves displayed gold and silver plate and great branches of light highlighted the cloths of estate. Another masque followed, in the style of Lombardy, with new velvet costumes, before the king and emperor departed Greenwich for London the following morning.[6]

A mile from the city, on a spot where two gold tents had been erected, they were greeted by the mayor, aldermen and dignitaries wearing their chains of office. Two drawn swords were borne before the king and emperor, who had changed into coats of gold embroidered with silver and were followed by Henry's men in purple velvet and Charles' men in red velvet, then the guards.

They were greeted by Sir Thomas More, who made an oration of welcome, before proceeding into Southwark, where the clergymen of the city were waiting in their copes, and heralds drew them onto London Bridge. A pageant at the start depicted two giants, Samson and Hercules, holding up a golden tablet, before a castle made of black and white, painted to look like marble, where Jason stood with the golden fleece, two bulls which let out fire and the richly dressed figure of Medea in a tower. At the Conduit in Gracechurch Street, a castle with two great gates, overseen by Charlemagne, awaited them, handing Charles the sword of justice and Henry the sword of triumphant majesty.[7]

Further pageants were situated at Leadenhall, where the figure of John of Gaunt presided over his descendants, and at Cornhill, where King Arthur and his round table were accompanied by music. At the Stock Market a garden full of flowers had been created, surrounded by water full of fish, and beyond it, the elements, stars and planets. Around the Great Conduit in Chepe (Cheapside), four galleries had been created of gold and silver cloth, four fair ladies sat in four towers and the arms of the emperor and king were displayed, as children sang.

More pageants told the history of England and Spain and depicted angels in heaven. Concluding his account, the chronicler Edward Hall does not neglect to mention the role played by the common people:

> Yet you must not forget ... how the citizens, well apparelled, stood within rails set on the left side of the streets and the clergy on the right in riche copes ... and all the streets were richly hanged with cloths of gold, silver, velvet and Arras, and in every house almost minstrelcy.

Such processions always had multiple audiences and players and were dependent upon the skills and effort of the guilds and their members, and the good behaviour of those gathered to watch.[8]

Other forms of visual display in the city streets relied upon certain figures whose appointments had strong performance elements. One of the longest-surviving medieval throwbacks was the fool, or jester. In January 1553, as part of the festivities for the twelve days of Christmas, King Edward's Lord of Misrule landed at the Tower.

A figure of mischief and fun, dressed in purple velvet lined with ermine and a robe of silver spangles, the Lord of Misrule was greeted by the Sheriff of London's jester, with his men, each wearing a white bow about their necks. Trumpets, bagpipes, flutes and drums played, and the fools danced and sang, before a proclamation was made about their arrival. The lord and jester gave each other gifts, and underwent a mock ceremony of knighthood before drinking toasts and riding about Chepe, where the cofferer cast pieces of gold and silver. It must have been a memorable day for those Londoners who witnessed it.

Another key entrance into the city was the annual Lord Mayor's Day, held in the sixteenth century at the end of October. Following the election of the new mayor, the successful candidate took to the Thames in a flotilla of decorated ships representing the guilds, with music playing and banners flying. In 1553, the new mayor was Sir Thomas White, of the Merchant Taylors, who docked to the sound of drums and flutes, all dressed in blue silk gowns, with matching caps and hose. The guild performed the pageant of St John the Baptist, before processing to St Paul's with torches and trumpets.

In 1562, the mayor was accompanied downriver by barges decked with streamers and banners, with drums, trumpets and gong, and was greeted in St Paul's by 'all the bachelors in crimson damask hoods, with drums and flutes and trumpets blowing, and sixty poor men in blue gowns with red caps, carrying targets, banners and standards'. There followed 'a goodly pageant with goodly music playing', and a dinner held in the Guildhall, with all the judges and 'many noble men and women' and music.[9]

Revelry was often announced in public, by proclamation, or in writing. In 1565, when Ambrose Dudley was married, the challenge for the joust was posted on the court gates at Westminster three weeks in advance. Of course, it was Dudley's intention to appeal to a literate, educated elite of competitors:

Yow that in warlike ways and deeds of arms delight,
Yow that for countryes cause or else for ladies love dare fight,
Know yow foure knyghts ther be that come from foreign land,
Whose haughtye hearts and courage great hathe moved to take in hand,
With sword, with speare and shield, on foote, on horse backe, to,
To try what yow by force of fight, or otherwyse, can do.
Prepare yourselves therefore this challenge to defend,

That trompe of fame your prowess great abroad may sound and send.
And he that best can do, the same shall have the price.
The day, the place, and forme and fyght, lou here before yowr eyes.[10]

In 1575, Elizabeth I visited her favourite, Robert Dudley, Earl of Leicester, at home at Kenilworth Castle. With their on–off relationship having lasted for over fifteen years, Dudley made a final effort to impress, in the hope of winning the queen's hand in marriage. Over the course of nineteen days, he entertained her at great expense, in a huge new tower with glazed windows, in the gardens he had redesigned to incorporate a huge lake, and all through his beautiful grounds.

Elizabeth's reception at the castle indicates the effort he went to, and the manner of display he created. She arrived around eight in the evening and was welcomed at the edge of the park by the figure of Sibylla, dressed in white silk, reciting poetry 'in the English rhyme and metre'. When she passed through the gates, a porter met her and conducted her through to the inner gate, near the base court of the castle. Here, she saw the Lady of the Lake and two nymphs, seated on a floating island in the middle of a pond, lit by torches, to the sound of music.

From the base court onwards, Dudley had constructed a bridge, 70ft long and 20ft wide, gravelled, railed and offering views of the entire estate. Seven posts were set along it at intervals, offering gifts to the queen, reputedly from the gods. First, there were caged birds from Sylvanus, god of Fowl; second, a silver bowl of fruit from Pomona; and third, a bowl with the ears of cereal crops from Ceres. On the fourth pillar were red and white grapes from Bacchus; on the fifth was a tray of fresh grass strewn with fish and seafood from Neptune; the sixth bore weapons from Mars; and the seventh was supplied with musical instruments from Phoebus.

Dudley's efforts impressed his queen, but she did not agree to his proposal. Out of all the visits Elizabeth made to the homes of her courtiers, who vied to outdo each other and almost went bankrupt in the process, the Kenilworth entertainments were the most spectacular.

❊

Local celebrations could be varied and unpredictable. In May 1549, Bishop Hugh Latimer hoped to stay overnight at a town on the way home from London and to preach there in the morning, which was a holy day. However, he found the church door locked and a parishioner told him, 'This is a busy day with us, we cannot hear you, this is Robin Hood's day, the parish is gone abroad to gather for Robin Hood.'[11]

Calendar dates like Midsummer's Eve, on 23 June, were marked, when bonfires were lit in the streets after sunset to purge the air and the wealthy set out tables 'with sweet bread and good drink ... with meats and drinks plentifully, whereunto they would invite their neighbours and passengers also to sit and be merry with them in great familiarity, praising God for his benefits bestowed on them'. The doors of English homes were adorned with green birch, fennel, white lilies and similar plants, with 'garlands of beautiful flowers' and 'lamps of glass with oil burning in them all the night'.[12]

Two different occurrences in London in 1563 highlight the colourful and dramatic nature of Tudor public revelry. On Easter Monday, following a sermon about French refugees, preached at St Mary Spital, the Bishop of Winchester led a procession of the mayor and aldermen, judges and sergeants, 'and many worshipful men and women', with the masters of the hospital carrying green staves in their hands, and the children of the hospital, boys and girls in blue coats and red capes.

That September, the mayor, aldermen and other dignitaries took part in quite another spectacle, 'after the old custom', when they hunted a hare and fox through the streets of the city. The pursuit of the fox lasted for a mile 'and after the hounds killed the fox at the end of St Giles, and there was a great cry for the death, and blowing of horns, before the party rode back through Lumbard street'.[13] The name of the central London district of Soho may derive from this practice – from the calls of the huntsmen – as the area was still countryside as late as 1536, when Henry VIII transformed it into a royal park. The pursuit of the fox, though, was taking place in at least a semi-built-up area. What the Londoners observing this process thought was not recorded.

In 1583, Philip Stubbes was critical of the fun and frolics of the people. He singled out May Day as an unruly occasion, when maidens were defiled in the woods:

but the chiefest jewel they bring from thence is their May pole, which they bring home with great veneration ... covered all over

with flowers and herbs, bound round about with strings from the
top to the bottom, and sometimes painted with variable colours ...
then fall they to leap and dance about it, as the Heathen people did.

At the end of the month, on Whit Sunday, ales were provided by the
parish, as Stubbes reports again: 'the Church wardens of every parish
... provide half a score or twenty quarters of malt ... made into very
strong ale or beer, [which] is set to sale in the church or some other
place assigned'.[14] Parish ales were held at other significant moments
of the year: bride-ales (bridals) at weddings; lamb ales during the lamb-
shearing season; leet ales when the manorial court was in session, and
other points, in order to raise funds for the Church.

A special dinner was usually held in early September, to mark the
return of the harvest, known as 'kern-feasts', 'mell-suppers' and 'hor-
keys'. Thomas Tusser's 1573 *Five Hundred Points of Good Husbandry*
instructs the local landowner that 'in harvest time, harvest folk, servants and all, should make, all together, good cheer in thy hall'.[15]

Good news prompted public celebrations. The birth of a royal baby
was marked by cannon fire, the ringing of church bells and free wine.
When Henry VIII learned that his rival, Francis I of France, had been
defeated by the emperor at the Battle of Pavia in 1525, command was
given to London's mayor that 'that night there should be a great bonfire at St Paul's church door, and there to be set a hog's head of red and
another of claret for the people to drink that would, for the good tid-
ings'. The following day, a 'great watch' was set throughout the city
as if it was Midsummer's Night and in every street a bonfire was lit.[16]
Likewise, to mark the death of Richard de la Pole, the Yorkist claimant to the English throne, who also died at Pavia, Bow Bell was rung,
followed by a peal in every parish church in London.

Events like All Hallow's Eve (Halloween) provided opportunities
for pranks and games. As Reginald Scot wrote in *The Discovery of
Witchcraft* in 1584:

some one knave in white sheet hath cozened an abused many thousands ... for in our childhood our mother maids have so terrified us
with an ugly devil having horns on his head, fire in his mouth and
a tail in his breech ... whereby we start and are afraid when we hear
one cry.[17]

Bonfires were lit, often on hilltops, in an attempt to drive away witches, who were increasingly feared and persecuted as the century progressed. At Christmas, and on other important days, wassailing, or drinking from a communal cup, was a common ritual. This form of drinking a toast, drawn from the Anglo-Saxon *waes heil*, or 'good health', might arrive on your doorstep with carol singers, or be carried into the fields or orchards to encourage the growth of crops.

Charivari, or rough music, was used on occasions when a community wished to express approval or disapproval. With participants banging household items together to make a disharmonious sound and taking part in a mock parade, they might exercise the weight of popular opinion when it came to an unsuitable marriage, acts of domestic abuse or deceit of any kind.

In a culture that was so highly visual, display in all its forms had meaning beyond the literal. From the pageants decorating streets during a coronation procession to villagers dancing around a maypole, signs and symbols conveyed meaning to the participants and the observers.

Revelry combined the elements of the visual and the active, and the preparation and the enactment, with the performance itself, as a live experience, engaged with at different levels of artifice and commitment. Most revels relied upon performers, either actors assuming roles, or monarchs and important figures following procedures as themselves. When it came to public spectacles and customs, individuals might commit to being performers, or observers, or move between the roles. The ways in which the Tudors interacted with different forms of revelry allows us to understand who they were and where they belonged in society.

❦ THEATRE ❦

It is easy to see how the masques, pageants and revels of the early Tudor court developed into the format we recognise today as Elizabethan theatre. Such early performances had clear characters, themes, costumes, scenes and sometimes even the scripted development of a story. In 1515, when Henry dressed in green and waited on Shooter's Hill to surprise Catherine and her ladies, and dined, played music and jousted, the court were acting a scene, in role, in costume, in character. Courtly tableaus such as the Garden of Esperance of 1517 and the Chateau Vert of 1522 used a formulaic narrative, predicated upon the theme of gender conflict and surrender, as metaphors for the games of courtly and romantic love.

The work of Nicholas Udall, initially taking the form of conventional verses for the coronation of Anne Boleyn, had developed by the 1550s into recognisable play form, in the comedy interlude *Ralph Roister Doister*. Taking the five-act structure that would become familiar in later drama, it pursued a courtship theme, with morality play-style characters such as Madge Mumblecrust and Tibet Talkapace. By 1561, Elizabeth watched *Gorbuduc* at Whitehall, by Thomas Sackville and Thomas Norton – a play developed at the Inns of Court with a more serious, political theme.

However, the presence of the queen could not guarantee a smooth performance. At the end of August 1565, Elizabeth was entertained by students of Christ Church College during her visit to Oxford. A range of comedies and plays were enacted before her, but *Arcite and Palamon*, possibly a version of the lost play by Richard Edwards listed as being in performance the following year, met with a tragic ending for, 'by the fall of a wall and wooden gallery' leading from the unfinished stairs to the hall, 'divers persons were sore hurt and three men killed outright, which came to behold the pastimes'.

William Harrison, who recorded the disaster at Oxford, was virulently anti-theatre, and stated, 'Would to god these common plays were exiled for altogether, as seminaries of impiety and their theatres pulled down as no better than houses of bawdry'. He believed it was 'an evident token of a wicked time when the players grew so rich that they could build such houses'.[1]

In 1579, Stephen Gosson published *Schoole of Abuse, Containing a Pleasant Invective against Poets, Pipers, Players, Jesters and Such Like Caterpillars of the Commonwealth*. His attack prompted many replies, especially in pamphlet form, but also Philip Sidney's *Defence of Poesy*, or *Apology for Poetry*, describing the art as creating a sublime reality and stirring men to virtue.[2]

Despite this mounting criticism, theatre was emerging as a profession. Formerly performed by tradesmen and gentlemen's servants, plays were being enacted regularly on Sundays at inns, drawing the crowds away from the churches, to the consternation of churchmen and Puritans. The council legislated that penalties be imposed upon any plays containing seditious or immodest content. It required all to be submitted for approval to the mayor in advance and actors to be licensed. To prevent disorder, the playhouses were forbidden from performing on Sundays and their performances had to take place during daylight hours, to enable the audience to travel home before sunset. When plague broke out in the city in 1574, entertainments were prohibited at the Guildhall 'to prevent the concourse of people from spreading the contagion', and frequently, as the disease recurred, the new theatres would find themselves ordered to close, for weeks or months on end, until the authorities deemed it safe to reopen.

The first English outdoor theatre, the Red Lion, opened in 1567 in Whitechapel, outside the city walls on the eastern side. Plays had been performed in the courtyards of inns, but the Red Lion had formerly been a farm, the garden of which was transformed into a single-storeyed performance space, with trapdoors and a tower. Ultimately, it proved to be too far out of the city, in a rural location, and did not survive beyond the summer season that year.

After that, the more successful Theatre opened in Shoreditch in 1576, the Curtain in 1577, the Rose in 1587, the Swan in 1595, the Globe in 1599 and the Fortune in 1602. Indoor venues continued to be used for the performance of plays, from the Inns of Court to Blackfriars, the base of the children of the Chapel Royal, at court and in private homes.

The full theatre experience, in the round, with the poorer people, or groundlings, paying a penny to stand in the pit and the wealthier seated in the galleries above, would have been a busy, noisy occasion. There was activity on all sides competing with that on the stage, and frequent changes of costume, stunts and dramatic effects intended to capture the unruly crowd's attention. Important visitors would place their chairs upon the stage, food and drink were sold, and brawls and business were conducted during the performance. Those that were built for purpose were brightly painted inside, with pillars painted to look like marble, stars and astrological signs upon the roof, curtains, trapdoors in the roof and floor, and basic props.

It has been estimated that up to 3,000 people might attend a single performance in the largest theatres, at the height of the summer season. Going to the theatre became as much about being seen, and being part of the crowd, as watching the play.

While violence could often feature on the Elizabethan stage, it broke out frequently in the audience, too. In April 1580, the Lord Mayor wrote to inform the chancellor that 'great disorder had been committed at the Theatre', and shared his belief that 'the player of plays ... tumblers and such like, were a very superfluous sort of men' and 'the exercise of the plays was not only a great hindrance to the service of God' but also 'a great corruption of youth, with unchaste and wicked matters, the occasion of much incontinence, practices of many frays, quarrels and other disorders within the city'.[3] His plea to have plays banned in the city was not upheld and the unruly behaviour worsened.

In 1592, the Lord Mayor reported a 'great disorder and tumult' in Southwark, which he attended and found 'a great multitude assembled', mostly apprentices and 'masterless men'. He issued a proclamation and dismissed the crowd, discovering that they had met under the pretence of attending a play.[4]

In the same year, the aldermen wrote to the Archbishop of Canterbury complaining of 'the daily disorderly exercise of a number of players and playing-houses ... whereby the youths of the city were greatly corrupted, and their manners infected with many evils and ungodly qualities, by reason of the wanton and profane devices represented on the stages'. In addition, 'apprentices and servants were withdrawn from their work' in order to attend a play, 'to the great hindrance of the trades and traders of the city', and the theatres abounded with 'the light and lewd disposed persons, as harlots, cutpurses, cozeners, pilferers etc who under colour of hearing plays, devised evil and ungodly matches and conspiracies which could not be prevented'.[5] The aldermen called upon the Master of Revels to take control of the situation, and plays were limited to those performed by the queen's private players.

⚘ ENACTING JUSTICE ⚘

Throughout the Tudor period, a constant presence of authority was maintained by the watch. Their job was, quite literally as their name suggests, to use their eyes and watch the streets to prevent and intercept trouble. A thirteenth-century statute required a body of trusted men to be appointed to serve under the constables and patrol the streets through the hours of darkness, locking the city gates, checking on lights and fires, apprehending drunks, loiterers and strangers. Sometimes this was seasonal, commencing at Easter and tailing off in the autumn months, and sometimes only until the small hours, such as the watchmen in *Much Ado About Nothing*, who plan to sit on the church bench until two 'and then all to bed'. Each London ward had its own watch, and other cities and towns employed groups of men according to their size. Coventry appointed ninety men to serve between 9 p.m. and the morning bell.

In 1571, the Merchant Taylors of London were issued with instructions to join with the Vintners to provide a watch at 'every gate and postern in the city', two men at every station from 6 a.m. until 5 p.m., stopping suspicious and idle people:

Firste at this daye, a Precept directed from the Mayor to the Master and his Wardens, concerninge the appoyntinge and nominatinge of some sufficient, able, and discreete men to joyne with the Company of Vinteners, who are likewise appoynted to set forthe other and able and discreete men to joyn with this Company in watche, on Monday nexte, beinge the 22nd daie of this instante monthe of October:

'We straightlie charge and commande you that you immediatelye upon the receipt hereof, do call and assemble together so many of your Companie as you shall think meete and expediente, and that ye take such order forthwithe among yourselves that ye appointe tenne sufficient, able, and discrete persones to joyne with the Companie of Vintners who are likewise appoynted to set forthe the tenne able men to joyne with you to watch at every gate and posterne hereafter named, that is to say: at Newgate two, at Ludgate two, at the Bridge two, at Billingsgate two, at Moregate two, at Cripplegate two, at the posterne beside the Tower two, at Aldgate two, at Bishoppsgate two, at Aldersgate two; and that they be ready uppon Munday nexte, being the 21st daie of this instante monthe, by sixe of the clocke in the morninge, and they theire continuallie to remaine from the said houre of six until five of the clocke at night, watchyng and havinge continually, duringe the sayde tyme, a vigillant eye to all and every suche suspect and idle persones as shall passe and returne in, at, and by the same gate, and upon suspicion to stay and examine them, and so manye as they shall fynde suspecte and faulty, to commit to warde under safe custodie untill our pleasure shall be knowne therein for their deliverance.'[1]

You could see the watch coming. They were equipped with padded doublets, helmets and an assortment of available weaponry, including staffs, pikes, spears or poleaxes. Assembling at a central point, often a guildhall, they were given a 'watchword', a prearranged password to identify other members of the watch. All able-bodied citizens were obliged to take a stint, and to fail to appoint watchmen was to break the law, and led to prosecution, as the constables of Earls Colne in Essex discovered in 1592, and Henry Edlyn of St Stephens, Westminster, did in 1600. Substitutes and stand-ins were permitted, so long as they were not foreigners.

Depending upon the nature of the offence, anyone causing suspicion was either escorted home, or detained overnight and taken before the mayor or magistrate in the morning. The *London Letter Books*, which extend through the medieval period into the first decade of the Tudor regime, are full of couples being surprised by the watch *in flagrante*.[2]

At times of civic crisis, the watch might find itself at the heart of unfolding drama. A young Thomas More, then acting as an under-sheriff of London, was part of the watch around St Paul's on the night of 4–5 May 1517. Several thousand young apprentices gathered to attack foreigners and free prisoners, and, although More managed to calm them, the residents fought back, sparking full riots. As Stow relates:

> The 17 day of Februarie at nyght, beinge Monday, was a great watch in the citie of London, so that ye Lord Maior, the sheriffs, and alder-men themselves were abroade in the streets all that nyght with great numbars of people; whiche great watche continued all that week. Whiche watche was for feare of an insurrection agaynst the strangers, whiche were in great numbar in and abowt the citie, as in all other port townes and havens of the whole realme, and still increased and do tyll this day.[3]

Extra watches were mounted in towns and cities across the south-east during the Pilgrimage of Grace in 1536 and Thomas Wyatt's rebellion of 1554. When Henry, Lord Darnley, husband of Mary, Queen of Scots, was discovered strangled in the grounds of Holyrood Palace after a big explosion in 1567, the local watch were on the scene and arrested a man who was lurking there. William Blackadder claimed to have been merely drinking nearby and the sound had prompted him to satisfy his curiosity, but he was known to be an associate of

Lord Bothwell, who was suspected of planning the murder, and who married Mary afterwards.

Elizabeth's suitor, the Duke of Anjou, also engaged in acts of watching, in order to protect her. In 1581, he 'caused all the roads to be watched in order to keep [your] Majesty informed of all he could learn which concerns her affairs', and uncovered a letter containing the plans of her enemies. He sent the original of the letter to Elizabeth herself.[4]

Under Francis Walsingham, a huge spy network was established across Europe to uncover Catholic plots attempting to assassinate Elizabeth and replace her with her cousin, Mary, Queen of Scots. The English Ambassador in France, Sir Edward Stafford, wrote to the Spymaster General about one such scheme, which was to be put in the hands of the 'searchers':

> There is a Spaniard here hath assured me that there are certain Spaniards in the Low Countries, directed by the Spanish agent here, that have a certain enterprise for the deliverance of the Scottish Queen, and that the said agent despatcheth him within twelve days to go to them where they be in Flanders, and so into England for that intent that they carry with them excellent engines, to carry under their arms with a certain wheel and cords in fashion of a ladder, to climb up and to come down the highest castle or wall that may be; that he will, if I give him letters of direction where they land, put them into the searcher's hands and their instruments. I have promised him 300 crowns if he do it, if they come for that intent.[5]

Ever vigilant, the watch was tasked to report anything suspicious, which, in Shakespeare's plays, could be anything from 'criminal conversation' (i.e. illicit sex) to ghosts walking on battlements. They might pursue a 'hue and cry' or vigilante group in pursuit of a burglar, in this case Falstaff, whom Prince Harry conceals behind an arras, or be summoned to break up a duel, as in the case of Romeo and Paris.

In Worcestershire in 1583, Thomas Smith murdered his neighbour and hid the body in his cellar, in order to steal the contents of his shop. It was around Christmas time, and at nearby Evesham a watch was held so 'that no misorder or ill rule be committed in the town'. Smith made the error of giving one of the watchmen the watchword 'see and not see', which aroused suspicion and led to his arrest.[6]

Occasionally, though, the watch could turn, and support those bent on civil disobedience. Its secret nature, and its excuse for being out after dark provided too great a temptation for plotters, who saw it as an opportunity to have free run of the city. In 1549, at the time of Kett's rebellion and other localised uprisings, Sir Thomas Smith wrote to William Cecil to complain of 'the evil state of the realm'. He had found that 'the watchmen are the great promoters of the rebellion' and suggested 'the appointment of one or two responsible gentlemen in each shire to enforce the King's proclamation'.[7]

The watch might also overreach itself in revelry if the numbers and spirits of the watchers grew too high. The traditional Midsummer's watch, which had been held every year, became unwieldy in 1539 when a great muster was made by the citizens at Mile End, all 'in bright harnesses with coats of white silk or cloth and chains of gold, in three great battailes, to the number of 15,000'. This huge number of revellers passed 'through the city to Westminster, and so through the Sanctuary and round about the park of St James and returned home through Oldbourne'. After this, the Midsummer watch was suspended, and did not meet again until after Henry VIII's death.[8]

The watch was literally extra pairs of eyes observing the streets. This echoed the public way the Tudor authorities used an audience when it came to punishment. Eyes were constantly watching, when it came to sin, crime and justice, creating a culture where private morality was a communal concern.

All manner of misdemeanours received correction in the most open forums, through the city streets, or at prominent locations such as marketplaces and churches. The main punishment meted out might be whipping, branding, wearing marked clothing, or a spell in the stocks or pillory. There was a powerful sense of shame for the guilty party, which could involve the exposure of secrets and the resulting loss of social stature.

The ritual humiliation was intended as a deterrent for those watching, as with the heads of traitors on London Bridge, but the crowd was complicit in the punishment through the act of seeing. Whether they liked it or not, the eyes of audience, from casual passers-by to those who might hurl insults or rotten fruit, provided a sense of societal condemnation. The public exposure of crimes also ensured that business credibility was lost, such as in the case of Thomas Elys, a 'dawber' or painter, who was condemned to stand in the pillory for forging a bond for £10.

The grisly display of human remains continued throughout this era too, and was not only confined to the spikes on the north side of the bridge. In April 1551, rebels from the West Country were 'drawn' on a cart from the Tower to Tyburn 'and there hongyd and quartered and their quarters sette aboute London on every gate', for all to see.[9] Judicial spectacle was a regular feature of the sixteenth century and the act of seeing sin had as powerful an impact for the Tudors as the wearing of a rich gown.

Offences against morality, especially sexual ones, were exposed and corrected through the public gaze. Elizabeth Judela was convicted of being a 'common bawde' in the 1480s and sentenced to be led from prison to the Pillory in Cornhill, with 'mistrely' and a 'rayhood' on her head and a white rod in her hand. There, her guilt was proclaimed aloud and she was conveyed through Chepe to Newgate.[10]

In 1490, Christine Houghton, alias Stone, who had been convicted as a 'common bawde and strumpet', was discovered within the city walls, and so was set in the pillory for an hour at a time on two separate occasions, before serving a prison sentence of a year and a day.

In January 1553, seven women were whipped 'at the cart's arse' for being 'vagabonds that wold not labour, but play the unthrifts'. That June, a pillar was set up at the Standard in Chepe and two young servants were chained to it 'because they had two wenches into their master's house' on a Sunday. For two days that summer, a cart was pulled about the London streets bearing a tailor and his sister, both with their heads shaven, for having an incestuous relationship that produced two children, after which they were both banished from the city.[11] In 1563, a parson was apprehended after 'using another man's wife as his own' and was carried to Bridewell through all the streets, with 'his breeches hanging about his knees, his gown and his hat borne after him'.[12] In 1563, the tinker Symsone's wife, dwelling in Southwark, was set upon two ladders outside St Margaret's Church, 'where she sat the space of one hour, greatly rejoicing in that her lewd behaviour'.[13]

The physical symbols of Tudor punishment, the stocks (seated) pillory (standing) gibbet and gallows were visual deterrents in themselves, without requiring the enactment of execution to remind citizens how to behave. In September 1563, when Elizabeth was at Windsor Castle, and the worst case of plague was raging that century, dramatic steps were taken to keep travellers out of the town. A 'new payre of gallows' was erected in the marketplace, 'to hang up all such as should come there from London', no parson or traders, 'upon pain of hanging without any judgement'. Any people living in Windsor who received goods from London were turned out of their homes.[14]

Corporal punishment could also highlight past offenders. In 1546, Thomas Wriothesley wrote to his fellow council member, William Paget, 'Certain of the thieves that stole Mrs Hutton's coffer are apprehended.' He observed that 'they are masters of the craft' because two of them were 'already burnt in the hand', having committed similar crimes before, and asked, 'Will the king have any of them executed about the court for an example?'[15]

Important prisoners on their way to trial and execution were often paraded through the streets, especially those born of lower rank, or who were perceived as needing to be humbled. When the imposter Perkin Warbeck was captured in 1497 and brought to Westminster, he was not chained or bound, but walked unfettered before the king's horse. After that he was regularly walked through the streets and the crowd's reaction to him was condemnatory, with shouted curses and jeers, in order that Perkin 'could tell better what he was'.[16] When he was convicted of treason two years later, he was drawn on a cart through the streets from the Tower of London to Tyburn, where he experienced a traitor's death of being hanged. Warwick was lucky to escape he graphic, bloody death meted out to traitors, based on the Treason Act of 1351, was defined as being:

> laid on a hurdle and so drawn to the place of execution, and there to be hanged, cut down alive, your members to be cut off and cast in the fire, your bowels burnt before you, your head smitten off, and your body quartered and divided at the King's will.

Those who numbered among the large crowds drawn to witness such events can hardly ever have forgotten them. Edward, Earl of Warwick, who had been convicted along with Warbeck, received the private death of beheading within the Tower, as the result of his royal blood.

The trials of Anne and George Boleyn, in May 1536, were held in the King's Hall in the Tower, with the intention of drawing a huge crowd. Imperial ambassador Chapuys estimated that around 2,000 people attended, seated on benches around the great scaffold that had been erected for the occasion. Their co-accused, Weston, Norris, Brereton and Smeaton, were carried by barge from the Tower to Westminster Hall, a huge space, and died publicly at Tyburn.

One of the most terrifying locations for trial was the imposing fifteenth-century Guildhall in the centre of London, reached only by procession through the streets. The reputed lovers of Catherine Howard, Francis Dereham and Thomas Culpeper, were arraigned there in December 1541, then executed at Tyburn, with their heads placed on spikes above the Thames.

The Protestant martyr Anne Askew was tried and condemned at the Guildhall in 1546, reputedly carried there in a chair as her limbs were broken by torture. Anne was later burned at Smithfield, where seats had been set out for court visitors and gunpowder bags tied about her neck to hasten her end.

Henry Howard, Earl of Surrey, was also tried at the Guildhall in 1546, accused of trying to dethrone Henry VIII and take control of his son, Prince Edward. He was beheaded on Tower Green.

In November 1553, Lady Jane Grey and her husband, Guildford Dudley, were put on trial for their roles in the Protestant plot to usurp Mary I that summer. They were led out of the Tower as part of a procession behind an axe bearer and their fellow prisoner, Thomas Cranmer, Archbishop of Canterbury. Tiny Jane was only 16 years old, and had initially resisted attempts to put her on the throne. She was dressed all in black, carried a Bible and was heavily guarded. Walking through the London streets, she was far more than a deterrent to anyone in the crowd who was minded to rebel. She was a symbol of the Protestant hope in England, which had been stymied by the accession of Mary and her Catholic Counter-Reformation, which undid all the religious reforms of the 1540s and early 1550s. Jane was also a former queen, albeit only briefly and uncrowned, but her walk to her trial echoed the fates of Anne Boleyn and Catherine Howard, whose executions had set a terrifying new precedent for unwanted women on the throne. The public display of the defeated Jane in

November 1553 played out the succession drama in an unparalleled visual spectacle of pathos and power.

The most extreme of all Tudor judicial spectacles was the Marian burning of live heretics, or martyrs to the Catholic faith. Between 1555 and 1558, Mary I made it her personal mission to enforce her faith upon her subjects, using public execution simultaneously as their punishment and the means of their salvation, before an audience. Even those who did not attend could not fail to catch the scent of flames, or the reported news in the marketplace, or see the woodcuts circulated on pamphlets.

Incredible and barbaric as it might seem to the modern mind, Mary's actions must be viewed in terms of contemporary ideas of salvation. As queen of England, she believed she had a genuine calling, a religious mission to return the country to the true path. Temporal, or earthly, life was considered merely a brief space before the soul's passage to eternal salvation or damnation. What really mattered was the afterlife.

It was part of Mary's Catholic doctrine that heretical souls could only be saved through the process of cleansing fire. Thus, Mary truly believed that the burning of unrepentant Protestants was not simply a punishment meted out to these individuals but also their salvation from their sin. By burning them, she was saving them. By saving them, she genuinely believed she was implementing a programme of national imperative.

The deaths were dramatic and disturbing, with the martyrs standing atop the pyre, often with bags of gunpowder strapped to them to hasten their demise. Although they were committed to their cause, and refused to recant to save their skin, the prolonged suffering of these individuals could turn even the hardest Tudor heart. In total, in 1555, seventy-six individuals were burned. There were eighty-seven in 1556, seventy-seven in 1557 and forty-one in 1558, making a total of 281, of which sixty-two were women. Thomas Cranmer, former Archbishop of Canterbury, was martyred in March 1556.

ꙮ PHENOMENA ꙮ

In 1569, a book was published entitled *Certaine Secrete Wonders of Nature Containing a Description of Sundry Strange Things, Seeming Monstrous in Our Eyes and Judgement, because We Are Not Privie to the Reasons of Them*.[1] It covered unnatural deaths, divine signs and warnings, monsters of land and sea, conjoined twins, weather, comets and dragons, water and plants, multiple births and more. The preface by the author, Pierre Boaistuau, explained the fascination with the topic:

> there is nothyng to be seen, which more stirreth the spirite of man, whiche ravisheth more his senses, whiche doth more amaze hym, or engendreth a greater terror or admiration in all creatures, than the monsters, wonders and abominations, wherein we see the workes of Nature, not only turned arsiversie, misseshapen and deformed, but [which is more] they do for the most part discover unto us the secret judgement and scourge of the ire of God.[2]

The work's significance, though, lies in the second half of the title. It includes the acknowledgement that these things 'seem' monstruous in the people's eyes because they were not 'privy' to the reasons of them; they did not understand them. Boaistuau presents these phenomena as oddities, while understanding there is a gulf between the visual spectacle and the scientific cause, in an attempt to make sense of the world. He had seen a flying fish in Paris, a strange creature he could not explain, but one which he had described for an illustration:

> This fishe or rather monster of the Sea, I haue considered with long viewe and iudgement, and have caused him to be drawne as neare as I can according to his naturall proportion, wherein I maye boldly preferre as witnesses aboue two hundreth personnes who sawe him in Paris, as well as I.[3]

The visually sensitive Tudors were particularly attuned to the occurrence of natural phenomena. These might be cases of extreme weather, astrological events, plagues, famines or babies born with physical irregularities, always considered as signs to be decoded. A comet was believed to portend terrible events, but what those events might be, and the reason for them, were interpreted differently depending upon the eye of the beholder. The direction, colour, length and shape of its tail would be noted, analysed, discussed and even drawn, before conclusions were reached.

Astrologers, astronomers, doctors, kings, mathematicians, scientists and the average Tudors all had their different suspicions of what such strange occurrences might mean, and might look for births, deaths, victories, defeats, misfortunes, accidents, floods and crop failures to follow. Often, one or more of these events obliged.

The possible range of interpretations was determined by specific context of the observation: the exact time, place, duration and speed, if applicable; what was happening in the wider world – and what the king wanted. Often it was prudent to interpret the unusual to fit in with a patron's aspirations. It could also prove lucrative, if perhaps only in the short term.

When Halley's comet appeared in 1531, it was believed to be a sign of encouragement for England to abandon the old faith for the reformed beliefs. The direction of comets' tails were thought to be of particular significance. In 1577, when a huge comet 'as bright as the moon' crossed the skies from the west, its red tail pointing north-east, it was judged to mean harm for the Russians and the imminent death of Ivan the Terrible was predicted. As it was, Ivan lived on until 1584.

In 1564 a particularly unusual sky was observed above England, starting in the north-east about eight in the evening, but could not be explained. Stow showed remarkable restraint in observing the facts without adding his interpretation:

> Very great lightes like great flames of fire, whiche shot forthe as it [were] gunpowder fired and spread out in a longe, from the northe easte, northe, and northe west, in divers places at once; and all met in the midst of the firmament, as it were, ryght over London, and descended somewhat west warde, and all the flames beynge there gatheryd, grew in to a redness, as it were a very sanguine or blood colour, and this continued till nine of the clock; and all the same nyght was more lighter than if the moon had shone moste bryght, whereas no moon shone that nyght.[4]

In contemporary records, significant events and bad weather are frequently juxtaposed, with the assumed causality this creates.

The 1499 compiler of an entry in the *Greyfriars Chronicle* follows the executions of Perkin Warbeck and Edward, Earl of Warwick, with 'and the same daye was grete flooddes, wynddes, thunder, lytnynges, wyche dyd moche harme and hurte in dyvers placys and countres in Ynglonde'.[5] No commentary is made, no connection drawn, because none is needed, but danger might have been incurred if the scribe had explicitly condemned the deaths. Contemporaries would have understood the relation of all the events.

Another favourite Tudor habit was the observation of the stars and planets. Chapbooks and manuals provided guides to understanding unusual behaviour in the sun, moon and stars, and possible interpretations of what this might mean. Thomas Tusser's collection of such observations of the natural world provided an early attempt to predict the weather, with parallels drawn with Elizabeth and her personal iconography. If the moon changed, keeping in its closet three days, like a queen, she was unlikely to be seen in her prime; if she appeared great, it was likely to shower; if small, there would be drought. If the moon was changeable or full, there would be a high tide; 'come it late or else soon, main sea is at highest at midnight and noon', and later in the creeks, 'through farness of running'.[6]

'Unnatural births' or the occurrences of twins and triplets might reflect trouble on two scales, either as signs of national instability or manifestations of sin in the community. Boaistuau's explanation for the existence of 'monsters', or such misshapen creatures, was the judgement of God upon the sins of the parents, usually from immodest or sinful sexual practices:

> It is moste certaine, that these monstrous creatures, for the most part do proceede of the judgement, justice, chastisement and curse of God, which suffreth that the fathers and mothers bring forth these abominations, as a horrour of their sinne, sufferyng themselues to run headlong, as do brute beastes without guide to the puddle or sinke of their filthie appetites.[7]

The thoughts of the mother during conception and pregnancy were considered particularly influential in shaping the formation of her child. Medical manuals of the early sixteenth century attempted to explain these phenomena in a number of ways. Eucharius Rosslin's *Rose Garden*, published in Zurich in 1513, contained illustrations of fully formed foetuses, side by side, while a 1530s translation of Hugh de Campenden's fourteenth-century poem relies on the theory that there were several different chambers of the matrix, or womb, allowing for multiple pregnancies:

> May any woman bear mo
> Children in her at once but two?
> A woman may bear kindly
> Seven at once in her body,
> For the matrice of woman,
> If that thou understand can,
> Hath seven chambers and no mo,
> And each is departed other fro,
> And she may have in each of tho
> A child and with seven go,
> If God's will be first thereto
> And the kind of woman also.[8]

These attempts to explain multiple births according to scientific causes did little to dispel the myths and concerns surrounding deviations from the perceived norm. In cases when the children survived, such concerns might be easily dismissed, but as a 'natural' and 'unexplained' phenomenon, unusual births captured the imagination and prompted the most elaborate and implausible hoaxes.

In 1547, a monstrous calf was displayed in the market at Newgate with two heads, four ears, four eyes, eight feet and two tails, where the mayor observed it, and commanded that it be cut into pieces and buried.[9]

Stow reported in August 1551 that a woman in Oxfordshire, lying in at the sign of the Eagle at Middletonstone, was delivered of a child with two heads, four hands and four feet, which lived for fifteen days. At the same place, a hen hatched a chick with two heads and four feet, and in the same month huge fish were seen in the Thames.

The case of Agnes Bowker's cat was publicised most recently by David Cressy,[10] and came to light in 1569 when a midwife reported that she had delivered a cat with food in its stomach. Agnes was in service and unmarried, and had attempted suicide at least twice during her pregnancy. The introduction of a cat was likely to have been a diversionary tactic to avoid a paternity scandal, but although the story was published in a pamphlet, it quickly died down, and what happened to Agnes afterwards is unknown.

The reporting of these occasions must be taken with a degree of scepticism, but such examples appear to be cases of conjoined twins, in the days before scans and modern techniques could detect irregularities. In some cases, though, individuals were clearly responsible for the creation of strange sights to send a deliberate message. One example of anti-Catholic propaganda in 1554 was that of a cat hanged on the gallows at Chepe, clothed like a priest, which was also held up before the preacher at St Paul's Cross.

Variations in weather also provided the Tudors with phenomena to interpret. Apparently, biblical-style plagues could affect England, like the one reported by William Harrison in 1583:

> Great harme done in England in diverse shires, by locustes, or 'grasshoppers' as we call them, which devoured the grasse, & consumed the pastures & meadowes in very pitifull manner: soche great nombers of crows also do come into those partes to feede upon those creatures, that they tread down & trample the rest, I meane, whatsoever the locust had left untouched. Not long before, if not about this time, also some places of the hundreds in Essex were no lesse annoyed with mice, as report then went, which did great hurt to corn and the fruits of the earth, till an infinite nomber of Owles were assembled into those partes, which consumed them all to nothing.[11]

As an astronomer and predictor of the future, Dr John Dee was a keen observer of the skies, recording changes in the wind, clouds and precipitation in his diary of the 1580 and '90s. On an August evening in 1581, he noted:

> a strange meteore in forme of a white clowde crossing galaxium, when it lay north and south over our zenith, this clowde was at length from SE to the SW sharp at both ends and in the west end it was forked for a while; it was about sixty degrees high, it lasteth an hour, all the sky clear about, and fair starshine.

In February 1598, he noted an eclipse: 'a clowdy day but with great darkness about nine, half moon'.[12]

A 1553 astrological text explained that such phenomena were divine signs and should be taken seriously as warnings:

> Eclipses, by the cognysion, congression, consentment, discordant, and regression of them, men maye predicte divers accidentes commynge to the worlde, as warres, mortalities, famines, contagious sickenesses, peace, abundaunce of goodes, mutations of realmes, and sects, death of Princes, tumultes of people, perturbations of public thynges, inundacions, earthquakes and lyke thinges, the whyche by the influence celestyall vertue of the Elementes, and puissance of the starres we see followe and fall on us.[13]

The Tudors looked to understand their world by perceiving the differences in it. Wherever something, or someone, deviated from expectation, a window of interpretation was opened; a space in which explanations could grow to fill a void of uncertainty.

Deviances from the natural world mattered, especially when it came to the limbs and lines of mankind, which they believed to be created in the image of God. At a time when God and nature were presumed to be working in tandem, any appearance of unnaturalness was considered to be a deliberate response to sins committed by the parents. After Anne Boleyn miscarried three and a half months into pregnancy, in January 1536, her enemies represented her lost foetus as being a misshapen lump of flesh, lending credence to the accusations of sexual immorality she faced the following May. However, as the century advanced and Humanist scientists developed concepts of the natural world, simplistic responses of condemnation gave way to a more complex understanding of genetics.

COMMUNICATION

❦ THE WRITTEN WORD ❦

Tudor handwriting has a beauty of its own. It curls and loops, with its bar and superscript abbreviations, in faded browning ink; its meaning often elusive to the modern eye. There is something so immediate about a handwritten piece too, something personal, even though the Tudors wrote in a formal, secretary style that followed strict rules. The personal touch is still evident in the knowledge that someone in the past sat down to etch out those marks by hand. There's an immediate connection implied by the process of one person committing thoughts to paper, for another person to read, even when separated by four or five centuries.

Medieval reading culture had centred upon the aristocracy and the manuscript-producing elite of the monasteries. It is difficult to estimate how many Tudors could read and write, especially among the middling and lower classes. Most of the definitive documents of their lives, such as deeds, debts, court proceedings, business transactions and wills, were dictated to clerks. Where it was required, a large percentage of official paperwork was signed by individuals using only a mark or initial.

As the sixteenth century advanced, though, the advent of the printing press, the effect of Humanist and reformist thought, the accession of two educated queens regnant, and other changing social factors all contributed to a rise in levels of literacy for men and women, so that modern academics have identified a surge in literacy beginning around 1560.[1]

If you had access to paper and ink and were able to write, or knew someone who could, letter writing was still the easiest way to communicate with someone at a distance. The physical practicalities of producing writing were a craft of their own. Juan Luis Vives, a Spanish Humanist scholar who lived in England in the 1520s, produced *Tudor School Boy Life*, a collection of dialogues in which the teacher describes the making of a quill pen, from goose or hen feathers.

The quill itself was best stripped of feathers and could be made smooth with saliva, or by rubbing on the coat or against the stockings:

> First of all, cleave the head on both sides, so that it is split in two. Then, whilst you carefully guide the knife, make a cutting on the upper part, which is called the crena, or notch. Then make quite equal the two little feet, pedunculos, or if you prefer to call them, little legs, cruscula, so nevertheless, that the right one on which the pen rests in writing may be higher, but the difference ought to be barely perceptible.[2]

Two techniques of holding the quill could dictate the speed of writing:

> If you wish to press the pen on the paper somewhat firmly, use three fingers, but if you are writing more quickly, with two, with the thumb and fore-finger, after the Italian fashion. For the middle finger rather checks the course and prevents it from proceeding too quickly, instead of helping it forward.[3]

Ink was usually made from oak galls, or oak apples, ground with water. Vives refers to an ink horn and a leaden mortar, which is filled from a two-handled ink flask. The pupil has learned to use a sponge or similar absorbent material to soak up ink and to dip his quill into that, but the teacher informs him that a more direct method is better, as 'if you dip the pen into cotton or silk-thread or linen, some fibre or fluff adheres to the nib',[4] the cleaning of which resulted in delay. If the matter is not drawn out of the nib, the writing will be blurred as a consequence.

When ink was unavailable, other methods of producing writing were necessary. In the most extreme case of the 1559 *Complaint of Rauff Allerton and Others Poor Prisoners Being Held in the 'Lolers Tower'*, their publisher claimed it was written in their own blood.

Writing tables, or tablets, had been imported since the fifteenth century and were used for temporary note taking. They followed the same principles as a wax tablet, but were sturdier, being made from parchment coated with varnish or gesso, to create a stiff surface that could be written upon with a quill or stylus and erased with a finger.

Initially ornately decorated, they began as gifts for the nobility, but towards the end of the century were mass produced for the middle classes to meet the increasing demand of a literate population who had benefited from the foundation of grammar schools and several generations of Humanist education. These were used to record on-the-spot thoughts, lists, financial transactions and things of importance, with an immediacy but a temporality, which Hamlet plays upon by mocking Polonius, saying he must set down the old man's wisdom in his tables.

Paper was first used in England in 1309, imported from France and the Low Countries, and gradually came to replace the thicker animal-hide parchment. England's dependency upon wool meant that it lacked the leftover rags from the clothing trade which were used in Europe to make the key ingredient of rag pulp and was therefore comparatively less successful in paper making.

The first English paper mill operated in Hertford between 1494 and 1507, and a second short-lived business during the sixteenth century found it difficult to compete with the quantity and quality of French imports. In October 1518, while Henry VIII was staying at Greenwich, he ordered five quires of paper costing 10d, half a quire of the finer paper royal, costing 3d, and one parchment skin, at a price of 3d, imported from across the Channel.[5]

Vives' teacher rejects the paper brought by his student as too rough and 'would check the pen so that it would not run without being hindered'. He advises the boy to 'leave this kind of paper, wide, hard, thick, rough, for the printers of books' as it was called Libraria, from its use in printing. Books made from it lasted a long time.

For academic use, pupils should not choose Augustan or Imperial paper, called Hieratica, which was used for religious books, but should buy the best writing paper from Italy, which was 'very thin and firm' or 'even that common sort brought over from France'. This could be bought in single blocks at 2d each. He should also buy blotting paper, known as Emporetica, made from the linden tree, to blot the ink, instead of relying upon bran, sand or scraping up the dust from the floor to scatter over it![6]

Paper which had unequal, rough or wrinkled edges should be trimmed neatly with the shears. It was quite a delicate undertaking to ensure paper was properly prepared, before even a word was committed to the page, so it is of little surprise that many Tudors opted to buy their paper ready-made.

When it came to writing, Vives's pupil complains that he can only fit six lines on the page. The teacher tells him not to leave such spaces between each line, to crowd them up more closely together, to watch the tails of letters like 'b' and 'p', and to write on both sides of the paper. When the ink was too thick to flow, they added a few drops of water or, better still, vinegar, although there was a danger that the acidity could eat into the surface of cheap paper.

Handwriting styles varied between the medieval secretary hand used in the Courts of Chancery and Common Pleas, to italic, roman, modern secretary and more decorative hands. By the 1570s, manuals of handwriting were being widely used in schools. It was important to keep a straight back and hold the hand upright while writing, otherwise 'humours flow downwards onto the forehead and eyes, whence many diseases are born, and whence too may come weakness of eyes'.

Letters were folded in upon themselves, making them into their own envelope, and sealed with melted wax, into which the imprint of a ring, fob or other device could be pressed. Bearing initials, a crest or personal device, this was an effective way of announcing the identity of the writer. One 1573 recipe lists a method of making red sealing wax with clear turpentine and wax melted together, with finely ground vermilion and salad oil added once it had cooled.

Family collections of letters such as those of the Pastons and Lisles, the Cecil or Rutland Papers, or the courtship letters of Henry VIII and Anne Boleyn reveal an array of purposes for writing, from friendship and love, to politics and business. An average family might accumulate receipt (recipe and remedy) books, household accounts, inventories, payments, business accounts, students' notes, miscellanies, commonplace books and fictional texts, often collated in manuscript form. The sixteenth century witnessed a proliferation of writing, of which a very small overall percentage has survived.

Another significant development in the history of writing, and many other social and cultural histories, was the ruling in 1538 that individual parishes must keep a written record of births, deaths and marriages. Before this, such events had gone largely unreported, save for the entries in family Bibles or references in letters. A nationwide system of recording these critical rites of passage was the starting point for understanding the country's demographic and has proved invaluable to historians since.

Despite conventional, linguistic and cultural idiosyncrasies, personal letters written by individuals are still the most immediate way for a modern reader to access the thoughts and feelings of the sixteenth century. Thus, shortly after Catherine of Aragon was widowed upon the death of her first husband, Prince Arthur, in April 1502, her mother Isabella's heartfelt letter to Ferdinand, Duke of Estrada, in an attempt to bring her daughter home, is still powerful after five centuries:

> You shall say to the King of England that we cannot endure that a daughter whom we love should be so far from us when she is in affliction, and that she should not have us at hand to console her; also it would be more suitable for a young girl of her age to be with us than to be in any other place. While telling the King of England that we know very well that where he and the Queen are, she would not lack either father or mother, you shall also add that we greatly desire to have her with us, urging whatever else may seem meet to you with a view to this. You shall request the King of England to give you authority to bring her here, and to appoint some principal person of competent age, who shall be fitted for such an office, to escort her hither.[7]

Equally, when Catherine wrote to her father, begging for financial assistance on 22 April 1506, her desperation is conveyed in this translation from a letter originally written in cipher:

> Has written many times to him, but has had no answer. Begs him to consider how she is in debt, not for extravagant things, but for food, and how the King of England will not pay anything, though she has asked him with tears. He had said that the promise made him about the marriage portion had not been kept. Is in the greatest anguish, her people ready to ask alms, and herself all but naked. Supplicates him to provide a remedy for all this as quickly as may be. Begs him to send her a confessor, as she cannot understand English, and has been for six months near death.[8]

The most extraordinary letters could come from strangers, especially for people in controversial positions of authority. At some point in

1533, a William Glover, dwelling with Henry Wyatt, father of the poet, wrote to Anne Boleyn to inform her that he had experienced a dream vision of her pregnancy. This was clearly written long after the details of her coronation and delivery of a daughter in September had been made public but claimed prior knowledge of a prophetic kind. The validity conferred by what Glover interprets as a divine visitation singling him out as God's mouthpiece explains his extreme impropriety in writing directly to the queen about such a personal matter:

> Once a messenger of Christ came to me, and commanded me to take a message to you, but I did not believe him. In three nights he came again, and I said I would do it, fearing he was my ghostly enemy. In three nights he came again, in angel form, and I promised to take the message, which was that you should have been Queen of England 10 yeares past. I left it with John Averey, master of the flagons to the King. When you had become Queen he bade me let it alone, but told Dr. Bruton of the message. After your Grace's coronation the messenger came again, and bade me tell you that you were with child … I told this to Dr. Bruton, and told him also that your Grace should be delivered of your burden at Greenwich. Dr. Bruton then wrote about it to Mr. Gwynne, your chaplain. Mr. Gwynne brought your almoner with him to me, but I was loth to tell them, and lay there three days. Now again the messenger has come to me, and commanded me to go or write to you, or else his master, Christ, would 'stryke'.[9]

An anonymous letter, this time written to William Cecil, Lord Burghley in 1571 warned of a conspiracy against the minister's life. He wrote on it, in his own hand, that it was 'a letter brought by the post of London':

> My Lord, of late I have upon discontent entered into conspiracy with some others to slay your Lordship. And the time appointed, a man with a perfect hand, attended you three several times in your garden to have slain your Lordship. The which not falling out, and continuing in the former mischief, the height of your study window is taken towards the garden, minding, if they miss these means, to slay you with a shot upon the terrace, or else in coming late from the Court with a pistolet. And being touched with some remorse of so bloody a deed, in discharge of my conscience before God, I warn

your Lordship of their evil and desperate meanings, and would far-ther declare the whole meaning, if I should not be noted of infidelity, being so near and dear unto me as they are. For the thanks I deserve, I shall, I doubt not, but receive them hereafter at your hands at more convenient time, when these storms are past; but lastly, I require your Lordship in God's name to have care of your safety.[10]

A similar threat was uncovered by Sir William Petre in March 1576, also by an anonymous missive placed in his path. Petre delivered it to Cecil, who endorsed it by writing upon it, 'Delivered to me by Sir William Petre, 20 March, I read it to the Queen Majesty at Greenwich':

Encloses a letter he found very early in the morning as he went from Paul's Church by Paul's Wharf to the water by the tavern there. It was sewn with black Paris silk. No creature was by, so he took and read it, and was never so afraid in his life. Beseeches Sir Wm. Petre to give it to the Queen.[11]

Frustratingly, the contents of the letter which had put Petre in such fear of his life were not recorded.

Outside the marital conventions of the aristocracy, personal letters are one place where it is possible to see the dynamic between public duty and private inclination. In 1574, Richard Neville had been hoping to marry the widowed Lady Elizabeth Frechvell and had asked the queen to intercede on his behalf. However, he had received the answer that 'she was not minded to marry, finding herself very unfit thereunto, through grossness of her body and daily increasing sickness', so had given up his pursuit. He requested instead that the queen take into consideration his thirty-six years of service and grant him the lease of a parsonage in Cuddesdon, Oxfordshire, a wish with which Elizabeth saw fit to comply.[12]

Semi-official letters could also be influential warnings when an individual was refusing to toe the line. In the remoter corners of the realm, it could bring pressure to bear from powerful peers speaking on behalf of the queen. Such a situation arose in 1575, when Lord North was angered by the ingratitude of the Bishop of Ely, who was resisting royal decrees. North's tone conveys his feeling more directly than any formal notification of dissatisfaction might:

> Suffer me, my Lord, I pray yow, to put yow in mind who it is that yow deny; is it our dread soverayne lady, oure most gracious & bountiful Mistress, who hath abled yow even from the meanest estate that may be, unto the best Byshopricke in Englande, a thing worth three thousande pounde a year. It is she unto whom yow have done no especial service as yet, nor any way shewed yourself specially thankful for her unspeakable goodness to yow. Ingratitude, yow know, my Lord, is noted among the common persons for a monstrous vice, and between the subject and sovereign, [it is] a horrible monster. If then this be true, that she hath rewarded yow with one of the best things of her realm, and yow on the other side deny her every trifle that she demaundeth, judge my Lord indifferently whether she can like this kindness or not, considering she taketh no rent from yow.
>
> My Lord, I wish yow from the bottom of my hart to shake of the yoke of your stubbornness against her Majesty's desires; to lay aside your stiff-necked determinations and humbly to reconcile [by yielding] yourself unto her known clemency. She is our God on earth; if there be perfection in flesh and blood, undoubtedly it is in her Maiestye. For she is slow to revenge and ready to forgive. And yet, my Lord, she is right King Henry, her father. For if any strive with her, all the Princes of Europe cannot make her yield. Again, whoso humbly and lovingly submitteth himself to her desire, she doth, and will, so graciously receive and recompense him, as every that knoweth her doth honour and entirely love her.[13]

The late-Elizabethan espionage network relied heavily upon letters, both in writing them and intercepting those written by their enemies. After years as a prisoner on English soil and several failed plots for her release, Mary, Queen of Scots was drawn into Catholic plots to replace Elizabeth with her in the mid 1580s. Some insight into the method by which letters were smuggled in and out of her household is provided by her agent, Thomas Morgan, who wrote to her in February 1585 when the system encountered a temporary hitch:

> About three months past, Fontenay sent a coffer to this country, in a secret place in the bottom of which he hid certain letters written

by the King her Majesty's son to her, and to the Duke of Guise, Monsieur de Mayne and the Bishop of Rosse. The said coffer was addressed to Du Ruisseau, but never opened by him until now, which is the reason why her Majesty's letters have been so long by the way.[14]

The smuggling of letters in coffers, or chests, and barrels was risky and open to error, like the failure of Du Ruisseau to open his coffer. The Throckmorton plot of 1584 had failed in its aim to remove Elizabeth and place Mary on the English throne, but as a result, she was moved and forbidden contact with the outside world. From this point, she was too dangerous to be allowed to live.

Walsingham set up a trap with a local brewer, who offered to conceal her letters in watertight compartments inside the stopper of a beer barrel. Then Walsingham employed a cryptographer, Thomas Phelippes, to decode any messages based upon the frequency of certain words and letters used in them. Eventually, Mary took the bait and responded, offering her full support to plans for Elizabeth's assassination. She signed it 'let the great plot commence' and sealed her own fate.

When William Cecil, Lord Burghley came to justify the death of Mary, Queen of Scots in 1587, he cited among his reasons the spread of dissent among the people, which had been facilitated by treasonous writings:

There was also at the same time discovered a practice – betwixt the French ambassador and a lewd young miscontented person named William Stafford, and one Mody, a prisoner in Newgate, a mischievous resolute person – how her Majesty's life should be taken away, and all in favour of the Scots' Queen. Anon, after this, also, followed a seditious general stirring up of the common people into arms, by spreading of billets in writing carried from one shire to another, and from town to town; which, though the justices of the country seeking to pacify, yet, as the same was stayed in one part, and like rose up again in another; and by these seditious practices to procure a rebellion, all the whole realm was greatly stirred.[15]

Letters could also take on great sentimental value, becoming mementos of lost times, places and people. In August 1588, when Elizabeth's long-term favourite, Robert Dudley, Earl of Leicester, was on his way to take the cure at Buxton, he wrote to her from Rycote, the home of the Norris/Norreys family:

> I most humbly beseech your Majesty to pardon your poor old servant to be thus bold in sending to know how my gracious lady doth, and what ease of her late pains she finds, being the chiefest thing in this world I do pray for, for her to have good health and long life. For my own poor case, I continue still your medicine and find that amends much better than with any other thing that hath been given me. Thus, hoping to find perfect cure at the bath, with the continuance of my wonted prayer for your Majesty's most happy preservation, I humbly kiss your foot. From your old lodging at Rycote, this Thursday morning, ready to take on my Journey, by your Majesty's most faithful and obedient servant, R. Leicester.

Next, Leicester moved on to Cornbury, a lodge he owned in Oxfordshire, still on his way to Buxton. He died there on 4 September. Elizabeth was devastated to learn of his death and shut herself away for days. After her own death in 1603, this letter was found among her personal effects, upon which she had written 'his last letter'.

☙ THE PRINTED WORD ❧

One of the greatest visual developments of the Tudor world was the explosion in the printing industry. The first press had been developed by Johannes Gutenberg in Germany as early as the 1430s, although it was not until twenty years later that he produced his first version of the Bible. New presses were set up across Europe, arriving in the Westminster workshop of William Caxton in 1477, Oxford in 1478 and St Albans in 1479. By 1500, it was estimated that 1,000 establishments existed worldwide that were able to produce printed matter of some form, either as full-length books or as simpler pamphlets.

By the advent of the Tudors, Caxton was already an expert translator and printer, having produced his own versions of Aesop, Chaucer, Gower and Lydgate, *The Golden Legend*, John Mirk's *Festial* and Nicholas Love's *Speculum Vitae Christi*. From 1485 until his death in 1492, he produced more poetry, romances like *Blanchardin and*

Eglantine, and spiritual works such as *The Craft for to Die Well* and *The Book of Divers Ghostly Matters*.

The earliest books, published before 1501 and known as incunabula, were finished by hand, with colour plates, marginal illustrations and capital letters. In addition, the books of Caxton, Richard Pynson and Wynkyn de Worde effected a standardisation of the English language, with greater consistency of spelling in comparison to what had previously been an aural, and therefore highly varied, tradition. It has been estimated that Caxton provided the first known usages of around 1,300 English words.[1]

The Reformation also contributed to the rise of literacy. Church murals were replaced by texts; the translation of the Bible into English and the proliferation of psalters and homilies replacing the old visual books of hours encouraged a greater personal connection with the written word. Literacy was embraced by the Church as a means of fighting heresy. It also enabled heretics to read and imbibe the messages of forbidden texts.

In 1535, the English reformer and printer, William Marshall, produced *The Defence of Peace*, his translation of a fourteenth-century anti-papal text. Marshall was also a confidential agent of Cromwell, who allowed the book's publication, in spite of its controversial and unpopular advocacy of the burning of religious images, such as was soon to take place at Cromwell's home in Chelsea.

Thomas Broke wrote to inform the minister of the public response, as 'the people greatly murmur at it'. Imperial ambassador Chapuys reported this to the emperor as an indication of the direction Henry VIII intended to take the English Church:

> There is a report that the King intends the religious of all orders to be free to leave their habits and marry, and that if they will stay in their houses they must live in poverty. He intends to take the rest of the revenue, and will do stranger things still.

Shortly afterwards, Lord Chancellor Audley judged that the text went too far and wrote to Cromwell:

> In the parts where he has been there has been some discord and diversity of opinion touching worshipping of saints and images, creeping at cross, and such ceremonies, which discord it were well

to put to silence. This book will make much business if it should go forth. Intends to send for the printer to stop them. It were good that preachers and people abstained from opinions of such things until the King has put a final order by the report of those appointed for searching and ordering the laws of the Church. A proclamation to abstain until that time would do much good.[2]

Audley's warnings came too late, as by that October twenty-four copies had been distributed among the monks of the Charterhouse, although these had been returned after three days. Jasper Fyloll complained of finding 'three or four foreign printed books of as foul heresies and errors as may be'.[3]

During the visitation to the monasteries, other dangerous books were sought out. John Horwood reported the discovery of a book by Alverius, 'which some think smells of the Popish pannier'.[4] In December that year, books of sermons by John Fisher, Bishop of Rochester, who had been executed that summer for refusing to swear the Oath of Succession, were recalled by the chancellor, along with 'other books containing error or slander to the King or to the diminution of his Imperial Crown, or repugnant to the Statutes of the Succession or for the abolition of the usurped power of the bishop of Rome'.[5]

Those who printed seditious material took their liberty, and their businesses, into their own hands. In June 1574, William Cecil and Robert Dudley, Lords Burghley and Leicester contacted Sir William Fleetwood, the recorder of London, to act against a Mr Bradborn. Fleetwood was required to go to Southwark 'very early in the morning' and apprehend Bradborn, 'dwelling near the sign of the Red Leg, a hat maker, and search his house for printing presses, letters' and anything else 'belonging to printing'. Fleetwood was also to seize all books and writings relating to religious matters and keep Bradborn 'a close prisoner till the Queen's further orders'.[6] However, upon executing his orders, Fleetwood found that no man named Bradborn existed there, and wondered if it had been an alias:

Between one and two o'clock in the morning, went to Southwark, and in Barmsey Street found the sign of the Red Leg, not far from the Bridge House. Being there with the Bridge master, perused the Beadle's book of all that part of Southwark, and found no such man

there abiding, neither master nor servant. Made secret inquiry of
the householders' names, their menservants and guests. Could not
find any such name as Bradborn, nor any likely to be suspected of
his conduct. Travailed in the search from two till five without letting any know the cause. Men thought it was Scotch spies. Has left
orders with Battes, the bridgemaster.[7]

Elizabeth had to issue a declaration in 1576 against a pamphlet printed
in Milan entitled *Novo Aviso*, which charged her with ingratitude
towards Philip of Spain, and with an intended plot against his life.[8]

Seditious books continued to be a problem throughout the sixteenth century. In 1579, a book entitled *A Discovery of the Gaping
Gulf* was printed, which 'very contemptuously intermeddled in matters of estate touching her Majesty's person' and her friendship with
the Duke of Anjou, 'the intention evidently being to cause a suspicion
of her Majesty's actions, as tending to the prejudice of the realm and
the subversion of the estate of true religion'. A proclamation from the
queen was published and all civic dignitaries called to assemble in
their halls to hear it read and collect all copies to be destroyed.

Mayors and aldermen continued their vigilance and, in April
1580, John Fagge, Mayor of Rye, searched a boat from Dieppe on
which 'certain little books called the Jesus Psalter to the number
of two dozen' were found and removed to safe custody.[9] Two years
later, another ship was intercepted, 'full of Popish and superstitious
books' hidden in a barrel of worsted yarn, and the miscreants were
apprehended and questioned.[10]

Books might contain other dangerous practices. Thomas, abbot of
Abingdon, reported the arrest of a priest, 'a suspect person with a book
of conjurations for finding hidden treasures, consecrating rings with
stones in them and for consecrating a crystal in which a child may
see things'. They also contained disturbing images, including a sword
crossed over a sceptre.[11]

Books and pamphlets could be aimed at specific patrons. Thomas
Nicholas wrote to William Cecil from the Marshalsea Prison in
November 1582 and entrusted the letter to a printer, who had recently
produced Nicholas' treatise, *Caesar and Pompeius*. Nicholas had
penned another tract while he was incarcerated about the prison experience, entitled *Monastical Life in the Abbey of Marshalsea*. Trying to
please Cecil, at a time when the queen was increasingly under threat

from Catholic plots, he claimed the pamphlet would 'terrify all the Papists in England'. Nicholas concluded by asking for the question of his imprisonment to be examined, as it was a 'great wrong'.[12]

The rise of pamphlets, and the quality of the writing in them, might cause concern. In 1562, Thomas Brice reacted to what he saw as a dumbing-down of poetry being sold in the shops, in a hilarious short piece entitled 'Against Filthy Writing and Such Delighting', with its casual xenophobia. Bad, prolific writing was apparently the trade of 'ethnics', but worse still, it was just bad art:

> What meane the rimes that run thus large in every shop to sell?
> With wanton sound, and filthie sense, me thinke it agrees not well
> We are not Ethnickes we forsoth, at least professe not so
> Why range we then to Ethnickes trade? come back, where will ye go?
>
> But for the vile corrupting rimes, which you confesse to wrighte
> My soule and hart abhorres their sense, as far from my delight
> And those that use them for their glee, as you doo vaunte ye will
> I tell you plainly what I think, I judge them to bee ill
> This boasting late in part hath caused, mee now to say my minde
> Though challenges of yours also, in every place I finde.[13]

Sometimes old books were viewed with caution, given the changing ideas and mores of the era. In Rye in 1487, an ordinance was made by the mayor and aldermen that no wardens were to make ordinances unless they were passed by the authorities, as a number of books had been circulated which had not been approved. The ordinances were cancelled and the leaves of the books on which they had been recorded were cut out.[14]

A century later, a different Mayor of Rye worried about the existence of:

> a book in parchment containing the customs of each town of the Ports, written in the Latin and French tongue ... in which is set forth in each of the customals the order to send process to the parts beyond the seas where the King of England hath league or amity ...

... which he took that 'the showing of so ancient a book cannot be hurtful' so long as the officials of Winchelsea agreed with its use.[15]

News was increasingly circulated by the public display of pamphlets as well as by vocal proclamations in the street. Although they were ephemeral and fragile, pamphlets were cheaper, easier and faster to make, and included fiction, travel stories, personal accounts and notable occurrences.

In Coventry in 1535, a John Robynse and three others were arrested for pulling down at night 'certain acts of Parliament and proclamations' that had been fixed to the market cross. He and his companions admitted to having done so after drinking at 'Roger's tavern' and the Panyer Inn.[16]

When Henry VIII was at war with Scotland in 1545, he recommended the use of posted warnings:

It would be well for such as make raids into Scotland, when they have despoiled any towns or states, to leave a written notice on the church door, or some other notable place therein, in the following or similar words: 'You may thank your Cardinal for this, for if he had not been, you might have been in quiet and rest, for the contrary whereof, he hath travailed as much as can be, to bring you to sorrow and trouble.'[17]

Book ownership increased throughout the Tudor period among the middle classes. When merchant John White of Bristol died in 1570, he left an impressive small library comprising fifty great books of law and scripture, twenty small books on varied English and Latin topics, two Bibles, two books by St Augustine, a testament, a herbal and a copy of *Fabyan's Chronicle*.

Books were symbolic of learning and class, but also spoke of the sixteenth-century struggle by which new ideas emerged from old. While the printed word in pamphlets had an immediacy and accessibility, the publishing of a book conferred an authority and permanence that was new to the Tudor age. The importance of sight, as well as education, to access this New World cannot be overestimated.

❧ MAP-MAKING ❧

Tudor maps are remarkable for their beauty and their idiosyncrasy. As the dynasty grew, so did their knowledge of the world. Explorers crossing the Atlantic and sailing around Asia brought back stories of new people and lands, unsure of exactly where they had been and how to relate this to an existing understanding of geography.

In August 1492, Christopher Columbus set sail across the Atlantic in an attempt to find a passage to India and China by sailing west, rather than east. Six weeks later, he set foot on an island in the Bahamas, which he named San Salvador, or 'Holy Saviour', later known as Watling Island. It was 5 miles wide and 13 miles long, and already inhabited by natives, adorned with gold jewellery, who were peaceful and vulnerable – and whom Columbus immediately thought of conquering. He recorded in his diary that 'they ought to make good and skilled servants, for they repeat very quickly whatever we say to them. I think they can very easily be made Christians.' Indeed, he acted on this notion, taking six natives back to Spain with him as slaves.

After San Salvador, he landed at Cuba, Haiti (Hispaniola) and the Dominican Republic. On arriving back in Spain, which had funded his mission, he travelled in procession to the court, drawing great crowds to see the natives he had enslaved, with their golden ornaments and painted bodies, and the exotic specimens and trays of cotton and gold. The youngest daughter of the Spanish monarchs, Ferdinand and Isabella, was the 6-year-old Catherine of Aragon, listening wide-eyed to these tales of adventure and riches.

But more than the gold and the parrots, the tobacco and the slaves, the New World offered the west an expansion of their imagination, an intellectual exercise that required a redefinition of what was known about the Earth, and England's place in it. Curious Tudors wondered where these marvellous places might be, and how to measure and display distance and direction; how to record their discoveries so that others could retrace their steps.

The old mappae mundi of the medieval world had been created primarily to illustrate tenets of classical learning, or show the relationship of England to Jerusalem, and depicted Europe and Africa in strange proportions. Sometimes, as on the most famous of all world maps kept at Hereford, the Garden of Eden was depicted in a circle on the edge, or features like Noah's ark were added, or the maps were populated with mythical figures.

Henricus Martellus Germanus had produced a world map in 1490, possibly influenced by an earlier, lost work by Columbus's own brother. Two years later, Martin Behaim created the first globe, which he called an earth-apple, the *Erdapfel*, and which did not feature the Americas. Both of these prioritised proportion and clarity over the myths and imagination which muddied the waters of earlier works. After the discoveries of late 1492, though, more accurate portolan maps were required to allow ships to navigate the newly discovered routes.

The first map to include the Americas was painted on parchment by a Spaniard, Juan de la Cosa, in around 1500, showing traffic across the Atlantic. However, despite three more maps being produced in the early years of the century, varying in style, design and colour, it was not until 1507 that the name 'America' featured on one, with the creation of the Waldseemüller and Ringmann work. This remarkably detailed depiction shows a slim American continent in two halves, Africa, Europe and Asia, along with longitude and latitude readings – although they are not always accurate. The map is designed with curved meridians and rises in the top right and left corners, enabling it to depict the entire known world. It is highly decorative, with a border filled with tablets of information, and real and mythological characters, including Ptolemy and Amerigo Vespucci, holding measuring instruments, the faces of the winds and foliate designs. The African continent contains drawings of a group of naked, wild men and a fairly realistic depiction of an elephant, but the whole design is black and white.

The 1520 world map of Venetian Pietro Coppo is the closest, thus far, to a recognisable world map in layout, style and colour. With its vivid blue seas and land masses coloured in brown, green, yellow and orange, it is instantly recognisable, if rather crude in depiction. Known as *De toto orbe*, it was part of an unpublished series of twenty-two maps, including an outline of the coast of America. The most sophisticated first atlas was produced half a decade later, in 1570, by Abraham Ortelius; its world depiction contained America in its entirety and a series of plates relating to every corner of the globe.

Individual maps of countries, cities and towns were also being made. The earliest printed map of London, dated 1574, by the

Munich-born Frans Hogenberg, gives us a colourful impression of the city as it was, probably in the 1550s, as it depicts the spire of St Paul's which blew down in 1561. In shades of orange, brown and green, it places four Elizabethans on the South Bank, with the bend of the Thames rising above them, dotted with tiny craft and the larger ships contained beyond the bridge to the right. The Square Mile is busy, between the Tower in the east and Whitehall in the west, while the Westminster complex is still predominantly rural, surrounded by gardens and orchards. A little expansion has taken place outside the walls to the north, and the South Bank has its few houses, but the urban sprawl feared by the late Elizabethans has not yet altered the structure of a city that looked largely unchanged from the arrival of Henry Tudor in 1485.

In addition to mapping the expanding world, sixteenth-century astronomers continued the tradition of reading the skies. In 1515, Nicholas Durer and Johannes Stabius produced a star chart of the northern and southern hemispheres, featuring the twelve zodiac signs and forty-eight constellations. For centuries, thinkers had been challenging the notion that the world was flat. By the thirteenth century, Thomas Aquinas assumed that his readership understood it was spherical. He knew of different methods by which this fact could be proven, by physicists observing the movement of heavy bodies towards the centre and by mathematicians studying the shapes of eclipses, but it was not until 1543 that Nicolas Copernicus published his theory that the earth orbited the sun.

Henry VIII's physician, Andrew Boorde, is well known among historians for his 1542 *Dietary of Health*, but his lesser-known work, the 1547 *Principles of Astronomy*, illustrates the overlap of the two professions. Each sign of the zodiac was associated with a different part of the body, and Boorde was adamant that no bloodletting should take place when the moon was in the sign relating to that part. Taurus was aligned with the neck, so no blood should be drawn from there in late April and most of May, then the following month of Gemini, the arms and hands should not be touched, and nothing taken from the breast while Cancer was in the ascendancy.

There were also times when it was inauspicious to administer
medicine according to the zodiac sign, so during the reigns of Aries,
Taurus and Capricorn, or the ram, bull and goat, which were creatures with double bellies, medicine would cause the patient to be
nauseous or vomit. It was better not to administer medicine when
the moon was in a hot sign, like Sagittarius or Leo, but 'to comfort
and help the virtue of retention' by waiting for a cold, dry sign like
Taurus or Virgo.[1]

The art of watching the planets and stars balanced on the dangerous
edge where astrology and divination met. It was customary to compile
the natal charts of significant figures, but it was considered treason to
predict or 'encompass' the death of a monarch and could lead to arrest
or even the death sentence. In 1553, a book of astrological divination by a Belgian physician, Arnold Bogaert, was published in London,
with the title *A Prognostication for Divers Years Ryght Utile and
Profitable to All Sortes of People, Wherein is Declared What Persons
Hath Moste and Leaste Dominacions over the Starres and Elementes,
Whereby the Judgementes of the Astrologiens Be Scarcely True,
Givynge Together Great Consolation to Those Who Muche Fear the
Constellations.* An introduction by the translator, John Cook, Clerk
of the King's Recognisances, urged readers to put their faith in the
Holy Scriptures, while the text encouraged the use of astrology to help
steer through dangerous times:

> In the same Astrologie we haue aboundantly proposed certayne
> great and true signes, signyfyinge many thynges, yet neverthelesse
> they be not to be feared, nor credited as gods: but to the ende that by
> divine signes we be admonyshed to know our selves, and from evyll
> threateninges to kepe oure selues.[2]

The book expresses an absolute conviction that the world was created
for the service of mankind and that all the elements were present as
symbols, to be interpreted, of God's plan:

> If you looke on highe, you shall see the divers movinges of the starres
> and elementes, lykewise theyr situations, distance, propertie, and
> yet so manye lampes burnyng, and two greate lightes, as in the day
> the Sonne, in the nyght the Moone, the whyche shininge and illu-
> minynge over all the worlde, be created for the usaige of man, and

to manifeste the glory of God. These be creatures and instrumentes wherby God enspireth his natural puissance accordyng to his wyll, and converteth to acyions suche as he hath predestinate.[3]

The Tudors were well aware that, to borrow Hamlet's phrase, there were 'more things in heaven and earth' that were 'dreamt of in [their] philosophy'. Thus, every strange thing in the world had an explanation, which on one level must have been reassuring, while on another, it was unsettling as a potential harbinger of danger. Mapping out the skies on paper was one way of imposing a system upon them, visualising relationships and transferring knowledge.

⚘ TELLING THE TIME ⚘

In 1912, workmen excavating a cellar in London's Cheapside came across a buried hoard of over 400 pieces of Elizabethan and Jacobean jewellery. Among the gems set in rings, brooches and on chains, the fan holders, scent bottles and cameos, the tableware of salt cellars and tankards, they discovered a large Colombian emerald, estimated to have been originally the size of an apple, with a hollowed-out centre. The cavity had been created to house a Swiss watch movement, created in around 1600, and signed by the maker, G. Ferlite.

Clock faces became frequently more visible through the sixteenth century. Most people did not own them, and still relied upon the hours of the watch, the rise and setting of the sun or the summons of church bells, but references to the hours of the clock become increasingly common.

A fictional dialogue written by Juan Luis Vives, set early in the morning, has one character ask another to open the window so the rays may fall upon the sundial, suggesting it was located indoors. Then he asks a servant to run quickly to St Paul's Square to observe the time on the mechanical clock and compare it with what he could read on the sundial. The methods of reading both devices were different: the mechanical clock's 'hand points a little after the hour of five', while the sundial's 'shadow is yet a little distant from the second line'.[1] Public clocks, set in squares and on the exterior of municipal buildings, would have set the time which individuals used to regulate their own timepieces.

One of the most famous was the clock at Hampton Court. The current large astrological clock in the inner court was installed in 1540, designed by Nicholas Cratzer and built by Nicholas Oursian, or Urseau, but there was clearly a clock of some kind pre-dating this. In February 1530, 40s was paid to the keeper of the clock and that July, a Westminster clockmaker received 20s for mending it. Cratzer had arrived in England in 1516 from his native Germany and collaborated with Holbein in producing maps, and tutored Thomas More's children in mathematics and astronomy, earning himself a place as Henry VIII's clockmaker and astronomer. Among his creations were sundials in Oxford colleges, one at Acton Court, near Bristol, and a portable dial for Wolsey.

Clocks were not merely functional, to help with timekeeping and prevent the owner from being late. They were the latest gadgets and status symbols, and as such, were incorporated into the most elaborate jewellery and cases, combined with other functions. As part of their on–off friendship and rivalry, Francis I sought out the most impressive gifts to outdo Henry VIII, one of which was a stately silver-gilt clock salt set with precious stones. Built in stacked-up ornate shapes with a statuette on top, it resembled a tiny fountain, the right size to sit on a dining table. The bottom section, a hexagon studded with Roman-style cameos, originally contained a clock mechanism, or dial, although no clock face is visible, while a well above it held salt for the king's food.

Other smaller clocks were in use in the royal palaces, as a jeweller's bill of 1530 shows, rewarding a John Lenger for supplying two of them among other items. Upon their wedding in 1533, Henry VIII presented Anne Boleyn with an intricate clock, engraved in silver, brass and bronze with the royal motto *Dieu et mon Droit*, coats of arms and symbols like fleurs-de-lys, scrolls, leopards, foliage and the new queen's falcon badge. In 1544, John Dudley clearly had access to clocks about his property in order to reply to the Privy Council that he had received their letters 'this night at nine of the clock'.[2]

By the 1540s, timepieces had been perfected and minimised so as to be able to fit in pieces of jewellery, like that found in the Cheapside Hoard. In 1541, Italian scholar Giglio Giraldi observed, 'I myself have often seen a watch, which admirably, showed the hours, placed in the handle of an eyeglass of Pope Leo X, of which he availed himself while hunting and traveling.'

Clocks were used in two ways. They were large, public devices, mounted in some accessible, popular location, which allowed for accurate timekeeping or, as small portable pieces, they were status symbols, mounted in jewellery, which also happened to tell the time.

In 1553, when Lady Jane Grey was imprisoned in the Tower for usurping Queen Mary, among the list of clothing and possessions sent to her from Westminster were three richly made clocks – two dials and an 'alarm'. The first clock was described as a 'fair striking clock, standing upon a mine of silver, garnished with silver and gilt, with a crystal at the top', but it was decorated with 'divers counterfeit stones and pearls', which were 'broken and lacking in sundry places'. The second was a 'little striking clock within a case of latten, book-fashion', engraved with a crowned rose and the royal motto *Dieu et mon Droit*. The third was set within a sable skin, with a head of gold set with rubies and diamonds, and two pearls hanging in the creature's ears, with gold feet and sapphire claws, two of which were broken. It was an unusual choice to embed a small clock in the gold collar of a fur, highlighting the decorative value of the timepiece as well as its practical use.

Although not described specifically as clocks, Jane also had a 'round striking dial, set in crystal, garnished with metal gilt' and another 'round hanging dial, with an alarm closed in crystal'. Her final piece, an 'alarm of copper garnished with silver, enamelled with various colours', was set in a box of silver, 'standing upon a green molehill, and under the molehill a flower of silver', all of which stood upon three silver pomegranates.[3] The slow passage of time for Jane in captivity did not go unmeasured.

The first English clock to bear a date was the gilded brass 1588 lantern clock made by Francis Nowe, in London. A refugee from the Low Countries, Nowe arrived in the city in 1571, and his technique has also been found upon a cup that survives from the two decades in which he worked as an engraver and horologist. The clock contains dials that mark out the regular time, the position of sun and moon and the time of the high tide at London Bridge.

Another brass standing clock, thought to date from around 1598, has been attributed to Nicholas Vallin, the London-born son of a Huguenot immigrant. This clock contains longitudinal readings for sunrise and sunset that show it was created in the south of England. It has brass pillars and a pierced, engraved dome.

⚘ RESTRICTED SIGHT ⚘

Sight was central to the Tudor dynasty. However, eyes were fallible. They could prove susceptible to illness and states of emotion, when they might play tricks upon the brain. Richard Burton's *Anatomy of Melancholy*, published in 1621 but still reflective of Tudor beliefs, states that spirits 'may deceive the eyes of men', just as the friends of young Hamlet fear when he sees his father's ghost appear on the battlements. However, it is also possible to read the old king as exactly what he appears to be: a messenger from beyond the grave, seeking revenge. Conversely, Macbeth's vision of the murdered Banquo, the floating dagger and Lady Macbeth's blood-spotted hands appear more like manifestations of internalised guilt, and mark steps along the path to madness. Burton confirms, 'Sometimes they think verily they hear and see present before their eyes such phantasms or goblins, they fear, suspect, or conceive, they still talk with, and follow them.'

There was little comfort for those Tudors who experienced vision impairment. Convex lenses had been used to assist reading by the Greeks and Romans, and the thirteenth century saw a range of texts published on optics, with the first recognisable glasses developed in Italy in the 1290s. England began importing reading glasses in the fifteenth century, concurrent with the proliferation of material flying off the new printing presses, but specific prescriptions were unknown.

Jean Poyner's 1500 *Book of Miniatures* contains an image of St Mark reading in round glasses with arms and thick yellow rims. The 1580s saw a swathe of publications on ocular matters, including Walter Bailey's treatise on his use of needles to break down the crystal deposits in cataracts, which must have been as painful as it was dangerous. Less agonising remedies for deteriorating vision included wine, eyebright (*Euphrasia*), wild sage and fennel.

What you looked at mattered too, and certain colours were thought to be beneficial or injurious to sight. In 1547, Henry VIII's physician, Andrew Boorde, considered:

> Everything that is green or black is good for a man to look upon it. Also to look upon gold is good for the sight, and so is glass, cold water and every cold thing ... and no hot thing ... is good for the eyes except woman's milk and the blood of a dove.[1]

The importance of eyesight in such a visually oriented culture is summarised in Romeo's comments about love: 'He that is struck blind cannot forget the precious treasure of his eyesight lost.'

In a letter written to Henry VIII from the French court in 1545, Sir Henry Wootton made reference to the use of a pair of glasses as illustrative of an argument:

> As for himself he was suspected without just cause, for, as for the French king, he said, it was well known how he had kept him in prison and how he had pursued him by sea to have slain him and his children and therefore any man might gather of what mind he ought to be towards him; and whereas some maliciously said he had received rewards of the French king he had not received the value of his spectacles (holding them up), and his son of Arras had refused benefices and great promotions offered by the French king.[2]

Eyesight, or the lack of it, could influence the appointment of individuals, and thus the course of their career. When it came to appointing the Chancellor of Ireland in September 1546, Henry VIII was informed that 'Henley is sick and has lost one of his eyes and the other is in danger, which makes him unmeet to be spoken with; and yet he is more fit than Chidley, "which wanteth already both the eyes that we would have".'[3]

In a domestic context too, failing eyesight was a cause for concern. Roger Manners wrote to William Cecil in 1578 to update him on the health of his mother: 'I suppose she can see much better than can Mr Edmond Hall, specially of the one eye. She saith she can see her way, and near-hand, can well know one man from another or discern a colour from another.'[4]

It should not be forgotten that the Tudor era was darker than ours. We are used to bulbs that simulate light as bright as day at the flick of a switch, streetlamps that blot out the stars, glowing cities that can be seen from space. The name of modern historian William Manchester's illuminating study, *A World Lit Only by Fire*, reminds us of the Tudors' complete dependence upon firelight during the long hours of darkness, with all the practicalities and dangers of maintaining the flames.[5] Instances of hearth-related injuries, deaths and destruction are high in dense urban centres like London, often related to women and children. Long, voluminous skirts and toddlers, combined with boiling pots and falling coals made the home a dangerous place. In 1577, Thomas Tusser warned his readers to 'feare candle in hay loft, in barne, and in shed, feare flea smocke and mend breech, for burning their bed'.[6]

Fire could represent the best and worst of the Tudor world. Flames in hearths were welcome signs of warmth and cooking; in forges and workshops they indicated productivity; and bonfires could mark ritual celebrations, such as on Midsummer's Eve. To a beggar on a winter's night, fire was a means of survival and the only way of preparing hot food. However, a blaze out of control, with the potential damage to overhanging wooden buildings, or in the close confines aboard a ship, must have been one of the most fearful sights to sixteenth-century eyes.

John Stow reported that in November 1564, the snuff of a young woman's candle fell upon some gunpowder, and the resulting explosion shook three houses in Bucklersbury and blew the back parts off.[7] The *Greyfriars Chronicle* for 1547 related how a great fire broke out in the Tower of London because a Frenchman had set a barrel of gunpowder on fire, which also burned himself.

Fire was an essential signal of danger, as when beacons were lit along the south coast in the 1580s when invasion by the Spanish was likely. The message spread from station to station, a glow on a hilltop, dependent upon the eyesight of the watchers. It was also an era that saw fires lit under the feet of martyrs and the burning of forbidden books.

The Tudors were dependent upon daylight. Their daily routine was dictated by the rising and setting of the sun and the cycle of the year. In an exchange between a teacher and pupil in Vives' dialogue, the teacher intends to 'open both the wooden and the glass windows, so that the morning shall strike brightly on your eyes'.[8]

According to Tusser, households would rise with the light, 'in winter at five a clocke, seruant arise, in sommer at foure is verie good guise', and retired 'in winter at nine, and in sommer at ten, to bed after supper both maidens and men'. Tusser's verses in his 1577 *Book of Husbandrie* evoke a world both restricted and dependent upon the natural world, exchanging one sense for another, 'as housewives are teached [sic] in stead of a clock, how winter nights passeth by crowing of cock'.[9]

Bedtimes in those cold months prefaced long dark hours without interruption. Wealthy Tudors could draw curtains around their bed, for privacy and warmth, but otherwise curtains were a luxury that rarely graced windows. Glass was a rarity, glazed in diamond shapes or 'quarrels' and set in lead lattices. Poorer dwellings filled their window frames with narrow laths, laced or nailed together, or thin horn strips, which let in very little light. By 1587, though, William Harrison was able to write that glass had become cheaper, and, therefore, more plentiful.[10]

City streets were dark too, with narrow lanes and the overhanging upper storeys of buildings casting shadows into the space below. Back in 1461 a proclamation ordered every freeman in London, 'from seven of the bell at night', to be on their way home in an attempt to deter thieves, beggars and loiterers, and make way for the watch. Elizabethan playhouses were instructed to finish their performances early enough to allow the audience to return home before nightfall.

Darkness was the perfect cover for immorality and crime, as the London Letter Books and local Assize Court records attest, but it also provided cover for those embarked upon the most shady acts of the queen's service. When engaged in war upon the Scots, Thomas, Earl of Surrey wrote to Wolsey from Newcastle about the night raids he had planned upon Scottish ports, which were being hampered by the wrong kind of moon. The moonlight was too bright, too early. Until the moon shone after midnight, not before, it was 'not possible to do any good exploits, but only to make small excourses'.[11]

Candles chased away the darkness for the Tudors, so their manufacture and supply were of great importance. In 1488, the master, wardens and 'good men of the craft of wexchaundlers' came before London's mayor and aldermen, asking that certain articles for the preservation of the craft could be approved. They asked that no member made items of anything but good and able wax, with sufficient wick, and that certain sized and shaped candles continue to be used for the correct occasion, such as in funerals and churches, as these would have been made specifically for that purpose, on pain of penalty.[12]

In 1578, there was concern that the dryness of the summer could result in low supplies of tallow, causing a peak in the prices, 'to the great burthen of the poorer sort'. Richard Pope, Mayor of London, wrote to inform William Cecil, therefore, that 'there is arrived at Harwich some good quantity of Moscow tallow', which had been bought by merchants for dispatch to foreign countries. Pope considered this 'a great pity, that this country should not be fully supplied, before any be suffered to pass hence'.[13] It would appear that Cecil agreed, as a few days later, Francesco Giraldi, the Portuguese ambassador, wrote to Cecil, requesting the transport of 5 or 6,000 weight of candles stopped by the customs officials.[14]

The Tudors' was a predominantly visual culture, from art and dress, to architecture and objects, spectacle and theatre, and the printed and written word. The look of things mattered in an aesthetic sense, but beauty was rarely appreciated out of context, for its own sake. Visual ornament was a sign of worth, usually in terms of social standing, and the lack of external clues was interpreted as a lack of substance.

The discovery of the New World and the explosion in printed material made available new bodies of knowledge to those Tudors able to access them. Yet this is not to suggest the Tudor era was an entirely surface or superficial culture. It was evidently a time when boundaries were being challenged and new identities explored. The evidence shows us a paradox of contrary impulses at the heart of Tudor life: the desire to climb the scale of rigid hierarchy and the will to avoid, escape and subvert such a structure. Within their wider social identities, Tudor men and women used the visual world to engage in acts of self-fashioning.

Painted in 1533, *The Ambassadors* by Hans Holbein depicts Dinteville and de Salve, two up-and-coming young men who were visitors to the court of Henry VIII. The image is crammed full of symbolism, referencing the men's position, their Humanist education and the latest scientific technology, all to enhance their social standing.

The top shelf alone of *The Ambassadors* is a still life of renaissance wizardry, containing a terrestrial globe; a shepherd's dial to measure the height of the sun; a quadrant for angles up to 90°; and a torquetum that conflates three measurements, horizontal, equatorial and ecliptic and a polyhedral sundial. The young men in the painting use this visual shorthand to appear sophisticated, smart and advanced.

Henry VIII, cartoon for the Whitehall frieze, 1537. Holbein's sketch is the only image that survives of his original painting of the king and his father. Here, Henry VIII still stands to the side, facing slightly to our right, not yet turned fully to the audience, as he would be in the final work. He appears imposing, masculine and regal in what has become an iconic image.

The Lady Eliot.

Clockwise from left:
Known as the *Portrait of a Lady with a Squirrel and a Starling*, Hans Holbein's work of 1527 depicts Anne Lovell, with its playful symbolism suggestive of his sitter's pedigree. The starlings are a pun on Anne's marital home of Harling and the gnawing squirrel features on the Lovell family arms; Lady Margaret Elyot, or Eliot, drawn by Hans Holbein, between 1532–34. Lady Eliot wears an English gable headdress and pendant, her eyes turned upwards. She is sketched loosely in chalk and pen upon paper, in preparation for her portrait; Lady Mary Guildford, by Hans Holbein in chalk, 1527. Facing the viewer, Mary has her eyes to the left and a slight smile plays on her lips as if she has been distracted by someone at the side, making this a far more intimate and playful depiction than the final, formal oil painting.

Painted in 1527, Sir Thomas More presents a sombre face to Holbein, with all the gravitas of his position echoed in his sumptuous costume and the draped fabric behind. He wears the livery Collar of Esses with a Tudor rose hanging from the end, signifying his allegiance to the dynasty.

A 1540 miniature by Holbein of Jane Small, *née* Pemberton, wife of a London merchant. As the flower in her hand represents, this image is likely to have been created to celebrate Jane's betrothal or marriage in her early twenties. Her simple but elegant outfit speaks of class and quality without overstepping the complex sumptuary laws regarding suitable dress.

Sir John and Thomas Godsalve, a Norwich-based father and son who were lawyers and associates of Thomas Cromwell. They were painted by Holbein in 1528, just after Thomas had entered Gray's Inn, representing a new portrait class of those who could afford to hire an artist and valued the possession of a self-portrait. Depicted in their work environment, they also helped celebrate their professional identities, in contrast to the images of the leisured upper classes.

This sketch, or cartoon, of Thomas More and his family, by Hans Holbein in 1527, is all that remains of his final work, which was later destroyed by fire. It captures the mood in the family home, showing the extended members located around More and his father, and the family's love of learning and music. The composition is unusually formal for the time, and the direct gaze of the family's jester is the only indication of the group's awareness of the artist.

Floor tiles in St David's Cathedral, Haverfordwest, Wales. Located before the altar, these high-status tiles have a repeating black diamond, or diaper, pattern, containing large and small circular designs in terracotta with gold foliate decoration.

The painted ceiling in the presbytery, St David's Cathedral. In 1540, the body of Edmund Tudor, grandfather of Henry VIII, was brought from Carmarthen to St David's and laid to rest in a prominent box tomb immediately below this ceiling, beside the shrine of St David.

Even the smaller domestic chimney stacks were made into a decorative feature at Hampton Court. Twisted, patterned and embellished, they proved that even the most distant, functional parts of the king's residence were worthy of ornamentation.

Completed in 1440, London's Guildhall provided an imposing central location for business and legal matters. It was the location of the trials of the Protestant martyr Anne Askew, Archbishop Thomas Cranmer, Lady Jane Grey and her husband Guildford Dudley, who were processed through the streets from the Tower for the crowds to see.

New gardens at Kenilworth Castle were designed by Robert Dudley for the visit of Elizabeth I in 1575. The medieval building and its grounds were transformed into a renaissance palace in the hopes that the queen would finally accept Dudley as a suitor. Allegorical figures met Elizabeth and conducted her to a pageant on a lake, and the event culminated in a firework display.

The estate at Kentwell Hall dates from the Norman period, although the moat house and service wing date from the early fifteenth century. The main building, facing three sides of the courtyard, was listed in 1563 as the 'new mansion house,' and home of the Clopton family, where historical re-enactments are held each year.

The Tudor House in Margate was built in 1525 and occupied by a yeoman farmer and his family. It was a building of status, with two chimneys, glazed windows and was originally surrounded by land. Partly based on the old medieval design of the long hall, it also had a more modern two-storey aspect, representing a transitional architectural phase.

Built around 1500, the Tenby Merchant's House is a narrow, three storey building combining workshop on the ground floor and living quarters above. Yards from the harbour, it housed a prosperous family in a thriving trade, waiting for the arrival of ships bringing more wares. The interior contains replica furniture and wall paintings.

Taken from the 1568 German *Book of Trades* by Jost Aumann and Hans Sachs, the following four images depict commercial interiors.

Here, the stonecutter sits before the window, using his foot to power the wheel that slices his work, the size suggesting these are probably precious stones for jewellery rather than masonry.

Interior of the apothecary's shop, with his jars of ingredients on the shelves and a potion being made up in a large, lidded pestle and mortar, while customers wait.

Workshop of the bookbinder with his large pieces of equipment and a book being assembled in the background.

An eyeglass maker measuring lenses for a customer. The diminishment or loss of eyesight could expose an individual to danger, exclude them from certain professions and prevent them from participating in a culture that defined itself visually.

Also included in the *German Book of Trades* is the fisherman, pursuing his catch as he balances a large net above the water. His image serves as a reminder of how significant fish and seafood were to the Tudor diet, whether fresh, dried or salted, especially on fast days.

Clockwise from right:
This late Elizabethan tomb depicts a lady in a
ruff and high hat, kneeling before her prayer
book. Such upright statues were common
representations of the deceased or their
mourners on post-Reformation tombs and
capture changing fashions; Holbein's design
for a cup for Anne Boleyn, featuring her device
of a falcon standing on a rose, four satyrs as
caryatids supporting the lid which is topped by
a crown; As court painter to Henry VIII, Hans
Holbein also completed a number of jewellery
designs, dating from around 1532, including this
pendant. His work followed circular, oval and
diamond shapes, and were set with sapphires
and rubies, emeralds and pearls.

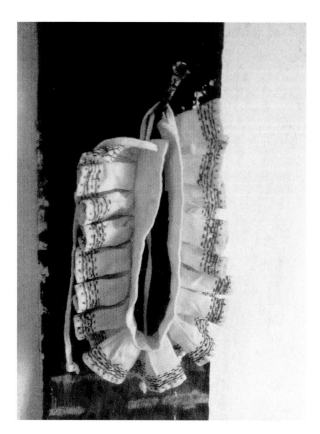

A reproduction, handmade soft collar, featuring blackwork embroidery, also known as Spanish blackwork, featuring black stitches on a white or cream fabric, common on shirts and chemises.

Standing at 15ft in diameter, the Hampton Court Clock was designed by Nicholas Crazter and made by Nicholas Oursian. It was installed in 1540 on the gatehouse to the inner court and tells the hour, month, zodiac sign, day of the year and phase of the moon.

Holy Trinity Church, Long Melford, was built between 1467 and 1497 and contains the tomb of Sir John Clopton, owner of nearby Kentwell Hall, who died in 1497. Located in the chantry chapel, the ceiling is decorated with a painted scroll running around the four walls, bearing the text of John Lydgate's poem 'Testament'.

Cloister, Gloucester Cathedral. Some of the most elaborately designed religious interiors were found inside the monasteries, such as the carving in the cloister at Gloucester. Monastic building projects continued right into the 1530s, when the sudden process of dissolution converted many into secular properties and such ecclesiastical wealth and treasures were lost.

Tomb of Prince Arthur Tudor, Worcester Cathedral. When the heir to the throne died at the age of 15 in April 1502, he was laid to rest in a magnificent chantry tomb adorned with heraldic stone carving, including the Tudor rose, the Beaufort portcullis, Prince of Wales' feathers, French fleur-de-lys and the pomegranate of Aragon.

Misericord, St David's Cathedral, Pembrokeshire. Hidden under the seats in the choir of most medieval churches lurked elaborately carved images of people, animals and scenes. Depicting folklore, old wives' tales and rude humour, misericords occupied a hidden space where vulgarity was permitted in the heart of the church. Some, like this example, named the individuals who had either paid for the seat or were entitled to use it.

PART II
SMELL

❧ UBIQUITOUS SCENTS ❧

Where did the Tudors encounter smells? Everywhere.

In a far less sanitised century than ours, people of all classes were exposed to many different odours throughout the day and night, every day of their lives. Smells pervaded each room of their homes: in clothing and bed linen; in the kitchen, over the fire and in the storeroom; in the latrines and laundry; opening the spice chest; in the distilling room and dairy; the glycerine of tallow candles wafting down church aisles.

Outside, they encountered smells in the air: from fires and plants; in the roads and fields; about town; by the stables and markets; arising from the rivers and rubbish tips and graveyards; and wherever animals lived and died. The odour must have been intense wherever farming and industry took place; where crops grew and were cut and stubble fields burned; where metal was mined and smelted; where beer was brewed; and where dyers submerged cloth in vats of urine.

There were smells resulting from life, birth and reproduction; from illness and bodily functions; from death and decay; as powerful indicators of potential dangers. The Tudors believed that pleasant smells could block foul ones, forming a protective shield to keep bad ones at bay, literally, as the scents did battle for dominance in the air.

However, this was the norm. Most Tudors would hardly have noticed the smell, as they were used to this assault upon their nostrils. In the modern world, our default setting is to eradicate many of our natural smells, and we fastidiously cover what we perceive to be unpleasant odours with manufactured scents such as air fresheners and laundry conditioner, deodorants and perfumes. Yet if we reflect upon the question, 'What is clean?' or 'What does it mean for a person or item to be clean?', even today, individuals might disagree. Standards of hygiene differ.

To the sixteenth-century nose, modern bodies and homes would probably smell overpoweringly strong from all the chemicals used, and most unlike the usual 'people' smell. Certainly, the definition of 'clean' was much more complex for the Tudors and overlapped with questions of practicality and health risks. The past was more willing to embrace natural odours and, as such, these were not only valuable signals of the state of a person's health, but also a part of individual identity. Such intimate smells as sweat and bodily fluids, illness, the hormone or subtle pheromone mix, changes in women's odours as part of their monthly cycle and the impact of diets upon bodily emissions, which varied by class, were all more immediate for the Tudors, even if they were experienced subtly, or unconsciously. The Tudors were not dirtier than us, but their standard of cleanliness was different, for a number of reasons.

Smells had intrinsic value beyond the way they were physically experienced. As shortcuts to emotions, they epitomised the obvious connections we still experience today: the aroma of food cooking could provoke hunger; while lavender might make for a good night's sleep; or the unmistakeable tang of rotten food was a warning sign from which the body recoiled; while the scent of fire in the air might induce fear, panic or action. For the Tudors, though, with a more limited olfactory palate than the modern era can replicate, smells arising from the natural world had particular significance, keeping them in tune with bodily health and the cycles of the natural world.

In the poetry and drama of the era, the sense of smell is frequently employed as a metaphor, but usually in a dichotomic way, either as an idealised lovers' symbol or to represent evil or sin. As Juliet says of Romeo, 'That which we call a rose by any other name would smell as sweet', highlighting the lack of power of names over physicality, which Shakespeare echoes in *Sonnet 54*, where 'the rose looks fair, but fairer we it deem for that sweet odour which doth in it live'. Claudius admits to his fratricide of old Hamlet in olfactory terms, 'O, my offense is rank, it smells to heaven', and for Lady Macbeth the persistent smell of blood meant that 'all the perfumes of Arabia will not sweeten this little hand'. When Hamlet killed Polonius and concealed his body, he teased that if the guard did not find him within a month, they would 'nose him as you go up the stairs into the lobby'.

Odours were typical in dramatic insults too, with the particular tangs of 'mountain goat' and 'the rankest compound of villainous smell that has ever offended nostril' used in *Henry V* and *The Merry Wives of Windsor* respectively. Trinculo admits in *The Tempest* that he smells 'all horse piss', at which his 'nose is in great indignation'. However, *Henry V* does move from the comic use of smells into the serious territory of perfume as a sign of common humanity: 'I think the King is but a man, as I am; the violet smells to him as it doth to me.'

This final observation reminds us of the communality of scent. Some perfumes might be affordable only to the rich, but a pauper might catch its notes in the wind. Smell could not be contained or classified according to rank; by definition it dispersed in the air, bringing information about the immediate environment which helped the Tudors to decode their world.

Smell could act as a powerful warning tool. Some of the Tudors' reactions to certain smells were instinctive and biological, such as the need to recoil from rotten food or carcasses, from which illness or disease might arise, while others were culturally acquired – like the scent of a favourite perfume or the church's incense – and were constructs of faith or class. In this way, smell was closely aligned to the sense of taste, especially in relation to food and drink, but both were functions of the need to guard the health when it came to the experience of the senses. How that health was understood, and maintained, was the result of a range of sixteenth-century beliefs about mankind's relation to the natural world.

ꙮ PIPE SMOKE ꙮ

Amid the mingled Tudor odours of woodsmoke and latrines, sodden straw and roasting meat, a new acrid, unfamiliar tone arrived towards the end of the era. Initially feared, then ridiculed and dismissed, the woody tones of the tobacco plant swiftly found favour among the elite, as a symbol of status and a cure for damp humours.

Cultivated in the New World, tobacco had been offered to Columbus as a valuable trade item back in 1492. It was observed to have soporific effects. One of the earliest Spanish settlers in the Americas observed:

> men with half-burned wood in their hands and certain herbs to take their smokes, which are some dry herbs put in a certain leaf, also dry ... and having lighted one part of it, by the other they suck, absorb, or receive that smoke inside with the breath, by which they become benumbed and almost drunk, and so it is said they do not feel fatigue. These, muskets as we will call them, they call tabacos.[1]

Tobacco was widely known in Europe henceforth, being prized for its reputed medicinal qualities, and curing the headaches of Francis II in the 1550s. Tobacco seeds were first brought to England by John Hawkins, who was smoking the finished product on an expedition in 1562: 'The Floridians ... haue a kinde of herbe dryed which with a cane, and an earthen cup in the end, with fire, and the dried herbs put together do smoke thoro the cane the smoke thereof.'[2] He claimed they could sustain themselves for four or five days by inhaling the smell alone, without food or water.

However, it was not until the 1580s that Walter Raleigh brought Virginia tobacco to England, giving rise to the apocryphal story that his servant doused him and his pipe with water, believing him to be on fire. Raleigh's contemporary, the playwright John Beaumont, described how he cultivated the plant:

> But if Raleigh denies himself the renown of being the first to bring the Indian's herb to his native country, he can fairly lay claim to the pleasure of having first planted it in Ireland. When he was Mayor of Youghall, and his abode the manor-house, he smoked his first pipe of tobacco in his garden, sheltered by the spreading branches of four yew trees that still may be seen forming a thatch-like covering for a summer-house. And in this Youghall garden he planted Ireland's first instalment of the Indian weed.[3]

As a new smell in the sixteenth-century air, and a corresponding new taste on their palate as they chewed the leaves, tobacco was unprecedented. It lingered in halls, clung to clothing and hair and, over time, stained the skin and teeth of those partaking regularly. However, unaware of the dangers that the modern world has uncovered, the Tudors interpreted it as a kind of new miracle cure, while rejecting its fellow import, the potato, as poisonous.

Medical textbooks rushed to proclaim the benefits of the plant. Its warming, dry nature appealed to contemporary medical theories of the four humours, making it a perfect antidote to cold, wet ailments. Spaniard Nicolas Monardes wrote in 1571 that the plant was first cultivated in Spain for its flowers, but that it had been found to cure over twenty illnesses, including colds, toothache, worms, halitosis, lockjaw, falling fingernails and cancer, while a text of 1573 described it as a 'sovereign healer of ulcers and sores' and rheums.[4]

In 1587, William Harrison described the way Englishmen smoked, rubbing their tobacco so dry that it became a powder, pushing it into the bowl at the end of the pipe 'and putting fire to it, they draw the smoke in through their mouths, which they puff out again, through their nostril like funnels, along with it plenty of phlegm and defluxation from the head'.[5] A different description of smoking was outlined by Mondares in 'an instrument formed like a little ladle, whereby it passeth from the mouth into the head and stomach' and was 'greatly taken up and used'.[6]

Objections were already being made to the smell by 1595, when Anthony Chute's *Tabaco* played devil's advocate to warn pipe smokers that their enemies would rise like woodcocks, crying, 'Fie, fie, how it stinks, smell you it not?' He also refers to a liquid made from the leaves being drunk, and another odorous method, that of placing green leaves on top of burning embers, to create a dry, fumigation effect which could improve 'all evils that come of cold effects'.[7]

By 1598, though, tobacco was so popular that Hentzner was able to write that the English were 'constantly smoking the nicotine weed' and 'they have pipes on purpose, made of clay'.[8] The account book of the Earl of Rutland for this year includes payments for one ball of tobacco in July, pipes costing 8d in October, and 2s 6d in November for an ounce of tobacco.[9]

The approximate price was 3d for a pipe full, the same cost as a ride in a wherry from Westminster to St Paul's or a cheap meal in a tavern, so it was not beyond the reach of the middle classes. The following year, 1599, *Gerard's Herbal* claimed that the tobacco plant was commonly grown in English gardens, 'where it doth prosper exceedingly, insomuch that it cannot be destroyed where it hath once sown itself and it is dispersed into most parts of London'.[10]

Sir John Beaumont celebrated the possible cerebral benefits of smoking in *The Metamorphosis of Tobacco*, calling it 'the great God of Indian melody' with the power to 'infume my brain, make my soul's powers subtle' and:

Give nimble cadence to my harsher style;
Inspire me with thy flame, which doth excel
The purest streams of the Castalian well.[11]

Tobacco was a new smell for the English, making a widespread appearance towards the end of the Tudor era, initially as an exotic, elite scent. It would have been identified at first in small pockets across the country, wherever sailors and travellers frequented, as an unusual foreign herb. Its adoption by Walter Raleigh and its circulation at court prompted a spate of medical publications on its health benefits, both as a curative practice and one which was pleasurable and improved mental agility. Thus, for most Tudors, the woody scent of Virginia tobacco was associated with status and good health.

⚘ FOUL BODIES ⚘

The Tudors did bathe, but they didn't necessarily get undressed for it.

In 1529, Henry VIII ordered a new bathroom to be built for himself at Hampton Court. The Bayne, or 'bain' tower, had a gilded ceiling and window seats, and a wooden bath (built by a cooper) attached to the wall, with taps dispensing hot and cold water. A stove in the next room ensured that there was a constant supply of the former. The bath was supplied by three conduits, which were fed by a spring and filtered out the sediment, before the water was carried along lead pipes over a distance of almost 3.5 miles. A similar bathroom built at Whitehall in the 1530s was equipped with thirty-five Holland linen towels, washing cloths, bathrobes, sheets for lining the tub, pails and sponges.

The king would have descended into the tub in his linen shift, ensuring that the kind of intimate washing or scrubbing of body parts with soap and water that we are used to in the modern world was unlikely to have taken place. When he rose from his bath, Henry was provided with clean body linen, which had been infused and strewn with fresh herbs by his laundress, Mrs Harris. For her annual salary of £20, she washed his clothing and other linen once a week, including bed sheets, towels, napkins and intimate cloths.

When Henry travelled, he was attended by others, such as in January 1530, when 'Sexton servant' was paid 9s 8d for washing the king's shirts 'and other of his necessaries'. The same Sexton washed his shirts again, and supplied shoes, ale and other items in April.[1]

Later in life, Henry installed sunken baths, perhaps to better suit his limited mobility. In the 1540s these were constructed at Whitehall and Woodstock, the latter of which was supplied by Rosamund Spring and, according to witness Thomas Platter, was cold in summer and warm in winter. Henry took the advice of his doctors and used herbal baths for medicinal purposes in the winter, retiring to bed afterwards in order to prevent colds and fevers setting in.

A book of recipes in the royal collection from the late 1510s, signed A. and T. Darcy, contained a holistic account of how a person might fall ill, and what the best preventative measures were:

> As through the default of good ruling and dieting in meat and drink, men fallen often into this sickness, therefore when the pestilence reigneth in country, the man that woll be kept from that evil, him needeth him to keep from outrage and excess in meat and eke drink, ne use no baths, ne sweat not too much, for all these openeth the pores of the body, and maketh the venomous airs to enter, and destroyeth the lively spirits in man, and enfeebleth the body; and sovereignly haunting of lechery, for that enfeebleth the kind, and openeth the pores that wicked airs may enter. Also, use little or nought of these: garlick, onions, leeks, or other such meats that bring a man into an unkindly heat. Also, suffer not greatly thirst that time, and if thou thirst greatly look thou drink but measurably to slake thy thirst; and the best drink were cold water, menged with vinegar or tisane. The poison enters at the pores in one of the 'cleansing places' of the principal members, i.e. heart, liver, and brain; and unless the patient is bled within 18 hours, it fastens on one place, and casts him into an ague, and maketh a botch in some of the three cleansing places, or near them.[2]

The danger was thought to come from open pores in the skin, which would allow infection to enter the body, and which responded to the stimulus of water. Thomas Moulton's *This Is the Mirror or Glasse of Health* of 1545 recommended people 'use no baths or stoves, nor sweat too much, for all openeth the pores of a man's body and maketh the venomous ayre to enter and for to infect the blood'.[3] Thus, during times of illness, Tudors were advised not to bathe and to keep their bodies covered from wrist to ankle.

When the Duke of Norfolk was ill with an ague (fever) in September 1569, he took a purgative and went to bed but delayed his return to court as he was 'afraid to into the air so soon'.[4] In 1582 the Earl of Arundel complained that he was forced to hurry away from his house because it was 'encompassed' by plague. He asked William Cecil to provide him with an alternative residence:

The air of my house in Sussex is so corrupt even at this time of the year as when I came away I left sick of hot agues. Wherefore the Bishop of Chichester being dead, and I wanting an house to remove unto, I beseech your lordship I may have the Bishop's house near Chichester to use till I may otherwise provide myself.[5]

Unhealthy airborne odours were blamed in 1502 for the death of Prince Arthur at Ludlow on the Welsh Marches, which was cited as being too damp and cold and unhealthily situated.

In 1533, after Henry VIII had banished Catherine of Aragon from court and was shunting her between different rural properties, he proposed that she live at Somersham Palace in the Cambridge Fens, surrounded by water and swamp. The last incumbent, Nicholas West, had complained that it was so dangerously located that people were unable to visit him without a boat or incurring great danger. Catherine's great ally, the Imperial ambassador Chapuys, described it as a house 'surrounded with deep water and marshes, which is, as she is informed, the most unhealthy and pestilential house in England and she, seeing the evident danger of it, refused to go except by force'. Catherine was reflecting contemporary medical advice by objecting, as Moulton advised people to 'avoid places where vapours arose from pools, marshes, muck heaps and tanneries' and to 'keep the air about you fresh and sweet smelling'.[6]

In his bathroom, just as in every other aspect of his life, Henry VIII was the exception rather than the norm. For practical reasons and their fears about their health, the ordinary Tudors did not bathe with any degree of regularity. The process of drawing a wooden tub to the hearth, heating pans of water and filling the lined tub would have been a lengthy and often prohibitive process. Bathing or swimming in rivers and ponds was no substitute and could not guarantee cleanliness or safety.

However, it would be incorrect to assume that the Tudors were dirty or smelly as a result. On the contrary, the many manuals, receipt books and accounts suggest that they prided themselves in keeping clean and smelling fresh, but that they went about it in different ways.

It is impossible now to authenticate the famous words that tradition has attributed to Elizabeth I, that she bathed once a month, whether she needed to or not. The bathrooms installed by her father were redesigned to her tastes, with water pouring out of oyster shells at

Whitehall and the room she bathed in at Windsor being lined with mirrors. The queen was very conscious of hygiene and unpleasant odours,
and paid particular attention to her hands, washing them before every
meal in perfumed waters. Beauty, though, was another matter entirely,
so long as it remained odour-free. When she advanced in age and
required layers of thick white lead to be applied to her face each morning, there was no corresponding face-washing routine for Elizabeth.
The previous day's ceruse was simply topped up to look fresh.

Baths were also considered auspicious in certain cases and at certain
times, although this did not always prove the case. An unusual female
medical practitioner, Susanna Gloriana, recommended that Mrs Bret
take a bath after six or seven years of failing to conceive. Rosemary
water was considered particularly efficacious for women's health and
gynaecological problems, baths of which were known as the 'bath of
life'. Within three hours of taking her bath, though, Mrs Bret had died,
and another doctor, the famous Simon Forman, calculated that the
moon had been inauspicious at the time the bath was taken. This
provided what was considered irrefutable evidence that Gloriana
had given bad medical advice, although the autopsy revealed a hard,
shrunken womb, more in line with a modern diagnosis of cancer.[7]
The timing of the bath was likely to have been completely coincidental but, for the Tudors, it would have been the fatal catalyst.

For the first half of the sixteenth century, Tudor men in London
might visit the communal baths or 'stews'. Most of these were situated on the South Bank, or on the north, close to the river, where some
of the alleys and lanes bore names suggestive of their presence. Here,
you could relax in a heated bath, taking its name from the French
word *estewes*, meaning a stove which was used to heat the tubs.

However, these were so closely associated with sexual immorality
that both Henry VII and Henry VIII attempted to close them down,
especially to check the spread of syphilis, then known as the pox. In
1506, they were shut down briefly, but found alternative locations or
pretexts for reopening, such as in taverns. In 1546, twenty-two stews
existed on Bankside, with names that sounded like inns, such as the
Antelope, the Bull's Head, the Cross Keys, the Little Rose, the Swan
and the Unicorn. That year, Henry VIII closed these establishments
permanently, ending the 'toleration of such dissolute and miserable
persons as have been suffered to dwell in common open places called
the stews without punishment or correction [for] their abominable

and detestable sin'. From this point onwards, prostitution moved into the taverns, so that reformer Philip Stubbes could call them in the 1580s, 'the slaughter howses, the shambles, the blockhowses of the Devill, wherein he butchereth Christen mens soules, infinit waies, God knoweth'.[8]

For those who did not frequent stews, rivers or ponds, and did not own a bath, Vives' description of the process of washing the body began with fetching the washbasin and pitcher. The pitcher should be raised high, so the water was able to 'drop out' rather than pour. He recommended that his charges wash the dirt carefully from the joints of the fingers, rub the eyelids and eyebrows and then rub the glands of the neck under the ears vigorously. The same water should be used to wash the mouth and gargle, then the student should dry themself with a cloth.[9] Such rituals often included the face, hands and feet, and must have been a regular, fast and portable element of the morning routine in most households.

Poorer people, especially those engaged in manual work, agriculture or industry, enough to leave them smelly at the end of a day's labour, dipped or swam in ponds, rivers and streams, even perhaps in the sea, where it was safe. This would have been seasonal and weather dependent, and the reputed health benefits of sea bathing that would become so popular in the eighteenth century were not yet being praised by doctors, although mineral baths were encouraged.

Individuals did drown regularly in rivers in the summer months, and in 1571, Cambridge University prohibited students from entering the river, whether to wash or swim. In 1576, a boy at St Osyth, Essex, pretended to be drowning in a millpond where he was bathing, prompting two of his friends to come to his aid, both of whom drowned in the process.[10]

❧ CLEAN CLOTHES ❧

The decisive factor for the Tudors when it came to bodily odours was the use of linen. It was the only item worn against the skin, in the form of smocks, shirts, shorts and hose, and was regularly changed and laundered. Linen absorbed sweat and grease and was recommended by Thomas Elyot's 1534 A Castel of Helth as the best fabric with which to rub down the body in the morning. Other fabrics like wool, silk or leather were not worn next to the skin and were changed and cleaned far less regularly.

Juan Luis Vives recommended shaking out stockings and then cleaning them with a hard fly-brush and to wear clean socks, because the moist smell of sweaty socks was offensive.[1] External garments were also turned inside out every so often, to present the cleaner side outwards, and must have absorbed the strong odours of common smells like soap and industry-specific smells, which overpowered any bodily scents that reached them. In 1559, soap imports worth over £9,700 came through London's ports, but these were almost entirely the alkaline, animal-fat soap used to wash clothing.

Keeping clothing clean was a particular challenge for a country where most people worked manually, exerted themselves significantly more than today, and washed less. Henry VIII's laundress was required to provide her own soap, usually a sticky black substance, and probably also the urine required for bleaching whites. Urine from red-headed, prepubescent boys was particularly valued for the task. It was sought out by those employed as fullers, who collected gallons of urine, and much of the day was spent treading cloth soaked in it.

The use of linen for undergarments was a partial solution. These were washed by housewives in wooden tubs, or by professional laundrywomen, with various soap solutions and combinations of herbs. Ashes were made into lye soap, or used as an individual agent, and were combined with lavender, roses, marjoram, egg yolks and fresh brook water to wash clothes which were laid flat on the ground, or over bushes, usually out of the sun to prevent the fading of colours. Expenses from Henry VIII's most intimate room, his closet, in 1546, include an additional 10s to his laundress, 6s for flowers, 16d for hooks and 6d for threads and pins.[2]

A recipe book for 1573 includes a violet powder treatment for woollen clothes and furs, which were far more difficult to keep clean and sweet smelling than linen. A variety of herbs including violets, cypress, galingale, dried rose leaves, cloves, lavender flowers, nigella and benjamin (benzoin gum) should be finely beaten, then sprinkled with a water of musk and rose, until 'it have drunk up the water', after which it should be stored in silken bags and placed among the clothes. When it came to linen, or napery, which was table linen, the same source recommended a powder made from dried seeds of sweet marjoram, with musk in the winter and dried rose petals in the summer, scattered among the linen. It took a particularly long time to prepare the roses to perfection:

> Moreover in the Sommer time, gather red Roses in faire weather, so soone as they be blowne and opened, laye them upon a Table, a Bed, or a fayre floroe of boards, and now and then remove them least they mould, and grow fusty, that you may have two peckes of them, then strewe them among and betweene the boughts and foldinges of your Linnen.
>
> Be sure that your linnen be everthrough dry ere ye lay them by, for else the Roses will grow hoar, let your coffer in a dry aire, and in the winter tyme, or in wet weather, when ye percieve your Roses to grow moyst, the put them into a pillow case or two, that they fall not out, and lay them vpon your bed between the Coverlet and the Blanket, all night, or else before the fire, let them dry, and strew them agayne. Moreover, ye must always have a bag full of dry Roses in store, kept in a dry air, for if he loose his rednesse, the looseth the rose his sweetnesse. Fynally, ye must euery yeare, put away your olde Roses, and occupye new, but keepe your sweet Bagges styll many yeares.[3]

The look of clothes mattered, not just the items of clothing themselves; the Tudors wanted their whites to be pristine, their colours intense and their garments clean and unstained.

Methods of cleaning survive in family receipt (recipe) books and contemporary advice manuals, such as the late-fifteenth-century German *Kunstbuch*, which contains instructions for caring for the clothing of a community of well-to-do nuns, who appeared to wear largely green, red, pink and brown, in taffeta, brocade, velvet and damask. They recommended removing stains by working in the yolk of an egg, which was then washed away with soap, before the garment was hung out in the air, but only in the shade so the sun did not fade the dye. Other stains might be removed by the water used to boil peas, or the ashes of grapevines or beech, while red shades should be boiled in slaked lime and colour could be intensified by washing in brook water.[4]

Drying clothing could be problematic. One house in London's Honey Lane had been leased out, but the new tenants had to respect the right of the next-door neighbour to lay out her washing to dry in their yard.[5]

Wherever possible, clothes were dried in the open air, and the washing line was not yet as popular as lying garments on bushes or flat upon the ground. Obviously, this was dependent upon good weather and risked the items being dirtied further by weather, passers-by, animals and birds flying above. The Agas Map, which depicts London in around 1561, shows women laying out their washing on the ground on Moor Field, just outside the northern stretch of the city walls. Ideal conditions were a private, enclosed space on a dry, sunny, slightly breezy day.

⚜ PERFUME ⚜

Perfume was not as exclusively applied to the skin as it is today. The Tudors' favourite spicy, floral, smoky and musky scents could be infused into items of clothing, burned in the form of pastilles and incense, or carried about in bottles on chains. It wafted out of churches and was raised to the nose to avoid contact with unpleasant odours, in the form of nosegays, muslin bags or pomanders. A beautiful little gold and enamel bottle was discovered among the Cheapside Hoard, with a screw top and chain, indicating its portability and the need for quick access to pleasant smells.

Perhaps the easiest way to carry scent with you was in the pomander, the *pomme d'ombre* or 'amber apple', where a sort of potpourri was contained within a hollowed cavity, or the item itself generated the scent. These ranged from simple, homemade devices, of a ball of rags stuffed with dried herbs, to dried apples or the more expensive oranges studded with cloves, to the high-end ornate metal balls filled with spice and perfume, suspended at the waist from a belt. Elizabeth's favourite combination was damask rose, benzoin and ambergris, and she often received such items as a New Year's gift.

A 1573 recipe book reveals some of the key ingredients used in pomanders and how they could be made at home. Benjamin (benzoin gum) and storax, a bitter gum from Syria, were required, with the Mediterranean bitter gum labdanum, beaten to a powder and boiled over coals with a little damask or rose water, until they were dissolved and soft, like wax. Then the residue should be rolled between the hands into a ball, along with cinnamon, cloves, ambergris, musk or civet oil; dissolved in a silver spoon over the fire; a little sweet water added; and the ball mixed together, until each ingredient was 'perfectly incorporated'. The ideal size for a pomander was 2oz, so the ball could be made into two if necessary, before being bored through with a hole and hung upon a lace.[1] This could then be tied to the girdle.

Powdered grains, pastilles or perfumes could also be burned to scent a room and drive away bad spirits. These might be in a small dish set above coals or on the fire. Benjamin and storax provided the gum base again for a pastille and, combined with powdered juniper, cloves or cypress, could be worked into a 'rownde of the bigness of a black sloe', which was then printed with a seal while it was still soft. One or two of these were cast upon a chafing dish of coals 'to purge all pestiferous infection and corrupt airs out of your house'. A sweeter smell was achieved through the addition of powder of amber beads.[2]

The Tudors used perfume to target areas that were recognised to be the origin of foul odours. One recipe 'to cure armhole stench' recommended plucking out the hairs and washing the armpits with a mixture of white wine and rose water, in which cinnamon bark had been boiled.

Waters specifically for hand washing also existed, including the most common rose water, but increasingly supplemented by the new herbs and spices brought back from the East and the New World: orange blossom water, jasmine, pine, cedarwood, nutmeg, vanilla, frankincense, sandalwood and cardamom. The expensive Castile soap was favoured by wealthy women, being made from olive oil rather than the smelly animal fat used to wash laundry.

A 1573 recipe for musk soap recommends:

> stronge lye made of chalk, and six pounde of stone chalk, four pounde of deer suet, and put them in the lye, in an earthen potte, and mingle it well, and kepe it the space of forty days, and mingle and stir it three or four times a daye, untyll it be consumed, and that, that remayneth seven or eight dayes after, then you muste put a quarter of an ounce of muske, and when you haue done so, you must al styre it, and it wyll smell of musk.[3]

Herbs and spices played a crucial role in keeping clothes and the air clean. These were applied to garments, used to infuse items, stuff pomanders, make perfume and burn on fires. Many were grown locally, in gardens and plots, or foraged for, while others were bought fresh or dried at market.

In the 1570s, the list of those recommended for distilling into waters included thistle, dill, endive, fennel, hyssop, mint, sage, saxifrage, strawberry leaves, sorrel, woodruff and other more obvious laundry choices such as lavender and rose. Other herbs and flowers in season were planted in knot gardens, in pots, or along walks to scent the air. These included bay, columbines, cowslips, daffodils, sweet briar, lilies, carnation, hollyhocks, lavender, marigolds, pansies, pinks, rosemary, sweet william, snapdragons, violets and stocks.[4]

In 1577, Thomas Tusser advised women to 'take heed when you wash' to 'wash well and wring well' and not to lack beating and to have 'an eye to thy bowl'. He offered them the rhyme, 'Go wash well, saith Sommer, with sunne I shall drie, go wring well, saith Winter, with winde so shall I.' He recommended that they seek out and use a variety of herbs to cleanse and scent the wash, dependent upon the season, including basil, camomile, cowslip, daisy, fennel, lavender, marjoram, roses, sage, tansy, violets and winter savoury.[5]

A beautiful, poetic recipe for 'Vinegar of Roses' was included in John Partridge's 1573 *The Treasury of Commodious Conceits and Hidden Secrets*:

In Sommer time when Roses blowe, gather them ere they be full spread or blowne out, and in dry weather: plucke the leaves, let them lye halfe a day upon a fayre boarde, then have a vessel with vineger of one or two gallons, put therein a great quantity of the said leaves, stop the vessel close after that you have stirred them well together, let it stand a day and a night, then divide your vineger and rose leaves together in two parts put them in two great Glasses and put in Rose leaves enoughe, stop the Glasses close, set them upon a shelfe under a wall side, on the Southside without your house where the Sunne may come to them the most parte of the daye, let them stande there all the whole Summer longe: and then strayne the vineger from the Roses, and keepe the vinegre. If you shall once in ten dayes, take and strain out Rose leaves, and put in newe leaves of halfe a dayes gatheryng, the vyneger wyll haue the more flavour and odour of the Rose. You may use in steade of vinegre, wyne and receiue ye vertue of the Roses, both at once. Moreouer, you may make your vineger of wine white, red, or claret, but the red doth most binde the belly and white doth most lose. Also the Damaske Rose is not so great a binder as the red Rose, and the white Rose lose the most of all: whereof you may make vinegre russet. Thus also, you may make vinegre of violets, or of Elder flowers.[6]

A recipe for 'an excellent water for perfume' from Peter Levens' 1582 *The Pathway to Health* recommended a very full list of ingredients: a handful each of basil, mint, marjoram, corn-flag roots, hyssop, savoury, sage, balm, lavender and rosemary, half an ounce each of cinnamon, cloves and nutmeg, and three or four sliced citrons, all infused in damask water for three days, before being distilled over a charcoal fire. When it was ready, and put into a clean glass, a fine lawn bag was suspended in it containing musk fat, civet and ambergris, and boiled with lemon peel, bay leaves and cloves.[7] Distilling, or still room, recipes involved the infusion, brewing or distilling of ingredients in simmering water, making something like a modern essential oil for use in perfume, cooking or medicine.

Herbs and spices were also used to infuse items of clothing. Levens has a recipe for perfuming gloves with oils of sweet almonds, nutmeg and benjamin, and grains of ambergris and musk, ground upon a painter's stone and applied to gloves pre-soaked in rose water. A comparable recipe uses two spoons of cedar dust, a handful of moss from an apple tree, linseed (flaxseed) and gum dragon, with the gloves drying out in the sun or wind. It was also possible to perfume gloves by laying them in powder made from ingredients such as orris root, ground cloves, anise seeds and musk.

A tired jerkin could be cleaned and scented, according to Levens, by mixing oil of benjamin, spike (French lavender) and olive oil, warmed by the fire and rubbed into the leather using sponges.

Perfumed bracelets were recommended for women who wished to 'take men your prisoners', by using damask rosebuds, musk, ambergris and civet.[8] These recipes make clear that there was an overlap between cleanliness and attraction.

Powerful scents not only concealed bad odours but were attractive in themselves. As the antithesis of bodily stenches, illness and decay, they fooled the nose into believing in the wearer's good health, and those using expensive ingredients represented status, even the exotic and exciting.

As travel horizons broadened through the sixteenth century, new, exotic ingredients came into use. Most of these found their way onto trading routes that passed through Venice and are recorded in the import and export accounts of that city. Ambergris was collected from the shores of the Indian Ocean and was used as a tonic and 'exhilarating cordial'; the heady scented musk came from Asia 'and wherever the gazelle is found'; civet was brought from hyenas in the East Indies, as was the *Tignames* plant whose flowers were used in fumigation; and *Calamus verus*, a reed with a bitter pulp, and the bitter gum storax were found in Syria.

Henry VIII's favourite scent was a mixture of ambergris and civet, which would have been mixed with a binding base of either honey, beeswax or sesame oil. One such recipe he would have favoured required a quarter of a pound of damask rosebuds, a quarter of a pound of benjamin (benzoin gum or tree sap), 20 grains of civet and 10 grains of musk. As he aged, and the ulcerated sore on his leg could be smelt from the next room, powerful scents became even more important to a king determined to preserve his dignity. A quantity of civet and storax, as well as a gold casting bottle for sprinkling perfume, were found at Westminster in 1553.[9]

✤ WASTE DISPOSAL ✤

A fresh supply of water was an essential component of keeping body, clothing, homes, streets and cities clean. Attempts to harness springs and rivers were made all through the Tudor period, as the infrastructure for transporting water was constructed. In 1491, a deed was granted to Hugh Clopton, Mayor of London, to 'dig and break ground, where and as oft as need shall require' in a close called the Mews, and a garden called the Covent Garden on the land of Sir John Fortescue, in order to convey water to the city by conduit pipes.[1]

In 1580, the Lord Mayor and aldermen of London met with a German engineer named Peter Maurice, who presented them with a scheme 'for supplying the city with Thames water by a mill, to be worked by the water-all at the return of the tide under London Bridge'. Maurice was granted his request and leased one arch of the bridge, for 10s annual rent, obtaining a second arch two years later. The mill proved a success and continued to be run by Maurice's descendants until 1701. In 1594, an attempt was made to supply the western parts of the city 'by a horse engine, erected with four pumps at Broken wharf in Thames Street' but it proved too expensive to maintain.

One of the problems with the Thames supply was the quantity of waste that Londoners cast into it. The mayor was frequently required to forbid 'the casting of refuse' into the water as well as fishing nets from being drawn between Wapping and Durham Place or any individual fishermen between the Temple to the Tower 'upon pain of imprisonment of their bodies and losing the said nets ... and the fishes taken with the same'. The nets were to be burned in Chepe as a warning to others.[2]

Elsewhere, the use of local rivers to wash domestic and industrial products was carefully observed. In an Essex village in July 1593, three fullers, John Ingram, George Sewell and Anthony Bland, were fined for washing:

> thicked baye [baize] in a river near the house of the said John, by reason of which the water in the river aforesaid has become very noxious and insalubrious to the great harm of divers of the Queen's subjects dwelling nearby; and of the said Anthony for throwing filth in the said river, to the great harm likewise.[3]

Other proclamations prohibited the casting of animal remains into the river or its tributaries, unless they were finely chopped:

> The proclamation, further, notifies the appointment of John Petite, grocer, as overseer of the Thames from London Bridge westward, and Robert Lilly as overseer from London Bridge eastward. Moreover, butchers are forbidden to cast any inwardes of Bestes into the river, but if they be cutte in to small pecys.[4]

It was difficult enough keeping one's person clean when passing through a city. As early as 1461, a proclamation forbade the casting of dung or rubbish into the open streets and a Sergeant of the Channel was appointed, one John Homecastell, who was to patrol the city with constables of each ward 'and wherever they find mud or unclean thing, to distrain those whose duty it is to remove it and not to surrender the distress until a fine of four pence be paid to the chamber'. Further ordinances were passed at the start of the Tudor period, in April 1486, that fines should be imposed upon those who were negligent in cleaning the streets.[5]

In advance of Elizabeth's visit in 1575, the citizens of Worcester were instructed that 'every person having any dung hills ... within the liberties, shall cause the same to be carried away within ten days next and so shall keep clean their soils and pave the same with all convenient speed'.[6]

There would have been an overpowering stench of faeces from the common latrines, or jakes, usually erected over a tributary of the River Thames, or a ditch which allowed access for the gong farmer to clear away the nightsoil below. Wealthy citizens were starting to build their own closets, but this was a luxury most people could not yet afford, relying instead upon using chamber pots or the public houses of easement. The stench associated with such work saw the gong farmer being handsomely rewarded but confined to specific locations in the town, and some suffered fatal accidents carrying out their duties, such as drowning or asphyxiation.

Royal toilets enjoyed more comfort and privacy. Small garderobes had been incorporated into castle walls since medieval times, allowing the waste to fall down into the moat, but the introduction of a close stool with a bowl below contained the smell. The king was attended by a Groom of the Stool, an apparently unenviable post which literally entailed supporting Henry's hygienic practices but allowed an unprecedented degree of proximity and trust between master and servant. The groom had to be ready in attendance with a bowl of water and sponges or towel for the king 'to wipe the nether end'. Given the surviving details of Henry's bowel habits, which were often of long duration or the result of purgatives administered by his doctors, considerable wiping must have been required.

The close stool was next to the royal bedchamber and housed a casket covered in black velvet, with padded arms and seat, a lid, red sides and a gold fringe, held together by 2,000 gold nails. Inside was a bowl made of pewter, which was discreetly removed and cleaned afterwards.

Servants at the palace had to use the communal toilets, with little or no privacy, such as the great house of easement at Hampton Court, which could seat twenty-eight individuals at once. However, some still continued to relieve themselves in corners, passageways and fireplaces. In despair, the palace officials chalked crosses on the walls in the most polluted places, in an attempt to deter people from befouling a religious symbol.

The accumulating stench in royal palaces, as the royal family, their court and servants slept, ate and produced waste, was only tolerable for so long. When Henry VIII was in residence, his ordinances specified that his chambers be cleaned in advance of him waking in the morning, so he would 'find the said chamber pure, clean, wholesome and meet, without any displeasant air or thing, as the health, commodity and pleasure of his most noble person doth require'. The floors were strewn with fresh herbs, then pastilles and more herbs were burned to sweeten the air, and only sea coal, imported from the north, was used in the king's rooms.

The courtyards were swept several times a day by scullions, as the dust could 'putrefy the air', according to Andrew Boorde, and proved 'very noisome and displeasant to all the noblemen'.[7] After a few weeks, the smell of the toilets, dirty rush floors and filthy corners of the palace was overwhelming, and the court would move on to their next residence, allowing for a thorough cleaning to take place.

As the sixteenth century drew to a close, filthy streets were still giving offence. Sir John Harrington, who invented the first flushing toilet in 1596, commented that 'even in the goodliest and stateliest palaces in the realm notwithstanding provision of vaults, sluices and gates, or pains of poor folk in swilling and scouring, yet still this same whoreson saucy stink'.[8]

There was also a further ring of smells encircling the city to welcome visitors. The medieval walls had been built alongside a defensive ditch, which was frequently used as a dumping ground, with the worst section becoming known as Houndsditch in the east for the high number of dead dogs that were discarded there. The street running past it was paved in 1503, but it was not until 1595 that it was first considered desirable to level the ditch.

Towns and cities would have had their own collection of smells as the by-products of industry, too. In locations where particular professions dominated the market, those areas would have stunk of the particular tang of the tannery or the smelting of iron. A list of London professions made in the 1480s highlights some whose particular scents would have been known to their neighbours – some pleasant, some less so – tallow chandler, pastiller, fishmonger, maltman, vintner, cooks, slaughterers, brewer, leather makers, tanners, dyers, gunpowder makers, bakers and more. In addition, the sheer number of animals being driven through the streets to slaughter, and the disposal of their remains, as well as the sale of fish at Billingsgate, must have given those districts a particular odour of their own. The proximity of live animals, sharing the streets and being reared in gardens and outhouses, even under the same roof for poorer folk, introduced their own range of odours pertaining to urine, faeces, sweat, bedding, feeding, illness and death.

The first blast furnace was built to smelt iron in Newbridge, Sussex, in 1494 by the river, as water was needed to drive the bellows and mechanical hammers. By the 1560s, a number of ironworks had been established in South Wales and the West Midlands, creating localised pockets of smell and sound.

In 1559, Elizabeth's council forbade the manufacture of sugar within the realm 'for it is counterfeit and unwholesome' and only imports that were as 'pure and simple as it cometh out of the cane' were permitted to be sold.[9] The woad makers were considered particularly offensive, as the woad from which they extracted the blue dye was related to cabbages and stank during the process of fermentation, with the result that woad makers were often required to live outside towns and not permitted within 5 miles if the queen was visiting.

Conflict could arise between industry and its neighbours. In 1604, John Eldricke of East Ham was reported by his neighbours for making starch near the highway, 'wherefrom there was so much stench that the air, because infected thereby, to the annoyance of the inhabitants'.[10]

The process of running a home created a range of odours. Most houses were structured around the hearth, and the varied smells associated with it must have permeated the property: filtering through walls and doorways; up the chimney; absorbed into material and wafting up the stairs. This must have been particularly the case when the building was comparatively closed up during the colder winter months.

Keeping a house warm required the burning of wood, peat, coal or other substances, each of which produced a particular scent, depending upon the type of coal or variety and quality of wood. The wealthy used sea coal as it produced far less odour.

Creating light out of darkness was achieved by the burning of candles, but only the richer people could afford the pleasant-smelling beeswax versions, and others had to make do with the smelly, fatty tallow, or even burning oil.

Where cooking took place on a general fire, rather than a designated room, such as a kitchen, bakery or scalding house, the odours of food competed with the other smells of communal living spaces, including those of waste, animals, cottage industries, laundry and storage.

Bed linen, pillows, mattresses, blankets and straw were more likely to be aired than washed, and the worst smells could be masked by other, stronger ones, like woodsmoke. Bedding would have had its own particular odour.

At the start of the Tudor era, the poorest individuals, or servants sleeping in their masters' hall, bedded down on straw, which accumulated waste, fire and cooking smells, urine, sweat and spillages, although practical historians re-enacting the domestic interior have observed that these smelled less offensive over time than they had anticipated.[11] Tusser commented in the 1570s that the bottom layer of rushes might lie undisturbed for years, suggesting any smell was not noticeable or problematic.

Mattresses might be stuffed with whatever an individual could afford, from down to straw, hay or barley, although the favoured lady's bedstraw – the yellow *Galium verum* – retained its sweet scent even when old and dry. Wormwood was also incorporated to deter lice and fleas, which were a continual problem.

Public buildings also suffered from bad smells due to a general lack of cleanliness, but also from the habits of their patrons. Erasmus visited an inn and spent some time in its common room, where travellers were encouraged to 'pull off your boots, put on your shoes, change your shirt'. Observing his fellows, Erasmus noted how:

> one combs his head, another ... belches garlic and ... nothing is more dangerous than for so many to draw in the same vapour, especially when their bodies are opened with the heat ... not to mention the farting, the stinking breaths ... and without doubt many have the pox.[12]

The only way to avoid the stench of a number of people in a small space was literally to stay away.

✿ DEATH AND DECAY ✿

Just as can be the case in the modern world, the Tudors' response to the smell of disease and decay was to recoil. This biological defensive mechanism is intended to create physical distance, to lessen the ability of any lingering infection to act and keep the unpleasant aspects of mortality, such as decay, liquefaction or the presence of parasites at bay.

In a more sanitised era, this impulse can be overridden because the work of the emergency services, the NHS, the nature of undertakers' work and our modern methods of cremation place the majority of such interactions at one remove. Our pets can be humanely put to sleep, the animals we consume are slaughtered behind closed doors and presented on supermarket shelves in neat packages, our dead are cleaned up, removed, neatly boxed.

For the Tudors, the proximity of decaying bodies, most typically of animals but also potentially of corpses, especially in times of plague, brought a justified degree of fear. Contact with a contagious body, through vermin or potentially infected air, was a danger that could prove life threatening to those not just in close proximity, but within a fairly wide range.

The smell associated with dead bodies was particularly noxious and challenging to the Tudors because of their belief that odours could carry infection. In the 1480s, one rural church had difficulty recruiting any men willing to move leprous bodies to their graves, which was quite understandable given the highly contagious nature of the disease but failed to solve the problem of burial.

The heady scent of incense may have gone some way to masking any unpleasant odours inside churches when mourners came to the funeral service, and the censers were no doubt swung over open graves too. Smoke was also considered a powerful barrier and restorer of health and was frequently wafted to cover foul odours or applied as a 'fumigation', being blown into various human orifices with the intention that the hot, dry smoke would dry wet diseases, or restore life to victims of drowning.

When it came to royalty, bodies were embalmed as soon as possible, especially as they might be lying in state for a period of time or need to travel a distance to their burial. Prince Arthur died in April 1502 at Ludlow Castle and was embalmed almost at once, with his organs removed, the body cleansed and 'dressed with spices and other sweet stuff', before being sprinkled with holy water. He was then removed from Ludlow to Worcester, a journey which took two days in bad weather. Those less fortunate, whose final resting place might be a pauper's grave or plague pit, would be doused in lime in an attempt to limit the spread of infection.

There was also a moral dimension that came with the odour of death, especially towards those who may have lived immoral or incontinent lives. Claudius almost fears the discovery of his murder of old Hamlet, as the 'offense is rank, it stinks to heaven'.[1]

Conversely, the spiritual purity of saints in the pre-Reformation world was often characterised by the natural preservation of their bodies after death. Relics were reputed not to decay and emitted a sweet smell, or else the smell emanated from the wounds of stigmata. Saints in this condition are referred to as myroblytes, and modern science suggests such a smell might have been created by a state of ketosis, brought about by the saints fasting.

For the Tudors osmogenesia, or the 'smell of sanctity', was described as being comparable with the scent of flowers. When visiting their shrines, pilgrims might buy flasks that supposedly contained the odour of the saint, which might be harvested by the monks and referred to as 'manna'. One such flask from the shrine of St Nicholas was opened in the twentieth century and revealed to contain vegetable oil. The shrine of St William of York was even fitted with little taps to allow pilgrims to fill a phial from it, and was in use into the Tudor period.

Illness, which brought with it a warning, or shadow, of death, had its associated smells. Towards the end of his life, Henry VIII's varicose leg ulcers were kept open by physicians in the belief that closing them would direct the evil humours inwards. As a result, they became prone to frequent infection, the stench of which was so bad it could be smelt from several rooms away.

The problem appears to have begun with his fall from horseback in 1536 and soon prevented him from travelling, as he wrote to the Duke of Norfolk, 'To be frank with you, which you must keep to yourself, a humour has fallen into our legs and our physicians advise us not to go far in the heat of the day.'[2] At one point, he was so ill that the French ambassador wrote, 'For ten to twelve days the humours which had no outlet were like to have stifled him, so that he was sometime without speaking, black in the face and in great danger.'[3]

The final illness of Henry's son, Edward VI, produced odours that spoke of his imminent demise. In June 1553, it was reported that his legs were so swollen he had to lie on his back and 'the matter he ejects from his mouth is sometimes coloured a greenish yellow and black, sometimes pink like the colour of blood'.[4] Over a month elapsed before his burial, in the heat of the summer months. However, rumours of Henry VIII's coffin exploding and leaking liquids, which were licked up by dogs, probably owe more to subsequent propaganda.

Sometimes, as Hamlet suggests when he tells the guards they will 'nose' the dead Polonius when going up the stairs, smell could be an indicator of crime. In October 1571, a Mother Margery, who dwelt in the almshouse in Rye, was suspected of witchcraft and the mayor ordered a search of her property. There was uncovered 'a good quantity of raw beef', creating a terrible smell, which Margery had been using as a form of magic: as the meat decayed, so would the bodies of those against whom she bore malice. She was driven out of the town, which 'had not been troubled since'.[5]

The stench of the beef, revealing and confirming Margery's crime, was correlative with her moral corruption, and its decay mirrored her own downfall. The smell of death and decay was a warning sign to the Tudors of potential danger and they responded with distance, attempts to eradicate the cause of the odour, and the use of powerful counter scents.

Closely allied to the sense of taste, smell was often dichotomised in the Tudor world. Odours and, by association, their point of origin, were categorised into extremes of pleasantness or unpleasantness. This was an understandable response to real and perceived dangers and a reflection of their greater proximity to the life cycle in its entirety. It was also a function of class, though, as the wealthier could afford to keep themselves removed from such processes by the employment of servants, greater privacy and better methods of transport.

The dirtier and smellier an individual, the lower down the social scale they appeared, reinforced by aristocratic practices of wearing white, starched or impractical clothing to indicate they did not engage in physical labour, and the use of scent, symbolic of luxury. Those who could afford perfumes made from expensive imported grains and spices wore it as another badge of status. Thus, the association of high-class sweetness and lower-class stench was reinforced as a literal and metaphorical distinction. For the Tudors, a sense of smell was useful in two essential areas: it helped to preserve their safety and to recognise and define class.

PART III

SOUND

❧ MUSIC ☙

The Tudor song 'Pastime with Good Company' features regularly in film, documentaries and re-enactment events set in the sixteenth century. Attributed to Henry VIII in around 1513 or before, its sound has come to typify the timbre and style of Tudor music to the modern ear, with its varied volume, trilling high notes and slightly 'raspy' edgy feel to the voices, singing in polyphonic harmony. It was also a hit in the sixteenth century, in England and Scotland and across Europe, where it was known as the 'King's Ballad'. Music was ever present in the Tudor world, in churches, taverns and streets, but also as part of the elite experience, marking courtly entertainment, ceremonial occasions, ambassadors' visits, feasts, Christmas revels and long evenings. Henry VIII particularly loved music, amassing a huge collection of hundreds of instruments and employing sixty musicians at his court by 1547.

Foreign musicians were particularly prized, especially those from Italy. They were invited to play at court and in aristocratic households, with which they could also travel for the entertainment of their employer. The 1529 Trevelyan family papers show the wages for the month of October, which include twelve trumpets at 16*d* a day, and four more trumpets at 8*d* a day, four lutists, three rebecks, three tabrets, two viol players called Hans Hasnet and Hans Highorne, and nine sackbutists, some with the foreign-sounding names of John van Vinche, John van Herten, Lewes van Wincle, John and Mark Antonia, and Ipolit de Salvator.[1]

The Trevelyan papers also list the monthly wages made to players at Mary I's court for the year 1555. There were two lutists, brothers named Philip and Peter van Welder, one harper called Bernarde de Ponte, one player of the rebeck, seven players of the viol, including one from Milan and three from Venice, four sackbutists, one bagpiper, one drumslade, eight minstrels and two 'singing men'. John Heywood was listed as a player on the virginals, with which Mary herself had impressed the French ambassadors by playing in 1520 at the age of 4. There was also Robert Reynolds, a Welsh musician, five 'interlude players' and, by midsummer, a flautist named Piro Guye.[2]

When Elizabeth visited Worcester in 1575, the trumpeters would have been busy announcing her approach and then her arrival, wherever she went, and were rewarded with the large sum of £1 10s. The drums and flutes, probably used for entertainment, received 5s and the generic musicians were paid 6s 8d.

Elizabeth was accompanied by Robert Dudley, who brought his own troop of musicians, who were rewarded with 6s 8d, in addition to whatever retaining fee he was paying them. Music clearly featured in the pageantry to welcome the queen to the city; £4 was paid to Mr Lupton 'for his pains for devising and instructing the children' of the choir, and those who gave speeches, and 31s 7d to Mr Heywood for providing entertainment with six children upon two stages. Elizabeth visited the tomb of her long-dead uncle, Prince Arthur, where there was 'great and solemn noyse of singing in service in the quire, both by rote and also, playing with cornets and sackbutts', followed by a reading and sermon.[3]

Tudor instruments were considered to belong to the loud or soft category, and the harsh notes of a trumpet or cornet were less prized than the soft, subtle tones of strings. Among the string family, the harp was usually smaller than the big free-standing instrument of today, but was strung across a triangular board. The lute was popular among the nobility and had between six and thirteen strings, while the fiddle was simple in design and easily portable, making it a common choice among the lower classes.

Various other prototypes of the violin were used, such as the little rebeck with its teardrop shape, the sound of which was compared to a woman's voice, and the vielle and very similar viol, which were like a violin but with a longer body, held on the lap or between the knees and played with a bow. There was also a cittern, or gittern, an ancestor of the modern guitar, strung with metal and shaped like a violin, and a psaltery, a triangular cross between a guitar and harp, from the zither family.

Among the percussion instruments were tambours, which were small drums of all shapes, and the related tambourine, with skin stretched across a frame, set with small cymbals round the edge. There was also a portable triangle, which was suspended and struck with a metallic stick, much like the modern version.

The harpsichord family contained the spinet, which was a smaller version of an upright piano with strings struck by hammers operated with a keyboard; the virginals, which were smaller and often lacked legs, needing to be placed upon a table; and the quieter clavichord, used as an accompaniment. Very similar in appearance, all these keyboard instruments tended to be referred to as simply 'virginals' or 'a pair of virginals', even though it was only one instrument and had a similar sound, paradoxically high and tinny but soft.

The wind instruments included the loud, medieval sackbut, an early trombone with a small bell flare and two parallel sliding tubes, and the shawm, a long wooden instrument with a double reed and bell flare, made in a variety of sizes. The trumpet, or buisine, and smaller clarion were the loudest, being used to summon and announce, and could be straight, curved or sliding. The flute and recorder were straight, small and portable, while the crumhorn was a similar instrument with a curved end and an encased reed which meant it only had the range of an octave.

Perhaps the most accessible and universal of Tudor instruments was the human voice, either singing alone or as part of a choir. The fashion in song was for polyphonic harmonies, taught to the royal choirs and in individual lessons, often to children. Writing in 1596, singing teacher William Bathe explained the importance of following simple rules when it came to learning to sing, and recounted his experience with pupils:

In a moneth and less, I instructed a child about the age of eight yeares, to sing a good number of songs, difficult crabbed Songs, to sing at the first sight, to be so indifferent for all parts, alterations, Clefs, flats, and sharpes, that he could sing a part of that kinde, of which he never learned any song, which child for strangeness was brought before the Lord Deputie of Ireland, to be heard sing: for there were none of his age, though he were longer at it, nor any of his time, (though he were elder) knowne before these rules to sing exactly.

There was another, that had before often handled Instruments, but never practised to sing (for he could not name one Note) who hearing of these rules, obtained in short time, such profit by them, that he could sing a difficult song of himselfe, without any Instructor.

There was another, who by dodging at it, hearkning to it, and harping upon it, could never be brought to tune sharps aright, who so soone as he heard these rules set downe for the same, could tune them sufficiently well.[4]

Bathe expands upon the types of notes, their location on the stave, their length and the difference between chords that were in harmony and those that were discord, the importance of timing and the need to have a great quantity of breath.[5]

The Tudor era saw the rise of composers as stars at the court. The early years of the dynasty resounded with the music of Robert Fayrefax, who led the Chapel Royal Choir with William Cornish at the Field of Cloth of Gold, and whose masses, songs and instrumentals were played at the courts of Henry VII and Henry VIII. Cornish was Master of the Children of the Chapel Royal.

Both died in the early 1520s, just before the influx of cultural and religious change, but their work continued to influence later musicians, especially Thomas Tallis, who worked at Dover Priory, Waltham Abbey and Canterbury Cathedral before he became a Gentleman of the Chapel Royal in 1543, serving all the subsequent Tudor monarchs. Tallis worked with William Byrd and Robert Parsons, who wrote a new kind of religious music to express the changes that had taken place in the faith. After Parsons' premature death in 1572, Tallis and Byrd were granted a licence for the printing of music and the musical score paper required for composition.

Towards the end of Elizabeth I's reign, John Mundy and Thomas Morley were among the first composers of Italian-style madrigals, or love poems set to music for a group of voices. While some works by the elitist musicians were heard in closed circles, some found greater audiences as popular hymns and are even still played today.

One source of music to which the lower classes had regular access were the town waits. Associated with a particular place, this was a local band summoned to play in the streets, at fairs, weddings and funerals, and other important occasions, or hired to entertain private citizens in their homes. The instruments they favoured were light and portable, such as the fiddle, lute, recorder and small percussion pieces. The performance of the waits was dependent upon context – the location and reason for playing – just as informal social 'music' was, stretching to include charivari or 'rude music', which was improvised with whatever items lay to hand to express public approval or disapproval.

There was also a strong oral tradition of public poetry and storytelling in taverns, pageants and upon temporary stages, extending the old morality play traditions. While these allowed for embellishment and interpretation, the Tudors valued the skill of recounting an old story far more than the imagination required to create a new one. As listeners, the Tudors would have to have been particularly adept audience members, with the ability to decode sounds in context.

⚘ MEASURING AND WARNING ⚘

A cockerel right under your bedroom window can crow at around 130 decibels, the equivalent sound of a small jet engine taking off. No wonder they were considered such an effective means of rousing sixteenth-century sleepers, with their distinctive cock-a-doodle-doo. The bird's call appears throughout the literature of the period, signalling the arrival of dawn as Hamlet watches his father's ghost disappear, or when Macbeth's porter goes to sleep, or when Richard III realises the day of battle has arrived.

Thomas Tusser described the cock's crow in 1577 as a means of passing a winter's night: he claimed they crowed a few times at midnight 'with pause to his neighbour, to answer betwixt', again at three, then again at Matins, which might be any time between three and dawn. However, they did not just limit themselves to the task of waking the world, but 'uttered their language as well they may', giving 'counsel' as long as they live. Tusser warned sleepy maids to rise before their employers had to wake them: 'Take heed good maid: mark crowing of cock, for fear of a knock … lest quickly your Mistress uncover you bare.'[1]

For those living in or near a monastic establishment, the hours of the day were marked out by the bells chiming for the canonical hours, the times fixed for prayer in the Catholic Church. Matins was the morning watch, often beginning at two or three and ending at dawn, although the bell would only be rung at the start of that period, not throughout. When the dawn arrived, usually around six or later in winter, marking the first hour of the day, the bell tolled for Prime, after which psalms were read. The third hour, Terce, was marked around nine in the morning, followed by Sext, at noon, both involving the reading of more psalms. The ninth hour, or None, was at three in the afternoon, followed by Vespers at sunset and Compline at bedtime, with the end of the daily cycle at Midnight Office.

Although not all monks would have attended all these occasions, the ringing of bells at three-hourly intervals throughout the day and night would have been a persistent reminder of the passing of time, and a considerable interruption to those living nearby. Otherwise, where the rules were being strictly obeyed, monastic establishments would have been characterised by song and silence.

Bells marked a call to prayers in the secular world, too. A visitor to London in 1580 heard upon arriving, 'a great ringing of bells in almost all churches going on very late in the evening, and also on the following days until seven or eight in the evening'. The visitor was told that 'the young people ... for the sake of exercise and amusement ... lay considerable sums of money as a wager, who will pull a bell the longest or ring it in the most approved fashion'. The churches had spent 'much money on harmonious sounding bells' and Elizabeth was 'very much pleased by this exercise, considering it as a sign of the health of the people'. The bells were not rung to mark death, he explained, but 'when a person lies in agony, the bells of the parish he belongs to are touched with the clappers until he either dies or recovers'.[2] This would incite everyone in the vicinity to pray for the invalid in their hour of need.

Bells would mark the time to rise in the morning and to go to bed. The evening curfew bell, rung between seven and ten, depending upon the season, was literally the time to *couvre-feu*, or 'cover the fire'. The centrally burning logs would be taken off and put to the side, with the cold ashes raked back over the heat, allowing the fire to smoulder safely. It might also then be covered by a curfew bell, a bell-shaped pot with vents to allow steam to escape, but not sparks. However, by Shakespeare's time, the curfew bell had lost its associations with fire and was merely a measurement of the day's structure, as Shakespeare refers to the waking bell rung at three or four in the morning as the 'curfew' bell. Intended to rouse workers in the summer, it was rung for an unpopular fifteen minutes.

During the Tudor period, the curfew bell was rung from the small wooden turret on top of the Bell Tower in the Tower of London. Shortly after, the city gates would be locked until dawn and the watch patrolled the streets.

Particularly in rural locations, the sound of the bell ringing out through the falling dusk, or in mist or fog, could also have guided people home. In 1512, the priest Roger Lupton only found his way back to Cropredy in Oxfordshire by following the sound of the bell.

He showed his gratitude by making a donation of over £6 for maintenance of the church's clock, by which the correct hour to ring the bell would have been judged.

Bells were one of the most significant and regular sounds of Tudor England. They emanated from the parish church, which was usually, geographically and emotionally, the heart of the village, and were scattered throughout towns – the city of Norwich boasted fifty-two churches. The volume of bells made them impossible to ignore, refusing to be contained by boundaries and cutting above the usual noise of the marketplace.

Bells were representative of the voice of authority and the bond in a community, and even sometimes a state of rebellion when a new, urgent sort of community attempted to rebel against the existing order. For rebels to take control of the parish bells in order to summon people to their cause was a bold and symbolic act.

Individual bells were even given names of their own, which might be engraved upon them, and their tone could be recognised by those who heard them regularly. The bells were like old friends, coming into the home and workplace, bringing reminders of the daily, domestic and the immortal. Although the early morning alarm might be resented, bells were welcomed and needed; they were not intrusive sounds, but were listened to, and helped give structure to the day and to life. With their multitude of meanings, bells helped order the world, and helped the Tudors function as part of a community.

❦ PROCLAIMING NEWS ❦

The most immediate and effective way of spreading news was by word of mouth. Proclamations were made by heralds, sheriffs, aldermen and clergy in marketplaces, at crosses and in pulpits, when important information needed disseminating. Those present would then go and spread the word.

When it related to cases of treason, or the enforcement of the law, ignorance was no defence, so it was the duty of every citizen to use the oral networks of every family, parish and community. In 1487, the impending invasion of the pretender Lambert Simnel prompted a royal proclamation to be read across the land:

> Forasmuch as many of the King our Sovereign lordes, for forged sub-
> jects be disposed daily to hear fained contrived and forged tidings
> and tales, and the same tidings and tales, nether dreding God nor
> his highness utter and tell again as though they were true to the
> great hurt of divers of his subjects, and to his grievous displeasure.
> Therefore, in eschewing of such untrue and forged tidings and tales,
> the king our sovereign lord, straitly chargeth and commandeth that
> no manner person whatsoever he be, utter nor tell any such tidings
> or tales, but he bring forth the same person the which was author
> and teller of the said tidings or tales, upon pain to be set on the pil-
> lory there to stand as long as I shall be thought convenient unto the
> Mayor, bailiff or other officer of any city, borough or town when it
> shall happen any such telling or reporting.[1]

Bells could be rung in times of local and national emergency: fire,
flood, accident, invasion, disaster. They were also rung to signal the
presence of leaders, the spread of dissent and a call to arms. Every
parish church had at least one bell, typically three or four but often
more: larger churches and cathedrals might have eight, ten or twelve.
Bishop Hugh Latimer said, in 1552, 'If all the bells in England were
rung at one time, there would scarcely be a single spot where a bell
would not be heard.'

Early in 1537, Robert Aske, who was the leader of the religious
uprising, the Pilgrimage of Grace, was passing through Yorkshire on
his way back from meeting the king:

> Early next morning, at Burton Statur, he passed over Trent into
> Marshland, Yorks., where the people were in great rumour. Seeing
> Aske, who, they heard, was a leader in Lincolnshire, they wished to
> ring their bells, but he advised them not to be the first to rise, but to
> wait till they heard Houden bells rung.[2]

When the Spanish Armada was sighted off Plymouth in August 1588,
the bells were rung, along with the beacons being lit, as the fastest way
to rouse the populace and gather the trained bands. Important royal
news was proclaimed in the same way, often to the accompaniment
of ringing bells or gunshots, to alert the populace of a development.

Reliance upon word of mouth could be flawed, and the further
one was geographically distanced from the source of the news, the

greater the uncertainty. When information was anticipated, it could
arrive prematurely. In the summer of 1553, Sir Philip Hoby was based
in Brussels as reports of the declining health of Edward VI filtered
through. On 25 June, he reported that the night before, 'there came to
them one Evered, the King's jeweller dwelling at Westminster', who
had come from Antwerp and told them that there, 'it was reported
for truth, and wagers were laid, not only that Edward VI was dead,
but also that Mary had succeeded'.[3] As it happened, Edward did not
die until 6 July, and Mary's succession was complicated by the proclamation of Jane Grey as queen. When Mary eventually rode into the
capital, all the church bells rang out in welcome.

Coupled with bells and gunshot, fireworks were popular with the
Tudors to mark special occasions. Franciscan monks had been the first
to experiment with saltpetre in the thirteenth century, creating 'a roar
of strong thunder and a flash brighter than the brightest of lightning'.
A display had been mounted to celebrate the wedding of Henry VII and
Elizabeth of York in 1486, ushering the dynasty in with a bang.

Perhaps the most dazzling pyrotechnic event of the sixteenth century, though, was held at Kenilworth Castle to mark the queen's
visit to Robert Dudley in 1572. While Elizabeth gazed at the coloured sparks, an unexpected wind made the fire rain down upon the
nearby town, burning houses to the ground, for which the queen
paid the occupants £25 in compensation. When she returned to
Kenilworth in 1575, for her more famous long stay, Dudley ensured
the display was safer. A letter written by an eyewitness, Robert
Laneham, described it as a:

> blaze of burning darts, flying to and fro, leams of stars Coruscant,
> streams and hail of fiery sparks, lightnings of wildfire on water and
> land, flight and shoots of thunderbolts: all with such ... terror and
> vehemence, that the heavens thundered, the waters scourged, the
> earth shook ... It would have made me for my part, as hardy as I am,
> very vengeably afeard.

The fireworks were so loud in the quiet countryside that they were
rumoured to have been heard 20 miles away.

A record made in the 1570s of ingredients kept in the Tower for the making of fireworks included camphor, sal ammoniac, vitriol, arsenic, mercury sublimate, roses, aqua vitae, linseed oil, verdigris, turpentine and asafoetida.[4] Contemporary manuals indicate that among the Tudors' favourites were rockets and fountains, so the visual impact of a display was equalled by its sound. Elizabeth enjoyed firework displays so much she appointed an official Fire Master of England.

Word of mouth was an important way of passing on important information. Even with increasing levels of literacy, the dominant culture was an oral one, with practical knowledge transmitted through speech. The court records are full of references to 'good fame', or a community's response to an individual, and corresponding recommendations or warnings concerning their morals or business, history or trustworthiness. What people said about one another mattered and could determine their reliability as a witness and their success in a field of work, even their marital chances.

When a woman named Joan found the body of Margaret Pilgrim in 1559, who had drowned, she was not considered as a potential murderer, being 'of good name and fame'.[5] Likewise, William, who found the body of a dead infant in 1589, 'indeed is, and from the time or his birth up to now, was of good name and fame'.[6] However, Agnes Mason of Great Baddow must have been unpopular in her community, as she was reported in 1590 as living 'idly and is of evil fame'.[7]

Word of mouth was an essential tool in the transmission of female knowledge. With men excluded from the birth room as common practice, it was the job of midwives, relations, friends and 'gossips' – godsibs or godparents – to use their collective wisdom of their own experiences and those they had witnessed. Through the generations, methods of dealing with and surviving labour were actively demonstrated and discussed.

Although a few remedies were committed to the page, these tended to be authored by male physicians, who lacked the practical experience of delivery, or confined to family receipt books for a limited audience. The significance of sharing histories and stories pertaining to birth, and those used to amuse and while away the long month of confinement, was central to the maternal experience. Oral networks such as these were rooted in generations and the interconnection of friends and family groups, especially in the smaller towns and villages. Speech could be a gendered experience, in contrast to the written word, and it was there that most 'unrecorded' Tudor women's contributions were made.

⚘ GOSSIP AND SEDITION ⚘

Many different forms of Tudor literature condemn gossip as a destructive activity and equate loose governance of the tongue with loose governance of the mind and body. The 1526 Tudor book of jokes, *The Hundred Merry Tales*, warns:

> The tongue should not run at large, but be hidden as a precious treasure. For of all the members of man, the tongue ill-ordered is the worst. The tongue blasphemeth God, the tongue slandereth thy neighbour, the tongue breaketh peace and stirreth up cruel war, of all things to mankind most mischiefull, the tongue is a broker of bawdry, the tongue setteth friends at debate: the tongue with flattery, detraction and wandering tales infecteth pure and clean minds.[1]

Thomas Tusser's 1577 'A Sonnet Against a Slanderous Tongue' concludes, 'No more doth good a peevish slanderous tounge, But hurts it selfe, and noise [annoys] both old and young',[2] but this did not deter the Tudor tongues from waggling.

In court records, voices are usually recorded in the form of direct speech when the spoken words were troublesome. This might take the form of gossip, of one neighbour slandering the good name of another, treasonous utterances against the monarch or opposition to religious tenets.

The proximity of houses in towns and the lack of privacy led to cases of words being overheard through doors, windows and in gardens, and often passed on to the authorities by neighbours. Other significant locations where gossip and slander were reported as taking place were taverns, marketplaces and churches. Those found accused could be sent to prison or whipped in public; if the offence constituted heresy or treason, they might even be condemned to death.

Sometimes, it was impossible to overestimate the importance of a few words. When the validity of Prince Arthur and Catherine of Aragon's marriage was being investigated in 1529 to establish whether Henry VIII had grounds for an annulment, the witnesses who had been present to hear the young groom's words in 1501 were summoned to repeat them.

The morning after the ceremony, Arthur had appeared flushed and thirsty, 'good and sanguine', calling for a drink as he had spent the night 'in the midst of Spain' and that it was a 'good pastime to have a wife'. His chosen phrase, 'in the midst of Spain', with its obvious physical implication, could refer to sex, or metaphorically to Catherine's company, and her body as the symbolic representation of Spain. It was likely to have been the boast of a shy young man, who did not wish to lose face before his friends, but almost thirty years later, the case turned around those words.

Arthur Willoughby was the man from whom the prince had requested a cup of ale, and made his deposition in 1529:

> He was five years in the service of prince Arthur, for five years before that in the service of the bishop of Durham, and before that time in his father's household ... and was present at the marriage of prince Arthur and lady Catharine. By favour of his father, lord Broke, steward of the King's household, he was present when prince Arthur went to bed on his marriage night in the palace of the bishop of London. In the morning the prince, in the presence of Mores St. John, Mr. Cromer, Mr. William Woddall, Mr. Griffith Rice, and others, said to him, 'Willoughby, bring me a cup of ale, for I have been this night in the midst of Spain;' and afterward said openly, 'Masters, it is good pastime to have a wife.' He, therefore, supposes that the marriage was consummated; and he heard that they lay together the Shrovetide following at Ludlow.[3]

In August 1535, after Henry had put Catherine of Aragon aside for Anne Boleyn, John Horsey of Bridgwater reported David Leonard, an Irish hooper, for saying, 'God save king Henry and queen Catherine, his wedded wife, and Anne at his pleasure, for whom all England shall rue.' He was sent to gaol to 'await the King's pleasure'.[4]

Two years later, a glover of Southwark named Richard Birche was overheard on a boat from London to Greenwich, saying:

The King and his Council had sent proclamations to the North that no children should be christened unless there were a tribute paid to the King, and many children were unchristened for a fortnight or three weeks because their fathers and mothers were not able to pay.[5]

An assorted group of men signed the letter containing this accusation, presumably those who had travelled in the boat with Birche: Ninian Saunderson, a citizen of London; Richard Corke, a citizen and armourer of London; Humfrey Sexton, a citizen of Limerick; and Thomas White, a servant of Lord Jasper Butler. His suggestion of the king's manipulation of this important rite was not appreciated, but what happened to him as a result is not recorded.[6]

Two other men, a priest called Thomas Anderson and Robert Jenyns of Rutland, deposed before Sir Everard Digby that John Gurle, the master of Manton, had said, 'The king used too many women to be able to get a child of his queen.' A priest employed in Gurle's house had also remarked that the 'king was a poller and shaver of the realm'.[7]

With all the rapid changes resulting from the Reformation, even those in positions of authority were concerned about misspeaking, especially in the public forum of the pulpit. Early in 1536, the Archbishop of York heard an alarming report from one of his servants about Sir Robert Constable. Reputedly, Constable was 'not content with certain words that he [York] wrote to Lord Darcy', regarding a certain Markham, which he denied: 'The said words were reported to the archbishop by credible men, with more.' The archbishop asserted that he had 'never heard anything of Markham' and supposed that Constable 'said this of good mind to appease them, but he has no need to make amends'. Now, the prelate was 'loath to speak in the pulpit anything for which he had afterwards to make amends'. He wrote that it would be 'great folly to speak there what he could not avow … to likely danger of the body and undoubted danger of the soul'. He prayed Constable to let the words pass.[8]

In 1560, after Elizabeth I had been on the throne for almost two years, the wife of her married favourite died in mysterious circumstances. She had made her preference known for her handsome Master of the Horse, Robert Dudley, keeping him constantly at her side and inciting rumour. That February, a barber from Totnes called John Whyte was in the house of John Leche, with three other men, when one Thomas Burley, 'known by the name of drunken Burley', had

said that 'Lord Robert Dudley did swive [have sex with] the Queen'.[9]
When, that September, Dudley's wife Amy was found at the bottom of
a flight of stairs at Cumnor Place with her neck broken, the finger of
suspicion pointed to Dudley and the queen. Elizabeth had to be above
such slander, so she banished Dudley from court, but tongues were
already wagging. A few weeks later, one Arthur Cotton cast asper-
sions upon the queen's intentions to a George Gunter:

> That ere this my Lord Robert's wife is dead, and she broke her neck,
> but it is in a number of heads that the Queen will marry him. If
> she do, you shall see a great stir, for my Lord is sure of the Earl of
> Pembroke, and the Lord Rich, with divers others, be ready, with the
> putting up of his finger, and then you shall see the White Horse
> bestir himself, for my Lord is of great power, but a man shall have a
> ruffian with a dag to dispatch him out of a shop.[10]

Elizabeth's marital situation continued to provide her subjects with
gossip. In 1564, John Hales, gentleman, was indicted for having 'pre-
sumptuously and contemptuously discussed both by words and in
writing' the question of the succession to the imperial crown in case
the queen should die without issue.[11]

The spoken word mattered in court. Witnesses were asked to rely
upon memory and recall and recount events accurately, often citing
examples of direct speech. Thus, words spoken in haste or drunkenly
in the tavern, or in moments of duress, could be represented, even
reinterpreted, by others and given a permanence, by being recorded
by court scribes. In 1588, Elizabeth Callys was a midwife in Essex,
attending the unmarried Ursula Cleveland during her delivery. Her
account summarises her own speech on that occasion, and repeats, as
far as she can be accurate, what Ursula said:

> This deponent says that, being with Ursula Cleveland at the time
> of her delivery, she demanded of her who was the father of her
> child, and the said Ursula would make her no answer at all; then
> this examinant urged her again to tell who was the father, 'and ye
> said Ursula wold make noe aunswere but onelie our father, which

answere she made unto her diverse tymes'. This examinant said
unto her, 'why thow naughty pack, thow hast heretofore saied it was
Sympson', and the said Ursula said 'Sympson, Sympson'; then this
examinant said unto her 'Thow saiedst allsoe it was Nobles', and
the said Ursula would say nothing thereunto. 'And ye said Ursula
beyng better recovered after her sowndinge, and before that she was
delyvered, saied divers tymes, Ah woe be to the Sympson: and this
examinant asked her where he had carnally to do with her, and she
said at Redfannes, and this examinant asked here where there, and
she answered 'In the Coate.'

The scribe added the circumstances of the confession: 'this deponent
says that at such time as the said Ursula uttered these words she was
in great peril of her life, and to her thinking more likely to die than
to live'.[12] Ursula herself added, under examination, that Sympson had
threatened her that 'if she did betray him, he would kill her'.[13]

In 1592, a murder plot was uncovered in Rothesthorne, near
Chester, when the conspirators were overheard finalising their plans
to kill fishmonger George Hall. The would-be murderers, 'certain lewd
people having little or nothing to live on', by 'devilish instigation and
bloody conspiracy', were overheard by Isabell Johnson, wife of James
Johnson, who repeated their words and gave evidence against them in
court. Hall had been too afraid to continue to trade and had stayed in
the houses of friends, as one local bailiff had released the conspirators:

> And forasmuch as said supplicant dare not travail for his living to
> markets to use his said trade of fishemonger neither come at his
> owne house havinge lain amongst his friendes this sixteen weekes
> past: consumynge his substance without any gaine to his utter
> impoverishment he having procured warrant of good abearing
> against the said wicked persons and caused theme arrested there-
> upon by one John Brachgirdell bailiff to the sheriff that now is.
> Which Brachgirdell favoring the said evill persons suffered theme to
> escape unbound. To your supplicantes great peril of life.[14]

Ultimately, George Hall owed his life to the presence of Isabell
Johnson, who had been in the right place at the right time to overhear
the plotters. The spoken word could condemn those who were not
careful about their audience.

❧ DOMESTIC SOUNDS ❧

Tudor homes lacked privacy and soundproofing in comparison with their modern equivalents. The poorer inhabitants, sharing communal space, were unable to avoid the familiar sounds of bodily functions: coughing, sneezing, snoring, belching and farting. Servants sleeping in their employer's hall; apprentices sharing the workspace; town houses with narrow partitions and families in close proximity all held different standards of personal space and acceptance or tolerance levels of noise. Something as intimate as sexual intercourse must have been overheard in many homes and dormitories, such as that in which Catherine Howard lived as a young woman, which later provided witnesses to her experience with men.

For everyone below the monarch's family, bath houses and toilets were communal, with the largest 'jakes' often seating a dozen or more. Sounds of illness, pain, grief and childbirth would also have been closer and more familiar, especially among larger, mixed households. Even those in attendance upon royalty, sleeping on the floor, at the foot of the bed or outside the door, had little privacy for their own bodily functions or protection from those of others. The sounds of life continuing must also have abounded: the wheels of carts, fires crackling, voices calling, singing, laughing, crying, arguing. Work would have generated noise too: cutting, building, scraping, spinning, water running, pans bubbling.

The sounds of animals and birds must have been very familiar to the Tudors, even in the cities: from the cockerel who crowed in the morning to birds singing at dawn and dusk, dogs barking, horses' hooves, rats scrabbling in the walls, pigs snorting and cats fighting. Cities and towns still provided a home to many creatures. Many more gardens existed in Tudor London than today, even attached to modest homes, where chickens or a pig were kept outside, dogs and cats roamed the streets, chasing vermin, and horses were stabled at inns, at large houses and in public stables. Most large towns had a slaughter market, to which animals were driven through the already crowded streets, in an unfamiliar, perhaps terrifying, final journey during which their voices must have been heard. The practice of chasing a fox through the streets, or the departure into the countryside in order to hunt, would have brought large packs of dogs in its wake with their excited yelping and barking, followed by the clatter of horses' hooves.

In the countryside, where most people lived on a farm of some scale, the sounds of animals were part of the daily routine. The first and last tasks of the day would be to feed the livestock, which might also be herded, sheared, moved or worked during the day. Oxen, cows, horses, sheep and pigs were the most commonly owned larger animals, whose bellows, bleats and squeals were a measure by which the farmer could judge the state of their health, comfort and compliance.

Outside the confines of farm and field, the woods might be home to smaller creatures like foxes and badgers, with their night-time cries, but also to stag, deer and wild boars. The Tudors would have known the cries of vermin caught in the claws of a bird of prey, the swoop of a falcon, the squeal of a stoat, the cry of an owl.

Tudor ears would have been finely tuned to familiar noises and swift to detect the unfamiliar. On 8 March 1581, Dr Dee recorded an unusual sound in his diary, which he was at a loss to explain. 'It was the eighth day, being Wednesday', he wrote, between ten or eleven at night, when he heard 'the strange noise in my chamber of knocking, and the voice, ten times repeated, somewhat like the screech of an owl, but more longly drawn, and more softly, as it were, in my chamber'. Later that year, on 3 August, he reported, 'All the night, very strange knocking and rapping in my chamber.'[1] Whether Dee was experiencing a supernatural phenomenon, hearing noises from next door or simply dreaming, the noise was significant enough for him to notice it as an oddity.

Sometimes sound was used as a cover for crime. The playwright Robert Greene accused professional ballad singers of drawing in crowds for the benefit of pickpockets, who then operated among them: 'This trade, or rather unsufferable loitering quality, in singing of ballets [sic] and songs at the doors of such houses where plays are used, as also in open markets and other places.' It was often the use of the human voice which led to the apprehension of such thieves, though. When a pickpocket was detected, the victim would shout out loud for help, drawing those around them into a public clamour called a 'hue and cry'. This worked on the premise that sound could travel faster than the thief, so all those in the vicinity were roused to help try to catch him.

Language, intended to connect, could also serve to create division, especially among differing nationalities. Living in Spain and speaking Spanish brought out the typical English xenophobia in serving man John Bradford, which he expressed in a letter of warning to leading members of the council in 1556. Mary I had then been married to Philip of Spain for two years:

> But in shewing what is pretended to the contrary declare unto you the way, if it please you to followe my counsell, how to preserve your lordshipes, and the whole realme, from most miserable bondage and captivite. I purpose to declare a part of the naturall disposicion of Spaniardes: certayne of their premeditate mischefs, and pretended treasons, not onely against your most honorable persons, but also agaynst the whole realme: so farre, as I haue heard, seene and proved, for the space of two or three yeares in their companye.
>
> My frendes putte me to learne their language and compelled me to live amongest them, because myghte knowe perfectlye, whether their nature were so vile, as men reported, or not. And I assure your lordshipes, and all my frendes, that the least reporte, that ever I heard Englishmen speake, by the worste of all Spaniardes, is nothinge to the vileness which remaineth amongest the best of that nation, except the kings majestie.[2]

Careful to avoid treason at the end, Bradford expresses the typical antagonism in Anglo-Spanish relations which came to fruition in the rebellion of Thomas Wyatt, the English piracy of the 1580s and the Armada. Yet, it is clear that language was a trigger for his latent dislike; by speaking Spanish, his feelings were intensified.

The Tudors would all have sounded different when they spoke. Busy streets in towns and cities must have been particularly full of the human voice, in all its different degrees of volume, timbre and pitch. Cosmopolitan places like London also received large numbers of visitors, with accents from the English provinces, Ireland, Scotland, Wales and overseas. Travellers and merchants from all around the known world landed at London's docks or rode up from the coastal ports, bringing their wares to court or to the marketplaces. The differences in English dialect would have been apparent, as is clear from the spelling variations of key words, with their shifts in vowel sounds, such as the Scottish favouring the 'i', where the English often used an 'e', and the harsher Scots 'qw' for the English 'w' or 'wh'.

Before the standardisation of spelling, words upon paper reflected their sound, so that even the names of people and places were fluid. The spelling in ambassadors' letters betrayed their roots, with Imperial ambassador Chapuys' spelling of Cromwell as 'Cremuel',[3] while Thomas himself often signed off as 'Crumwell'.

According to the Tudors' use of words in poetry, especially when the syllabic rhythm or the rhyme depends upon them, it is possible to identify shifts in pronunciation. Most silent letters today were pronounced in the sixteenth century; for example, words ending with '-ng' and '-ght' had each of those letters sounded, as were the 'k' in knight and knot, the 'w' in sword, the 'b' in lamb, while the 'h' was often dropped, in the French style for honour, hour and heir.

The Tudor soundscape was one dominated by natural elements: the human voice and expression, animals, and even the weather, mixed with a balance of ordered and unordered sounds. Those reflecting order were the ringing of bells, church and monastic chanting and hymns, theatre, performance, news and music, in which the human voice or instruments were used to deliver a message or an experience. By contrast, conversation, gossip, rabble, riot, work and transaction noise were more occasion driven, with less planning and often to the detriment of the peace.

The experience of sound was an internal one, specific and local, understood by relating it to context. Sound was also a social barometer: to judge class and origin; to assess obedience and the mood in the streets. Listening required a process of evaluation in the individual to understand, assess and prioritise sounds as indicators of their immediate environment. Sound is difficult to recapture. It is of its moment: brief, ephemeral and uncontainable. Through the transcription of Tudor music, the modern world is able to hear the sounds that pleased the sixteenth-century ear, but the soundscape of the twenty-first century, with all its technological intrusions, bears little resemblance to that of our forebears.

PART IV
TASTE

❦ DINING HABITS ❦

Nothing evokes the experience of royal Tudor cooking quite like the kitchens at Hampton Court Palace. Thousands of modern visitors traipsing through those red brick walls connect with the past through its appeal to their senses – the smell of woodsmoke, the texture of bread, the sound of the fire crackling – transporting them back in the busiest hub of the palace, where the most sumptuous of feast days and the leanest fast days of the Catholic calendar were catered for.

Extended in 1529–32 to feed hundreds of members of the court, the kitchens covered a huge area of 3,000 square feet and fifty-five rooms, far larger than what is on display to the public today. When stretched to their maximum capacity, such as entertaining the French ambassadors in August 1546, they catered for 1,300 members of the royal household and 200 of the French company. A Spaniard in the entourage of Philip, husband of Mary I, described them as 'veritable hells, such is the stir and bustle in them ... there is plenty of beer here, and they drink more than would fill the Valladolid river'.[1]

When it comes to Tudor food, twentieth-century cinema created a visual feast in the minds of its viewers. The image of Charles Laughton as the obese Henry VIII, gnawing on bones and throwing them to his dogs while his courtiers politely look away, has established an inaccurate caricature of a man who was, in reality, fastidious in his habits, picky with food for reasons of health and who displayed exquisite table manners. It is partly the figure of the king in later years which has overshadowed the decades of his prime, partly our desire to correlate the Tudors with extravagance, fantasy and the fulfilment of physical appetites, as well as a sense of nostalgia for the past that allows this depiction of gluttony to persist. But the Tudors' consumption of food was far more nuanced, symbolic and central to their identities than this cartoonesque image suggests.

The Tudors would be the first to admit they had healthy appetites. The late-Elizabethan traveller Fynes Morison believed this was due to the geographical location of England: 'The situation of our region, lying near unto the north, doth cause the heat of our stomachs to be of somewhat greater force: therefore our bodies do crave a little more ample nourishment than the inhabitants of the hotter regions are accustomed.'[2]

There is no doubt that the mealtimes of royalty were lavish and excessive. Surviving menus list dozens of items per course – and hundreds of people might be fed daily, up to fourteen courses on special occasions. The first course of one fish-day meal served to Henry and Catherine of Aragon in 1526 comprised soup, herring, cod, lampreys, pike, salmon, whiting, haddock, plaice, bream, porpoise, seal, carp, trout, crabs, lobsters, custard, tart, fritters and fruit.[3]

The king's table was a canvas for the display of his wealth, just as much as his body was hung with cloth of gold and jewels. A king was served with luxurious food, dyed bright colours, painted with gold leaf, stuffed and dressed and carved from marchpane (marzipan) purely for decoration because that was considered an essential reflection of his position.

Sumptuary laws regulated food just as much as clothing, in a direct correlation relating to the display of wealth. Where they were restricted as to the fabrics, yards, colours, adornments and makers of the clothes they wore, the wealthy classes were not supposed to spend more than one-tenth of the worth of their property on their annual food budget.

In May 1517, new regulations stated that a cardinal may have nine dishes served at one meal; a duke, archbishop, marquis, earl or bishop could have seven; London's mayor and aldermen, Knights of the Garter, abbots and other lords might have six; and those with an income between £100 and £400 could have three. One dish equated to one whole large animal or bird, such as one swan, one bustard or one peacock; or four medium creatures like partridge or woodcock; or eight smaller ones such as quail; or twelve tiny ones, such as larks.[4]

A decade later, a feast given by Cardinal Thomas Wolsey for the French ambassadors comprised a multitude of main dishes, followed by over 100 marzipan subtleties in the shapes of buildings, animals, people and a chess set. Likewise, when William Warham was invested as Archbishop of Canterbury in 1505, the subtleties included the interior of an abbey with a range of altars. The sumptuary rules could be broken if you were the king's most important minister, or if you were hosting important guests such as ambassadors, or a wedding.

The most indulgent piece of culinary display was the Tudor banquet. These first appeared in the ordinances of 1494 and were similar to the 'void' of wine, wafers and spices, which were consumed at ceremonial occasions, with an intended warming effect to aid digestion.

It was the job of the usher to inform the spicery of the king's intention to hold such a display and to prepare the spice dishes, to notify
the cellar so that wine and cups might be warmed in advance, and to
summon the necessary servants.

The serving of the void, which developed into the banquet, took
place at the end of the meal in a different room, which allowed for
the hall to be cleared. Only an exclusive, intimate selection of guests
were invited, as a mark of favour, and it was conducted with great
ceremony, employing the best plate. A magnificent banqueting house
was built by the French for the 1520 Field of Cloth of Gold in the
shape of a rotunda with a circumference of 240 paces, covered with
powdered velvet and hung inside with tapestries, but the corresponding English version was not completed in time to be used that June.

Such display was often literally that – display. It did not mean that
all the food would be eaten, or even half the food. The expectation was
that a range of dishes would be sampled, more like the Greek mezze
style, and the considerable remainder distributed among the servants
or the poor at the gates, as Harrison outlined in 1587:

> The chief part likewise of their daily provision is brought in before
> them (commonly in silver vessels, if they be of the degree of barons,
> bishops, and upwards) and placed on their tables, whereof, when
> they have taken what it pleaseth them, the rest is reserved, and
> afterwards sent down to their serving men and waiters, who feed
> thereon in like sort with convenient moderation, their reversion
> also being bestowed upon the poor which lie ready at their gates in
> great numbers to receive the same.[5]

The important role of almoner to the royal household, or to a wealthy
lord, is no longer in use. It represented the distribution of alms in the
form of money, clothing or food as an act of that family's hospitality
and charity – an act of good lordship. Whatever food was left on the
plate was called the 'manners' and it was customary for the guests at
banquets to leave their trenchers or bread platters, rather than consume them all.

The work of the almoner occurred at the interface of material
wealth and spiritual benefit, whereby the excess of the rich man
served both to heighten his status and to feed the poor. The Tudors
saw no paradox in this: it was the right and entitlement of the rich

to live in luxury, rather than eschew it, but it did their souls good to share their leftovers. There was no sense of equality of rights, that all individuals might share the same food, but rather that everyone received food appropriate to their God-given rank – and was grateful for it.

For the wealthy, food was a social statement. Its quality, quantity, colour and imaginative presentation had to be worthy of the king's table. Meals were conducted according to a strict social hierarchy, even ritual, with precedence of diners and their manners established in behavioural manuals and ordinances.

Food was divided into portions, or messes, usually between four or six diners, and taking more than your fair share was the height of bad manners. It was customary to bring your own knife and spoon, and to spoon soft food on to your trencher before wiping your spoon down, and to pick up pieces of meat with the thumb and two fore-fingers. Higher-status diners were given a linen napkin to wipe their fingers on.

Writing in 1534, Erasmus advised diners to wash their hands, sit still and not shift from side to side, to place the hands upon the table while waiting, not in the lap or on the trencher, to wipe the fingers on a napkin, not your clothes, and to place larger pieces of food upon the trencher.[6] The Elizabethan *Schoole of Good Vertue and Book of Nurture for Children* recommended:

> For rudeness, it is thy pottage to sup
> Or speak to any, his head in his cup.
> Thy knife see be sharp to cut fair thy meate
> Thy mouth not too full when thou dost eat
> Not smacking thy lips as commonly do hogs
> Nor gnawing the bones as it were dogs
> Such rudeness abhor, such beastliness fly
> At the table behave thyself mannerly.[7]

In 1587, William Harrison recorded the routines and habits of the upper classes at table. The nobleman, his family and close guests were seated in the hall on the principal tables and an additional allowance was made for the chief officers and household and 'inferior guests', who could number between forty and sixty and included 'such poor suitors and strangers as oft be partakers thereof'.

Harrison noted the fashion for French chefs in the 1570s, particularly 'musical-headed Frenchmen and strangers', who produced whatever produce was in season for the table. The menu was very meat heavy, especially after the abolition of the old fish days, 'since there is no day in manner that passeth over their heads wherein they have not only beef, mutton, veal, lamb, kid, pork, coney, capon, pig or ... some portion of the red or fallow deer, besides great variety of fish and wild fowl'.

Each dish was carried first to the 'greatest personage that sitteth at the table', after which 'it descendeth again even to the lower end' so that everyone might have a taste, although the quality and size of the portions would clearly diminish by the time it reached the bottom of the table, assuming it did reach that far. Gentlemen and merchants might dine on a couple of dishes, or five or six if they had company. After a minimal breakfast, the nobility dined at eleven and then had supper at five or six, merchants about an hour later, husbandmen dined at seven or eight, and the universities at nine or ten at night. 'As for the poorest sort, they generally dine and sup when they may.'[8]

Feeding the king or queen required its ritual, depending upon the occasion. Sometimes a monarch chose to dine in their private chamber and the food was prepared in a privy kitchen located below or nearby, from where it could be swiftly delivered still piping hot. Alternatively, the meal might be served in the presence chamber, to a monarch seated at the high table, under a canopy of estate, announced by trumpets before an audience.

Henry VII and Elizabeth of York preferred to dine publicly in the great hall, but Henry VIII and Elizabeth I increasingly sought privacy for their meals. A sketch in the style of Holbein, made in the 1540s, shows Henry VIII dining in his privy chamber, seated alone at a trestle covered in a white cloth and being served on both sides. Of the dozen or so onlookers, no one else is seated, and certainly no one else is eating. The sewer would wash Henry's hands in warm, scented water and dry them with linen, before the servers would present the dishes on bended knee.

The sense of spectacle arising from the king's meal is a reminder of the ritualised, divine aspect of his bodily functions, combining his status and humanity through his separation and specialness when it comes to basic needs. The courtiers and servants would have to wait to be fed later, when the king had finished, and when it suited him.

If their names had been included on the bouche of court, they were entitled to two meals a day, at ten in the morning and four in the afternoon. The Lord Chamberlain placed them according to rank in either the great hall or great watching chamber, in one of two sittings. This meal was prepared by the great kitchens and might be tepid by the time it had made its journey along the corridor and up the stairs. Bouche of court also entitled an individual to beer, wine, bread, candles and firewood.

Fynes Morison assessed that:

In number of dishes and change of meat, the nobility of England do most exceed ... what great provision is made of all manner of delicate meats from every quarter of the country ... also jellies of all colours mixed with a variety in the representation of sundry flowers, herbs, trees, forms of beasts, fish, fowls and fruits, and thereunto marchpane wrought with no small curiosity, tarts of divers hues, conserves of fruit, foreign and home-bred, suckets, marmalades, sugar-bread, gingerbread, and florentines.[9]

By way of contrast, the dinner provided for the poor at St Martin's Priory, Dover, consisted daily of two messes of bread, meat and drink to a pre-specified number of the 'honest' poor: five on the 5 March in one sitting and fifteen in another, and fifteen on another date in April, in commemoration of the dead, although the prior's obligation was only for two people daily.[10]

❧ ON THE MENU ❧

Ask a Tudor what they ate and you would know who they were – and probably what time of year it was. The ingredients of their meals, the style of food and the quantities were indicators of social standing, role, location, season, supply and age. When Juan Luis Vives described the breakfast of a schoolboy in the 1520s, he listed a piece of bread with butter and dried figs, or dried but not pressed grapes, 'for fresh grapes besmear the fingers of boys and they spoil their clothes, unless he should prefer a few cherries or golden and long plums'. This quick, easy meal, requiring little or no preparation, was replicated by millions upon rising, although the choice of fruit reminds us of Vives' Spanish roots.[1]

While the availability of some food remained constant through the year, others were dependent upon seasonality, and certain phases of the year were thought to better suit particular types of food, depending upon the Galenic balance of the humours. The 1508 *Book of Kervynge* contained a suggested menu for flesh days in the period beginning with the feast of St John the Baptist on 24 June and lasting until Michaelmas, at the end of September, so from midsummer until the autumn equinox. The first course was a pottage of vegetable gruel and frumenty with venison and pestelles of pork with green sauce, followed by roast capon and swan with entrails. The second course began with pottage, then moved on to roast mutton, veal, pork, chickens, pheasants, pigeons and heron, with fruit and other baked meats. The pheasant and heron should be arrayed in the manner of a capon, but done dry without any moisture, eaten with salt and powdered ginger. All birds with open claws like a capon should be attired and arrayed like a capon.[2]

Through the autumn, from Michaelmas until Christmas, a different diet was recommended. The first course opened with pottage, with beef, mutton, bacon or pestelles of pork, or with goose, capon, duck, swan or pheasant, with tarts or baked meats or chines of pork. The second course had more pottage, followed by roast flesh of mutton, pork, veal, pullets, pigeon, teal, woodcocks, plovers, curlew or heron, roast venison, thrush and baked meats. The carver was advised to remove the skin first, then carve reasonably for the lord and lady, especially for the lady, 'for they will soon be angry for their thoughts be soon changed, and some lords will soon be pleased and some will not'. If they ate any 'stinking thing', the carver was to ensure 'it is made so clean with the water that all the corruption is clean gone away'. Skin was not considered wholesome to eat, and creatures that swam in rivers should be cleaned, while the field and wood birds were dangerous, as they ate foul things like worms and toads.[3]

The 1545 *A Proper New Book of Cookery* recommended each food in its season. Brawn was best from a fortnight before Michaelmas until Lent. Beef and bacon were good at all times, as was mutton, although mutton was worst from Easter to midsummer. 'A fat pig is ever in season. A goose is worst in Midsummer and best in stubble time, but when they be young green geese, then they be best.' January and February were the months to eat veal, although it was good for the rest of the year, while lamb and kid were at their tastiest between Christmas and Lent. Hens were best between November and Lent, woodcocks from October, but a fat capon was always in season. Peacocks, pheasants and grouse were best when young, mallards and teal were good after a frost, quails and larks were always in season, as were conies (rabbits), hares and does, although a barren doe was best eaten in winter.[4]

A recommended menu in A Pr*oper New Book of Cookery*, with the items served in the 'correct' order, shows the percentage of meat dishes, the kinds of sauces accompanying them and the frequency of certain ingredients, including the Tudors' favoured meat and fruit combination:

The servise at dynner:
Brawne and mustarde.
Capons stewed or in white brothe.
A pastie of venison upon brothes.
A chine of beef & a breast of mutton boyled.
Chewettes of pies of fine mutton.
Three greene geese in a dishe/sorell sauce.
For stubble goose/mustard & vinegar.
After all hallowen daie/a swanne Sauce chaudell.
A pigge.
A dubble ribbe of beef roasted/sauce pepper and vinegar.
A loine of veale or a breast. Sauce oranges.
Halfe a lambe or a kid. Sauce oranges.
Two capons roasted. Sauce wyne and salte/ale and salte
Two pasties of fallow deere in a dishe.
A custarde.

Second course:
Peacoke. Sauce wyne and salt.
Two conies or half a dozen rabbittes. Sauce mustarde and sugar.
Half a dozen chickyns.
Half a dozen pigions.
Mallarde. Sauce mustard & vergis.
Teal. Sauce mustard & vergis.
Gulles. Sauce mustard & vergis.
Storke. Sauce mustard & vergis.
Herons. Sauce gallentyne.

Crane. Sauce gallentyne.

Curlew. Sauce gallentyne.

Bitturn. Sauce gallentyne.

Bustarde. Sauce gallentyne.

Pheasant. Sauce water and salte with onions sliced.

Half a dozen woodcockes. Sauce mustarde and suger.

Half a dozen partriches.

A dozen of quailes.

A disshe of larkes.

Two pasties of red deere in a disshe.

Tarte.

Gingerbread.

Fritters.[5]

The expenses for Henry VIII's household at Greenwich in October 1518 cover the catering for Henry, Catherine of Aragon, his daughter Princess Mary, his sister Mary, Duchess of Suffolk, two papal legates, the French, Spanish and Venetian ambassadors and a number of nobles of the realm. Six bakers were required to produce 3,000 loaves of bread at a cost of £4 7s 4d, along with 3 tuns of wine and 6 tuns of ale.

The main kitchen was supplied with eleven beef carcasses, fifty-six sheep, seventeen veal, three pigs, four hogs, one fresh sturgeon, various gudgeons, eels, crayfish, pikes, ox and calf feet and a flitch of bacon. The department for fowl received five dozen Kentish capons, seven dozen coarse capons, twenty-seven dozen chickens, fifteen swans, six cranes, partridges, pheasants, plovers, teal, pigeon, quails, larks, geese, peacocks and 'quick birds'. These were to be cooked up with supplies of butter, eggs, apples, cream, milk, frumenty, curd, onions, oatmeal, berries, quinces and barley.[6] The salseria, or sauce-making department, ordered flour, mustard, vinegar, verjuice and herbs, suggesting quite a sharp, acidic palate.

Then, the ingredients for the king's personal quarters became more luxurious, including 188lb of sugar, 1 gallon of rose water, 5lb of pepper, almost 13lb of cinnamon, 6lb of ginger, 3lb of cloves and mace, 1lb of nutmeg, 10oz of saffron, 35lb of dates, 26lb of prunes, 31lb of small raisins and 32lb of almonds. If there was any doubt that this shopping list was for the king's table, the list proceeded to long and small comfits, 4lb of succates (suckets) or sweets, 4lb of the expensive and elusive green ginger, marmalade, gilded lozenges, damask water,

powder of anise and liquorice, pears and honey.[7] Such ingredients
serve as a reminder that many Tudor dishes featuring meat or fish
also combined a sweet element, such as the sweet-sour 'egerdouce' of
fish, combining honey and dried fruit with vinegar or red wine, or the
pickled herring and fruit pie, or spicy chicken in orange sauce found
in contemporary recipe books. The traditional ingredients for mince
pies, as the name suggests, was diced beef or veal, with apples, raisins,
dates, currants and lemon peel.

The most extravagant of all royal catering took place during
June 1520, when Henry VIII and Francis I erected temporary ovens
and kitchens in fields at Guînes and Ardres, near the Field of Cloth
of Gold, in northern France. Henry's pavilion contained his own private kitchen and its associated offices. A list surviving in the Rutland
Papers, a nineteenth-century collection of various documents,
includes a privy pantry and hall pantry, privy cellar and hall cellar,
privy and hall butteries, pitcher house for plates and pots, a room for
silver scullery plates, a spicery, a ewery and confectionary divided by
a partition, scullery, saucery, wardrobe for the beds, chandry, jewel
house and a room for John Shurley, the cofferer, and clerks of the
green cloth.[8] The cellar contained 'some 3,000 butts of the choicest
wines in the world ... malmsies and other wines, the best that could
be found in Flanders and France' and all visitors were 'compelled both
to eat and drink', and 'never was such abundance witnessed as in this
house'.[9] Venetian ambassador Soardino observed:

> Then when the most Christian King banqueted there, the eating
> and drinking witnessed were incredible, and the odour of the
> viands very noisome; and on those occasions there was an addi-
> tional and marvellous display of costly and beautiful plate, as
> mentioned in the description of the first banquet given to the most
> Christian King. As usual in England, the wooden floors of the hall
> and chambers were strewed with rushes, so that the planks could
> not be seen.[10]

The English retinue comprised around 5,000 souls, who each needed
to be fed at least twice daily, requiring a continual, vast operation
from dawn until well after dark. Outside the pavilion, a small village
of tents housed additional 'halls' to accommodate cooking, so they
were constructed at a distance for reasons of safety and comfort.

There were ten houses, some with hearths, 'to serve for working houses and larders'; two houses and two halls for the poultry; a scalding (boiling) house, scullery and mill; two large ovens, six ranges and a working hall for the pastillers and other subtlety makers; three more larders and two halls for the accommodation of kitchen staff, and various other offices. If this was not enough, local houses were hired to provide additional locations for the production of food. Two houses were hired at Guînes for the clerk of the kitchen, at a cost of 2s 8d, and for the counting house; two others at Guînes and Newnam Bridge for six weeks to act as butcheries at the cost of 23s 4d. The house of Cornelius Baker in Calais, possibly already a bakery, given his surname, was leased for 26s 8d, to act as a bakery. Mr Yerford's wool shop was taken over at a cost of 10s to be a pantry, and three other properties temporarily became the spicery, chaundry and waffry.

Among the banquet items consumed at the Field of Cloth of Gold in 1520 were 4,000 wafers used to build subtleties, a number of sticks of sugar candy, almost 10,000 pippins, 5,500 oranges, 200 lemons and 4 gallons of gooseberries. Nearly 10,000 eggs were consumed, 562 gallons of milk, 432 gallons of cream and extra cream for the king's cakes.[11]

Officials and members of the king's household were granted wholesome but more limited fare. In 1533, the diet of the cofferer, comptroller and clerk of the kitchen was set out by days of the week, at a time when the eating of meat was limited by the Church. From Sunday to Thursday, their dinner consisted of beef, mutton, pig, goose or other meat dish, with veal or pork and a bakemeat, while their supper was boiled mutton or beef, roast mutton, hen or pullet, lamb, rabbit or similar. On Friday and Saturday, they dined on ling, salmon, whiting and plaice, with a 'reward' of rabbits, pigeons, tarts or fritters, sole or flounders, and supped on similar, with a 'reward' of wild fowl or tart. In the morning, afternoon and night, they were allowed bread and ale, making a total of £1 4s 7d for their weekly food per head. Added at the end of this was the information that 'the diet of ladies is the same as the preceding', while gentlemen and gentlewomen were permitted a menu costing 18s 5d a week.[12]

The Northumberland Household Book of 1512 reveals that the Percy family ate quite modestly for an aristocratic house. Breakfast was taken at noon and on fish days, the lord and lady had a loaf of bread, two fine manchet loaves, two pieces of salt fish, six baked herrings, a dish of sprats, a quart of beer and one of wine. Their children ate half a loaf of household bread, manchet, a piece of salt fish, three white herrings, a dish of sprats, a dish of butter, a quart of beer and one of wine. On flesh days, the fish was substituted for a chine of mutton or boiled beef. The family came together at six in the evening to eat supper together.[13]

When Sir Thomas Wriothesley was in Abbeville in 1514, he was entitled to 14s a day for each of his four servants and the daily livery for a Garter King of Arms. This gave Wriothesley four dozen bread(s), one cheese, four septiers of wine, two pieces of beef, one whole sheep, four capons, two rabbits, a pig, four wildfowl, 4lb of lard, twenty-six pears, half a dish of raisins, hippocras, 2 quarts each of white wine and claret, a box of comfits, a box of quince marmalade and expenses for his horse, fire, bed and lodgings.[14]

In October 1582, William Stanton at Hereford Castle recorded the diets of its keepers at William Cecil's request. The Lord Keeper Sir Nicholas Bacon and his assistants, Sir Richard Sackville, Sir Walter Mildmay and Sir Ambrose Cave, all dined at the same table for dinner and supper in the large chamber assigned for the Star Chamber. They were served two messes of meat, or two of fish, with the remainder feeding their gentlemen and servants, twenty-eight or thirty in all, although additional beef or mutton was prepared in case this should not go far enough. Their table was covered with a carpet and set with plate, pewter vessels and napery owned by the Star Chamber, and they drew their wine from the same source, amounting to 1 tun of Gascon claret, 1 of red and 1 of white. In addition, the deputy steward supplied them with beer and ale, while their salted fish came from the queen's storehouse at Westminster. A London supplier, Robert Jorden, brought poultry and fresh fish from Cambridge daily. Thus, the household was supplied with essentials befitting the rank of the queen's servants, even when employed away from the court.[15]

The traveller Fynes Morison stayed at the house of a knight north of the Berwick border into Scotland in 1598:

I was at a knight's house, who had many servants to attend him, that brought in his meat with their heads covered with blue caps, the table being more than half furnished with great platters of porridge, each having a little piece of sodden meat; and when the tables were served, the servants did sit down with us; but the upper mess, instead of porridge, had a pullet with some prunes in the broth. And I observed no art of cookery, or furniture of household stuff, but rather rude neglect of both, though myself and my companion, sent by the Governor of Berwick upon bordering affairs, were entertained in the best manner. The Scots ... vulgarly eat hearth-cakes of oats, but in cities have also wheaten bread, which, for the most part, was bought by courtiers, gentlemen, and the best sort of citizens ... They drink pure wine, not with sugar, as the English, yet at feasts they put comfits in the wine, after the French manner: but they had not our vintners' fraud to mix their wines.[16]

The diet of a captive queen still managed to reflect her rank. In 1585, the penultimate full year of her life, Mary, Queen of Scots' kitchen expenses included six dozen manchets, eight dozen cheat breads, 353 tons of beer, 28 tons of Gascoigne wine, 158 beef carcasses, 1,441 sheep, 712 pigs, barrels of salt salmon, over £9 of pikes, £48 of barbel, 17,862lb of butter, 73,250 eggs, poultry such as capons, chickens, cocks, hens, geese and pigeons, and fish like herrings, salt eels, sprats, ling, cod, salmon and stockfish.

Among the condiments and ingredients Mary favoured were salt, salad oil, vinegar, verjuice, mustard, yeast, dates, oatmeal, cream, milk, herbs, roots, ale and suet. Her spice cupboard contained pepper, fine and cosarse sugar, almonds, prunes, currants, cinnamon, mace, nutmeg, raisins and 'raisins of the sun'. An allowance made for the spices served at Mary's funeral banquet in February 1587 included pepper, saffron, cloves, mace, cinnamon, ginger, nutmeg, sugar, dates, currants, oranges, lemons, rice, rose water, cherries and biscuits.[17]

Those living in religious orders were expected to follow strict guidelines about what could be consumed, and when, as part of their vows of abstinence and the Catholic calendar. Those living off monastic charity were also catered for according to their dependent status, as described in the ordinances for the almsmen of St Peter's, Westminster.

At dinner, each man would receive a farthing loaf, a quart of ale, which also cost a farthing, and as much flesh or fish as the season required, to the cost of half a penny, with four men sharing a mess between them. The poor women were put to work to 'provide and make good and wholesome pottages for the said poor men and their self, and serve every one of them at their dinner with one mess of pottage'. To create the pottage, a kind of soup that could include almost anything, the women were permitted an unappetising weekly allowance of oatmeal, salt, salt fish and mustard. The men had an additional allowance of a pot of ale and unlimited bread, which they were allowed to consume in their chambers, for suppers and 'drinkings'.[18]

As is revealed by the *London Letter Books*, the consistory court records and, eventually, the 1535 investigation into the monasteries, *Valor Ecclesiasticus*, those being fed in religious institutions were not always following the rules. Jasper Fyloll reported to Cromwell from the Charterhouse in October that year that the monks were eating too much: 'The meal that now serves twelve, would then serve twenty persons honestly', and lay stewards and servants should be able to eat flesh in their hall or parlour while the monks sit in their frater, and share one mess between four.[19] The contents of their meals from 10 to 13 October was outlined:

> Sunday at dinner: every monk had furmentye, a hot pie of lampreys, and three eggs; the lay brothers, salt fish and cheese. Monday: monks and lay brothers alike had pottage of herbs, plenty of Suffolk or Essex cheese, and three eggs. Tuesday: furmenty, oysters, and a piece of ling for each monk and lay brother. Wednesday: pottage of herbs, a great whiting, and two eggs; for the lay brothers, pottage, oysters, and a whiting to each man.[20]

As the monasteries increasingly came under question, some of the monks flouted the culinary regulations. Richard, abbot of Winchcombe, reported the offenders under his roof to Cromwell:

> On Thursday in the first week of Advent two of my brethren, dan Walter Aldelme and dan Hugh Egwyne, ate flesh, contrary to custom. I called them before me and my brethren in the chapter-house, and imposed penance, which they refused to obey, saying they would eat flesh next Friday if they might have it. I told them that imprisonment was the punishment for disobedience; which they little regarded, and I have therefore committed them to custody till I hear further from you.[21]

✳

When it came to the diets of those lower down the social scale, less variety was on offer. Among the middle classes, meat was still the most desirable food, coupled with bread and ale and supplemented with condiments and extras. In 1577, Thomas Tusser suggested that the modest Christmas dinner of such a family might be:

Good bread and good drinke,
a good fire in the hall, brawne,
pudding and souse, and good mustard withall.
Beefe, mutton, and porke, shred pies of the best,
pig, veale, goose and capon, and turkey well drest;
Cheese, apples and nuts, jolly Carols to heare,
as then in the countrie is counted good cheare.[22]

Many people, in professions, service, monasteries or poverty, had little choice over what they ate. The quantities supplied to feed an enclave of 500 men at Blackness, eating two meals a day, estimated by Sir Richard Cavendish in September 1546, were a seventh of a peck of bread, 3 quarts of beer, a 21lb piece of beef, one fish for two messes, or four men each, stockfish at the same rate, 1.5lb of butter, 1lb of cheese and their share of forty flitches of bacon.[23]

The meals of poorer people were dictated more by what was available and would have fluctuated seasonally, affected by the success of the harvest and the survival of livestock. A basic breakfast of bread would be followed by pottage made from onions, leeks, cabbages, oatmeal or whatever was available, boiled up with a small piece of meat or fish, enlivened by herbs, with more rye or wheat bread and ale. The family's pig, cow or sheep would have been slaughtered on Martinmas Day, 11 November, and divided up into sections to be boiled, salted and preserved, in order to take them through the winter. Every part of the animal would have been used, including the organs, head, feet and bones.

❧ SPECIFIC FOODS ❧

Status was not the only factor that dictated what the Tudors ate. Specific diets were recommended by contemporary dieticians, according to age, illness and the Galenic theory of the four humours, thought to dictate the balance of health and correspond with the properties of the natural world. *A Compendious Regiment, or A Dietary of Health*, written by monk, physician and traveller, Andrew Boorde, gives insight into the benefits of individual food items, their use, preparation and varieties in 1542.

The main ingredients for the middle classes upwards were meat and fish. Boorde considered that of all nations, England was best served with fresh and all manner of salt fish. He considered that sea fish with scales or fins were the most wholesome, followed by those from rivers and brooks, while those from standing water might have fed upon mould. Older fish were better to eat, as their flesh was softer and easier to digest, the only exception being porpoise. Salt fish was 'not greatly to be praise[d] specially' and would 'cleave to the fingers' while being eaten. The skin of fish was to be 'utterly abhorred' because it caused the growth of viscous phlegm.[1] Fish, in general, were cold in nature, provided little nourishment and should not be eaten in the same meal as meat.

Fishermen had to obey the strict rules about where and when they might catch their wares. In 1485, the mayor and aldermen seized and burned 'false nets' as a warning to those fishing unlawfully. The following May, they added an ordinance regarding the size of fish caught, ordering that barbel, flounder, roach, dace, pike and tench were permitted but that the immature fish be put back in the river.[2]

Some creatures were exclusively reserved for the consumption of the rich or royalty. The ownership of swans had been restricted in 1482 to those over a certain income, and possession was recorded by a series of nicks in the beaks of the birds. Any birds without nicks reverted to ownership of the Crown, for whom it was a favourite delicacy at Christmas. Hentzner described how the swan lived 'in great security, nobody daring to molest, much less kill, any of them, under penalty of a large fine'.[3]

Likewise, the porpoise was an aristocratic treat, often eaten with mustard. In 1498, Henry VII served one to a group of visiting ambassadors at the vast cost of 21*s* and, two decades later, Wolsey made one the centrepiece of an official banquet.

Beef was the Tudors' meat of choice, although not everyone was in a position to choose. Meat was a rare luxury for the poor, who might save a joint for a feast day and eke out the offcuts in several days' pottage. Boorde favoured veal, or young beef, as older meat could 'engender melancholy' or even cause leprous tumours. Dried, cured beef, saved from the annual Martinmas slaughter on 11 November and hung in the smoke house, may 'fill the belly and cause a man to drink' but could also give him a gall stone.

Veal was considered the most nutritious and easily digested of all the meats. Mutton was palatable if the sheep was fat and had been raised in a good pasture, while lamb was full of moisture and should be avoided by old men, save those who were 'melancholy of complexion'. Boorde took his cue straight from the Bible in stating that pork was an unclean meat, as pigs lay upon 'filthy and stinking soils' and should be allowed to bathe in rivers, like in Spain and Germany. Eating 'an old hog not clean kept' would 'engender gross blood' and upset the stomach. Bacon, though, was good enough for carters and ploughmen, as they were always labouring in the earth and dung, and was best eaten with eggs.

Hares, too, were considered unclean in the Bible, so they should be considered sport and left to the hounds to devour, although rabbits were tender and wholesome. Old physicians used to advise against venison as bringing on melancholy or choler, but Boorde concluded that, as it was a lord's dish, 'I am sure it is good for an Englishman', as it 'doth animate him to be … strong and hardy'.[4]

Birds featured regularly on the Tudor table. Boorde considered that pheasant was the best, although partridge was the quickest digested, provided comfort to the brain and stomach and increased the libido. Woodcocks, quails, plovers and lapwings should be eaten in moderation as they might encourage melancholy humours, and cranes were to be avoided as engendering evil blood. Bustards, shovellers and bitterns were a better choice, but wild fowl living by water were of 'discommendable nourishment'.

Boorde recommended birds reared in captivity, especially the capon, as nutritious and easily digested. In the winter, a hen was the best choice, while a pullet (a chicken under a year) or a chicken (one over a year) suited the summer months best. Although the flesh of a cockerel was hard to digest, a broth or jelly made from it was restorative. Pigeon was good for a choleric or melancholy man, duckling was better than duck and peacocks were hard on the stomach. Smaller birds were good and light to eat – the lark was best, but sparrows should be avoided, along with all those fowl who ate spiders, as they could contain poison.[5]

There was always a pan of pottage simmering away on the Tudor stove. A kind of rich soup, it suited all tastes, ages and classes, and could be a simple stock that was added to, day after day. Boorde found that pottage was 'not so much used in all Christendom as it is used in England' and it seems to have been eaten, in differing varieties, both sweet and savoury. It was made from the juices or water in which meat was cooked, with oatmeal, chopped herbs and salt added. The herbs, he commented, 'if they be pure, good and clean', not withered or infected, as often happened 'through the corruption of the air' in times of pestilence, 'doth comfort many men'. He recommended a stew or gruel made in a pot with oatmeal and no herbs, which could 'do little displeasure' and relaxed the belly.

Furmenty was a variety of pottage made with wheat and milk. It was more difficult to digest, but could strengthen a man, although Boorde advised against combining this with meat, as 'flesh soded in mylke is nat commendable'. Pease pottage was better than one made with beans for it was more easily digested, although both could cleanse the body. Bean pottage was crude fare, as it had been found to 'increase grosse humours', including flatulence.

Almond milk and rice pottage was a good dish for women, as it was considered to be hot and moist in character and could comfort the breast, mollify the belly and restore and comfort nature. Weak men, or those with feeble stomachs should eat a variety of pottage brewed in ale and consider the addition of hemp seed and shrimp, which comforted the blood. The sweetest type of the dish was honey sops, although these were not good for colic and could encourage other digestive illnesses.[6]

On the whole, Boorde considered dairy products to be beneficial to health, so long as they were consumed in the right way, at the right time. Hens' eggs should be divided in two parts: the yolk was considered to be 'cordial' and hot, according to the theory of the humours, while the white was 'viscous and cold' and slack of digestion, so did not engender good blood. Poached eggs were the best but should be eaten at night. If they were eaten in the morning, they needed to be tempered with salt and sugar. Roasted eggs were acceptable, so long as they were fresh; fried eggs were 'nothing'; duck and goose eggs were to be avoided; but those of the pheasant and partridge were admirable for good health.

Butter should be eaten in the morning, ideally before meat, although in combination it was nourishing for the breast, lungs and belly. Eaten any time later during the day, as the author had observed the Dutch do, caused the fat in it to swim about in the stomach and the excess would rise and cause 'eruptions', and it should be avoided at all times by those with an ague or fever, as it inflamed the liver.[7]

There were four main types of cheese. Green cheese was named for its newness, not its colour, and its high whey content made it cold and moist. Soft cheese, not too old or new, was hot and moist. Hard cheese, hot and dry, was 'evil to digest', and 'spermyse' was made from curds and the juice of herbs.[8]

Tastes changed, though. At the start of the century, curds were favoured in the typical soft, creamy late-medieval palate, but as the years advanced, these were increasingly neglected in favour of harder cheeses, which were brought to London from the counties where they were produced, highly coloured with saffron or marigold. Parmesan imported from Italy was enjoyed by the Elizabethans.

Whichever cheese was favoured out of the four, only a little of the best should be eaten:

> But take the best cheese of all these rehaersed, if a lytel do good and pleasure. The overplus doth engendre gross humours for it is harde of dygestyon, it maketh a man constipated and it is not good for the stone. Cheese that is good ought not to be harde nor too softe, but betwixt both, it should not be tough nor brutal, it ought not to be sweete nor soure, nor tart, nor to salt, nor too fresshe, it muste be of good savoure … not full of eyes nor mites, nor magottes.[9]

The type of bread a Tudor ate revealed their social status. William Harrison described how the gentry grew their own wheat for white bread, producing the finest manchet loaf from 8 uncooked ounces of the purest white flour. Second to this was cheat, or wheaten bread, which was yellowish or grey with the coarsest of the bran removed, and third was ravelled, a cheap, darker bread with less pure wheat.

Brown bread contained all the fibre 'and it is not only the worst and weakest of all the other sorts, but appointed in old time for servants, slaves and the inferior kind of people to feed upon'. Sometimes this was mixed with corn, to make miscelin bread, which made it slightly less rough and dry.

However, worse options did exist. The poorest people relied upon flour made from rye, barley or even, during one of the terrible harvests of Elizabeth's reign, ground peas, beans, oats, lentils or acorns.[10] In 1535, the quality of bread and the number of individuals being fed by God's House in Portsmouth was declining following the appointment of a new master:

> The poor people have not their bread baked and drink brewed as was wont to be done; but the present master has carried all the brewing and vessel to a farm a mile from the house, so that the poor people are in manner undone. The mayor ought to see the weight and goodness of the bread and ale. However high the price of corn, the bread and ale ought to be of the same goodness, but the master serves the people with very coarse bread and small drink. The house may spend yearly of temporal lands £80, whereof six poor men and six poor women have 6d. apiece, and a priest has his wages. Every fortnight they have seven loaves of bread and five gallons of ale apiece. The present master may spend 800 or 900 marks a year, and keeps no hospitality, which is a great decay to the town.[11]

The production of bread, as with most guilds, was highly regulated. In 1486, the bakers were required to report any guild members who were charging too much for their loaves, or producing too much, except for at Christmas time, or were 'regrating' wheat, or making loaves adulterated with other corn, or brown-bread bakers making white.[12]

By 1493, it was necessary to regulate that all bread 'hawked' around the city, meaning bread sold outside the official guild channels, should be forfeited and disposed of. The sale of bread by foreign bakers was restricted at the same time, and they were not permitted to trade after midday.[13] At the same time, the London bakers complained that 'foreign bakers bought and sold bread made of evil and unwholesome paste, and passed it off as bread made by the petitioners', and requested that the wardens have the right to search premises and seize such offending loaves.[14] The angry guildsmen were back again in 1495, complaining about bakers from Stratford driving into the city and selling their wares in the marketplace, and succeeded in having their activity also limited to before midday.

Fresh, dried and treated fruit was widely available to the Tudors. In season, their gardens and marketplaces provided homegrown delicacies, supplementing the bland diet of the poor and being stored, pickled, dried, preserved and distilled for the coming winter months. Recipes abound with raisins, prunes and dates for sweetness, with homegrown quinces, grapes and gooseberries stewed up with meat.

William Harrison listed 'the most delicate apples, plums, pears, walnuts and filberts' in 1587, as well as new varieties which had been planted in the last forty years, 'almonds, peaches, figs and corn-trees [cherries] in rich men's orchards', 'capers, oranges and lemons', and even wild olives growing in England.[15] All classes could enjoy some degree of what nature offered, if they had access to a plot of land or could forage, with strawberries and cream described as the poor man's banquet. Only the rich could afford far more exotic delicacies, such as the imported citrus fruits, and the gardeners of aristocratic country estates regularly harvested supplies to transport to wherever in the country the court may be.

Harrison believed that the geographical variety of fruit and vegetables was part of a divine rationing scheme:

How many strange plants are daily brought to us from the Indies, America, Tabrobane [Ceylon], Canary Isles and all parts of the world ... in respect of the constitutions of our bodies, they do not grow for us, because that God hath beStowd sufficient commodities upon every country for her own necessity yet, for delectation sake unto the eye and their odoriferous savours unto the nose, they are to be cherished.[16]

He credited the skill of English gardeners in cultivating native varieties and mixing them with new plants, improving upon nature. They had developed a new art form, treating plants and their various needs with the same skill as doctors tending to their patients:

We have in like sort such workmen as are not only excellent in grafting the natural fruits, but also in their artificial mixtures, whereby one tree bringeth forth sundry fruits, and one and the same fruit of

divers colours and tastes, dallying as it were with nature and her
course, as if her whole trade were perfectly known unto them: of
hard fruits they will make tender, of sour sweet, of sweet yet more
delicate, bereaving also some of their kernels, other of their cores,
and finally enduing them with the savour of musk, amber, or sweet
spices, at their pleasures.

Divers also have written at large of these several practices, and
some of them how to convert the kernels of peaches into almonds,
of small fruit to make far greater, and to remove or add superfluous
or necessary moisture to the trees, with other things belonging to
their preservation, and with no less diligence than our physicians do
commonly show upon our own diseased bodies, which to me doth
seem right strange.[17]

In 1578, Thomas Martin wrote to William Cecil to report on action
that Martin had taken in Cecil's garden, after finding it neglected:

According to my promise I have sent a note of such notable practices
for orchards, gardens, and ponds, and other like things of commodity and pleasure as my poor skill could attain unto. And because I
have many of your lordship's fruit trees 'mozy', and 'some to rot,
and other some sick of the gall, or of the worms, and such other
diseases which the very best trees are subject to', I have prescribed
in writing sundry remedies for the same, and did partly admonish
your gardener and steward thereof. At what time I brought six other
pearmain trees to be then presently set amongst your cherry trees,
which fruit of pearmain is of that excellency that Sergeant Baram,
and also Harris, her Majesty's fruiterer, did cut off 40 heads of the
rennet to graft the said pearmain upon with 'cyons' [scions] which
they had from me. I have sent herewith a basket of the fruit, and
trust to present likewise of the said apple and the pond pear at Easter
and Whitsuntide next.[18]

Knot gardens developed from the end of the Tudor period, planted
not only for their visual impact in complex geometrical shapes which
replicated carpets, but also for their scent. Many followed a formal
design, within a square, hedged by a sweet-scented box in part of the
garden of a large estate, but the principle of planting medical and culinary items for scent was replicated on many scales.

Knot gardens, as opposed to vegetable gardens, were planted close to houses, as a letter from Peter Kemp in 1561 explained: 'For the many different scents that arise from the herbs, as cabbages, onions etc are scarce well-pleasing to perfume the lodgings of any house.' Gardens that were attached to most domestic properties would have had a percentage given over to growing scented plants, divided by gravel paths. They represented more private versions of the old monastic gardens, in which the attributes of specific leaves and flowers were valued and cultivated for use in the sanatorium. The pungent tastes of marjoram and thyme, rosemary and hyssop, lemon balm and camomile found their way onto the Tudor table from the knot garden.

❧ DRINK ❧

Tudor drinking habits varied considerably from those of modern England: tea was unknown to them and although the first ground coffee beans were introduced to England by the Levant Company, possibly as early as 1583, it appears not to have been drunk until considerably later. Sir Anthony Shurley wrote the first description of Turks drinking it in Aleppo in 1599:

> They sit at their meat, which is served to them upon the ground, as tailors sit upon their stalls, cross-legged, for the most part, passing the day in banqueting and carousing, until their surfeit, drinking a certain liquor, which they do call Coffe, which is made of seede much like mustard seede, which will soon intoxicate the brain like our Metheglin.[1]

In another culinary oversight, Columbus may have brought back cocoa beans from the New World as early as 1502, but their potential was not spotted in England. Drinking chocolate, with added spices, sugar, honey and chilli, took off first at the court of Spain, as observed by Jose de Acosta:

> The Spaniards, both men and women that are accustomed to the country are very greedy of this chocolate. They say they make diverse sorts of it, some hot, some cold, and some temperate, and put therein much of that chili, yea, they make paste thereof, the which they say is good for the stomach and against the catarrh.[2]

The Tudors considered milk to be a dangerous drink, reserved only for children, and best consumed in the morning. Fresh cows' milk, whey and buttermilk, taken straight from the dairy or pasture, could cleanse the gut, lift melancholy and alleviate pain in the breast and lungs, but it could cause 'gurgulations' in the belly and was best avoided by men of a sanguine humour. The best way to take milk was with lumps of bread soaked in it, and a little sugar added. Goats' milk and women's breastmilk was considered a good restorative and helpful for those 'in a consumption'.[3]

In 1534, Thomas Elyot enthused about the properties of pure water, 'not only because it is an element, that is to say, a pure matter, whereof al other licours have their original substance, but also for as much as it was the very natural and first drinke to all manner of creatures'. He stated, 'We have seen men and women of great age' who never drank anything but pure water, particularly in Cornwall, 'although that the country be in a very cold quarter', which proved that 'if men from their infancy were accustomed' to it, moderately used water 'should be sufficient to keep natural moisture'.[4] In practice, though, the Tudors appear not to have drunk much pure water, if 'pure' water might be obtained. It was feared that water could carry disease, and although rainwater or distilled water can be found in recipes, it was boiled in the process of preparation.

The drinks most commonly appearing on Tudor menus and in cookery were boiled, distilled or alcoholic, with the bacterial dangers purged away. Ale was drunk even at breakfast and by children, in watered-down quantities, but beer was viewed with suspicion and less widely enjoyed. The hops in it categorised it as a 'cold' humour and were far less preferable than the 'hot' qualities of wine, which were considered closer to the body's natural fluids.[5] By Elizabeth's reign, it was being brewed in three strengths: single, double and double-double, although the queen halted production of the last, very strong, kind in 1560.

Cordials, syrups and tisanes made from flowers, fruit and herbs were drunk for pleasure and for their reputed medicinal benefits. Other Tudor favourites were mead, made from fermenting honey, metheglin, which was mead with honey, spices or citrus flavouring, and perry, a cider made from pears – although Andrew Boorde advised against drinking all fruit-based ciders, which 'engendered evil humours' and gave people wrinkles.

The drink often used at royal ceremonies was hippocras, another form of spiced wine, warmed at the edge of the fire, with cinnamon, cloves, ginger, nutmeg, honey, anise, citrus slices or any other combination, not too dissimilar to modern mulled wines.

Wine featured freely, both red and claret, white and sweet wine, used in cookery and at table, sometimes watered down to drink with spices or sugar. Andrew Boorde wrote in 1547 that 'wine moderately taken doth comfort the heart. And all good and temperate drinks, the which doth engender good blood doth comfort the heart. All manner of cordials and restoratives and all sweet and soothing things doth comfort the heart.'[6]

From the time of the Norman Conquest, wine had been produced from vineyards grown on English soil, with a surge of production in the twelfth and thirteenth centuries. By 1509, there were 139 vineyards in England and Wales, eleven of which were owned by the Crown, fifty-two by the monasteries and sixty-seven by independent landowners. The Dissolution of the 1530s impacted the local monastic supply, but by this point the industry was in decline. Imported wine sales grew, especially from the different regions of France and Germany, and the dry Spanish sack, although a 1600 health manual warned that 'sacke doth make men fat and foggy'. Anjou, Poitou, Gascony and Guienne were considered to be the best wine-making regions.

The Tudors added honey, sugar and spice to create 'bastard' wine, which referred to its sweetness. The cellar of Anne of Cleves' home in 1556, at Blackfriars, contained three hogsheads of Gascon at £3 a tonne, 10 gallons of malmsey, costing 20d per gallon, 11 gallons of muscadel at 2s 2d each and 10 gallons of sack, costing 16d per gallon.[7]

The accounts of the Field of Cloth of Gold of 1520 list great quantities of malmsey, romeneyes, muscadel, camplet, Gascon, Rhenish and 'French' wine, as well as ale and beer for the king's consumption. It appears that brewing was taking place at or near the English camp at Guînes, too, with payments to Edward ap John, overseer of the brewhouse at 'Medlewe'; to suppliers of hops and malt; renting the cellars; and to an individual for making hippocras in his cellar and for the grinding of wheat and oats.[8]

With all this alcohol being consumed, no matter how watered down, the literary trope of the merry drunk in Elizabethan drama comes as no surprise. Sir Hugh Plat included a recipe for the prevention of drunkenness in his 1594 *A Jewel House of Art and Nature*:

Drink first a good draught of sallet [salad] oil, for that will float upon the wine which you shall drink, and suppress the spirits from ascending into the brain. Also what quantity soever of new milk you drink first, you may well drink thrice as much wine after, without danger of being drunk. But how sick you shall be with this prevention, I will not here determine, neither would I have set down this experiment, but only for the help of such modest drinkers as sometimes in company are drawn, or rather forced to pledge in full bowls such quaffing companions as they would be loth to offend, and will require reason at their hands.[9]

The dangers of drinking too much, and speaking too freely, were apparent in an incident from April 1536, explained to Cromwell by Rowland Morton. A priest of 'little reputation and less discretion, of no promotion or learning ... chanced to be in light company in an alehouse and on his ale-bench', spoke certain words that resulted in him being committed to Gloucester Castle.[10]

❦ TASTE BUDS ❦

What did Tudor food actually taste like? Perhaps the most valuable source for understanding the sixteenth-century palate is contemporary cookbooks with their combinations of flavours and methods of preparation, which have allowed historical re-enactors to extrapolate and recreate Tudor dishes. An analysis of cookbooks dating from the end of the fourteenth century through to the end of the sixteenth shows the sameness of the tastes, in comparison with those of the twenty-first century.

With a few exceptions, dishes were prepared with ingredients or in sauces that made them predominantly milky, spicy, sharp or sweet, and the same handful of herbs reoccur in the vast majority of sweet and sour recipes. Barely anything escaped the popular cinnamon or ginger, blanched almonds or almond milk, lashings of salt and sugar or, if the household could afford it, a good dose of saffron, which would also colour the dish. Yet it is possible to observe a change in the flavours and ingredients as the era advanced, with more stodgy medieval-style fare at the advent of the Tudors, and fresher, sharper tastes used at the end.

The late-fifteenth-century *The Gentyllmanly Cokere* (Pepys MS 1047) favours a blend of sweet, sharp and milky flavours. Meats were usually cooked in sweet sauces, such as the capons stewed with saffron, wine, dates, raisins, sugar and powdered ginger, or the goose in red wine and ginger, or chicken stuffed with raisins, herbs, saffron and salt. Eels were cooked in saffron and ale, white fish with blanched almonds and sugar, peacock in ginger sauce, duck in honey mustard and herring with herbs and currants and served in a mustard ale sauce. As an alternative to a sweet style, meat and fish might be presented with sharp tastes, more to the modern palate. Salmon was cooked in a mixture of both, with the cinnamon and ginger offset by vinegar and salt, lobster eaten with vinegar, pike in hot mustard alone, and sturgeon and gurnard in pepper and vinegar.

The compiler includes many recipes of meat laid on 'sops' or toasted bread soaked in a liquid, which was usually almond milk, with saffron, sugar, wine and salt. Rice was also flavoured with almond milk, saffron and salt; vegetables were almost drowning in butter; poached eggs simmered in milk, ginger and saffron and were topped with cheese; while a galantine, or sauce, comprised breadcrumbs soaked in vinegar with the familiar ginger, cinnamon and pepper, but also the more unusual sandalwood and galingale. The writer adds that if this may prove too sharp, 'and if hit be to terte put more sugar ther to and that will amend hit'.

The palate of this household, or compiler, was not very varied. Much of the food would have tasted of cinnamon and ginger, both similarly warming spices, with a considerable amount of cloying milky and heavy dishes. Saffron was an expensive spice and it is used with consistency in this text, but otherwise the ingredients suggest the book's title: this was the range of food being consumed by the family of an early Tudor gentleman.[1]

A second recipe, or receipt, book of the late fifteenth century (Harleian MS 5401) favours a more sweet and milky palate, with a greater range of dishes, especially sweets, and more fish. The occasional meat dish was cooked in sweet spices, such as capon in ginger and cloves or saffron, but these are few and far between. The menu is dominated by fish: pike, fish broth, fish jelly, salmon, conger, whiting, lampreys, mussels, oysters, fish tarts, gurnard and eels, cooked in sweet sauces made of almond milk, saffron, ginger, cloves, galingale and wine. An exception is the caudle of mussels, which comes in a sharp-sweet combination of almond milk, vinegar and verjuice. Another recipe for eels makes the unusual pairing of saffron and mint, with parsley, ale and pepper.

Whoever compiled the collection included a number of almost cloyingly sweet dishes. White mortrew sauce was made from almond milk, with fine white breadcrumbs, honey and saffron; berleggs with cream of almonds, rice flour, ginger and saffron; charlet with pork, milk, eggs, ale, almond milk, ginger, saffron and sugar. Milky dishes dominate this section: roasted milk with saffron, cut into thick slices; blancmange with almond cream; meat, wine, vinegar, eggs, galingale, cloves and mace; almond-milk flans; cheese wrapped in nettles; milk jellies; rice pottage; sops in milk; and defoyles with cream, eggs, sugar, saffron and salt baked in pastry cases. The unusual mon ami was a cream dish boiled with saffron, sugar, eggs and butter, decorated with violet flowers, and the blanc de Surre, or white of Surrey, combined cow's milk, egg yolks, fine wheat bread, rice flour, cumin and saffron. Fruit dishes also feature, with pears in sweet wine syrup; fig fritters; fruit rissoles; apple tarts; stewed prunes with honey and galingale; and pears with cinnamon and anise.

Occasionally, a dish stands out for being different to the dominant palate, such as the sharp sauce madame, to accompany goose, made from sage, parsley, hyssop, savory, quince, pears and garlic. MS 5401 reflects a milky sweet palate, with a sweet tooth well catered for, and bland dishes that would have been rich but easy to eat. Perhaps this was personal preference, or a specific diet for an invalid.[2]

A Proper New Book of Cookery, dating from 1545, caters for a similarly sweet, milky palate, with the predominant ingredients being almond milk, saffron, ginger, sugar, cloves and salt. Sweet dishes include a cream and rose water snow; blancmange; apple pie with cinnamon; custard with dates and raisins; fruit and flower tarts like gooseberry, marigold and borage; and eggs in 'moonshine' or rose water. Meat dishes are flavoured with a restricted range of spices, mostly cinnamon, vinegar, sugar, pepper, salt and ginger, but also with fresh herbs or green vegetables like rosemary, thyme, parsley, savory, spinach and lettuce, as well as dates and raisins. A 'Stew after the Guise of beyond the Sea' sounds more exotic than its mutton, wine, onions, ginger, cinnamon, cloves, mace and salt suggest.[3]

John Partridge's 1573 *The Treasury of Commodious Conceits and Hidden Secrets* offers recipes for the table, treats for the storeroom and a range of cures and mixtures for health and hygiene. Its meat dishes are typical, with capon, chickens and pheasants baked with cloves, ginger, egg yolk, pepper, salt, cinnamon and verjuice, although the fruit-and-meat combination marries chicken with gooseberries. The majority of recipes are sweet. A marchpane, or marzipan, of almonds and rose water, constructed into shapes with the use of wafers and sugar, is followed by instructions for how to gild it in gold leaf. There are also recipes for baked quince in blanche powder; quinces and plums in syrup; conserves of roses and acorns, marmalade of green ginger, and syrups of various herbs and spices, including endive, nutmeg and musk.[4]

By the end of the century, a shift has occurred away from spices towards a fresher, more vegetable and herb-based cuisine, as found in Thomas Dawson's 1596 *The Good Housewife's Jewell*. Increasingly, meat is flavoured by garden ingredients instead of dried spices: larks are boiled with spinach, endives, pepper, cloves, cinnamon and verjuice; rabbits with parsley, sweet herbs, pepper and currants; and chickens with grapes, rosemary, thyme, marjoram, savory, hyssop and verjuice. Mutton is married with cabbage and lettuce; chicken with sorrel; plovers with spinach and parsley; teal with spinach and onion; although the throwback capon broth with prunes and dates was thickened with almond powder and the leg of mutton came with a pudding of parsley, pennyroyal, cinnamon, currants, cloves and mace. The old mortis recipe remains, made from chicken, milk, rose water, sugar and blanched almonds, but there is also a black pudding from oatmeal, blood, herbs, leeks and spices. The inclusion of 'A Strong Broth for Sick Men', with its blanched almonds, capon brains, cream and rose water, suggests a diet designed to cater for a particular individual.[5]

One possible reason for the shift towards the greater inclusion of vegetables in the latter half of the century was a shift in class tastes. Further detail was offered by Raphael Holinshed in 1548, who commented that 'melons, pumpkins, gourdes, cucumbers, radishes, parsnips and turnips', which had previously been eaten mostly by the poor, were starting to be eaten 'as dainty dishes at the tables of delicate merchants, gentlemen and the nobility who make their provision yearly for new seeds out of strange countries'.[6]

As late as the 1580s, such basic 'wortes' like carrots, turnips, cabbages and parsnips were still being sown as high-yielding crops to feed the poor, referred to by Thomas Cogan in his *Haven of Health*, as the 'common meat among the common people, all the time of autumn, and chiefly upon fish days'.[7] Such vegetables formed the basis of the universal pottage, developing a distinction between these and the more delicate melons, gourds and suchlike, which were planted with foreign seeds.

The Tudor taste buds appear to favour creamy or milky dishes, with almonds, cream and sugar, sweet but mellow spices like cinnamon, mace and ginger, and sharp verjuice and vinegars with their meat, fish and spices. While fruit appeared in recipes from the start of the period, often as an accompaniment to protein, fresh and dried fruit-based dishes increased in popularity and variety in tandem with the inclusion of more vegetables.

A slight shift towards the replacement of spices with herbs occurs at the end of the century, but many of the old favourites are still present. One constant, though, is the sheer number of dishes that were flavoured in some aspect by cinnamon. In some meals, almost every plate would have tasted of it, making cinnamon the dominant flavour of the Tudor palate. Compared with modern tastes, a Tudor meal would have been stodgy, heavy and samey.

Providing for the favoured tastes was not easy, and the cookbooks do not reflect the meals of the majority, rather the elite, who could afford their expensive ingredients. In 1526, John Blagge, a London grocer, acknowledged a debt of £596 for spices he had purchased in Antwerp: mace, large, at 19s 8d per pound; others at 16s 6d and 14s 6d; cloves 9s 6d; cinnamon, large, 7s 8d and others 5s 4d; 'grains' 2s 6d; pepper 2s 4d; verdigris 12d; ginger calico 22d; nutmegs 4s; almonds, three balls weighing 1,084lb at 18s 6d = £10 6d; rice, two bags weighing 680lb at 13s = £4 8s.[8]

By the advent of the Tudors, the spice trading routes were well established. Expensive, imported spices were very much a valued commodity and status symbol, as well as a favoured ingredient. The majority to arrive in English ports came from Venetian ships, whose merchants traded in the markets of Alexandria and Damascus, bringing ginger from Malabar, cinnamon from Ceylon, pepper from India, cloves from Malacca, wormwood from Persia, galingale from the East Indies and green ginger and brown sugar from Palermo.

Homegrown produce was also supplanted by superior foreign versions or replaced as English supply dwindled. Saffron came from Italy, rhubarb from Persia, syruped fruits from Palermo, currants from

Patros and dried prunes from Naples.[9] These catered to the English palate and were so treasured that they were kept locked inside special cabinets, the key of which was usually in the hands of the mistress of the house.

In 1535, Lady Lisle's agent in London, John Hussey, was sourcing spices to send her in Calais, but the sugar was proving expensive and some of the spices were powdered:

> I send the spices you wrote for in Philip Crayer's ship, John Davy, master, in a sugar chest 12 sugar loaves, a piece of great raisins, a topnet of figs, 4 dozen quarriers, and 4 dozen staff torches. The spices amount to £8. 18s, according to the prices of the grocer's own hand, enclosed in my Lord's own letter. I am bound to pay before I leave. Sugar is very dear, and likely to be dearer ... The bowls, trays, pestle, and trenchers will come by the next ship. You may send Mr. Skerne some cloth for kerchers or embroidered sleeves ... Some of your spices are powdered, as cinnamon, etc.[10]

❦ SWEETS ❦

Without doubt, the Tudors loved their sweets. Sugar became the most desirable ingredient, purchased in large cones with small pieces broken off as required. It features early in the records, with half a dozen ships noted as having arrived in Venice carrying loads of Madeira sugar, and that the price of sugar had fallen in Cyprus, Alexandria, Syria and other ports. By 1503, English markets favoured the sugar produced by Sicily to those of Madeira and the Levant.

Elizabeth I's famously black teeth belie the estimated average consumption of around 1lb a head, which seems comparatively small in the twenty-first century, but as with all luxury foods, the wealthy could afford a larger share. The sixteenth-century sugar obsession did not cause too much concern, though, as it had been given the stamp of health by Andrew Boorde in 1542, who wrote that 'all meates and drinkes the which is sweet and that sugar is in, be nutrytyve'.[1]

Recipes from Partridge's 1573 book include syrups, jams, marmalades and suckets, drawing on the naturally occurring sugars in fruit, but also adding sugar, honey, their favourite cinnamon and other sweeteners. A conserve of roses, or other flowers, used the unopened buds, 'somewhat before they be ready to spread', ground in a mortar, with 3oz of sugar for every 1oz of roses.[2] Violets were also a favourite, preserved with double the amount of sugar as the roses required, stored away in a stoppered bottle.

Other popular herbal conserves include borage, rosemary, succory, elderflower, sorrel and acorns, which called for the addition of honey, all of which were considered of benefit to the health. The most popular fruits were strawberries, damsons and cherries. Marzipan, or marchpane, was baked into edible shapes as well as the imposing subtleties or warners (literally warning of the feast's arrival) that impressed diners, and could be painted, dyed, decorated with fruit, nuts or flowers, or covered with gold leaf.[3]

Marmalade was also a favourite treat for those who could afford it, made from expensive, imported oranges or, more cheaply, from home-grown fruit. One recipe used ripe quinces, a common Elizabethan fruit shaped like a pear but bright yellow, which had been used in cookery since Roman times, although it is less well known now. The quinces were mashed and boiled, as if they were to be used in a tart, with sugar and rose water, and then cooled until it was set.[4] The recipe's author suggested that it could be gilded like marzipan, which was sometimes applied with a feather or a brush made from hairs from a rabbit's tail. When quinces were not available, or needed to be supplemented, good ripe apples could be included too. Marmalade could also be made with ripe damsons, pears, strawberries or similar fruits, boiled in the same way with sugar and sweet water.[5]

Succades of fruit peel were another popular treat. The rinds of oranges and lemons were boiled repeatedly until the water contained no bitterness before they were preserved in syrup and stored in a glass or pot. 'Green' ginger probably referred to young ginger, rather than any greenish colour, and was made by covering ginger in sand, five fingers thick, and sprinkling it with water twice a day until it was soft. Then it should be washed, scraped and placed in a syrup in a pot of stone.[6]

The Tudor sweet tooth was catered for by lozenges or boiled sweets made from sugar and rose water, cooled until hard, with any spices or powders of the cook's choosing. Then, they could be cut into diamond or lozenge shapes and covered with gold leaf, applied by a rabbit's tail. Similarly, manus christi was both a sweet syrup and another type of boiled sweet, with ground pearls stirred into it, gilded and then sweetened with almonds or butter. Crystallised or candied fruits were made in the distilling room, or still room, using cherries, apricots, peaches, grapes and oranges. The Tudors also enjoyed 'jumbles', or biscuits made in the shape of knots, with rose water and aniseed or caraway seeds, and 'kissing comfits', boiled and hardened from gum tragacanth, sugar and rose water. Thomas Elyot's 1534 *Castel of Helth* also includes liquorice and pistachios.[7]

The recipe books show the popularity of cream and cream-based dishes with the Tudors, both from cows and cream of almonds. A special, rich dish of cabbage cream was made from layers of clotted cream with sugar and rose water sprinkled between them. Cream and sugar was a favourite combination but eaten 'more for a sensual appetite than for any good nourishment', and Boorde had known banquets of strawberries and cream which had 'put men in jeopardy of their lives'.[8]

White pots, caudles, rice puddings, snows, fools and syllabubs were flavoured with ginger, cinnamon, mace and saffron, with the addition of fresh or dried fruit and flowers. Possets were made from milk or cream, thickened with eggs, ground almonds and grated Naples biscuits, flavoured with sack or a similar wine.

Nuts provided another source of sweetness and were grown in Tudor gardens in fashionable nut walks or nutteries. Almonds were an exception, being imported from abroad in order to cater for the huge quantities used. Walnuts, chestnuts and filberts were eaten alone, as accompaniments to fruit and cheese or incorporated into dishes.

Elizabeth's famously blackened teeth were not only a reflection of her sweet tooth but a statement of high class; in her ability to afford such treats. It was a fashion that her court aped.

⚘ EATING OUT ⚘

The restaurant had not truly evolved by the advent of the Tudors, but fast food certainly had. From the pie seller, balancing his tray and shouting his wares down the street, to the open-fronted stall that was little more than a shelf in front of a bakery, to the cook shop where you could sit down and eat a bowl of pottage and meat, England's towns and cities provided for their inhabitants when they needed to eat in a hurry. Equally, the influx of visitors to urban hubs, especially on market days, brought a whole new swathe of customers who needed something quick and hot to eat. The fifteenth-century poem, 'London Lickpenny' elaborates on the options:

> When I hied me into East Cheap:
> One cries ribs of beef, and many a pie:
> Pewter pots they clattered on a heap;
> There was harp, fife, and sautry
>
> Yea, and we shall be right welcome, I dare well say,
> In East Cheap for to dine;
> And then we will with Lombards at passage play,
> And at the Pope's Head sweet wine assay.
> When I hied me into East Cheap:
> One cries ribs of beef, and many a pie:
> Pewter pots they clattered on a heap;
> There was harp, fife, and sautry.[1]

London's cook shops and inns were mentioned as far back as the reign of Henry II and in the poetry of Chaucer. The Cook of *The Canterbury Tales* was renowned for his skills in boiling chicken, making powdered marzipan tart with galingale, roasting, seething, boiling and frying, and baking excellent pies.

From the limited references, it appears that many were centred around the Cheap district, the long street bisecting the city east–west, where markets where held, proclamations read and punishments enacted – where the most people gathered, food was required. A 1522 interlude, *World and the Child*, mentions dining in East Cheap, where the characters would be welcomed, followed by a game of 'passage' and drinking sweet wine at the Pope's Head tavern.[2] Shakespeare makes Mistress Quickly landlady of the Boar in East Cheap, an establishment in existence before 1537, which was destroyed in the Great Fire of 1666.[3]

However, the cook houses were not confined to Cheap. While walking in Westminster one night in the 1510s, Thomas More noted the number of food outlets that served those associated with the court. 'Whithersoever we cast our eyes, what do we see but victualling-houses, fishmongers, butchers, cooks, pudding-makers, fishers, and fowlers, who minister matter to our bellies?'[4]

Bake and brew houses catered to the poor and the public, as mentioned in John Stow's *Survey of London* in the 1590s. The Bridge House had originally been a store for wheat and grain, but recently ten ovens had been installed – six large and four half the size of those – to bake bread 'to the best advantage for relief of the poor citizens, when need should require'.[5] A nearby property, named Goldings, had been given to the city by a former mayor and in its place there was now 'a fair brew-house, new built, for service of the city with beer'. Stow also noted in Bridge Ward that the great stone house with arched gates, formerly the property of the prior of Lewes, had been turned into 'a common hostelry for travellers' at the sign of the Walnut Tree.[6] In Basing Lane, in Breadstreet Ward, another large old house, 'built upon arched vaults, and with arched gates of stone, brought from Caen in Normandy', was now 'a common ostelry for receipt of travellers commonly and corruptly cammed Gerrards Hall' and, in recent years, the hall was altered and 'divers rooms are made in it'.[7]

Cook houses might also be called upon to supplement the meals of great households, even that of the king or queen, such as in 1577, when Lord Keeper Bacon of Gorhambury paid London cooks £12 to help provision the house ahead of Elizabeth's visit. In Juan Luis Vives' dialogues, Apicius works at an eating house called the Poultry Cock and is hired by a private citizen to cater for a wedding.[8]

The number of taverns, or alehouses, serving ale and a basic meal, increased in number in the later decades of the sixteenth century: in Canterbury, they doubled between 1577 and 1596. As new urban centres for meetings, socialising and cheap food, they also became venues for the performance of actors and players, for whom their courtyards offered a convenient space, or ballad singers, jesters and game players who utilised the presence of the drinkers.

The Dissolution of the Monasteries and the resulting closure of the hospitality they offered created a new market to cater for the needs of travellers, and while those passing through could benefit from a meal and a bed, such venues also attracted locals and began a tavern culture where friends might meet away from home. The alehouse also provided a venue for the celebration of rite-of-passage events, which had previously been located in churches: betrothals, engagements, wakes, christenings, marriages and churching feasts.

✥ SUPPLY ✥

For the Tudors, what appeared on their table was always dependent upon supply. This might have been as simple as herbs picked outside the kitchen window, or fresh fruits brought to court from the countryside, or the arrival of carts bearing flour, to the more exotic ships bearing spices. Weather, seasons, price and human error might all affect the menu.

Ingredients were always best sourced as close to the kitchen as possible, but often foodstuffs had to be transported by road on carts, as slow as that was. As a result, it was difficult to keep some items fresh, so salted or smoked fish was more popular away from the coast, and shellfish proved notoriously dangerous.

A lot of trade went from the English ports and fields to the markets of the capital. In 1535, John Green of St Osyth in Essex received a permit from the collector of customs, to bring twelve cheeses, six seams of wheat and ten dozen Calais skins to London for sale,[1] and another St Osyth man, a monger, or grocer, John Wade, was licensed by the collectors of customs in Ipswich for wheat, rye and cheese.[2]

When the officers of Yarmouth were asked by William Cecil to name the quantities of victuals passing through the port, they admitted that the prices were higher than usual, with white herrings at 30s a barrel, and red herrings 10s, and these were in short supply, as the year had proved 'very troublesome for men to fish'.[3] That autumn though, Yarmouth recorded a variety of unusual goods arriving, suggesting that traders were seeking their luck elsewhere in the current dearth of fish, buying nails, vinegar, spices, cotton wool, gowns and mantles, women's hose, soap, flannels, coal, salt, cabbages, iron, hops and onions.[4]

Provisioning large establishments could be the most difficult, but while the court always received gifts and could commandeer local resources, other institutions could prove tricky to supply. When Sir William Fitzwilliam was responsible for stocking the garrison at Guînes in 1524, he estimated a quantity of beef, mutton, ling and other fish to feed 1,000 men for a period of six weeks, including the costs incurred in transporting them to Calais, suggesting that suppliers across the Channel in England were being preferred over those near Guînes in northern France. Wolsey thought the costs of movement were too large, but Fitzwilliam assured him that it would cost

2s to transport an ox and 4d for a sheep, but he found himself unable to estimate costs for butter and cheese.[5]

Down at Dover in 1537, the king's labourers were going hungry, according to John Golde, although he could not uncover the reason why:

> This day we were of laborers 280 and more, and of tide men 94. Our butchers are ready to give over their shops. Of the brewers we can get no drink. The King must leave off the men for lack of victuals. You must find a remedy before you come down, for you never see the case that here is ... I have inquired at Hyde concerning the butcher's behaviour and this day could not substantially find the fault, where this scarcity was. We have much need for the redress of corn.[6]

Anthony, Lord Roos, was responsible for sending supplies to Calais in January 1545, including 100 weight of cheeses, 50 barrels of butter, 400 quarts of wheat and 500 of malt, but he was aware of the dangers, writing to Lord Cobham that these would 'be with you as soon as God sends wind and weather, if not intercepted by enemies'. More malt had been ordered too, but it was not available yet, 'there being such a small store that we had much ado to furnish the quantity now sent to Boulogne'.[7]

When Edward Baesh was estimating amounts required to supply the queen's ships in harbour for a whole year in 1564, he commented that 'as old experience teaches him, it is far better and cheaper to make provision from the bakers, brewers and butchers by agreement at prices to be arranged monthly according to the plenty or scarcity of the articles' instead of giving a supplier a commission, which could result in the royal purse being charged too much and the provisions being too little.[8]

The council was concerned in February 1574 about 'the daily rise in the price of corn and all manner of victuals'. Following a bad harvest and a dearth of produce, the council had foreseen the problem and 'provided well', but their best-laid plans had failed when it came to 'the transporting of beer' and the forestalling of corn coming from the ports. After the city of London ordered 4,000 quarters of wheat, the price suddenly rose from 12 and 13 groats to 15 and 16, 'and some markets were left almost destitute of corn'. Emergency measures were required, wrote Sir Thomas Scott, especially to sustain the poor through the summer:

If, as in some parts spoken of, such as have corn brought by turns a certain quantity every market day, the markets might conveniently be served till Whitsuntide or Midsummer, when the poor people, by the warmth of the year, the fruits of the earth, and the increase of cattle, might be sustained.[9]

In 1545, the Scots were blamed for the dearth of supplies on the border as they were 'daily coming into the realm whereby victuals upon the frontier wax scarce', so Henry VIII agreed that his local wardens should devise some remedy.[10] However, England and Scotland were then engaged in the hostilities of 'the rough wooing', following the Scots' defeat at the Battle of Solway Moss. Warfare impacted upon the availability and movement of supplies, as Sir William Petre found in Calais the following year. 'Victuals,' he wrote, 'especially flesh, are dearer than during the wars, owing to the restraint in England, which is straiter and otherwise than hath been accustomed.' Petre's deputy prayed him to send schedules of the numbers of beef and mutton killed weekly, and the live numbers remaining.[11]

Important households required a constant stream of deliveries in order to maintain the lifestyles of the aristocracy. The expenses of Sir Thomas le Strange in one month in the 1520s included:

1st week. Sunday: a pig, 4d.; 14 rabbits and 2 hernsewes [heron] of store. Monday: a pig, 14 rabbits and 2 hernsewes of store, and 1 hare. Tuesday: 10 rabbits and a hernsewe of store; 4 dotterels, 3d.; 2 mallards, killed with the cross-bow. Wednesday: a sole, 1d. Thursday: 12 rabbits and 2 hernsewes of store; 2 mallards, killed with the cross-bow; 12 dotterels, 9d. Friday: 1 sole, 1d. Saturday: a sole, 1d.; a salmon trout, 2d.; 3 cod, 13½d.; ¾ of a ling, 6¾d.; fresh cod, 4d.; plaice, 6d.; crabs, 1½d.; 150 eggs, 9d.; butter, 18 cakes of store; 6st. of beef, 2s. 9d.; half a veal, 10d.; a quarter of veal of store; a mutton, 3s. 4d.; a lamb of store; pigeons, 1d.; 3 b. wheat, 21d.; 5 barrels of beer, 5s. 10d.[12]

Even the household of the disgraced Thomas Wolsey in 1529 was recorded as consuming 621 beasts between Easter and August, 363 in August and September, 430 oxen and 181 mutton in October and 728 beasts in November, at a cost of £204 17s.[13]

Important households were not immune from the difficulties in procuring specific supplies. John Draper, prior of Christchurch, Canterbury, wrote to thank Lord Lisle in 1535 for sending him two storks, one of which had been delivered alive by the servant but the other was drowned on the way, although the meat was good. Draper had nothing to send in return, except for an ox, which he had dispatched alive to Lisle's ship. He had planned to send salmon, both barrelled and baked, but 'could not send them because Swifte was in trouble'. Exactly what Swifte had done, and why it impacted the delivery of salmon, was not stated.[14]

The diet of the nobility was particularly targeted in 1543, following 'a great mortality happening among the cattle'. There was such a dearth of beef that a sumptuary law was passed by the London Council 'to restrain luxurious feasting'. It was ordained that the mayor should be limited to a maximum of seven dishes at dinner and supper; aldermen and sheriffs were to have six; the sword bearer four; and the mayor and sheriff's officers three, with a penalty of 40s being incurred for every additional dish.[15]

Another emergency in supply arose in 1582 when 'the wheat of Sussex hath this harvest greatly failed, being much light and smitten', so the price had risen to 23s or 24s per quarter. Thomas Blank, Mayor of London, requested that three ships at Faversham, the *Rowe* of Newcastle and the *Burre* and *Marie Katherine* of London, were prevented from sailing with their 1,500 quarters of wheat, as it was needed.[16]

Sometimes dearth was preceded by a glut of a certain item. One year, it was recorded by Harrison that saffron was so plentiful that the inhabitants of Walden (Saffron Walden) 'said in blasphemous manner' that 'God did now shit saffron', but some of the offenders died soon after as beggars, and twenty years later 'there was so little of this commodity, that it was almost lost and perished in England'.[17] The production and popularity of saffron had tailed off by the mid-sixteenth century, although it was still used by the wealthy, and Sir Francis Drake believed that what kept the English people 'sprightly' was their 'liberal use of saffron in their broths and sweetmeats'.

✳

Food items were often given as gifts, between families, communities or as part of patterns of allegiance, where the sharing of luxury food was a status symbol. Royal and aristocratic figures attracted both luxury and practical gifts, as the giver could afford, to win favour, but also to provision their table while they were staying in particular locations.

In 1527 Henry VIII's illegitimate son, the 8-year-old Henry Fitzroy began to cultivate a friendship with James V of Scotland, who was then 15, by sending him a suitable gift. James replied, thanking him 'for his honest present for the game of hunting' and sending, in return, 'two brace of hounds for deer and smaller beasts'. He also offered, 'if the Duke take pleasure in hawking', to send 'some of the best red hawks in the realm' when the season was right.[18]

In 1535, Henry VIII attempted to curry favour with Emperor Charles V by sending him something for his table. John Gostwyk wrote to Cromwell, explaining that he had discharged his duty: 'On Tuesday last, I delivered to the Emperor's ambassador as fat a stag as I have seen in my life, for which he has given you and the king hearty thanks.'[19]

Wherever a monarch travelled, they attracted gifts. Elizabeth of York's privy purse accounts for 1502 show the range of items she received while at Richmond Palace in March and April. The givers of gifts were not always wealthy, either:

John Goose, 'my Lord of York's fool' brought a carp.

The daughter of the keeper of the King's Place at Westminster gave almond butter.

A servant of the prothonotary of Spain brought a gift of oranges on the same day that a poor man brought oranges and apples, and a poor woman brought butter and chickens.[20]

After Elizabeth had moved to Greenwich in April, she continued to receive offerings from those close by, when a servant of William Bulstrode brought wardens, a kind of large pear. When she moved to the Tower in May, the queen was sent rose water by the 'Abbess of the Minoresse [sic]', and at Richmond later, a Frenchman sent apples, Lady Bray sent puddings and a servant of the prior of Hitchin brought apples and a 'quysshyn [cushion]'.[21]

When Elizabeth I was staying at Richmond in the autumn and winter of 1578, she received a number of varied gifts. Sir Harry Lee sent two doves, Mr Lewis Dyve four pheasants and four little cheeses and Mr Edmonds two pheasants. These gifts tended to be taken from the land and livestock of locals, who dispatched them to the queen with their servants. Game was a common, fresh treat, sometimes live but often dead, to be taken directly to the royal kitchens. Deer, pheasants, woodcock, plovers, larks, rabbits and chickens appeared regularly in the list compiled by William Cecil to record what was received, often for purposes of giving the benefactor a small, monetary reward. Locals also sent what little gems they had sitting in their larders for the benefit of the queen: cheeses, puddings, pasties, pies and pots of jelly.[22]

❧ DANGEROUS FOODS ❧

The tomato and potato were two new arrivals at the Elizabethan court, brought by travellers to the New World. The red-fleshed sweet potato is thought to have arrived first in 1564, with the return of John Hawkins from Hispaniola and the coast of Guinea, described by Richard Hakluyt twenty-five years later as 'the most delicious roots that may be eaten and do exceed our parsnips or carrots'. The common or white potato arrived later, probably after 1580, but before its inclusion in *Gerard's Herbal* of 1597, but it was scarcely used for a century or more.

The tomato received an even less warm welcome. Classified by Italian herbalist Pietro Mattioli as part of the deadly nightshade family, the 'golden apple' tomato was renamed the 'poison apple' and avoided. The tomato's high acidity also reacted with the lead in pewter plates and did result in some cases of lead poisoning, for which the humble fruit was blamed. *Gerard's Herbal* did the tomato no favours either, describing it as rank and stinking, but admitting that the fruit was not poisonous, although he thought the leaves and stalk were. They were grown in English gardens from the 1590s – not to be eaten but for their beauty.

Real cases of poisoning in the Tudor era were scarce. In February 1531, John Fisher, Bishop of Rochester, and his household and guests at Lambeth ate a meal which included a dish of pottage. Afterwards, a number of the diners became ill and two died: a member of Fisher's household and a woman who had sought alms at the gate. Fisher had either been fasting or had not been hungry and did not partake of the meal.

A Richard Roose, who was not employed as a cook but had been present in the kitchen, was arrested for having cast some powders, or yeast, into the pottage as it was being prepared. He was subsequently questioned in the Tower and tortured on the rack, where he confessed to having added a powder that he believed to have been a laxative into the dish.

Contemporary chronicler Edward Hall suggests that Roose was the scapegoat for someone who had sent him out of the room briefly while poison was added or convinced him to add a substance he believed was fairly innocuous. He thought the intended target was Fisher, because of his opposition to the king's divorce. Roose suffered the horrific death of being boiled to death at Smithfield.

In 1546, James Butler, Earl of Ormond, the man who the Boleyns had intended for Anne, was invited to dine by John Dudley at his London home of Ely Place. During the meal, he and seventeen members of his household were poisoned, with James dying nine days later. As Earl of Ormond and a key player in the Irish family feuds of the day, he did not lack enemies, but there was no apparent cause for Dudley's involvement, and no accusation was made against him.

It may or may not be purely coincidental that Dudley's family experienced their own case of poisoning a few years later, when his son Guildford married Jane Grey on 25 May 1553 in a busy ceremony at Durham House. The French and Venetian ambassadors were invited to the 'very splendid, and royal, wedding, with a large gathering of people, and of the principal [people] of the realm', but the cook preparing the food made an error when making a salad. 'Sallets', or salads, contained more ingredients than today and often described any vegetable dish, but in this case the cook mistakenly 'plucked one leaf for another'. Guildford and several of the guests fell ill as a result, and Guildford at least continued to experience symptoms into the middle of June.

Royal food was tested carefully for poison before it reached the monarch's table. This intensified from the 1560s when Elizabeth was a target for Catholic plots, with Francis Walsingham uncovering her enemies' intention to introduce a foreign substance into her meals. Cecil insisted that she was not to accept any gifts of perfumed gloves. All perfumes and cosmetics were to be tested by her ladies, no underwear was to touch her skin and no unauthorised people were allowed near her wardrobe.

In August 1568, Franchiotto, an Italian, professed his forty loyal years of service and devotion to the queen before warning her 'that the advices she has recently received are not by any means to be despised' and begged her 'to exercise great watchfulness over her food, utensils, bedding and other furniture, lest poison should be administered to her by her secret enemies'.[1]

An attempt to poison Elizabeth's betrothed 'Monsieur', then the Duke of Alençon, in 1575 reveals the easiest way to administer poison, and its dramatic effects:

> As the attempt upon his life will be variously reported writes himself the true facts. Last evening there was served at his collation some wine so strongly poisoned that immediately the Sieur de Thore, his cousin, and others drank it they were taken with such violent vomiting that but for prompt help their enemies would have had the satisfaction they desired. Begs Dr. Dale to inform the Queen of England that he is well now.[2]

Poisons could be subtle and difficult to taste, masked by opposing scents and tastes. The French physician Ambrose Pare wrote in his treatise on poisoning in 1585 that it was hard to avoid poison because 'by the admixture of sweet and well-smelling things, they cannot easily be perceived even by the skilful', so those who 'fear poisoning ought to take heed of meats cooked with much arts'. He described one method used by poisoners – introducing dangerous elements into a pomander, which released a wave of poison every time the wearer moved.

Accidental poisoning as the result of food being mouldy, infected or incorrectly prepared rarely arose, or were not considered worthy of mention. The Tudors seem to have managed well enough without modern methods of refrigeration and storage, with their wet and dry larders, their use of syrups and spices to preserve and mask tastes, and their dishes that adapted to availability, like pottage. Where cases of poisoning occurred, whether deliberate or not, additional items were deliberately introduced into the meal or were incorrectly identified. Along with their understanding of the Galenic theory of the humours, the Tudors understood that certain foods could harm, and avoided those they did not trust.

Candles were central to the Tudor experience, illuminating their religious and domestic spaces, and their long, dark nights. Placed upon the altar, they took on a religious symbolism, representing the presence of Christ and the light of salvation, providing hope amid the darkness occasioned by fear and illness, witchcraft and devilry. Richer people could afford cleaner candles which smoked and smelled less, while the poorer folk made theirs from tallow.

A quick and effective way of spreading news was by the lighting of beacons, particularly at night. By placing these metal cages at prominent locations, filling them with kindling and setting them alight, simple warnings could be made visible from miles away, establishing a national network. In 1588, beacons along the south coast were responsible for the rapid spread of news about the approaching Spanish Armada.

The Tudors lived in an expanding world, but recording this process was a challenge. After Christopher Columbus' voyage to America in 1492, map-makers developed more sophisticated representations of the known earth in their mappae mundi, as fresh travellers brought back more detailed information. Such maps were often highly decorated and featured information or representations of mythical creatures or personifications of the wind.

Above left: Hampton Court's reproduction of a Tudor railed garden demonstrates one of the ways that nature was tamed for human pleasure. With carved heraldic beasts, flowers and walkways laid out with rails painted in royal white and green, it was an ornamental, additional outside room attached to the palace.

Above right: By contrast, Hampton Court's knot garden was more about utility than beauty. Named after the intricate, geometrical patterns laid out in the planting, knot gardens contained herbs, fragrant plants and useful flowers, for use in the kitchen, around the house and in medicine.

The hearth was the centre of every Tudor home, from richest to poorest. It offered not only warmth, light and comfort, but the opportunity to prepare food, drinks and cures, to assist in the care of clothing, and in domestic industry. Whilst being the main life force, it paradoxically was also the greatest source of danger and death in the home, with accidents occurring in cramped city dwellings on a regular basis, some of which proved fatal.

Roses were a universal commodity in Tudor times. They were a representative symbol of the dynasty, objects of beauty, sources of perfume, stuffing for pomanders, dessert flavourings, medicine ingredients and had their petals candied. The highly prized Damask roses were used to scent water for handwashing, often gifted to the king or queen.

Cinnamon, in the form of bark strips and powder, was a popular Tudor ingredient, thought to have warming properties. It was used in all manner of medicines and dishes as well as in the *voidée*, a spice dish used on religious and ceremonial occasions, along with wine. The main supply was shipped to England from Indonesia, until Magellan discovered it in the Philippines.

Inside the still room, or distillery, at Kentwell Hall, Suffolk. Flowers, herbs and other ingredients were ground, boiled, steamed, filtered and transformed, to preserve their essences to be used as perfumes, cures and ingredients. The mistress of the household oversaw this work, and a distillery attached to a house was a sign of status.

Pomanders, such as the one pictured here, might be homemade from simple ingredients or bought from gold and silversmiths. Filled with herbs and sometimes containing a ball of solid perfume and spices, they were carried or hung from the waist to ward off bad smells. The simplest were a piece of dried fruit, such as an orange or apple, stuck with cloves and suspended on a ribbon.

A group of singers, from the 1568 *Book of Trades*. Not much singing is taking place in this leafy arbour, but the group appear to be examining copies of a musical score, one of which, sitting on the table, is marked Bass.

The lute, affordable, accessible and portable, making it the most common instrument of the Tudor era. Whilst it could be played in the marketplace or to celebrate the harvest, it might also represent social mobility, such as in the case of Mark Smeaton, whose talent brought him to Henry VIII's court despite his humble origins.

The church of St Peter and St Paul, Lavenham, Suffolk, is typical of the wealth developed in late medieval England as the result of the wool trade. By Tudor times, many East Anglian towns had such a church in the perpendicular style, ornamented to display the standing of local families. At the centre of this trade, Lavenham was one of the most thriving locations, where the evidence of its past prosperity can be found in its religious and domestic architecture.

Tudor cities were full of narrow, winding lanes, flanked by tall, overhanging buildings. This created a dark, dirty and often smelly environment at street level. Like York's famous Shambles, which was dedicated to butchery, many lanes were named after the specific trades that operated there.

The English countryside was littered with sheep, revealing the nation's largest export and source of wealth. Providing meat, lambs, butter, milk and cheese, sheep were fairly low maintenance and were more common than people. The Tudors were used to the sights, sounds and smells of animals with whom they lived in close proximity to, from their birth to slaughter, and the disruption of whole herds being driven through the streets to market.

The two-storeyed banqueting house at Melford Hall, Suffolk, is set in the outer wall of the estate, and was used as an alternative venue for the fashionable final course of a meal featuring sweet dishes such as pastries, tarts, jellies, custards and cream.

The dairy at Kentwell Hall, Suffolk. Milk, cream, cheese and curds were made in the dairy, which was lined with tiles or stone to keep it cool and easy to clean. Although cows were prized, it was the more affordable sheep who provided the Tudors with most of their dairy products. Like the distillery, the dairy was often the province of women, supervised by the mistress of the house.

A variety of herbs and dry ingredients were grown in Tudor gardens, from single beds and pots on windows sills to garden patches, to full herb and knot gardens, used dried or fresh, according to season.

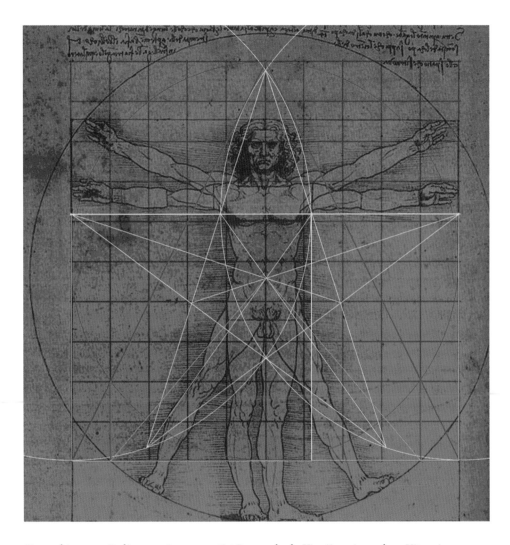

Created in 1490, Italian renaissance artist Leonardo da Vinci's universal, or Vitruvian, man depicted the ideal proportions of the human body. To achieve this, the artist measured a number of male models in Milan, considering the workings of the body to be a microcosm for the universe, reflective of its ideal state. Da Vinci's image captures the body shape that was recreated in artworks and sculpture across northern Europe and helped shape the aesthetic behind the depiction of kings.

Falconry was a popular sport among the Tudor aristocracy, who used the opportunity to display their skills and status. Birds were hooded until they were required to perform and would sit upon a gloved arm, to be encouraged to fly and return, to hover or hunt, before an audience. Manuals were written about the care, rearing and training of birds of prey.

Little Moreton Hall, Cheshire, a moated and timbered manor house dating from 1504, contains a long gallery, running along the entire length of the top floor of the building's south range. Lined with windows on both sides, the gallery was intended to facilitate exercise when the weather was poor, but its weight has caused the beams on the floors below to warp and buckle.

Ludlow Castle, the marital home of Prince Arthur and Catherine of Aragon from December to April 1502, set on the Welsh border. The castle was considered to have contributed to Arthur's premature death as the result of its wet climate and unhealthy vapours.

Once used profusely in England, saffron was farmed in Essex and Cheshire, although the industry was waning by the sixteenth century and the three red stigmas of the crocus flower were imported from the east instead. It was popular as a flavouring and colouring in wealthy Tudor dishes, especially dessert such as jellies and custards.

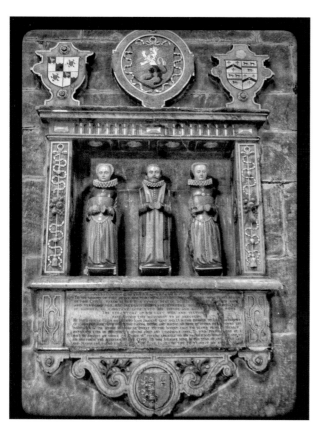

Memorial in Chester Cathedral to Thomas Greene, Mayor of the City, who died in 1602, and his wives Ellen and Dorothie. The wives are identical, but painted in different colours, while Greene wears his ceremonial robes; all three have wide, white ruffs.

As in this Doom scene, at Waltham Abbey, Essex, pre-Reformation church interiors were painted with visions of heaven and hell in graphic detail and colour, intended to inspire the congregation to good behaviour. Such visual reminders featured significantly in the lives of a largely illiterate community who attended church on a regular basis.

Tomb of Sir William Cecil in St Martin's Church, Stamford, Lincolnshire. His head rests upon an embroidered pillow, with his long beard, modest ruff and red cloak lined with ermine. Elizabeth I's chief advisor for years, he wears golden armour and clasps his staff of office as he lies under a splendid double canopy tomb on a marble base, topped with heraldic devices. It is a tomb which proclaims his importance.

This ape doctor with a urine flask is depicted on a misericord in Holy Trinity Church, Stratford upon Avon, as a warning against quack doctors. The diagnosis of illness by examining the colour and texture of a patient's urine, or urinalysis, was commonly used throughout the Tudor era.

The double tomb of Elizabethan couple Sir Edward Denny and his wife Margaret in Waltham Abbey, Essex. Denny died in 1601 and Margaret commissioned the tomb, although she did not fill her place beside him until 1648. Depicted in colourful detail in their best clothing, and lying on their sides, the pair project a far more physical presence the figures on traditional, reclining tombs.

PART V

TOUCH

☙ THE HUMOURS IN BALANCE ☙

In Tudor England, survival frequently depended upon physical strength and good health. As part of a more physically exuberant culture, whether labouring, hunting, riding or fighting, with life-threatening diseases recurring year after year and limited medical assistance in cases of accident, illness and childbirth, keeping healthy was a delicate balancing act for the sixteenth-century man, woman and child. The best path was a combination of dietary and astrological advice, a heavy weighting of prayer and avoiding excess in all things.

As Thomas Elyot outlined in his 1534 *The Castel of Helth*, the Galenic theory of humours underpinned sixteenth-century under-standing about the workings of the body and mind and how it related to the natural world, resulting in some unusual conclusions about the best way to maximise health and treat illness. Each individual body contained a mixture of the four humours; sanguine (blood), phleg-matic (phlegm), choleric (yellow bile) and melancholy (black bile), which broadly corresponded to four states: heat, cold, moisture and dryness, and the four elements: earth, air, fire and water. Usually one type was slightly more prevalent, but some individuals were believed to experience a great imbalance, resulting in the dominance of cer-tain characteristics or combinations, such as hot and dry, or hot and moist. This might be the result of natural disposition towards one type, illness or infection, the result of diet, or exposure to extreme temperatures or external factors.

A sanguine individual, with an excess of blood, was predominantly hot and moist, and ruled by the air. They were characterised by 'car-nosity' or fleshiness, and addicted to matters of the flesh, having large appetites for food, drink and sex. They had plentiful hair, which might be red or reddish, while the face was pale and ruddy, with red cheeks, and their veins and arteries were large and their pulse strong. They slept a lot and had vivid dreams of either 'bloody' or pleasant things, had perfect digestion and sweated profusely. Quick to anger, they pro-duced 'red and gross' urine and bled copiously.[1]

The direct opposite of a sanguine man was one of a phlegmatic dis-position, being cold and moist, governed by the element of water. He was soft and flabby, with narrow veins and a weak pulse, with a white complexion and much 'plain' hair. He slept 'superfluously' and dreamed of watery or fishy topics, was slow and dull when it came to thought and learning, displayed cowardice, and his digestion was weak. He produced abundant white spittle and his urine was thick and gross, white and pale.[2]

The choleric man, of yellow bile, was hot and dry and ruled by fire. He was lean in body, with face and skin either red as fire or sallow, and hair black or dark, or auburn, and often curly. He required little sleep but dreamed of fire, fighting or anger, and was often constipated and produced a strong-coloured, clear urine. His wit was sharp and quick, his voice sharp, the pulse swift and strong and, overall, he was a hardy fighter.[3]

The melancholy man, filled with black bile, was cold and dry, with the sign of the earth. He was prone to misery, as the name suggests. He was lean and his skin was hard, with 'plain' and thin hair and 'dusky' in colour. He was timorous and fearful, spending much time worrying and seldom laughing. His dreams were full of fears and he was stiff, or fixed, in his opinions, with a weak pulse and slow, poor digestion. His urine was watery and thin.[4]

Each of these elements could affect the different parts of the body, regardless of what an individual's dominant body type might be. The brain, the complexion, the heart, liver, stomach and genitals could each be taken over by one of the four combinations. Thus, the hot stomach could digest well, especially hot, spicy flavours and hard meats, but light meats might be 'corrupted' by their system and generally the appetite was poor and slow. The cold stomach craved food, but although this person loved cold meat and drink, it grew sour and damaging inside him and was poorly digested, and he could not stomach hard meat. The moist stomach was seldom thirsty but still craved drink, which led to superfluous, dangerous drinking, and delighted in moist meats. The dry stomach was always thirsty but only required a little drink and ate dry meats.

Elyot also identified four physical phases relating to the humours. Surprisingly, he considered adolescence, or youth, to last until the age of 25, during which the body was growing and was in a hot and moist state. Between 25 and 40, what Elyot called 'Juventute', the bodily condition of heat and dryness resulted in perfect growth; at the age of 40 to 60, 'Senectute', the body was cold and dry and 'decreasing' until old age arrived after 60, usually cold and dry, but 'accidentally moist'.[5]

The four elements crucial to health, air, earth, fire and water, could also be altered by external factors. The quality of the air might be influenced by certain stars, great bodies of stagnant water, carrion 'lying long above ground' or 'much people in small room lying uncleanly and sluttishly'. Certain winds could bring wholesome air, such as one blowing from the northerly direction, which was thought to prolong life and expel ill vapours, while wind from the east was temperate and lusty. Southern winds, though, were corrupting and created ill vapours, while that from the west was mutable 'which nature doth hate'.[6]

The primary treatment for an imbalance of humours was through diet. All edible substances were considered to also conform to Galenic theory, containing the four qualities of heat, and could react to the same in the human body, so particular foods were to be avoided by those who understood their specific disposition. The choleric man should not eat too much garlic, onion, rocket, leeks, mustard, pepper, honey, sweet meats or drink too much wine.

An individual whose humours were in perfect balance might begin to exhibit symptoms of choler if they overindulged in these items. The same was true for the foods associated with phlegm, which were all 'slimy and cleaving meats', new cheese, all fish, the inner organs of animals, lamb, cucumber and rape seed.

The melancholy man should avoid beef, boar, goat and hare, salted meat and fish, pulses except for white peas, coarse brown bread, 'great fishes of the sea', old flesh, old cheese, thick wine and black wine.[7]

Equally, the internal qualities of each food – hot, cold, moist and dry – could affect the organs in any well-balanced body, for better or for worse. The diagnosis of foods was based upon their appearance, textures, flavour and origin, as well as the belief in the theory of 'signatures', in which nature had left a visual key or clue in every foodstuff to indicate its intended use. Thus, when a food was cut in half, its cross-section could suggest the shape of the heart or lungs, and vegetables growing into phallic shapes were good for the reproductive health. Direct correlations existed too: animals' brains were good fuel for the human brain and consuming their organs could directly help those whose corresponding organs were weak.

To prevent the 'juices' of the body from thickening, Elyot advised the avoidance of musty rye bread, unleavened bread and cake bread, great sea fish, shellfish and beef kidneys. Also off the list were pig's liver, all round vegetables, sodden milk, cucumber, sweet wine, deep red wine, garlic, mustard, origanum, hyssop, basil, fennel, cheese, hard-boiled or fried eggs, chestnuts, green figs, unripe apples, peppers, rocket, leeks and onions.[8]

Certain foods were thought capable of hurting the teeth due to their content. These included very hot meat, sweet meats, nuts and sweet drinks, hard meat, radish, bitter meat, milk, leeks, fish fat and lemon. The eyes were affected by mustard, all pulses, sweet and thick wines, hemp seed, very salty meats, garlic, onions and radish, as well as drunkenness, lechery and reading immediately after supper. People suffering from wind should avoid all beans, cucumber, herb juices, figs, mustard and poorly made honey.[9]

Many foodstuffs were actively beneficial for the health when used in the correct context, even some unusual ones that were rarely or never used in cookery. Galingale, marjoram, mint, nutmeg, musk, rosemary, rose, peony, camomile, hyssop and rue were thought to be good for the head. Cinnamon, saffron, cloves, mace, mint, musk, nutmeg, rosemary, marjoram, borage, ground coral, pearls and 'the bone of the heart of the red deer' were good for the heart. The liver was aided by wormwood, agrimony, saffron, cloves, endive, raisins, fennel, violets, lettuce and rose water, while hyssop, liquorice, raisins, almonds, dates and pistachios improved the lungs.

It comes as no surprise that the Tudors believed the herb eyebright to be beneficial to the sight and eye health, along with fennel, vervain, roses, celandine, agrimony, cloves and cold water. The stomach was best served by nutmeg, pistachios, quince, saffron, coral, agrimony, galingale, cloves, coriander and 'the inner most skin of a hen's gizzard', as well as the expected mint, which may have actually achieved results.[10]

John Partridge's 1573 *The Treasury of Commodious Conceits* was also predicated on the belief that the right diet was essential in keeping the four humours in balance. His numerous cures applied the properties of particular food items to the body, internally or externally, with directions about their properties and effects. Certain items were believed to be stronger in terms of the humours and were classified in degrees of strength. Roses were considered to be cold and moist in the second degree, thus they could be laid upon a burning sore and calm a fever in the stomach. Lilies, however, were cold and dry in the third degree, 'so sayeth Galen', so made a plaster for burns and scaldings, as well as being able to remove freckles and spots. Rosemary, hot and dry, could make you merry, rid you of evil dreams, remove worms from the teeth, aid gout, cleanse the complexion and reduce swelling, amid a myriad of other miracle cures.[11]

One of the principal methods used by physicians to diagnose illness was by the examination of a patient's urine, usually gathered in a flask. Charts were created to compare the differing colours and degrees of cloudiness or clarity, and this was related to astrological charts, known as 'volvelle', to determine the most auspicious time for treatment.

Partridge's brief treatise of urine was intended 'to judge by the colours, which betoken health, which betoken sickness, and which also betoken death'. This was part of a wider diagnostic tool for, as he explains, sickness dwelt in four parts of the body: the womb, head, liver and bladder.

The ideal urine, betokening perfect health, was clear in the morning, red before meat, white after meat and not too thick. 'Thick' (presumably concentrated) urine indicated a headache, while fat, white and moist urine pointed to quartan fever. Bloody urine meant that the bladder was hurt by some rottenness, but someone peeing blood without pain may have trouble with their veins.

Women's urine was an entirely different matter. If it was clear and shining, even silvery, and if she urinated frequently and was off her meat, she was likely to be pregnant. Strong, white, stinking urine indicated illness in the reproductive organs, which were likely to be 'full of evil humours', but women with dark, golden urine were full of lust and desire for a man. If a woman's urine 'hath colour of stable cleansing', she was likely to have the fever and would die within three days, but urine of the colour of lead in a pregnancy meant she had lost her child.[12]

As well as correcting the diet, the main way Tudor physicians restored the balance of humours was through bloodletting. Bad humours infecting the blood were released by an incision in the vein, usually in the wrist, but sometimes in the ankle, 'whereby the blood, which is the cause of sickness or grief to the whole body' could 'pass'. Rather than weakening an invalid, it was thought to relieve them, as they were too full of blood, which led to a fulness or inflammation, expelling what was 'contrary to nature'.

In August 1504, the young widowed Catherine of Aragon fell ill while visiting the king at Greenwich Palace, 'suffering from ague

and derangement of the stomach'. She returned home but was 'rather
worse' when she got there, suffering alternately from sweating and
chills, losing her appetite completely, developing a cough and her
complexion changing 'completely'. The physician, who 'generally
bleeds well', purged her twice and made two attempts to bleed her,
with no success.[13]

Boorde believed that those who ate and drank to excess were most
helped by bloodletting, while those who were temperate, 'keeping
good diet', did not need this. They were helped instead by 'bathes,
exercise, walking, and riding moderatly. Also unctions with oyles and
oyntments called Diaphoretice, which by evaporation, doe shortly
evacuate the fullnes.'[14]

❧ PLAGUE AND SWEAT ❧

In April 1501 Arthur, Prince of Wales, the intended future king of
England, died at the age of 15. Newly married to Catherine of Aragon,
Arthur was based at Ludlow Castle on the Welsh Marches, where
his last public engagement was during the celebrations for Maundy
Thursday on 24 March. The prince may have been distributing money
to the poor, or even assisting in the traditional foot washing, as was
customary. At the time, it was recorded that a 'great sickness' was in
the area, which may have been the plague, or more likely the sweat, a
particularly virulent and dramatic illness that had arrived in England
in 1485 and was known to kill within hours. Symptoms of the illness included cold shivers, headaches, muscle pain, dizziness and
exhaustion, which quickly gave way to a high temperature and the
heavy sweating that was the main characteristic for sufferers. Thirst,
delirium and palpitations followed, after which there was a final
exhausted collapse.

While the cause of the sweating sickness is still unknown,
contemporaries blamed poor sanitation, and sources describing the
outbreak at Ludlow referred to a 'malign vapour which proceeded
from the air'. Catherine's mother, who had never visited the town,
described it from Castile as an 'unhealthy place', which may refer
to information contained in lost letters from her daughter or in
retrospect after her illness. Typically, it seems to have affected
upper-class adults, and the cramped, dirty living conditions in

castles supports rather than refutes claims that it was related to hygiene. The curse of poor sanitation and water supplies was avoided in Henry's London palaces by the peripatetic nature of the court, but the prince and princess had then been in residence at Ludlow for three uninterrupted months.

As a result of what had happened to his elder brother, Henry VIII had a particular horror of the sweat. When the illness raged through his court in 1517, claiming the lives of Lord Fiennes, Thomas, Lord Grey of Wilton and Henry's Latin secretary, the Italian Humanist Andrew Ammonius, who was 'carried off in eight hours', Henry fled. The Venetian ambassador reported that he was 'keeping aloof' at Windsor with his physician and favourite gentlemen. 'No one is admitted on account of the disease, which is now making great progress.'

Wolsey also fell ill in 1517, apparently for the fourth time, vowing to undertake a pilgrimage to Walsingham when he recovered, although the ambassador noted he had 'a troubled countenance and bent brow' and 'profuse perspiration'. The malady, claimed Hall, was so cruel that it 'killed some within three hours, some within two hours, some merry at dinner and dede at supper'.[1] Oxford and Cambridge universities suffered such losses that the Michaelmas term was cancelled and 'the kyng kept himself ever with a small company and kept no solempne Christmas', lamenting the deaths of his people.

In 1528, when another virulent outbreak claimed the life of Henry's close friend, William Compton, his beloved Anne Boleyn also fell ill, removing to her family home at Hever Castle. Hidden away in the countryside with a skeleton staff, Henry wrote to her having heard 'the most afflicting news' and saying he would 'willingly bear the half of yours to cure you'. He sent her one of his own physicians and beseeched her to 'be guided by his advice'.[2]

Specific cures against the sweat were included in *A Book of Receipts*, created in 1528 by physicians T. Darcy and A. Darcy for Henry VIII, and likely with his input, as is evident from other entries. The ingredients included endive, marigold, nightshade boiled 'in conduit water' and sweetened, or treacle, mace, 'water of dragons' and powdered unicorn's horn (narwhal tusk) 'and let him keep him by taking clothes off him little by little, till he be dried up and let him use wholesome meats'. It was also important that the patient follow the rules for recovery:

How the patient shall behave himself when he hath ended his sweating. – Let the keeper of the sick beware of the breath of the patient in his sweat; also let the clothes be well aired and washed; and because he shall be faint and distempered after his sickness, he shall eat no flesh nor drink wine for the space of one week, but let him use this comfortness for the heart; – as conserve of bugloss or red roses, and specially he shall drink three or four days after he hath sweat, morning and evening, three quints of the juice of sorrel, with one oz. of conserve of sorrel, mixed together, and so forth, with all besides that is comfortable for the heart.[3]

The sweating sickness continued to plague Tudor England in regular outbursts, usually in the summer months, until the final recorded cases in 1551. Diarist Henry Machyn recorded that 'the seventh day of July began a new sweat in London' and, three days later, 'the king's grace [Edward VI] removed from Westminster unto Hampton Court for there died certain beside the court and cause the king's grace to be gone so soon'.

Many London merchants and 'rich men and women, and young men and old'[4] contracted the illness, including the two young sons of the Duke of Suffolk, Charles and Henry, aged 15 and 13, who died within an hour of each other at the Bishop's Palace at Buckden in Hertfordshire, where they had gone to escape infection.

After the disappearance of the sweat in 1551, as suddenly as it had appeared, the greatest danger became the plague, transmitted by fleas carried by rats. This caused devastation in fourteenth-century England, after being brought on ships from the Far East.

The symptoms of bubonic plague were fevers, headaches, buboes (swellings) in the neck, armpit and groin, vomiting and aching joints. Few who contracted it survived, and the proximity of people living close together in towns led to a rapid spread of the disease, and recurring bouts in sixteenth-century Europe, especially in 1500–03, 1518–31, 1544–48, 1563–66, 1573–78 and 1596–99. The Tudors believed that sweet-smelling odours were helpful in countering infection, and carried nosegays and pomanders to that effect, but the distinctive beak-nosed physician's costume was not invented until 1630.

In 1563, Ambrose Dudley, Earl of Warwick, was laying siege to the French at Le Havre, but was forced to retreat when plague broke out among his men. Returning home, they brought the infection back to the English garrison 'where great multitudes were swept away by it'. It was also raging in London, and although the magistrates legislated to restrict movement, over 20,000 people died, resulting in 'a dearth of provisions, and scarcity of money from the stagnation of business, to the increase of the general distress'.[5]

When plague broke out in Bristol in 1575, after the St James Fair that July, it continued unabated for six months, claiming almost 2,000 lives. When cases began to rise again in the spring of 1585, it was decreed that all stray and 'unnecessary' dogs were to be killed, in order to prevent another outbreak in the summer, indicating the common belief that cats and dogs spread the infection.[6]

In 1582, the bailiff and jurats of Hastings acted to try to prevent the spread of infection from London to the south coast. They wrote to the Mayor of Rye to cancel a fair that was due to be held between the two towns that November:

> forasmuch as at this present time the city of London is grievously infected with the plague, a disease very contagious and infectious, by reason whereof, through the great concourse of people thither resorting, and buying of wares amongst those as were infected with the same disease, many towns and places hereabout in the country, by their own folly, are infected with the same.

They feared that the same would happen in Hastings 'through the resort of some unruly people out from some infectious place' and so the fair 'shall not be kept'.[7]

Numerous remedies were invoked against the plague, but one of Henry VIII's own devising survives from 1528:

> The king's medicine for the pestilence. Take a handful of sawge of vertue, a handful of herbe grace, a handful of elder leaves, and a handful of red briar leaves, and stamp them together, and strain them in a fair cloth with a quart of white wine, and then take a quantity of ginger, and mingle them all together, and drink of that medicine a spoonful every day, nine days together, and after nine days ye shall be whole, for the whole year, by the grace of God. And if it fortune that one be sore taken with the plague before he hath drunk of the same medicine, let him take the water of scabies, and a spoonful of betony water, and a quart of fine treacle, and put them all together,

and cause the person to drink it, and it shall put out all the venom; and if it fortune that the botch do appear, then take of leaves of briars, elder, and mustard seed, and stamp them all together, and make a plaster thereof, and lay it to the sore, and it shall draw out all the venom, and the person shall be whole.[8]

Henry's recipes also include a method for making the unusual 'philosopher's egg', which was made with saffron, herbs and grains of unicorn horn, which could be kept for twenty or thirty years, although the exact way the thing was used is not clear:

A proved medicine against the pestilence, called the philosopher's egg. – Take first an egg and break an hole in one end thereof, and do out the white from the yolk as clean as you can; then take whole saffron and fill the shell therewith by the yolk, then close it at both ends with two half egg shells; then rake it in the embers till it be so hard that you may stamp it to fine powder in a mortar, shell and all; then take as much white mustard seed as the weight of the egg and saffron is and grind it as small as meal; then take the 4th part of an oz. of a dittony root, and as much of turmontell and of crow nuts one dram; stamp this three sundry times very fine in a mortar, and then mix them three well together; after that take as a thing most needful the root of angelica and pimpernel, of each one drachm, and make them to powder and mix them with the rest; then compound herewith 4 or 5 grains a quantity of unicorn's horn if it be possible to be gotten, and take so much weight as all these powders come to of fine treacle, and stamp the same with the powders in a mortar, till they be all mixed and hang to the pestle, and then it is perfectly made; put this electuary in glass boxes, and you may keep it 20 or 30 years; the longer the better.[9]

❧ PAIN AND SUFFERING ☙

The Tudors' rudimentary pain relief, drawn from such herbs and spices as they valued for the task, was at best harnessing natural qualities of plants like mint or camomile, but at worst little more than a placebo. Short-term pain, such as wounds or headaches, might be soothed by the application of clysters and ointments. Teeth might be pulled out or treated for worms and women in labour offered a range of charms, amulets and, before the Reformation, holy relics.

There was little relief for long-term conditions and the many 'wasting' diseases that carried off the Tudors, beyond the oblivion offered by alcohol and the happy accidents sometimes arising from a correct diagnosis and remedy. Nor were the true causes of suffering understood, being frequently framed within a divine scheme of trial and salvation, rather than having scientific roots.

Specific remedies targeted localised pain through the application of the humoral theory, and bloodletting allowed the suffocating vapours or bad blood to leave an overburdened body. However, when such efforts failed, and the pain remained, one remedy particularly used by Henry VIII as a cure for most ailments was the use of suppositories or 'purges' to 'void', 'siege' or evacuate the bowels, releasing all toxic matter retained by the body. As his physician Thomas Elyot recommended in 1534:

> If the head be heavie, or the eyes dimme, or if there be paine felt of the colicke, or in the lower part of the belly, or in the hippes, or some cholerike matter or phlegm in the stomacke. Also if the breath be hardly fetched, if the belly of himselfe sendeth forth nothing, or if being costive, one feeleth ill savour or bitterness in his mouth, or that which he maketh hath an horrible savour, or if abstinence do not at the first put away the fever, or if the strength of the bodie may not sustaine letting of blood, or else the time therefore convenient is past, or if one haue dronke much before his sicknesse, or if he which oftentimes unconstrained hath had great sieges, be suddenly stopped. In all these cases, and where it is painfull to vomit, and in gnawing or frettings of the stomacke: finally, in all repletions, where a man cannot or will not be let blood or vomit, it is expedient to provoke siege by purgations, which are to be received by two wayes: upward at the fundament by suppositories or clysters: downward at the mouth, by potions, electuaries, or pilles.[1]

Suppositories, or 'purgations', took the form of a solid pill made with honey, pitch, soap, wax or gum, or with root vegetables, figs, raisins and the leaves of green mercury, and were placed in the 'fundament to the great end' for half an hour. 'Clysters' were liquid, made from milk, oil, wine or sodden milk, with herbs or gum, 'having properties to make soft, dissolve, draw forth or expel matter'. It was often applied warm 'by a little pipe of gold or silver, ivory or wood ... called a clyster pipe'.[2] Elyot considered it to be a 'convenient and sure' medicine and least harm came of it.

Discomforts of the physical body were sometimes intensified by cures. A letter sent by Lord Edmund Howard detailing his body's intimate disfunction after taking Lady Lisle's medicine for a gallstone reveals just how unfortunate some of the results could be:

> Madame, so it is I have this night after midnight taken your medicine, for the which I heartily thank you, for it hath done me much good, and hath caused the stone to break, so that now I void much gravel. But for all that, your said medicine hath done me little honesty, for it made me piss my bed this night, for the which my wife hath sore beaten me, saying it is children's parts to bepiss their bed. Ye have made me such a pisser that I dare not this day go abroad.[3]

Besides the many recipes available to rebalance the humours, the Tudors were aware of the benefits of the newly revived cure of taking the waters. Spa resorts such as Bath, Chester and Buxton, which offered hot or mineral-rich water for invalids to drink or bathe in, became increasingly popular among the Elizabethan aristocracy. John Leland's account of England in the 1540s describes the three different bathing experiences available in Bath: the King's Bath in the city centre had a long arcade for both sexes and was popular with the elite; the Hot Bath and the warm Cross Bath were used by poorer people and those with skin conditions and were both situated near the hospital.[4]

In June 1577, Robert Dudley, Earl of Leicester, and his brother Ambrose, both in their forties, were advised by their physicians to drink and bathe in spa waters. Dudley recommended the same for Cecil, chiding him for not taking care of himself, 'think[ing] it would be good for [you], but not if [you] do as they hear [you] did last time, take great journeys abroad 10 or 12 miles a day and use liberal diet with company dinners and suppers'. The Dudley brothers were staying with Lord Shrewsbury and had but one or two dishes at most and took the air 'afoot or on horseback'. Cecil was urged to come next year, but not bring too many people with him, as the house was small and 'a few fills it, and hard then to keep sweet'.[5]

The Earl of Sussex, though, had a completely different experience of the waters at Buxton in August 1582. He found the well so cold, 'by reason of the ill weather', that he was unable to use it, except very seldomly. Yet he goes on to add that he had started with 3 pints a day and had increased daily until he reached 8 pints, and was then descending again, by a pint a day, until he was back at 3.[6] In 1586, Charles Paget was advised that visiting a spa was the best remedy to cure his 'stone'.[7]

The increasing Elizabethan fashion for spa treatments is evident in the publication of Walter Bayly's *A Brief Discourse of Certain Baths of Medicinal Virtues* in 1587, extolling the benefits of Newnham Regis, in Warwickshire. To uncover the secret health benefits of the waters, Bayly had distilled, filtered and evaporated them, finding that there remained 'a certain residence [sic] in colour whitish, and in taste somewhat salt' which, placed upon a hot iron, 'doth forthwith become clearer and white'. He also suspected the presence of other elements: 'There is no small suspicion, that some parts of iron also are mixed with these waters. For daily much iron ore is found everywhere in places near adjoining. And hard by these fountains, a kind of clay is found of colour like to rusty iron.' It was the presence of this combination that Bayly believed responsible for the many cures he had witnessed:

> For I my selfe being there present, am an eyewitness, that one, which by long obstruction had a scirrous splene many yeeres, by the use of these waters recouered his perfect health. Likewise I did see another, which being subject to a strangurie, by means of a stone in his bladder, when no other helpe could serve, the drinking of this water brake the stone, and the man was in short time healed. The like successe haue I there seen in divers other affects, as namely in women's whites, in the gonorrhaicall passion, and in all inward exulcerations, both of the reins and the bladder, so that I may boldly conclude, that these baths are not vtterly void of iron.[8]

In the early Tudor years, before the Reformation, those suffering from pain or misfortune were likely to undertake a pilgrimage to a local or distant shrine and make offerings and prayers there for their well-being. Holy wells were also significant pilgrimage destinations, where people might drink or wash afflicted body parts in natural springs.

The use of such water was associated with mystical acts of faith, but Bayly's later style of physician's analysis represents a more scientific approach to the treatment of ailments.

Drinking medicinal 'waters' was a common resort for those suffering from a range of ailments. In the 1550s, printer Robert Wyer reissued a text by the thirteenth-century Roger Bacon, with recipes for mixing waters for all kinds of ailments from commonly available ingredients. Mint water was recommended for those experiencing liver and urine trouble or bad breath, lack of appetite, heart failure, worms, coughs, milk stoppage in breasts and difficulties with the womb. The common pain of gout, likely caused by the overrich meat, alcohol and dairy diet of the upper classes, was to be cured by taking 'the flesh of a fox, and cut it right small' and distilling it, before rubbing the liquid into the body.[9]

Elyot's *Castel of Helth* was one of the first medical works to present a connection between mental and physical health. The individual with melancholy humours had always been associated with sadness and low moods, while the sanguine character was reputedly swift to anger, but these were considered aspects of their integral composition. Elyot recognised the extent to which 'passions of the mind' might affect physical health and endanger well-being. If a man experienced immoderate emotions, 'they do not only annoy the body and shorten the life, but also they do appear and sometimes loose utterly a man's estimation'. They were capable of bringing a man 'from the use of reason' to the displeasure of God. The cure was not entirely physical. The afflicted required the 'help of physic corporal' and 'the counsel of a man wise and well learned in moral philosophy'.[10]

Thomas Moulton's *This is the Mirror or Glasse of Health* had certain recommendations for someone who had 'lost their mind', including the juice of marigold, sage and wormwood, drunk with white wine, cold, in the morning for five days, or the more drastic step of shaving off the hair and binding it with 'archangel' and letting the patient sleep. It was anticipated that afterwards, 'when he waketh, he shall be right weak, and sober enough'.[11] Yet, this method treated the condition entirely as a physical one, without making any connection between physicality and emotion.

※

Beside the sweat and plague, the Tudors feared the pox. If it did not prove fatal, as it did in around one in three cases, it could leave the face disfigured with pits and pock marks. In October 1562, after four years on the throne, Elizabeth was at Hampton Court when she was taken ill with a bad cold, which rapidly descended into a fever. She concluded a letter to Mary, Queen of Scots that day by saying she was to take a hot bath, in an attempt to cure herself. In just seven days, her condition worsened so significantly, with the tell-tale pustules breaking out over her body, that her life was feared for. Smallpox had been claiming victims among the queen's ladies, and her diagnosis sent the court and council into chaos over the problem posed by her succession, to the point that Elizabeth herself appointed her favourite, the then highly unpopular Robert Dudley, as Lord Protector in the event of her death.

Numerous cures for the pox were available. Thomas Moulton, in his *Mirror or Glasse of Health*, recommended drinking a mixture of celandines, saffron, pepper, stale ale and mace, or applying salves made of the highly toxic white lead, verdigris, mastic gum, raisins, mercury, turpentine and oil, and when the blisters appeared, to treat them with butter, cumin, black soap, rue, sheep suet, the gall of an ox and salt.[12] However, Elizabeth's doctors used the 'red treatment' from Japan, which involved wrapping her in red cloth from the neck down, which was believed to prevent scarring of the skin.

After several days in a coma, Elizabeth rallied and began to improve, although she was still left with faint scarring. Later, these pits would be filled with a mixture of wax, turpentine and fat, painted over with white lead. The queen's faithful servant, Mary Sidney, who nursed her throughout, also caught the disease but was left terribly disfigured. When her husband, Henry, returned from France afterwards, he found her transformed:

When I went to Newhaven I left her a full faire Ladye in myne eye at least the fayerest, and when I returned I found her as fowle a ladie as the smale pox could make her, which she did take by contynuall attendance of her majesties most precious person the skarres of which (to her resolute discomforte) ever since hath don and do remaine in her face, so as she lyveth solitairilie sicut Nicticorax in domicilio suo [like a night-raven in the house] more to my charge then if we had boarded together as we did before that evill accident happened.[13]

In 1569, the Duke of Norfolk was incarcerated in the Tower for treason, having plotted to marry Mary, Queen of Scots and overthrow Elizabeth. While languishing, awaiting justice, the would-be bridegroom, who was only 33, tried to use ill health as a plea for sympathy and to argue his innocence, as proof that he was not fit for any marriage. That October, Sir Henry Nevill wrote to William Cecil on Norfolk's behalf:

> The Duke [of Norfolk], finding himself not well, and fearing to fall into his disease which he had this last year, was very desirous to write unto my Lords, hoping thereby to obtain some more liberty, as either the wall or the gallery. His stomach is very much troubled with water, which takes away his suppers from him, and causes him to swell in the body, which he thinks is [for] lack of his usual walks.[14]

Norfolk wrote to the queen himself that December, claiming his memory and health were affected by imprisonment and that he hadn't realised how 'unpleasant' his potential marriage to Mary had been to Elizabeth:

> Sir Henry Nevill delivered to him by mouth certain articles which he trusts he has answered as far as his ill memory will suffer him. It was never good but is grown much worse by want of health since his imprisonment. Now that he sees how unpleasant this matter of the Queen of Scots is to her Majesty, he never intends to deal further therein, and will not refuse to yield any assurance the Queen shall please to command. As for marriage any other where, although his ill-health and the place he is in is unfit to think of any such matter, yet hereafter, as he shall find it best content her Highness, he will the sooner apply himself thereto for the Queen's satisfaction. Prays deliverance 'out of this dolorous house'.[15]

At the same time, the Bishop of Ross wrote on behalf of Mary, Queen of Scots, who was also suffering from what was diagnosed as the suffocation of her womb, and her letter to Norfolk confirmed the intended union between them:

> The Queen of Scots hath been sore vexed with pain of her side, which engendereth continual vomits. The cause thereof as considered by

the doctors, is only suffocacio matricis, quia desinit esse mater, which they affirm to be a common disease to virgins and young widows. She fears that her sickness shall cause the Duke of Norfolk displeasure, and therefore hath bidden him to write to the Duke her most hearty and loving commendations. The Duke's letter, token, and credit, sent with him, was her only comfort; she regarded little the Queen of England's letter, for it was no better worth, as may be seen by the double of it. – Sheffield, December 11.[16]

Sir Henry Nevill tried to gain sympathy for Norfolk and his poor state of health again the following February:

On behalf of the Duke of Norfolk, who, feeling his sickness grow upon him, and that his body inclines to the state he was in before, requests the Queen's permission to go to his own house to 'enter into the diet,' for the unfitness of that kind of physic to be taken in the Tower their Lordships well know.[17]

Norfolk was executed in June 1572 for his role in various plots against Elizabeth.

Old age presented its own set of ailments. Elyot characterised those in this period of life as experiencing:

Difficultie of breath, rheumes with coughes, stranguilion, and difficultie in pissing, ach in the ioyntes, diseases in the raines, swim-mings in the head, palsies, itching of al the bodie, lacke of sleepe, moysture in the eyes and eares, dulnesse of sight, hardnes of hearing, tissicknes or shortnes of breath.[18]

Again, Elyot's answer lay in balancing the diet in line with the humours, as choler could affect an old man of phlegmatic or melan-choly nature, in winter time in a cold country, in completely different ways than it would 'one young and lusty in the hot summer, in the countries where the sun fervently burneth'.[19] Roger Bacon, reissued in the 1550s, even had a cure for ageing that was aimed specifically at women:

For to please, and for to make these women to seeme more fairer, and younger unto their husbandes, and for to kepe them from goinge in to fornicacion, and adultre, it is suffred to use of some waters the which maketh the visage fayre and whyte ...

These simple waters be of the floures of bees, waters of the seede of melons, waters of the floure of elder, water of the floure de lys, water of the root of iris and of Dragontine and of the root of sygilon salmonis.[20]

When cures and waters failed, and more direct intervention was required, a barber surgeon was called in. Licensed by Henry VIII in 1518, the first professional body was the College of Physicians, which was then a somewhat all-encompassing term. The profession had developed by 1540 to unite the barbers, who would shave and trim, bloodlet, lance boils, cleanse ears and extract teeth, with the surgeons, who performed surgery, making each area of expertise exclusive, with dental surgery being the only area of overlap.

Surgery, without anaesthetic, was a painful and perilous process and a developing art, for which four public 'teaching' dissections were made each year, to better understand the workings of the body. Of the many texts published on anatomy and surgery, John Banister's 1575 *A Needful, New and Necessary Treatise of Chyrurgerie*, with experiments of his own, daily practised, is typical.

His particular speciality was the treatment of ulcers, typically in conjunction with the humoral theory. To treat a 'deep and crooked ulcer', he recommended that:

incision is to bee made from the orifice to the bottom of the Ulcer, chiefly if the hollowenes be along or naere the skinne, else if the imminent danger prohibit the same in the bottome, at the least it ought to be opened, and annointed with a mundifying unguent.[21]

Rates of survival in surgery were dependent entirely upon the skill of the physician, the nature of the illness or wound and a huge amount of good luck. If the patient survived the process and infection did not set in, the next few days were critical.

Although the average life expectancy in Tudor times was lower than today, brought down by factors like infant mortality, fatalities in battle and accidents and childbirth, a significant number of people

still achieved their three score and ten years. Advancing age complicated health conditions and pain and could interfere in their ability
to fulfil their duties, prompting those afflicted to ask for relief. In
1495, Roger Grove, a netmaker, and John Tailor were discharged by
Henry VII from serving on juries as they were both over 70 years old,
as was John Gyva, an ironmonger, who proved to be infirm.[22]

A century later, Laurence Swettenham of Somerford, who 'had been
and continued one of the high constables' of the district, requested
'tender consideration' for he was 'very aged, corupulent, grieved with
sickness and other infirmities and not able to travel, neither on horseback nor on foot', and requested to be discharged from his position.[23]
Likewise, John Lloyd in 1595 had 'long served her majesty in her wars'
and now, 'partly in respect of age and partly of other infirmities on
body', was unable to continue.[24]

⚕ SEX, PREGNANCY AND BIRTH ⚕

When it came to sexual health, both in terms of sexual desire and the
ability to procreate, the Tudors categorised individuals by the same
humoral theory. Those of a hot disposition had a 'great appetite to the
act of generation', lots of pubic hair and often produced male children.
Those whose genitals were defined as cool had little appetite to sex,
slow growth of hair about the members and engendered female children. People defined as being of the moist category had abundant seed,
but it was thin and watery, which could apply to both sexes, as wom-
en's eggs were considered a kind of seed, but believed to be released
upon orgasm, rather than as part of the monthly cycle. Those who
were dry produced little seed, but it was thick in substance. Those
with the highest sexual appetites were those with the combination of
hot and dry qualities, but they were also known for their 'swiftness in
speeding of the act' and being 'soon therewith satisfied', while those
who were hot and moist could be 'hurt' by abstinence.[1]

Thomas Elyot's 1534 *Castel of Helth* gave very precise recommendations about what to eat and when, depending upon the season, in
which diet and sexual activity are closely associated:

From the 12th day of December, at the which time the day is at the
shortest, until the 9th day of March, which doe continue 90 dayes,

rheumes and moystures doe encrease, then meates and drinkes naturally very hot, would be moderatly used. Also to drinke abundantly
Wine without allay, or with little water, and to use hilaritie: the
companie of a woman is not unwholesome to the bodie.

From the ninth day of March unto the 25th day of Aprill, sweet
phlegm and blood doe increase: therefore use thou things having
much juyce and sharpe, exercise the body diligently, then may ye
use safely the companie of a woman.

From the 20th day of Aprill, to the 14th day of June, choler increa-
seth, then use all things that are sweete, and doe make the belly
soluble, forbeare carnall companie with women.

From the 14th day of June, at which time the day is at the longest,
unto the 12th day of September, doth melancholy raine, forbeare
carnal company, or use it moderatly.

From the 12th day of September, unto the 17th day of October, do
abound phlegm and thin humours, then would all fluxes and dis-
tillations be prohibited, then all sharpe meates and drinkes and of
good juyce, are to be used, and carnall occupations should then be
eschewed.

From the 17th day of October, to the 12th day of December, increa-
seth grosse phlegm, use therefore all bitter meates, swéet wines, fat
meate, and much exercise.[2]

Sex was generally thought to be beneficial to both men and women
in physical and emotional terms. The denial of natural urges was
believed to foster wasting illnesses or lead to suffocation in accumulated reproductive fluids, with vapours from women's wombs causing
the 'green sickness'. However, getting the timing right was crucial, as
too much, too soon, was considered highly dangerous.

Margaret Beaufort survived delivering the future Henry VII at the age
of 13, but she never bore another child and intervened to prevent the
marriage of her granddaughter Margaret from taking place too soon.
The love match of Margaret of Austria with John, Prince of Asturias,
(brother of Catherine of Aragon) had lasted only six months in 1497,

with contemporaries citing their overenthusiastic lovemaking as the cause of his decline. Two months into the marriage, observer Peter Martyr wrote that John was 'consumed with passion' and was looking pale. His doctors urged him to 'seek a respite in the incessant acts of love' and warned that his increasing weakness was compromising his health. He died at the age of 19. When Catherine married Arthur in 1501, the question of whether they should live together as man and wife was hotly debated before Arthur's parents relented and permitted it, but after his premature death almost six months later, the inevitable gossip arose about his new wife's voracious appetite.

As a young widow, Catherine received very mixed messages. On one hand, the Church prized virginity as the highest of all states of womanhood, closely followed by the chaste life of widowhood. On the other, contemporary medical understanding dictated that such conditions could be injurious to women's health and advocated a return to the marital state in order for the impulses of women's sexually ravenous bodies to be properly satisfied.

The womb was categorised as being of a cold, damp nature, which craved the corresponding hot, dry seed of a man, with the woman's 'crooked instrument' designed to help them satisfy their 'foul lust'. Frequent references to Catherine suffering from fevers and being purged and bled, as well as her daily swings between 'cold and heat', would have been diagnosed in this light. Using her astrological sign of Sagittarius to suggest treatment, Catherine's warm, dry and choleric nature would have been balanced with foods that were believed to possess qualities of coldness and wetness such as lettuce, melons and cucumbers. Abstaining from sex was considered to provoke illness, melancholy and misbehaviour in women; effectively, the patriarchal medical system advocated sex as a means of control within marriage.

We might be mistaken for assuming that sex for the Tudors was the same as sex today, that the actual experience does not differ. This is true only to an extent. Approaching sex with a completely different attitude to the freedoms of the twenty-first century, the Tudor man and woman would have been following a complex code of rules that gave their encounters a different significance.

A number of sexual practices were considered sinful, in religious terms and also in the folklore that described the conception and appearance of children, which was the ultimate aim, and with so many prying eyes and ears at court, the king's and queen's morals and practices would need to have been exemplary – privacy is a modern luxury. Intercourse in the missionary position, between husband and wife, was considered the least of many potential evils, for purposes of procreation and to prevent men from seeking satisfaction elsewhere.

Other forms of sexual gratification, including oral or anal sex, foreplay or masturbation, and any other form of 'unnatural' fornication and 'carnal thoughts', were seen as sinful, as they did not result in pregnancy and were believed to result in birth defects. Sin, of course, may have been a powerful aphrodisiac for some, and court records prove that these Church laws were frequently broken. Likewise, sex during certain days of the Church calendar, or during menstruation, was supposed to produce small, unhealthy children.[3]

John Barrough addressed a lack of libido in married couples in his 1590 *The Method of Physicke*, as an essential act for procreation:

> They which be married, and cannot use the act of generation, because of the sluggish impotencie and weakness of their members: coming of a colde distempure wherewith they be vexed, or of some other cause: such ought to exercise the nether partes, and to use meates that doe heate and engender good humours, as is the flesh of hennes, capons, partrich, feasauntes … and specially sparrowes, cockes stones and such like … good nourishing meates, but also windy meates are good for him, as be chickens, beanes, scalions, leekes, the roote and seede of persneppes, pine nuts, rape rootes and such other like. Also the egges of partriches doe stirre up carnal lust. Let the patient sleepe in a soft bedde, and let him reade thinges that doe stirre vp lust, or let him heare them read. Let his privie members be continually chafed and rubbed with oyles, ointmentes and other heating medicines.[4]

However, evidence exists for the Tudors enjoying sex within the defined perimeters. *Jacob's Well* outlines contemporary expectations for moderate, appropriate sex:

> for wedlock truly knit, truly kept and used in order, is of such virtue that it keepeth their flesh from deadly sin. If you use your wife or husband as your sweetheart in intent, only for lust … not for love, nor the fruit of wedlock, nor to be honest, but as an unreasonable beast … beware of the fiend.

The text also reminded married couples that foreplay could lead to impurity and sin: 'When you feeleth or toucheth with mouth in kissing, with hand in groping, and with any member of thy body ... that stirs you to lust and sin, then you enter into ... wickedness.'[5] This was echoed in the *Book of Vices and Virtues*, which advised against any 'use of one's wife' that went against 'the order of wedlock'.[6]

It was considered imperative for a woman to 'emit seed' in order to conceive, so in that eventuality her husband was charged with arousing her body by 'smoothly stroke his lady, breasts and belly and excite her'.[7] A fourteenth-century text advised a man to 'arouse a woman to intercourse' by speaking, kissing and embracing her, 'to caress her breasts and touch [her] between the perineum and vulva and to strike her buttocks with the purpose that the woman desires ... and when the woman begins to speak with a stammer, then they ought to copulate'. Another technique suggested by a medieval advice manual was 'froting' (fretting) or rubbing, 'when a man hath great liking between him and his wife in bed'.[8]

The Tudor dilemma of elective virginity and the absence of sex is most obviously embodied in Elizabeth I, the famous Virgin Queen. From her very first Parliament in January 1559, the question of her marriage was raised, and continually postponed or rejected by the queen, with the Spanish ambassador de Feria writing, 'The more I think about this business, the more certain I am that everything depends upon the husband this woman may take', while the German ambassador stated that her 'wish to remain a maid and never marry is inconceivable'.[9]

Yet Elizabeth did not feel the need to conform to expectations of her gender, especially when their disadvantages were painfully apparent to her, commenting, 'I like so well of this estate [spinsterhood] as I persuade unto myself there is not any kind comparable to it.' Through her long reign, and even when she was in her forties and the chances of childbearing were slim, Elizabeth flirted with the idea of marriage. She may well have wanted to be married on a personal level, she may even have fallen in love, but at heart she knew that it involved a compromise that would forever alter, undermine or actively destroy the autonomy that was essential to her queenship. It may have been deliberate policy to send out mixed messages to keep the pleas of her councillors at bay. By remaining single, though, she made no unfortunate foreign alliance, alienated none of her subjects, maintained the

integrity of her kingdom and self, did not die in childbirth, and did not
have to bow to any man. She remained married to her subjects and
was the only governor of her destiny.

Sexual activity could prove difficult to regulate amongst Elizabeth's
subjects. Church and Assize Court records abound with cases of broken
betrothals, adultery, 'lewdness' and illegitimate pregnancies, especially
when young people could not afford to marry until their mid or late
twenties, a whole decade after the onset of sexual maturity.

In 1598, the case of a servant named Ann Prescodd was brought
before the justices of the peace in Worcester. Ann had been impreg-
nated by a fellow servant, John Hey, who 'knew her to be with child'
and did 'frequent the company of the said Ann', and made 'divers and
sundry promises' to her, but after the secret was discovered, he 'did
not only deny that promise of marriage to her ... but also most unhon-
estly doth absent himself'.[10]

Perhaps the most convincing argument against marriage was the
danger of pregnancy, which was fraught with risks from the start.
Diagnosis was an imprecise science, and the symptoms of other illnesses could easily be mistaken for the signs that usually indicated
conception had taken place. In some cases, even experienced women
were not certain of their condition until the first foetal movements
or 'quickening' took place, in the middle of the second trimester.
Catherine of Aragon experienced a phantom pregnancy in 1509–10,
withdrawing into her lying-in chamber with a swollen belly.

In September 1554, Mary I's menstruation ceased, and she started
putting on weight. In Tudor terms, at 38 she was old for a first-time
mother, having reached an age when her contemporaries were grand-
mothers and had even begun the menopause. As the weeks passed,
though, she became increasingly convinced that she was pregnant and
delighted at the prospect of bearing an heir.

In January, Parliament passed an act making Mary's consort, Philip
of Spain, regent in the event of Mary's death in childbirth, and for the
provision of education for any such children. However, Philip was not
entirely convinced that his wife had conceived, expressing doubts in
letters to his brother, but he still signed the circulars that had been
produced in advance to spread the news.

At the end of the month, a false report reached London that she had delivered a prince, so bonfires were lit and bells rung in celebration. But then the bells went quiet and there was no prince. Weeks later, Mary was observed in the garden, 'stepping' so well that her delivery date was rapidly revised. May and June passed and then her swollen abdomen began to go down, probably as the result of an infection or pseudocyesis, a phantom pregnancy.

In the summer of 1557, Philip left England for the final time and Mary was once again convinced that she had conceived. This time, though, there was no bustle of excitement, no sharing of her news and no preparations made at court, but Mary still clung to hope. The following March, she made her will, 'thinking myself to be with child … foreseeing the great danger which by God's ordinance remain to all women in their travail of children', and appointed Philip as regent during the child's minority. By 1 May, it was clear that there was to be no child. Increasingly, Mary was unwell, she could not sleep and suffered from an excess of black bile. Her death soon after, in November 1558, suggest that the symptoms she had mistaken for pregnancy could have been caused by cancer.

Childbirth was a risky business for women of all classes. Queens made an elaborate ritual of it, with specially prepared rooms decked out according to the ordinances devised in 1486 by Margaret Beaufort, which created a warm, sealed environment, full of blankets and cushions, with the walls and windows covered with tapestries, fires constantly burning and provocative influences and images removed.

A queen would take mass, followed by a banquet or void of wine and spices, before processing into confinement with her ladies, and remaining behind closed doors until the child arrived. Reading, dice and cards would have helped while away the time, as would playing music and singing or watching her ladies dance, as well as the regular prayers. Until the desperate delivery of Jane Seymour, lengthy and difficult, resulted in her death, no male doctors were permitted to wait upon the queen, but midwives were hired and rewarded handsomely for their work. Aristocratic women might retreat to their parents' home for lying-in, to draw upon their familial network of support, especially for a first child. Otherwise, babies arrived whenever they were ready; in beds, streets, fields and in church porches.

Pain relief was confined to herbs, wine and prayer, although the practice of chewing willow bark may have helped, given its role in the development of the modern aspirin. Women and infants did die in the process of delivery, with a variety of historians' estimates placing maternal mortality somewhere between 1 and 5 per cent.[11]

The risk of injury and infection was doubled, given the somewhat scanty post-partum care and conflicting advice. While Jane Seymour bled to death after a huge rupture in 1537, probably as the result of retaining part of the placenta, her physicians commented that she had been allowed to indulge her appetite. A second of Henry VIII's wives was also lost shortly after delivery, when Catherine Parr died from puerperal fever days after delivering her daughter by Thomas Seymour in September 1548.

☙ VIOLENCE ❧

Numerous sources give the impression that the Tudor era was one of physicality: riding and hunting, movement and labouring, in pastimes and sports, and in terms of discipline and abuse. Physical brutality existed on a daily scale, from casual attacks on animals to serious or fatal accidents; from the beating of children and apprentices, the rights of men to discipline their wives, assaults and fighting in the streets to forced entry to property, criminal damage, rape and murder. Regular attempts were made to curb lawlessness and those convicted suffered the penalties, with comparable corporal and capital punishment, but the sixteenth century was far less restrained by rules governing physicality than the modern world.

Cases of domestic assault feature with frequency in the Assize Court records. In May 1581, Helen Frotier of Rye, wife of John Frotier, a lockyer also of Rye, came before the mayor and 'complained of the injuries, wrongs and rigorous usage of her' by her husband, so that she was 'lamed in her limbs but also standeth in continual danger of her life'. She intended to leave him and go to Rouen, in France. Regarding Helen's conduct towards John, the mayor and jurats commented 'that the said Helen, ever sithens we have known her, hath behaved her-self well and honestly towardes the said John Frotier, hir husband, in every respecte as hath becomyd a dutefull wiff, and lekewise towardes all other persones to our knowledges'. John Frotier was known to be 'a very drunken and beastly person and hath from tyme to tyme con-tynually beaten and marvaillous evilly treated the said Helen, his wiff, whereof she hath often complaynid and we often tymes have punished him for his lewdness and yet no amendment followeth'.[1]

Female servants were particularly vulnerable to cruelty as unrelated dependents living at the mercy of their employer's good will. In 1589, Margaret Clarke, spinster of High Leigh, told the justices in Chester that while she was a servant to John Wilkinson, his son Thomas treated her 'evilly' and beat her 'very cruelly ... without any cause and threatened to cut her throat and to burn her'. Terrified by his threats, she had approached his father, John, after whose 'advise and counsel', she brought a warrant of the peace against Thomas.[2]

Male servants could prove to be aggressors, but it was a particularly unpleasant and foolish individual who was violent towards their employer. In 1582, Martin and Rachel Skinner complained about the behaviour of their servant, Thomas Yeldham:

First the said Rachel affirms that about six months past having just occasion to reprove the said Thomas for his lewdness he answered her that hereafter he could be worse than ever he had been and do worse than ever he did; and the next morning meeting with his dame in her shop, she being great with child, he gave her such a thrust against the shop chest that in her conscience he was the very and only occasion of the death of the child, and put her in great peril of death.

Martin sent him on an errand to one Chapman, a poor labourer, to have him to work the next morning, and upon his return, having tarried somewhat longer than cause required, his master asked him where he had been. Then said the said Thomas, standing very near to his said master and facing him boldly with his hat on his head 'whether did you sende me I have been with Chapman', and his master, 'seeing this malaperte boldeness of his over saucy servant, did with the back of his hande gyve him a blowe on the eare, the boye having a waster [a cudgel] in his hands made an offer as if he wolde strike agayne, where upon his master followinge hym to take away the waster, the boye closed with him and castinge his legge between his masters, and they stryvinge together, he overthrew his master and broke his legg in sonder.[3]

✳

Rioting and malcontents were identified and dealt with by the local authorities, with the support of the monarch. Early in his reign, Henry VIII was obliged to write to the Mayor of Southampton after having received a disturbing report from the Bishop of Winchester:

> We to our no little misconsternation and displeasure perceive that a great commotion and riotous assembly hath now at this season been made and presumptuously attended by diverse seducers and evil disposed persons of our said town as well in breaking down certain dykes there as also in the bold justification of the same to the disturbance of our peace and the perilous example of other light and wild minded people.

Henry urged that the offenders be 'speedily repressed and punished as accordeth with justice'.[4]

Sometimes specific individuals were to blame, as was the case in Chester in 1573, where:

> Thomas Coppock of Rostorne ... is a very unquiet and disordered person not only in his words but also in his deeds that is a common drunkard, a reeler, a swear, a brawler and a sower of dissention amongst neighbours much like to set neighbour against neighbour ... contrary to the Queen's majesty's peace and laws.[5]

Other times it was circumstances, like the unruly soldiers awaiting transport in Bristol, who were so prone to fighting and killing that the mayor erected a gibbet in 1579 in order to scare them.

The most famous riots of the era were those which took place on May Day 1517, when a group of apprentices turned against foreigners living in the city. An inflammatory speech at St Paul's Cross called on 'all Englishmen to cherish and defend themselves, and to hurt and grieve aliens for the common weal'. Rumours flew of intended attacks on May Day, prompting the mayor to call an emergency meeting at the Guildhall, but the debate went on too long and it was late in the day when permission was granted to impose a curfew with military support.

The Venetian ambassador put the number of rioters at around 2,000, bracketing them together as apprentices and bandits, although a number of London citizens also joined the fray. Barricading the city gates, they forced the mayor to release prisoners from the gaols before they attacked and sacked the homes of foreigners.

The rioting escalated and Henry was woken from his sleep at Richmond to be informed of the event, dispatching Wolsey, the Duke of Norfolk and his son, the Earl of Surrey, to quell the insurrection. Order was restored to the streets at three in the morning and something between seventy and 300 rioters were arrested.

Foreigners were rarely popular among the xenophobic English, who rose up under Thomas Wyatt in protest when Mary I planned to wed Philip of Spain in 1554 and who grumbled at the courtship of Elizabeth I by the Dukes of Anjou and Alençon. In August 1582, the Spanish ambassador:

> going in his coach through Fenchurch Street, was assaulted by boys who were playing with their bucklers and who followed him and his men, hurling stones, old shoes, etc. at him. So he was fain to turn the course of his waggon as fast as he could by Lime Street where the Lord Mayor dwelleth. Thereupon they fled.[6]

Violence might also arise when individuals were resisting arrest. In 1587:

> Arthur Herrys, esquire, sheriff, by his warrant ordered a certain Thomas Martyn, his bailiff itinerant in that behalf, to arrest a certain Robert Fawkes alias Faxe of Rayleigh, yeoman, being named in the aforesaid writ and warrant, and to be taken and arrested at the suit of John Porter of a plea of trespass; by virtue of which warrant the aforesaid Thomas Martyn, bailiff, took and arrested the said Robert at Rayleigh in the market place there on the 15th of April as above-said and would have kept him safely. Which same Robert with force and arms assaulted the said Thomas and beat him, and violently and victously rescued himself from the custody of the said Thomas and went a large, in contempt of the writ and warrant aforesaid.[7]

One of the ways in which lawlessness was addressed was with the trained bands, established in 1573. Volunteers between the ages of 16 and 60 were assembled in regional groups for training two days per month or a week per quarter, being paid for any time they spent away from their work. The majority of the remainder of men in the age bracket were classified as belonging to the untrained bands, who received no training and were only mustered in emergency situations like rebellion or foreign wars.

However, the proliferation of court cases featuring affray, assault and murder attest to the Tudors' propensity to be the instruments of their own definitions of justice, in immediate and decisive ways, in the belief that they were justified in doing so. The watch, sheriffs and trained bands of the era did not provide sufficient deterrent when it came to a Tudor bent upon the all-important revenge, or clearing of their name, or restoration of their stolen goods, all of which were critical to sixteenth-century concepts of identity. It was in the affront to their standing in the world that Tudor violence must be understood.

✤ IMPRISONMENT ✤

The restriction of an individual's liberty, usually in punitive conditions, was the ultimate act of control against the Tudors' exercise of their own physicality. Imprisonment might be the result of lawbreaking, but in the Tudor age, it could also be collateral damage from the realpolitik of the court.

In 1499, the surviving Yorkist heir, Edward, Earl of Warwick, was executed after having been incarcerated for fourteen years. As the son of George, Duke of Clarence, and a nephew of Richard III, Warwick was the next immediate male claimant, but was held in the Tower from the age of 10. Chronicler Edward Hall commented that he had so long been kept 'out of all company of men, and sight of beasts, in so much that he could not discern a goose from a capon'.[1]

His fellow prisoner in the Tower was Perkin Warbeck, the pretender from the Netherlands, whose attempt to invade England with Burgundian, Irish and Scottish help led to his arrest in 1497. When Henry VII sought to marry his eldest son Arthur to Catherine of Aragon, a condition imposed by the Spaniards was that all pretenders to the throne be removed to ensure the couple's future safety. As a result, the pair were linked in a fabricated plot and met their deaths that November, Warwick on the block and Warbeck by the hangman's noose.

On 17 March 1554, Henry Radcliffe, Earl of Sussex, and Sir William Paulet, Lord High Treasurer, arrived at Whitehall to escort Princess Elizabeth to the Tower. The associations of this, connected with her mother's fate eighteen years before, proved too much for the princess.

Terrified that her execution was imminent, she begged for time to write to her sister, composing a letter to remind Mary of a promise she made last December that Elizabeth would 'be not condemned without answer and due proof' and asked her 'to let me answer afore yourself'.[2] She signed it from 'your highness' most faithful subject that hath been from the beginning and will be to my end', and scored lines across the unused paper beneath, in order to ensure no false information was added once it was out of her hands. In pleading for an audience, she could not refrain from mentioning the fate of Thomas Seymour, still raw, from five years earlier:

> If any ever did try this old saying – that a king's word was more than another man's oath – I most humbly beseech your majesty to verify it in me, and to remember your last promise and my last demand: that I be not condemned without answer and due proof. Which it seems that now I am, for that, without cause proved, I am by your Council commanded from you to go unto the Tower, a place more wonted for a false traitor than a true subject. Which though I know I deserve it not, yet in the face of all this realm, appears that it is proved. Which I pray God I may die the shamefullest death that ever any died afore I may mean any such thing. And to this present hour I attest afore God (who shall judge my truth whatsoever malice shall devise) that I never practised, counselled nor consented to anything that might be prejudicial to your person any way or dangerous to the state by any mean. And therefore I humbly beseech your majesty to let me answer afore yourself and not suffer me to trust your councillors ... afore I be further condemned.
>
> ... in late days I heard my Lord of Somerset say that if his brother had been suffered to speak with him, he had never suffered.[3]

Elizabeth's letter only bought her a few hours. As she wrote it, the tide turned, and the barge was unable to embark from Whitehall until the next day. So it was on Palm Sunday, in the pouring rain, that Elizabeth was conducted downriver to the Tower, under arrest.

Collapsing on the privy stairs, she addressed her guard, insisting that they bear her 'witness that I come in no traitor but as a true woman to the Queen's majesty as any now is living, and thereon will I take my death' but she 'knew her truth to be such that no man would have cause to weep for her'.[4]

Some sources state that Elizabeth was placed in the same rooms where Cardinal Fisher had awaited his execution in 1535, and above those of Sir Thomas More in the Bell Tower, while others place her in those rooms where her mother had awaited her fate. Elizabeth was catered for according to her state, but the constant fear of accusations and imminent condemnation contributed to making it a time of intensity and terror that she would never forget.

Elizabeth's protestations went in vain. Her removal was urged upon Mary by Emperor Charles V as a necessary step to secure peace in the kingdom ahead of the arrival of the Spanish bridegroom. She was repeatedly questioned about her involvement in the uprising and her intentions, but her interrogators were mindful that they faced their potential future queen, and some were influenced by her great uncle, William Howard, and treated her with less harshness than Mary may have wished.

On 19 May 1554, the eighteenth anniversary of her mother's execution, Elizabeth was released from the Tower and taken by 100 royal guards, led by Sir Henry Bedingfield, to Woodstock Palace in Oxfordshire. Her popularity with Londoners was asserted when a large crowd of well-wishers turned out to cheer her progress, and many others appeared along the route for the same purpose. She remained there, living in seclusion and constantly in fear of her life until the late spring of 1555, when Mary believed herself to be pregnant and summoned her sister to be with her for the delivery.

Despite her early experiences, Elizabeth used incarceration as a punishment when her ladies and relatives transgressed. In the years immediately after her succession, her cousin Catherine Grey was first in line to the throne and a potential diplomatic bride for the Scottish Earl of Arran. However, Catherine fell in love and conducted a secret marriage with Edward Seymour, Earl of Hertford, with only his sister as witness. Shortly afterwards, Seymour was sent abroad by the queen, and Jane Seymour, their witness, died. Catherine was left pregnant and alone. She confided in Elizabeth's favourite, Robert Dudley, who informed the queen.

Elizabeth was furious at the secrecy of the match, given Catherine's status as heir, the disruption to Anglo-Scottish relations and the threat posed by any sons she might bear. Catherine was imprisoned in the Tower, where she bore her son, Edward, and upon her husband's return to England he was sent to confinement there too. Although they were supposed to be kept apart, the keeper of the Tower allowed them conjugal visits, with the resulting birth of a second son, Thomas, a year later, much to Elizabeth's fury. The union was forcibly dissolved in 1563, making both sons illegitimate, after which Catherine was removed to live under house arrest in the country until her death from consumption at the age of 28.

In 1565, Catherine's sister Mary Grey made her own secret marriage, despite having witnessed her sister's heart-breaking drama unfold. After Catherine's sons had been ruled out of the succession, Mary was technically next in line to the throne, when she married the queen's serjeant porter, Thomas Keyes, a huge man of well over 6ft tall and a widower with six or seven children.

Determined not to have her marriage invalidated, Mary ensured the presence of a number of witnesses, but it was the social standing of the groom that was problematic. Mary was put under house arrest for the remainder of her life, but Keyes was placed in solitary confinement in the Fleet, where he wrote to Cecil about being restrained in a cell of tiny dimensions and that his meat had been soaked in a substance used to treat mange in dogs. Keyes was eventually released, but the pair were never reunited, living separately in exile from the court.

In the autumn of 1591, Elizabeth 'Bess' Throckmorton and Walter Raleigh were married in secret after Bess fell pregnant. Their child was born the following March, and, despite their denials, Elizabeth became aware of the marriage and sent both to the Tower. Walter was released after a month, and Bess after six months, but instead of asking forgiveness and returning to court, they chose to live together in the country and went on to have more children.

Prisons were a holding place for those awaiting trial as well as those who had already been convicted. In Tudor London, serious criminals were sent to Newgate Gaol, while lesser criminals, debtors and people of standing were incarcerated at Ludgate, the upper portion of the

most westerly of the city gates. Newgate was capable of housing over
300 prisoners, in poor conditions, while Ludgate was smaller, with
only fifty inmates in the 1550s.

By the 1580s, there were around eighteen prisons in London, the
largest of which were the Fleet, on the Fleet River, on the western
side of the city; the Clink in Southwark, owned by the Bishop of
Winchester; and the Marshalsea, for debtors, also in Southwark.

Tudor sources reveal that the prison system was open to abuse
by those in charge. In 1533, the 'poor citizens prisoners in Ludgate'
compiled a petition for Cromwell 'complaining of injuries inflicted
upon them by Thomas Holland, keeper of the prison, contrary to the
articles contained in the table for the good rule and quietness of the
said prisoners':[5]

1. That whereas he is bound to take no more of any prisoner for a
feather bed with blankets, sheets, and coverlets than one penny a
night; yet if there lie two or three in one bed he takes a penny of each.
He also exacts a halfpenny a night of each man where three lie in a
couch, instead of a penny a week; for he says his couches are beds.

2. The keeper distributes the alms given to comfort us prisoners at
his own discretion, and retains so much in payment of the debts we
owe him that we get little or nothing.

3. The keeper uses the women's ward to wash bucks in, by which
the whole house is annoyed, and the women constrained to pay 3d.
a night for chambers, contrary to the table.

4. Whereas every freeman is allowed by the table to bring in his bed
or couch freely: the keeper 'appointeth them to a vile place, called
the Lumbardy,' to the annoyance of those that lie there.

5. Every prisoner going abroad has to pay the keeper 8d. a day, and
find the keeper's servants in meat and drink, who force him to spend
largely at taverns, so that it costs him 18d. or 20d. a day, and at night
2d. is required of him for his supper.

6. Whereas the poor prisoners used to have 'in the hole under gate'
a prisoner elected by themselves to ask alms for them: the keeper

will suffer none there, because he says the hole is not strong enough, though he has enough money by the house to amend it.

7. The keeper will not provide small beer for the prisoners, but drives them to drink good ale, to their great cost; moreover, it is brewed and mingled by the tapster by night, and not wholesome; nor do they give fair measure. "And if any man show the tapster his evil demeanour in that behalf, then he is ready to be wroken and to fight with them, and haleth and pulleth the poor men by the heads."

8. He sells them faggots at 1*d*. each, and will not provide coals at 1*d*. a bushel according to the table, nor allow prisoners to send out and buy faggots for themselves.

9. If any be sick, and call for drink in the night, they are not attended to, and some have died from this cause.

10. When in an ill temper he draws the men out of their beds or puts them in irons without mercy.

11. If a prisoner's wife come to see him, and she be a pretty woman, he will by crafty means 'labor to fulfil his foul lust'.[6]

Another complaining prisoner, Randall Tytley, wrote to Cromwell in September 1535, having been a prisoner for five years in 'Bread Street Counter', when one of Cromwell's servants arrived, asking the inmates how they were kept and telling them to 'write to your good mastership for remedy' if they were not 'well ordered'. Tytley duly wrote and sent a complaint to Cromwell, 'for doing which the keeper sent him to Newgate, where he is likely to die of the sickness of the house'.

At Bread Street, the prisoners were overcharged for their beds, and debts were charged at exorbitant rates, with anyone running one day into arrears being 'thrust into the hole and kept till he has sold all his clothes'. If friends brought in supplies of food, the keeper prevented them from being passed on to the prisoners as it would interfere with his own sales to them. After this cruelty, many were sent to Newgate, 'which has been the murder of many a tall man and true, able to do the King service'.[7]

Also in 1535, Thomas Burnett, a sailor, petitioned Cromwell because of a broken promise. He had been told that upon Cromwell's return to London he would be set at liberty, but the failure to do so meant his wife was forced to visit him in prison and 'was so infected that she died, and her child also'.[8]

Richard Jonson and his wife had been brought from Essex to Fulham and imprisoned by the Bishop of London for about a year, 'and compelled to abstain from flesh ... besides being so scantily fed that they would sooner have died'. Nothing had been proved against them, and the king commanded the bishop to release them, but instead they were moved to Colchester and imprisoned in the Abbey of St John, 'worse than before', until they managed to escape.[9]

In 1597, George Gatcliffe was being held in Chester Castle on a warrant to the constable of the castle for good behaviour, 'the cause I know not for which I was so committed', and he had not been permitted by the constables to speak with his accuser, a Randall Manwairing. He considered this to be 'a manifest wrong done unto me by them' for which he humbly craved the assistance of the justices to release him.[10]

A spell in prison could be very dangerous, even fatal. In 1580, Colchester Gaol in Essex was an especially deadly place in which to be incarcerated. At the spring inquisitions that year, the coroner heard how one prisoner, Nicholas Cole, who had been detained on suspicion of felony, died of 'le plage' by 'divine visitation'.

Katherine, wife of William Rundall of Ipswich, who was then a prisoner in Colchester Castle for helping another man escape, had become 'sick of a fever' and died, while Henry Jones, committed for felony, was also claimed by fever and William Warner had died after being 'sick of an ague', all by divine visitation.[11]

The loss of liberty posed a significant difficulty for the Tudors, often resulting in discomfort, illness and even death, due to the cruelty of prison keepers and the poverty of their conditions. Individuals could be arrested on a whim, without explanation, trial or the right to confront their accusers, and deprived of basic rights for an indefinite period of time. It is interesting to note that Thomas Cromwell was enquiring into the state of prisons in the 1530s, but those who sought to act upon his lead found themselves penalised further. This state was determined by a top-down pattern, which saw members of the aristocracy, and even royalty, subject to similar confinement and impoverished circumstances on the vaguest of suspicions, without proof.

The show trial of Anne Boleyn and her five co-accused; and the imprisonment, arrest and execution of the aged Margaret Pole in 1541; the torture of heretic Anne Askew in 1546 and the treatment meted out to Elizabeth's cousins and courtiers embedded a system in which injustice and brutality were justified in the eradication of danger or disruption. The rights, and even the life, of an individual mattered less than the need to protect the state or keep the peace.

⚜ POVERTY ⚜

Many Tudors would have known the intense, gnawing physical sensation of hunger and the bitter, bone-penetrating pain of cold. For all the era's professed charity and alms, the poor were constantly being demonised and legislated against in sixteenth-century England. Instead of eliciting compassion, as the visible symbols of the medieval wheel of fortune, or opportunities for the charitable good deeds so encouraged by the old and new faiths, the poor, homeless and the starving were perceived instead as a challenge to the Tudors' world theory that everyone had a place in the world, knew what that place was, and remained in it.

It began in 1494, when Henry VII's Vagabonds and Beggars Act ruled that:

> Vagabonds, idle and suspected persons shall be set in the stocks for three days and three nights and have none other sustenance but bread and water and then shall be put out of Town. Every beggar suitable to work shall resort to the Hundred where he last dwelled, is best known, or was born and there remain upon the pain aforesaid.

Beggars were punished by public humiliation, starvation and relocation, simply for being poor.

In 1530, laws were tightened even further, and penalties became harsher. On one hand, there was a recognition that the old, sick and infirm could not work, so they were licensed to beg, but anyone asking for help without being licensed would be whipped. In 1536, worse penalties were added – losing an ear for a second offence and death for a third.

The closure of the monasteries in the 1530s removed an essential safety net against poverty in Tudor England, with the resulting rise in vagrancy and subsequent legislation, such as the 1547 branding of vagrants with a 'V'; Edward IV's 1552 list of licensed beggars and appointment of an alms distributor in each parish; and Mary I's 1555 directive that beggars wear badges.

In 1569, the sixteen beadles belonging to the London hospitals were required to 'clear the streets of vagrants and sturdy beggars' and take them to Bridewell, the first house of 'correction', while the sick, lame, blind and aged were taken to St Bartholomew's and those under 16 to Christ's Hospital. The beadles were given regular circuits to walk, but the system failed, so the first city marshals were created to fulfil this role. St Bartholomew's and St Thomas' Hospitals, originally part of the monastic closures, were re-endowed and funded by taxes, in order to provide correctional facilities to accommodate and cure the poor.

Elizabeth's 1563 Relief of the Poor Act required every household that was able to contribute to the regular poor collections, suggestive of a more compassionate approach, and the start of a full-scale social policy. However, this was balanced by punitive measures against those 'sturdy' or 'professional' beggars, who were classed as 'repeat offenders'. They were burned through the ear for a first offence, but might afterwards be fined the huge sum of £10, which was way out of their reach, or simply hanged.

Later, steps forward were made when a directive of 1572 allowed parish officials to register those most in need and assess how much assistance they required per week, and the 1575 Poor Act required parishes to provide employment and houses of correction, where individuals might do useful work.

A full Act for the Relief of the Poor was finally created in 1597 and revised in 1601, in which the 'impotent' poor, defined as being 'old, impotent, lame or blind', were accommodated in almshouses and poor houses, and given a weekly allowance. The able-bodied poor were employed in a house of industry and provided with the necessary materials to work, poor children became apprentices, and the idle poor, or vagabonds, went to houses of correction, or to prison.[1]

In the 1580s, William Harrison identified three different types of poverty:

> With us the poor is commonly divided into three sorts, so that some are poor by impotence, as the fatherless child, the aged, blind, and

lame, and the diseased person that is judged to be incurable; the second are poor by casualty, as the wounded soldier, the decayed householder, and the sick person visited with grievous and painful diseases; the third consisteth of thriftless poor, as the rioter that hath consumed all, the vagabond that will abide nowhere, but runneth up and down from place to place (as it were seeking work and finding none), and finally the rogue and the strumpet, which are not possible to be divided in sunder, but run to and fro over all the realm, chiefly keeping the champaign soils in summer to avoid the scorching heat, and the woodland grounds in winter to eschew the blustering winds.[2]

In 1575, John Awdelay published *The Fraternity of Vagabonds*, in which he catalogued different types of poor, cheats and thieves, in an early kind of rogues' gallery, each with their own unusual name, specific to the Elizabethan age:

A Ruffeler.
A Ruffeler goeth wyth a weapon to seeke seruice, saying he hath bene a Seruitor in the wars, and beggeth for his reliefe. But his chiefest trade is to robbe poore wayfaring men and market women.

A Prygman.
A Prygman goeth with a sticke in his hand like an idle person. His propertye is to steale clothes off the hedge, which they call storing of the Rogeman: or else filtch Poultry, carrying them to the Alehouse, which they call the Bowsyng In, and there sit playing at cardes and dice, till that is spent which they haie so fylched.

A Frater.
A Frater goeth wyth a like Lisence to beg for some Spiritual house or Hospital. Their pray is commonly upon poore women as they go and come to the Markets.

A Quire bird.
A Quire bird is one that came lately out of prison, and goeth to seeke service. He is commonly a stealer of Horses, which they terme a Priggar of Palfreys.

A wilde Rogue.

A wilde Rogue is he that hath no abiding place but by his colour of going abroad to beg, is commonly to seeke some kinsman of his, and all that be of hys corporation be properly called Rogues.[3]

Ruffelers and Quire birds aside, anyone, even royalty, could experience poverty. In 1505, following the collapse of her betrothal to Prince Henry, the young widow Catherine of Aragon was so poor as to be unable to feed her servants. In March, she complained of 'the misery in which she lives', explaining that if she had 'contracted debts for luxuries, the king might have reason not to pay them' but she had been 'forced to borrow, otherwise she would have had nothing to eat'. That September she wrote to her father on behalf of her six ladies who had come with her from Spain and 'have served her right well, without her giving them a single maravedi', and she had nothing to offer them as dowries. By December, she was describing herself as 'destitute' and unable to buy clothing, 'each day her troubles increase' and she had 'lost her health'. The following April, she approached Henry VII and 'asked him with tears' now in the 'greatest anguish', with her people 'ready to ask alms and herself all but naked'. Things had not improved for her by 1508, when she appealed to her father:

Things here become daily worse and my life more and more insupportable, I can no longer bear this in any manner ... It is impossible for me any longer to endure what I have gone through and am still suffering from the unkindness of the king and the manner in which he treats me ... My necessities have risen so high that I do not know how to maintain myself, for I have already sold my household goods, as it was impossible to avoid it ... Some days ago, speaking with the king, he said to me that he was not bound to give my servants food, or even to my own self, but the love that he bore me would not allow him to do otherwise. From this your highness will see to what a state I am reduced, when I am warned that even my food is given me almost as alms.[4]

Catherine's dire financial situation was alleviated in June 1509, when the newly succeeded Henry VIII honoured his promise and married her. Her daughter, Princess Mary, was later to suffer penury as a result of her father's displeasure, as did her sister, Elizabeth.

In 1535, when Henry was married to Anne Boleyn and Mary was out of favour, John Gostwyk was approached by Sir Edmund Bedingfield, steward of Mary's household, asking for money, as he was 'clean without'. The household debts amounted to £1,000, of which £200 was due to the fishmonger in London and £180 to the grocer.[5] After her mother's fall, young Princess Elizabeth lacked clothes, having grown out of those she owned, requiring her governess, Lady Bryan, to write to Henry VIII requesting more, as 'she has neither gown nor kirtle nor petticoat nor linen for smock'.

Tudors of all walks of life frequently depended upon the patronage system and struggled to make ends meet. In 1535, Peter Rede was fighting against the Turks, but various misunderstandings and miscommunications had left him in need:

> Pray send me some money; 40s. a year will not keep me in hose and shoes. I must sell my cloak if Mr. Masun come not within 15 days. I will not borrow of Weldun; he warned me out of my master's service. Now I am in again, for I got the French ambassador to speak to my master, who said he never gave Weldun commission to put me out.[6]

Those in a position of influence could use it on behalf of their poorer relatives in order to secure them a career or alleviate suffering. At the same time Peter Rede was asking for help, Sir Henry Knyvet wrote to thank Lord Lisle 'for your kindness to my poor kinsman this bearer', for employing him as a soldier, in quest of which the poor man had used up all his money and resources. Knyvet asked 'that he may continue with your Lordship in house for a season ... having his meat and drink there'.[7]

The official records are full of letters from individuals asking for help. A Walter Graver appealed to Cromwell in the 1530s for 'some small gift which will enable him to prosecute literary pursuits at either university or London'. He had been teaching for two years at Croyland but 'the climate is so unwholesome that he would rather die than pass a third summer there'. Graver explained he was 'too poor to live at the university otherwise ... was 24 years old' and 'his body before he came to Croyland sufficiently strong and his thirst for learning insatiable'.[8]

At a similar time, Lord Sandys also approached Cromwell on behalf of a 'poor woman', a widow who had been asked to vacate her sheep farm. Sandys had supported her marriage, but the husband had died intestate, leaving his wife to pay his bills and administer the property.[9]

In 1594, Robert Scragge asked the justices at Chester for help, being a 'poor orator' with a wife and 'many small children', who had maintained himself by 'handy labour without offence to the parish'. His family lived in a small cottage built on waste land in Swettenham, 'long before the statute made against erecting of cottages', but it was still pulled down and the family were forced to shelter 'in a hollow place upon the same waste' and asked permission to build a new cottage which would be left standing.[10]

Prompted by the same harsh ruling, Rauff Hassall asked the Chester Assembly for a licence to build on the waste land at Little Hassall 'one cottage for a dwelling house' for three sisters, 'having spent their times in service and now by reason of their ages not able any longer to serve and to continue the same for a dwelling house during the lives of the same'. He assured the justices that Johanna, Ellen and Alice Hall were 'of honest and good behaviour and have no convenient place elsewhere to live in'.[11]

In 1601, Thomas Moore of Claynes and his family were destitute and asked for alms:

> Whereas your said petitioner having bene many yeares visited with sickness and infirmities, and his poore wife and their two children, being now in most miserable and wretched estates, and altogether unable to get theire owne livinges, and by reason thereof, all his goodes and substance are spent and gone who hath made his abode in Claynes aforesaid, for and during the terme of sixteene yeares laste paste, and now cannot use any other meanes for the releiving of himself and his family, but must of necessitie perishe, unlesse they may be aided by your good worships, in this theire said wante, wherefore his humble suite is, requestinge your good worships to order, that the said poore man may have some weekely allowance within the said parishe, towardes the releivinge of him and his said poore family, and therein they all will howerly pray to God to recompence you.[12]

In 1601, Eleanor Reeve, a 'lame cripple' who had always lived in Odingley, was forcibly turned out of her home of three years by Thomas Sales 'ever since which said time [she] hath been and yet is destitute of any place of abode and hath been diverse nights enforced to lie there in the streets', until the church wardens promised to take some 'convenient course to relieve [her] in her extremity'. Despite her condition, Eleanor professed herself 'always willing to the uttermost of her health and strength to labour truly towards her finding'.[13]

A pamphlet of 1591 recognised that winters were particularly hard for the poor, beginning earlier for them than for the rich, as they had 'no money nor credit', so lacked 'coals and wood and be faine to stand and starve for cold while old pennifathers sit and waste themselves by the fire'. It was also to be feared, continued the author, that 'through the extreme cold divers poor men shall die at rich men's doors', as the old forms of charity, alms and pity were 'exiled ... as a sign of Popish religion'.

Wounded soldiers, ex-servants and the maimed struggled for survival, particularly in the aftermath of war and in the second half of the century. Ports were overcrowded when large numbers of soldiers were billeted there, awaiting the arrival of a wind or tide. Cities like Dover, Portsmouth and Southampton bore the costs of men departing for France, and Bristol for Ireland. In 1581 alone, the city of Bristol was forced to spend £4,000 on the expenses and ships for departing soldiers. The churchwardens and inhabitants of Barthomley Parish in Crewe received an annual sum of 34s for the 'relief and maintenance' of prisoners and maimed soldiers from Chester, but requested assistance in 1599, as the quantities of men were so great that it had pushed them into debt.[14]

Individual cases of charity, and families saved from poverty, show the isolated acts of compassion that characterised this era, but they had not yet resolved into any form of welfare system or general benefit system. Even as the Tudor era drew to a close, the belief still persisted in the correct place of individuals, according to what the modern world recognises as 'just world theory' – the rich man at his table, the beggar at his gate, even if that beggar was dying of cold and hunger.

❧ WEATHER ❧

Weather was a significant physical factor in Tudor England. On a daily basis, its manifestations such as temperature, precipitation and wind were experienced first as bodily sensations, and secondly through its impact on the immediate structural and natural world. At its worst, it could ruin crops, prevent journeys and create structural damage. Extremes of weather might also be responsible for individuals experiencing illness, contribute to accidents or even cause death.

Dr John Dee's diaries display an unusual sensitivity to the weather. The vagaries of temperature, wind and sun often feature in his entries from the 1580s, when he notes that his wife was out walking in 'very great showers of rain', or that they had experienced continuous showers for two days, or there was snow before noon, or the wind 'came east after five weeks most part west'. One September, he recorded 'a terrible tempest of wind, south by wests, this afternoon and all the night following, a great storm of wind at north-west', while another September, four years later, brought 'tempestrous, windy, cloudy, hail and rain at three of the clock afternoon'.[1]

Severe structural damage might arise from storms, as when the steeple of St Paul's was struck by lightning, which sent fire raging through the cathedral. Between one and two on the afternoon of 10 June 1561:

> was seene a marvellous great fiery lightening and immediately issued a most terrible, hideous crack of thunder, such as seldom hath been heard ... directly oved the city of London. At which instant the corner of a turrent of the steeple of St Martin's Church within Ludgate was torn and divers great stones cast down and a hole broken through the roof and timber.

People on the bank of the Thames and in the outlying fields:

> affirmed that they saw a speare-pointed flame of fire running through the top of the shaft of St Paul's steeple, and some ... did feel a marvellous strong air or whirlwind with a smell like brimstone coming from Paul's church and withal heard the rush of stones which fell from their steeple into the church.

The devastation swiftly progressed:

> Between four and five of the clock, a smoke was espied by divers
> to break out under the bowl of the shaft ... but suddenly after, as it
> were in a moment, the flame broke forth in a circle like a garland
> ... and increased in such wise that within a quarter of an hour, or a
> little more, the cross and the eagle on the top fell down upon the
> south cross aisle.

The London Council feared for the destruction of people and property,
'considering the hugeness of the fire and the dropping of the lead',
and tried to seal off the church. About 500 Londoners helped to fill
and carry buckets of water but soon, 'it pleased God also at the same
time both to turn and calm the wind, which afore was vehement'.
The flames were still burning that evening, when they were sighted
by the queen all the way out at Greenwich, finally being subdued at
ten o'clock.[2]

One serious impact of unseasonal weather was the ruination of
crops and livestock. John Reppes suffered a setback to his fortunes
in November 1563 when many of his sheep were lost, 'owing to the
last storm breaking their banks', which also meant that 'fowlers have
no leisure to lay for fowl' and he could only send his correspondent,
Bassingbourn Gawdy, a crane and two mallards.[3]

Disaster was narrowly averted when Sir William Courtenay was
in Devonshire, in 1535, during heavy rainfall. He made an inspec-
tion of all the weirs on the River Exe 'and found them all faulty'.
Had the weirs been destroyed suddenly, Courtenay believed the
resulting flooding around the town of Exeter would have led to some
2,000 people dying from want of bread.[4]

The chances of the Tudor dynasty had almost been entirely ruined
by bad weather back in 1483. Henry VII's original plan had been
to oust Richard III that autumn with the assistance of the Duke of
Buckingham, who had amassed a large Welsh army in anticipation
of Henry's return from exile in Brittany. Rain and flood prevented
Buckingham's army from crossing the River Severn, resulting in
his capture, and the Breton fleet was beaten back from the coast.

It would have been easy to see the hand of God at work in these events, justifying Richard's kingship or the necessity for delaying the plan. Astrologers believed that certain days, hours, weather and circumstances were auspicious for life, health and success, so they consulted almanacs and the stars, to provide readings about 'lucky' and 'unlucky' days to travel.

Catherine of Aragon experienced terrible weather when attempting to sail from Spain to England in the autumn of 1501. Her fleet first tried to put to sea on 17 August, but the conditions in the Bay of Biscay were so severe that all but one were beaten back with torn sails and leaking hulls. While Catherine was forced to wait at the Spanish port of Laredo until the weather improved, Henry VII sent one of his best captains, Stephen Butt (or Brett), to await the appearance of her ships and guide her into port.

The weather was so bad that almost six weeks elapsed before it was judged safe to leave, and the fleet finally set sail on Monday, 27 September. However, they weighed anchor at five in the afternoon and although the weather 'was favourable at first, it changed after midnight', when they were overtaken by thunderstorms and huge waves. After that, there was a storm every few hours and 'it was impossible not to be afraid', but they sailed on for another six days through the notorious Bay of Biscay and around the tip of Brittany. Eventually, they entered the Channel and the coast of England came into sight. On Saturday, 2 October, at around three in the afternoon, the Spanish fleet drifted into harbour at Plymouth.

When Henry VIII's younger sister, Mary, was due to embark for her marriage to Louis XII of France, in September 1514, 'the wind was turbulous and the weather foule', keeping her ships at Dover. On 2 October, a brief lull in the wind allowed the fleet of fourteen ships to set sail, dividing between them her ladies, wardrobe, possessions, treasure, horses and the baggage of her companions. Such cargos were always split between ships to ensure that all would not be lost in one go. When they were halfway across the Channel, the wind rose again and scattered them, some to Calais or Boulogne, some to Flanders and some, including the 900-ton *Lubeck*, were wrecked with around 100 drowned. At the other side, a seasick Mary was carried ashore by Sir Christopher Garnish.

In April 1530, Richard Dolphine was being encouraged to set sail from Hull by Thomas Wolsey, who was at Peterborough and unaware of the terrible weather off the north-east coast. Dolphine attempted to explain the folly of embarking at the present time:

> On Easter Day last (17 April), received your letters, dated Peterborough, 15 April, wondering we do so long tarry here, and stating that the wind and weather were propitious with you. They are not so with us. You allege that the masters and mariners of our ships are, at this feast of Easter, at home with their wives and children, and that is the reason of our long abode. If the wind had served us, there is never a shipmaster but should have kept his Easter at Hull.[5]

The nature of travel during Tudor times meant that the problems created by the weather were ever present. In January 1559, Edward, Lord North, wrote to William Cecil that he 'cannot come as yet through the thunderstorms'.[6]

The following January, the Duke of Norfolk was at sea off Flamborough Head, 'whence he was driven by stress of weather to put back into the Humber mouth'. The next day he put to sea again, but three days later was 'separated from the others by violent weather' so that some were forced to seek shore.[7]

In February 1560, Thomas Challoner was attempting to communicate with William Cecil from France, but 'three or four of his last letters have by contrary weather been stayed at Dunkirk'. When Cecil was awaiting a report from Valentine Dale in January 1564, Dale seized 'the opportunity of a messenger' to write to Cecil that 'he has been compelled to remain at Dover, waiting for a favourable wind'.[8]

One occasion when the terrible weather in the Channel proved useful to English fortunes was on the invasion of a Spanish fleet in August 1588. When Philip II's armada of 130 ships was defeated at the Battle of Gravelines, a westerly wind threatened to wreck the survivors off the coast of Zeeland, but a change in the wind's direction sent them north instead and, pursued by the English, they were forced to round the top of Scotland in their attempt to return to Spain. Caught in the Gulf Stream, they were wrecked off the coast of Ireland, where the ships were looted and around 5,000 sailors drowned, prompting Philip to say, 'I sent the Armada against men, not against God's winds and waves.'

✳

Daily life, health and domestic affairs could be hindered or facilitated by bad weather. Those experiencing illness not only avoided travelling during cold, wind and rain, but actively sought windows of opportunity when the weather was fine. Arthur Throckmorton was ill in February 1583, writing that 'if the weather and ways wax [grow] fairer, [I] will go up [to visit] tho' it were in his litter, as being nearer his native air, he may recover his health'.[9]

In September 1588, 'unreasonable foul weather' prevented Edward Juliarde of Tolshunt, Essex, from travelling to visit his friend, Gawdy, and 'reporting verbally his conference with his sister touching Gawdy's suit'.

In most cases, the fury of the elements was treated as an inconvenience, best avoided. Occasionally, it was interpreted in the context of divine interventions, such as God's influence upon the wind direction when St Paul's was on fire, which was a benign act of salvation. The converse might be assumed, though, too. In August 1572, the mayor and jurats of Rye, in Sussex, called for public prayer and fasting 'in consideration of this unseasonable weather, a token of God's great displeasure threatening no small miseries and calamaties to fall upon us and that for our loose life and neglecting to do our duties as we ought to serve God'.[10]

The Tudor era experienced some extreme temperatures, during which the Thames might freeze solid, enabling the famous Elizabethan Frost Fairs. The year 1564 experienced 'a sharp frost, which began on St Thomas' day [21 December] and continued till the third day of January', when the thaw set in. John Stow reported that the frost was so 'sharp' that:

> even men went over the Thames as safe as on the dry land, not only between Westminster and Lambeth, but in all places between Lambeth and the Old Swan ... coming a land safely, thanks be to God, where they would ... and the same new years' even, being Sunday, people played at the foote ball on the Thames by great numbers. On new years' day ... divers gentlemen and others set up pryckes [targets] on the Thames and shot at the same and great numbers of people beholding the same standing at the pryckes as boldly, and thanks be to God as safely, as it had been o' dry land.

By Baynard's Castle, 'costardmongers' (apple sellers) were playing at dice for apples and people swarmed all over the river, until the thaw, when it was 'so sodaynly consumed'.[11]

William Harrison described 'a great snowstorm' which fell in 1578:

A Cold winter, and ere long there falleth a great snow in England, whose driftes, in many places, by reason of a Northest winde, were so deepe that the mere report of them maie seeme incredible. It beganne in the 4 of Feb and held on uvntil the 8 of the same month; during which time some men & women, beside cattle, were lost, and not heard of till the snow was melted and gone, notwithstanding that some sheepe and cattle lived under it, and fedd in the places where they laie, upon soche grasse as they could come by. Upon the 11th also of that moneth, the Thames did rise so highe, after the dissolution of this snow, that Westminster hall was drowned, and moche fishe left there in the palace yard when the water returned to her Channell, for who so list, to gather up.[12]

⚘ THE FARMER'S CYCLE ⚘

Large numbers of the Tudors lived far closer to the land and experienced the changing seasons in a more direct way than in the modern world. Bad weather crept into poor dwellings, rivers flooded and froze, fields had to be ploughed, crops needed to be sown, animals cared for, repairs undertaken and harvests brought in. William Harrison described Britain's soil as 'very fruitful, and such indeed as bringeth forth many commodities', although it was most inclined to feeding and grazing than the 'bearing of corn'. He estimated that, on cultivated land, an acre yielded about 16 or 20 bushels of wheat or rye, 36 bushels of oats and a little less with mixed crops of peas and beans and corn.[1]

The cycle of seasonal tasks necessary to sustain life for those dwelling outside the town was physically demanding. Tusser's seasonal guide provides a parallel with the medieval illustrated books of hours, typified by the *Tres Riches Heures du Duc du Berri*. Their bright illuminations reflected the labours of the month in a typically southern-European climate and a particular social elite:

January – Feasting
February – Sitting by the fire
March – Pruning trees, or digging
April – Planting, enjoying the country or picking flowers
May – Hawking, courtly love
June – Hay harvest
July – Wheat harvest
August – Wheat threshing
September – Grape harvest
October – Ploughing or sowing
November – Gathering acorns for pigs
December – Killing pigs, baking

Around 90 per cent of all Tudors worked on the land, as yeomen or husbandmen renting the land they farmed from the gentry, or labourers, who owned nothing, but rented themselves out daily for a fee. A life spent working the land was hard, physical and precarious, following an annual cycle and the vagaries of the weather.

The early months of the year began slowly, with a lull created by inclement weather, a time of feasting and sitting by the fire, when cottage industries, repairs, clothes making, and similar pursuits were followed. Yet there was still land, buildings and animals to be managed, particularly those besieged by the elements, and repair work to complete.

The agricultural year began properly with the new official calendar year, on Lady Day, 25 March, usually around the onset of spring and the lengthening of days. The hard work of ploughing the fallow fields with a team of horses began, followed by the planting of seeds and the harrowing of the field, or covering it over with soil and dung, which was gathered from the stables.

Vegetables and herbs were planted in the garden, ahead of the summer months, and the work of the dairy began again, following the milking of the cows. Tusser described March and April as 'breeding months', which saw the arrival of the first baby animals, especially lambs and chicks, which would guarantee meat and eggs, but could require a hands-on approach to their delivery and rearing.[2]

The hay harvest was ready in June, cut by teams of men walking through swinging scythes, with women and children gleaning after them. The success or failure of the hay determined how well the animals would be fed through the next winter, and any additional supplies could be sold. Lambs were weaned and sheep milked and then sheared.

The grain harvest in August depended on the weather and required several dry days. The wheat needed threshing, winnowing, sifting and sieving afterwards. Fruit and nut picking followed in late September, but not too soon, as Tusser cautioned with his little aphorism, 'September blow softe, till fruit be in loft', and the advice that:

> The Moone in the wane, gather fruit for to last, but winter fruit gather when Michaelmas is past … Fruit gathered too timely will taste of the wood, will shrink and be bitter, and seldome prove good: So fruit that is shaken, or beat off a tree, with brusing in falling, soone faultie will be.[3]

Farm-reared animals were driven into the woods between September and November to forage for beech nuts, chestnuts and acorns, as a way of fattening them up, a practice known as pannaging. This also helped turn the soil over to allow for new growth.

Martinmas Day, 11 November, was the traditional day for the slaughtering of farm animals, usually a pig, for the coming winter, although Tusser places it around 'Hallontide' (Halloween). The proper butchering, draining, skinning, salting, smoking and storing of a creature like a boar or cow took a considerable time with as minimum wastage as possible.

There were still other tasks to be done at this time, gathering firewood, weeding gardens and fields, cutting bracken for animals' winter beds and collecting and drying reeds to mend thatch. Channels and ditches might need to be dug to limit flooding or regulate the watering of crops. The fallow fields needed reploughing before the winter seeds were sown (perhaps wheat and rye) and fertilised with animal dung and bird droppings. The survival of the family during the winter months, with their short, dark, cold days, depended upon the work they had done that year in laying down stores. Tusser recommended hard work as a means of keeping warm and fed: 'No labour, no sweat, go labour for heat.'

The enclosure of common land was a constant problem throughout the Tudor era, reducing the amount of land available for small farmers to sow or graze animals upon. This could lead to disputes about long-standing rights, which could lead to the failure of farmsteads to survive if practical solutions were not found. In 1576, the Star Chamber arbitrated between Lord Richard and Thomas Francke on one side, and Sir Thomas Barrington on the other, all of Hatfield Broad Oak. By the agreed terms, Sir Thomas was to relinquish his role of forester of Hatfield to Lord Richard, in return for Richard conveying to him a fee in timber and trees. Thomas was to be permitted to enclose 16 acres a year, for a cost of 33s 4d, and to give Richard an additional £5 for rents and works needed. Richard and his heirs were to provide timber for Thomas and his family, but was to have the meadow called Lords Marsh, 'lately sown with mustard seed', and pasturage for his deer. Thomas was to have common pasture in the forest for 140 sheep, twenty steers or heifers, ten calves, ten horses or mares with their foals, ten colts or geldings and thirty swine, and to receive annually three bucks and three does from the forest.[4]

In the same year, 1576, the Essex Michaelmas sessions indicted John Coleman of Coggeshall, a labourer, for:

> breaking into the close of Henry Warner of the same, husbandman, at the same, and pulling up the hedge and enclosure of the said close by the roots, so that the beasts of the neighbours of the said Henry adjoining his close destroyed and ate his grass growing there.[5]

In 1580, George Greatehead of Brentwood had been ordered to take down a 'pale' which was encroaching upon the queen's highway leading into the town, on pain of forfeiting £10. However, it was reported that he had 'set up again the same pale and doth maintain the same to the annoyance and hurt to the queen's way', resulting in him being ordered to remove it by Easter 'and that from henceforth he do not maintain any pale or other enclosure there'.[6]

By 1600, William Vaughan believed that the old farming way of life was over:

> There is no life more pleasant than a yeoman's life, but nowadays, yeomanry is decayed, hospitality gone to wrack, and husbandry almost quite fallen. The reason is because landlords, not content with such revenues as their predecessors received, nor yet satisfied that they live like swinish epicures quietly at their ease ... do leave no ground for tillage, but do enclose for pasture many thousand

acres of ground within one hedge, the husbandmen are thrust out of their own, or else by deceit constrained to sell all that they have.[7]

In *A Marvellous Combat of Contrarieties Malignantly Striving in the Members of Man's Body*, written by William Averell in 1588, a dialogue between the hand and tongue attempts to resolve the question of which of them works harder. The tongue complained of having become enslaved to the demands of the belly and back:

> Like fooles we haue made the Belly and Backe our Lords, with great labour we get and provide all things may please them: poore soules we have no rest, sometime the Belly commandeth one, sometime the Backe another, one saith to ye Foote, arise sluggard, awake, the other to the hand, bestirre thee apace, get me some meate, prepare mee some dainties, fetch me some wine, lay the Table, the day passeth, the time goeth, and I haue eaten nothing: Hunger and Thirst my two enemies come & threaten my death, the one on the one side, the other on the other, and therefore except you speedely help me I die, and these are their dailie and usual complaints.[8]

The hand agreed, having suffered the extremes of temperature in their service, and left particularly unappreciated for all its constant efforts:

> I labour sundry ways to maintaine them. In the Winter I suffer cold, in the Summer I endure heat, my joynts are benumbed with the one, and dryed with the other, I labour day and night to procure for the both what I can and yet they are never satisfied ...
>
> Yea, for though I labour today to feede the one, and travaile tomorrow to clothe the other, yet if I do not the next day, and the next day also give them still, they complayne of myne idlenes, of mine injustice and negligence: saying I am unnaturall, unkinde, slothfull, and given to ease, and that I forget the ende wherefore I was made, which is, (they say) to serve them in all necessities, what said I?[9]

The foot joins the debate, believing itself to be the most hardworking of all the members, having to fetch and carry constantly:

> How do I trott up and downe, and as a Porter together with my fellow, am forced to beare uppe the rest of the members. Whatsoeuer

must be had, I am the Messenger to fetch it, is there any dish to feede the Belly? then must I runne to buy it, is there any fine apparrell fashionable for the Backe? be it neuer so farre, I must trudge for it. And albeit ye the waight of the members which nature hath gyuen be sufficient to charge & ouerburden my feeble force, yet must I haue a loade devised by arte, to oppresse the weakeness of my slender joynts, so that I thinke my burden heavier than Aetna, or the weight of the Heavens upon the shoulders of Atlas, with griefe hereof my bones consume, my sinewes shake, my humours dry up, and my joynts quake, like as when two weake Pillars beare uppe the burden of a heavie house.[10]

Humorous as Averell's conceit is and, ironically, accessed by the literate few unlikely to have been engaged in physical labour, the dialogue reminds us that the majority of the Tudors were constantly engaged in the work of survival. Much of it was preparation for harder times to come and the agricultural and farming work that ensured there would be food on the table, fuel, crops and animals provided for in the coming months. A spell of bad rain, or a drought, or the loss of the family's pig, or a rise in prices, could tip a household into debt or difficulty. Most people living in Tudor England, dependent upon the land for their livelihood, understood how precarious survival could be.

⚜ SPORT AND GAMES ⚜

The Tudors loved their sports. Hawking, hunting and archery were particular favourites with Henry VIII and Elizabeth I and their aristocracy and gentry. However, these were pleasures strictly reserved for particular classes. Butts or 'pryckes' were frequently set up on village greens for target practice, and the lower classes were actively encouraged to develop their skills with the longbow, but hunting in the royal forest and the sport of keeping expensive birds was an elite pursuit.

And they were pursued with commitment. Gregory Cromwell wrote to his father in September 1535 to excuse himself for not having written for such a long time, because 'he had not rested one day, but has either hawked, or hunted, or passed the time with gentlemen of the country'.[1]

A hawking and hunting manual of 1596 outlined the methods, care and medicines required by a hawk, suggesting that it be bathed every third day in summer or once a week in winter, and to ensure it was fed hot meat afterwards. To make a hawk fly 'with a good courage in the morning', it should be fed hot meat the night before, which had been washed in urine, but if the bird was 'fully gorged', corns of wheat should be concealed in its meat. A hawk with gout needed to be fed a hedgehog and one with mites should be treated with wormwood.[2]

Horses were central to the Tudor world: as a means of transport, for their strength in labour and for recreation and hunting. Everyone would have known how to ride and the status conferred by horse ownership varied from the poor family's single workhorse pulling the plough, to the rich man's stable of imported Barbary or Almayne thoroughbreds.

A 1566 horsemanship manual by Thomas Blundeville outlined the various types of horses, how to choose and care for them, breeding and rearing them. Addressing his work to Robert Dudley, Elizabeth's Master of the Horse, Blundeville identified the ideal features of the animal:

A good horse should have legges straight and broad, his knees great, lean and plaine, his thighs full of sinews, the bones whereof would be shorte, equall, iuste and well proportioned, his shoulders, longe, large, and full of fleshe, his breast, large and rounde. The ideal horse would have a necke rather long then short, great towardes the breast, bending in the midst, and slender towardes the heade, eares small or rather sharpe, and standing right up, beynge of a just length and largenes, according to the stature of the horse, his forehead, leane and large, his eyes, blacke and great. His jawes should be slender and leane, his nostrils so open and puffed up as you may see the red within, apt to receive ayre, his mouth great, and finally, his whole heade together woulde be lyke a sheapes heade.[3]

The English had a considerable history with the longbow: as an essential first line of attack in battle; as a means of killing prey either as sport or to eat; and as a competitive sport. A formidable defence during the Hundred Years War, the longbow was obligatory from the 1360s, when an ordinance required Englishmen between 16 and 60 to spend Sundays and holidays 'not in pointless amusements such as football, bowls, tennis and dice, but in shooting at the butts'.

The smaller crossbow was phased out to make room for the long-bow, with Henry VII banning them in 1503 among the lower orders, to ensure the correct weapons were being used. In 1513, the longbow proved its worth in the defeat of the Scots at Flodden, and Henry VIII reinforced the regular Sunday practice in 1515, ordering that butts were erected and maintained in all towns.

Longbows of around 6ft 6in were found in the wreckage of the *Mary Rose*, which sank in 1545. An analysis of the skeletons recovered from the ship revealed the presence of ninety-two archers who showed repetitive strain injuries in the shoulder and lower back, correlative with lifelong use of the bow.

Roger Ascham's book on the art, *Toxophilus, the School of Shooting*, of 1545 describes it as important for youth to practise, as 'the most honest pastime in peace', so that they might 'handle it as a most sure weapon in war' and 'I graunte you, shooting is not the worst thing in the world, yet if we shoote, and time shoote, we are not like to be great winners at the length'. His book covered topics including how to hit the mark, by 'shooting aright' and 'keeping a length', which came by 'knowing things belonging to shooting' and 'by handling things belonging to shooting' such as standing, drawing, holding and loosing.[4]

In 1574, details about the different kinds of bowstaves were sent to William Cecil. Traditionally made of yew and standing about the height of a man, bows were also made from imported wood. There were four main types of wood then in use: the first was formerly a monopoly owned by the emperor and grown near Salzburg, from where it was conveyed by boat down the Main and Rhine and on to England, where it was sold at the Steelyard for £15 or £16 per 100 trunks. The second originated in Switzerland and was only £3 or £4, and the third came from Denmark and Poland, but was of inferior quality, being mostly hollow wood filled with sap due to the cold climate, and sold for £4 or £5. The final kind, grown in Italy and imported by Venetian merchants, 'is the principal finest, and steadfastest wood, by reason of the heat of the sun which drieth up the humidity and moisture of the sap'.[5]

As the century progressed, though, bows were increasingly being replaced by guns and were used more for recreational purposes. Humfrey Barwick's *A Brief Discourse, Concerning the Force and*

Effect of All Manual Weapons of Fire and the Disability of the Long Bowe or Archery, in Respect of Others of Greater Force Now in Use praised the musket as being of 'great force' and a 'much feared ... terror to the best armed ... it will kill the armed of proof at ten score yards ... and the unarmed at thirty score'.[6] However, when it came to the threat of invasion in 1588, when it was feared that the Spaniards might land on English soil, the trained bands were summoned, and a significant number were wielding a longbow.

For the Tudors, life was an intensely physical experience, its quality dependent upon the health and liberty of the body, and its duration determined by the avoidance of serious illness, disease and accident. Football, cricket and tennis were played, and Henry VIII famously enjoyed wrestling. Not all these forms of exercise were approved, being seen as too violent or distracting people from work or training. Sir Thomas Elyot wrote in 1531, 'Wrestling is very good exercise in the beginning of youth ... but in football is nothing but beastly fury and extreme violence.'[7] The puritanical Philip Stubbes denounced 'all mixed, effeminate, lascivious dancing' as 'utterly unlawful to Christians, to chaste and sober persons ... I have heard many impudently say they have chosen their wives, and wives their husbands, by dancing. Which plainly proveth the wickedness of it.'[8]

EPILOGUE

Just like ours, the Tudors' experience of the world was immediate and unavoidable, regardless of class, age and location. Their physical environment defined and influenced them in ways too subtle and infinite to be untangled and established the framework of their mental geography. The experience of life, of having a physicality, literally occupied every moment of their being from birth until death, ranging between the subconscious and the overwhelming.

Tudor identities were a composite of the flavours of their food and drink; the spices they might afford; the fabrics and adornments they were permitted to wear; the space they occupied, its decoration and objects; the sounds of voices, of music or warnings; the smell of perfume, fire or candles; the sensation of illness and pain. These things were sometimes joyous, and celebrated, sometimes a nuisance to be endured or a terrible agony, but our understanding of their frequency allows us to see the Tudors as real people and map our experiences over theirs, in a way that more detached methods of analysis cannot.

Paradoxically, understanding the Tudors' physical world allows us to better understand their minds. While they recognised the limits of their perceptions, the Tudors saw this point as the commencement of the divine plan, with God as cause and justification for everything. Yet their reasoning and methods were largely empirical, and tracing their origin shows us the processes of their thought. The material world was the context, the stage upon which sixteenth-century men and women carved out their identities, in response to what they saw, heard, smelt, tasted and touched. By these means, they made sense of the world, and depicted it in ways that have kept it alive and accessible across five centuries.

NOTES

SIGHT

PEN AND BRUSH

The Ambassadors

1   Foister, Susan, *Holbein's Ambassadors: Making and Meaning* (National Gallery, 1998); Hervey, Mary Frederica Sophia, *Holbein's Ambassadors: The Picture and the Man* (Nabu, 2010).

Strutting Kings

1   Skidmore, Christopher, *Edward VI: The Lost King of England* (Weidenfeld and Nicolson, 2008).

2   Nichols J.G. (ed.), *A Collection of Ordinances and Regulations for the Government of the Royal Household Made in Divers reigns ...* (Society of Antiquities, 1790).

3   Sharpe, Reginald R., 'London Letter Book L' in *Calendar of Letter Books of the City of London* (HMSO, 1912).

Portraits in Courtship

1   *Calendar of State Papers* (CSP), Spain, Vol. 1 (1505) 436.

2   *Ibid.*

3   Wilson, Derek, *Hans Holbein: Portrait of an Unknown Man* (Pimlico, 2006).

4   Hall, Edward, *Chronicle* (J. Johnson, 1809).

5   CSP, Spain, Vol. 13 (July 1554) 7.

Family Groups

1   Allen, P.S. (ed.), *The Complete Letters of Erasmus* (Oxford University Press, 1906).

Pen Portraits

1   *Calendar of the Cecil Papers*, Vol. 1, 642.

2   Byrne, Muriel St Clare, *The Lisle Letters* (Penguin, 1981).

3   *Calendar of the Cecil Papers*, Vol. 2, 119.

4   *State Letters and Papers* (SLP), Henry VIII, Vol. 2, 395.

5   Riddell, Jessica Erin 'A Mirror of Men': Sovereignty, Performance and Textuality in Tudor England 1501–1559 (unpublished PhD, Queens University, Canada, 2009).

6   Ives, Eric, *Anne Boleyn* (Blackwell, 2005).
7   Sanders, Nicholas, *De Origine ep Progressu Schismatis Anglicani* (1585).
8   *Calendar of the Cecil Papers*, Vol. 3, 88.
9   *Ibid.*, Vol. 2, 717.
10   *Ibid.*

CLOTH AND THREAD

Early Tudor Peacocks

1   Anon., *A Pleasant Dialogue or Disputation between the Cap and the Head* (1565).
2   *Calendar of the Cecil Papers*, Vol. 1, 475.
3   Hazard, Mary E., *Elizabethan Silent Language* (University of Nebraska Press, 2000).
4   SLP, Henry VIII, Vol. 3, 869.
5   *Ibid.*, Vols 2 and 3, various.
6   CSP, Venice (June 1515) 624.
7   Hall, *Chronicle*.
8   Kipling, Gordon (ed.), *The Receyt of the Ladie Kateryne* (Oxford University Press, 1990).
9   SLP, Henry VIII, Vols 2 and 3, various.
10   *Ibid.*
11   *Ibid.*
12   Nichols, J.G., *Inventories of the Wardrobe, Plate, Chapel Stuff Etc of Henry Fitzroy, Duke of Richmond, and of the Stuff at Baynard's Castle of Katherine, Princess Dowager* (Camden Society, 1855).
13   SLP, Henry VIII, Vol. 9, 413.
14   Byrne, *The Lisle Letters*.
15   SLP, Henry VIII (1536).
16   Madden, Frederick (ed.), *Privy Purse Expenses of the Princess Mary* (William Pickering, 1831).

Clothing as Battleground

1   SLP, Henry VIII (February 1545) 196.
2   *Ibid.*
3   Vergil, Polydore, *History of England* (Camden Society, 1846).
4   Sanders, *De Origine ep Progressu* ...
5   CSP, Spain, Vol. 4, No. 2, 1003.
6   *Calendar of the Cecil Papers*, Vol. 1, 153.
7   Tanner, J.R., *Tudor Constitutional Documents* (Cambridge University Press, 1922).
8   Wagner, Anne and Sherwin, Richard K., *Law, Culture and Visual Study* (Springer, 2013).
9   SLP, Henry VIII (August 1535).
10   *Ibid.* (October 1535) 651.
11   Harrison, William, *The Description of England* (1587).

12   Riello, Giorgio and Rublack, Ulinka (eds), *The Right to Dress: Sumptuary Laws in a Global Perspective* (Cambridge University Press, 2019).
13   Burton, Elizabeth, *The Early Tudors at Home* (Allen Lane, 1976).
14   Sharpe, 'London Letter Book L'.
15   Cox, Noel, 'Tudor Sumptuary Laws and Academic Dress: An Act against Wearing of Costly Apparel in 1509 and an Act for Reformation of Excess in Apparel in 1533', *Transactions of the Burgon Society*, Vol. 6 (2006) Article 2 (New Prairie Press, 2016).
16   SLP, Henry VIII (December 1526) 2743.
17   Byrne, *The Lisle Letters*.
18   Jonson, Ben, *Every Man Out of His Humour* (1599).
19   Harrison, *The Description of England*.
20   Stubbes, Philip, *The Anatomy of Abuses* (1583).
21   Baldwin, R., *A New History of London, including Westminster and Southwark* (London, 1773).
22   Von Klarwill, V. et al., *Queen Elizabeth and Some Foreigners* (John Lane, 1928).

Clothing, Gender and Sexuality

1   Ferris, Lesley (ed.), *Crossing the Stage: Controversies on Cross-Dressing* (Routledge, 2005).
2   Beard, Thomas, *The Theatre of God's Judgements* (T. Whitaker, 1642).
3   Harrison, *The Description of England*.
4   Brandt, Sebastian, *The Ship of Fools* (1494).
5   *Ibid.*
6   Anon., 'An Homily Against Excess of Apparel' in *Certain Sermons or Homilies Appointed to be Read in Churches in the Time of Queen Elizabeth* (1623).
7   Cressy, David, *Literacy and the Social Order: Reading and Writing in Tudor and Stuart England* (Cambridge University Press, 2006).
8   Levine, Laura, *Men in Women's Clothing: Anti-Theatricality and Effeminisation 1579–1642* (Cambridge University Press, 1994).
9   Warnicke, Retha M., *The Marrying of Anne of Cleves: Royal Protocol in Tudor England* (Cambridge University Press, 2000).
10   D'Estoile, Pierre, *Registre-journal du règne de Henri III*, edited by Lazard (Schrenck Droz, 1992).
11   Ferris, *Crossing the Stage*.
12   *Ibid.*
13   Howard, Jean E., 'Cross Dressing, the Theatre and Gender Struggle in Early Modern England', *Shakespeare Quarterly*, Vol. 39, No. 4, Winter 1988, pp. 418–40.
14   Ferris, *Crossing the Stage*.
15   *Ibid.*
16   *Ibid.*
17   *Ibid.*
18   *Ibid.*

19   SLP, Henry VIII, Vol. 9 (November 1535) 288–310, 861.
20   Ferris, *Crossing the Stage*.
21   *Ibid.*
22   *Ibid.*
23   *Ibid.*

Ordinary People's Clothing

1   *Calendar of the Cecil Papers*, Vol. 1, 556.
2   Oxfordshire wills: will.oxfordshirefhs.org.uk
3   *Ibid.*
4   *Ibid.*
5   *Ibid.*
6   SLP, Henry VIII (August 1535) 105.
7   *Ibid.* (September 1535) 362.
8   *Ibid.* (1535) 768.
9   *Ibid.* 858.
10   Various, Essex Record Office online.
11   SLP, Henry VIII (August 1535).
12   *Close Rolls*, Henry VII, Vol. 1, 139ii.
13   Harrison, *The Description of England*.
14   SLP, Henry VIII (1519).
15   *Calendar of the Cecil Papers*, Vol. 1, 473.
16   *Ibid.*, 442.
17   Harrison, *The Description of England*.
18   Byrne, *The Lisle Letters*.
19   SLP, Henry VIII (1535) 794.
20   Sharpe, 'London Letter Book L'.
21   Goodman, R., *How to Be a Tudor: A Dawn to Dusk Guide to Everyday Life* (Penguin, 2006).

BRICK AND FIELD

How England Looked

1   Sneyd, Charlotte Augusta, *A Relation, or Rather a True Account, of the Island of England: With Sundry Particulars of the Customs of These People and of the Royal Revenue under King Henry VII, Around the Year 1500* (Camden Society, 1884).
2   SLP, Henry VIII (August 1535).
3   Harding, V. and Wright, L. (eds), *London Bridge Selected Accounts and Rentals 1381–1583* (London Record Society, 1995).
4   Baldwin, *A New History of London*.
5   Bernard, George W., 'The Dissolution of the Monasteries', *History* Vol. 96, Issue 324, 2011, p. 390.
6   Skidmore, *Edward VI*.
7   Leland, John, *The Itinerary of John Leland in or About the Year 1535–45* edited by Lucy Toulmin Smith (George Bell, 1907).
8   *Ibid.*
9   Tanner, *Tudor Constitutional Documents*.

10 *Ibid.*
11 *Ibid.*
12 *The Customs of Rye and Hereford* (HMSO London, 1892).
13 Hentzner, Paul, *Itinerarium* (1598).
14 *Ibid.*
15 Stow, John, *Survey of London* (Everyman, 1912).
16 Sneyd, *A Relation.*
17 Baldwin, *A New History of London.*
18 Stow, *Survey of London.*
19 Baldwin, *A New History of London.*

Royal Buildings

1   SLP, Henry VIII (August 1535) 110.
2   Hentzner, *Itinerarium.*
3   Stow, *Survey of London.*
4   *Ibid.*
5   Camden, William, *Annales Rerum Anglicarum*, (ed. T. Hearne), (Oxon, 1717).
6   Hentzner, *Itinerarium.*
7   SLP, Henry VIII (June 1520).
8   *Ibid.*
9   *Ibid.*
10 *Ibid.*
11 *Calendar of the Cecil Papers.*

Rich and Poor

1   Stow, *Survey of London.*
2   *Ibid.*
3   SLP, Henry VIII (August 1535) 66.
4   *Ibid.*
5   *Calendar of the Foreign Papers, Edward, Mary and Elizabeth*, Vol. 1 (1559), edited by Robert Lemon (HMSO, 1856).
6   *Calendar of the Cecil Papers*, Vol. 1, 587.
7   Harrison, *The Description of England.*
8   *Ibid.*

Inside the Home

1   Scott, A.F., *Everyone a Witness: The Tudor Age* (Scott and Finlay, 1975).
2   Harrison, *The Description of England.*

Possessions

1   Hentzner, *Itinerarium.*
2   *Ibid.*
3   *Ibid.*
4   *Ibid.*
5   *Ibid.*

6   *Calendar of the Cecil Papers*, Vol 1.
7   *Ibid.*, 475.
8   SLP, Henry VIII (January 1532).
9   *Trevelyan Family Papers* (Camden Society, 1853).
10   *Ibid.*
11   Oxfordshire wills: will.oxfordshirefhs.org.uk
12   *Ibid.*
13   *Ibid.*
14   Inventory of Henry Fitzroy and Catherine of Aragon.
15   *Calendar of the Cecil Papers*, Vol. 1, 252.
16   *Ibid.*, 434.
17   *Ibid.*, 475.
18   SLP, Henry VIII (January 1545) 31.
19   Oxfordshire wills: will.oxfordshirefhs.org.uk
20   *Ibid.*
21   *Ibid.*
22   *Calendar of the Cecil Papers*, Vol. 2, 108.
23   *Ibid.*

Working Interiors

1   Emmison, F.G., *Elizabethan Life* (Essex Record Office, 1976).
2   *Ibid.*
3   *Ibid.*
4   Sharpe, 'London Letter Book L'.
5   SLP, Henry VIII (1545).
6   Tusser, *The Book of Husbandrie* (1577).
7   *Memorials of the Guild of Merchant Taylors* edited by C.M. Clode (Harrison, 1875).
8   Bury St Edmunds Guildhall Records, 1520–21.
9   Baldwin, *A New History of London.*
10   *The Remembrancia 1579–1664*, edited by W.H. Overall and H.C. Overall (E.J. Francis, 1878).

Religious Interiors

1   Sneyd, *A Relation.*
2   Erasmus, Desiderius, *In Praise of Folly* (publisher unknown, 1511).
3   Leland, John, *The Itinerary of John Leland.*
4   Unspecified, *Art and Visual Culture: Medieval to Modern* (Open University Press, 2016).
5   Sneyd, *A Relation.*
6   SLP, Henry VIII.
7   *Ibid.* (January 1520).
8   SLP, Henry VIII, Vol. 9 (August 1535) 42.
9   SLP, Henry VIII (August 1535) 168.
10   *Ibid.* (September 1535) 434.
11   *Ibid.* (October 1535).
12   *Ibid.* (November 1535) 756.

13 *Ibid.* (1535) miscellaneous.
14 Stow, *Survey of London.*
15 SLP, Henry VIII (1535); miscellaneous (1618).

CROWD AND RITUAL

Entrances and Exits

1   *Wriothesley's Chronicle Volume 2* edited by William Douglas Hamilton (Camden, 1877).
2   SLP, Henry VII (1488) 21.
3   Kipling, *The Receyt of the Ladye Kateryne.*
4   *Ibid.*
5   *Ibid.*
6   SLP, Henry VIII (June 1520).
7   *Ibid.*
8   SLP, Henry VIII, Vol. 12, 8.
9   *Ibid.*, 58.
10 Hentzner, *Itinerarium.*
11 Nichols, J.G. (ed.), *Chronicle of the Greyfriars* (Camden, 1852).
12 Nichols, J.G. (ed.), *The Diary of Henry Machyn* (Camden, 1868).
13 *Ibid.*
14 SLP, Henry VIII, Vol. 1, 20.
15 *Ibid.*, 4.
16 *Ibid.*, 5.
17 Records of the Drapers' Company.
18 Sharpe, 'London Letter Book L'.

Revels

1   Hall, *Chronicle.*
2   *Ibid.*
3   SLP, Henry VIII (1511).
4   *Ibid.* (January 1518).
5   *Ibid.*
6   Hall, *Chronicle.*
7   *Ibid.*
8   *Ibid.*
9   Stow, *Survey of London.*
10 *Ibid.*
11 Latimer's Sixth Sermon delivered before Edward VI.
12 Stow, *Survey of London.*
13 *Ibid.*
14 Stubbes, *Anantomy of Abuses.*
15 Tusser, *The Book of Husbandrie.*
16 Nichols, *Chronicle of the Greyfriars.*
17 Scott, *Everyone a Witness.*

Theatre

1   Harrison, *Description of England*.
2   Gosson, Stephen, *Schoole of Abuse* (1579).
3   Baldwin, *A New History of London*.
4   *Ibid.*
5   *Ibid.*

Enacting Justice

1   *Memorials of the Guild of Merchant Taylors*.
2   Stow, *Survey of London*.
3   *Calendar of the Cecil Papers*, Vol. 2, 1113b.
4   *Ibid.*, Vol. 3, 99.
5   MacMillan, Ken, *Stories of True Crime in Tudor and Stuart England* (Routledge, 2015).
6   SLP, Edward VI, Vol. 8, 33.
7   Stow, *Survey of London*.
8   *Ibid.*
9   Sharpe, 'London Letter Book L'.
10 Stow, *Survey of London*.
11 *Ibid.*
12 *Ibid.*
13 *Ibid.*
14 SLP, Henry VIII.
15 *Ibid.*, Vol. 21, No. 2, pp. 12–30, 60.
16 Wroe, Ann, *Perkin* (Vintage, 2010).

Phenomena

1   Boaistuau, Pierre, *Certain Secrete Wonders of Nature* (Roger Fenton, 1569).
2   *Ibid.*
3   *Ibid.*
4   Stow, *Survey of London*.
5   Nichols, *Chronicle of the Greyfriars*.
6   Tusser, *The Book of Husbandrie*.
7   Boaistuau.
8   Rösslin, Eucharius, *The Rose Garden* (Germany, 1513). English translation: Ray, Thomas, *The Birth of Mankind* (London, 1540).
9   Cressy, David, *Agnes Bowker's Cat: Travesties and Transgressions in Tudor and Stuart England* (Oxford University Press, 2001).
10 Stow, *Survey of London*.
11 Harrison, *The Description of England*.
12 Dee, Dr John, *The Private Diary of John Dee*, edited by J.O. Halliwell (Camden, 1842).
13 Williams, C.H. (ed.), *English Historical Documents 1485–1558* (Routledge, 1997).

COMMUNICATION

The Written Word

1   Cressy, *Literacy and the Social Order*.
2   Vives, Juan Luis, *Tudor School Boy Life* trans. by Foster Watson (J.M. Dent, 1908).
3   *Ibid.*
4   *Ibid.*
5   SLP, Henry VIII (October 1518).
6   Vives, *Tudor School Boy Life*.
7   CSP, Spain, Vol. 1, 343.
8   *Ibid.* 1506 appendix.
9   SLP, Henry VIII, vol. 6 (1533); miscellaneous (1599).
10 *Calendar of the Cecil Papers*, Vol. 2, 2.
11 *Ibid.*,1567.
12 *Ibid.*, 213.
13 Brice, Thomas, *Against Filthy Writing* (1562).
14 *Calendar of the Cecil Papers*, Vol. 2, 339.
15 *Ibid.*, Vol. 3, 143.

The Printed Word

1   www.bl.uk/medieval-literature/articles/william-caxton-and-the-introduction-of-printing-to-england
2   SLP, Henry VIII (1535) 523.
3   *Ibid.*
4   *Ibid.*, 723.
5   *Ibid.*, 963.
6   *Calendar of the Cecil Papers*, Vol. 2, 207.
7   *Ibid.*, 209.
8   *Ibid.*, 429.
9   *Customs of Rye and Hereford, 13th Report*, Appendix, part IV (HMSO London, 1892).
10 *Ibid.*
11 *Calendar of the Cecil Papers*, Vol. 2, 551.
12 *Ibid.*, 1268.
13 *Customs of Rye and Hereford*, fo. 238b.
14 *Ibid.*
15 SLP, Henry VIII (1535) 883.
16 *Calendar of the Cecil Papers*, Vol. 1, 109.
17 *Calendar of the Cecil Papers*, Vol. 1, 109, 23–44.

Map-Making

1   Boorde, Andrew, *Principles of Astronomy* (1542).
2   Bogaert, Arnold, *A Prognostication for Divers Years* (John Cook, 1553).
3   *Ibid.*

Telling the Time

1 Vives, *Tudor School Boy Life*.
2 *Calendar of the Cecil Papers*, Vol. 1, 1544.
3 *Ibid.*, 475.

Restricted Sight

1 Boorde, Andrew, *A Compendious Regiment or Dietary of Health* (Robert Wyer, 1547).
2 SLP, Henry VIII (February 1545) 191.
3 *Ibid.* (September 1546) 155.
4 *Calendar of the Cecil Papers*, Vol. 2, 607.
5 Manchester, William, *A World Lit Only by Fire* (Sterling, 1992).
6 Tusser, *The Book of Husbandrie*.
7 Stow, *Survey of London*.
8 Vives, *Tudor School Boy Life*.
9 Tusser, *The Book of Husbandrie* .
10 Harrison, *The Description of England*.
11 SLP, Henry VIII (1513) 23b.
12 Sharpe, fo. 225–26.
13 *Calendar of the Cecil Papers*, Vol. 2, 636.
14 *Ibid.*, 637.

SMELL

Pipe Smoke

1 Hakluyt, Richard, *Diverse Voyages Touching the Discoverie of America* (publisher unknown, 1582).
2 *Ibid.*
3 Beaumont, John, *The Metamorphosis of Tobacco* (1602).
4 *Ibid.*
5 Harrison, *The Description of England*.
6 Beaumont.
7 Chute, Anthony, *Tabaco* (William Barlowe, 1595).
8 Hentzner, *Itinerarium*.
9 *Rutland Papers* edited by John Manners and William Jerden (Camden, 1842).
10 Gerard, John, *Gerard's Herbal* (1597).
11 Beaumont.

Foul Bodies

1 Nicolas, Nicholas Harris, *Privy Purse Expenses of Henry VIII 1533* (Camden, 1827).
2 SLP, Henry VIII, Vol. 2, appendix to preface.
3 Moulton, Thomas, *This Is the Mirror or Glasse of Health* (1545).
4 *Calendar of the Cecil Papers*, Vol. 1, 1334.
5 *Ibid.*, Vol. 2, 1223.
6 Moulton, *This is the Mirror*.

7   Kassell, Lauren, *Medicine and Magic in Elizabethan London: Simon Forman, Astrologer, Alchemist and Physician* (Oxford University Press, 2001).
8   Stubbes, *Anatomy of Abuses.*
9   Vives, *Tudor School Boy Life.*
10   Essex Record Office, St Osyth, 1576.

Clean Clothes

1   Vives, *Tudor School Boy Life.*
2   SLP, Henry VIII (September 1546) 179.
3   Partridge, John, *Treasury of Commodious Conceits and Hidden Secrets* (publisher, 1573).
4   *Kunstbuch* (Frankfurt, 1566).
5   Keene, D.J. and Harding, Vanessa (eds), *Historical Gazetteer of London before the Great Fire* (Centre for Metropolitan History, 1987).

Perfume

1   Partridge, *Treasury.*
2   *Ibid.*
3   *Ibid.*
4   Tusser, *The Book of Husbandrie.*
5   *Ibid.*
6   Partridge, *Treasury.*
7   Levens, Peter, *The Pathway to Health* (1582).
8   *Ibid.*
9   *Calendar of the Cecil Papers*, Vol. 1, 475.

Waste Disposal

1   Sharpe, 'London Letter Book L'.
2   *Ibid.*
3   Essex Record Office, Q/SR 125/34.
4   Harding and Wright, *London Bridge.*
5   Sharpe, 'London Letter Book L'.
6   Stow, *Survey of London.*
7   Boorde, *A Compendious Regiment.*
8   www.hamptoncourt.com
9   *Calendar of the Cecil Papers*, Vol. 1, 578.
10   Essex Record Office, Q/SR 170/57.
11   Goodman, *How to Be a Tudor.*
12   Erasmus, *In Praise of Folly.*

Death and Decay

1   *Hamlet*, Shakespeare.
2   SLP, Henry VIII (May 1538) 995.
3   *Ibid.* (June 1537) 77.
4   CSP (April 1553) 28.
5   *Customs of Rye and Hereford.*

SOUND

Music

1   *Trevelyan Family Papers.*
2   *Ibid.*
3   Stow, *Survey of London.*
4   Bathe, William, *A Brief Introduction to the Skill of Song* (1596).
5   *Ibid.*

Measuring and Warning

1   Tusser, *The Book of Husbandrie.*
2   Harrison, *The Description of England.*

Proclaiming News

1   Sharpe, fo. 234b.
2   SLP, Henry VIII (1537) 6.
3   *Calendar of the Cecil Papers*, Vol. 1, 460.
4   Collier, John Payne, *The Egerton Papers* (Camden Society, 1840).
5   Essex Record Office, T/A 428/1/1.
6   *Ibid.*
7   *Ibid.*, Q/SR 113/36.

Gossip and Sedition

1   Anon., *The Hundred Merry Tales* (1526).
2   Tusser, *The Book of Husbandrie.*
3   SLP, Henry VIII, 1529.
4   *Ibid.* (August 1535) 136.
5   *Ibid.* (1537) 62.
6   *Ibid.*, 125.
7   *Ibid.*, 126.
8   SLP, Henry VIII (January 1536) 33.
9   *Calendar of the Cecil Papers*, Vol. 1, 801.
10   *Ibid.*
11   *Ibid.*, 968.
12   Essex Record Office, Q/SR 104/59a.
13   *Ibid.*, Q/SR 104/59.
14   *Ibid.*, QJF 22/½5.

Domestic Sounds

1   John Dee, *Private Diary.*
2   Bradford, John, *The Copye of a letter, Sent by Iohn Bradforth to ... the Erles of Arundel, Darbie, Shrewsburye, and Penbroke, Declaring the Nature of the Spaniardes, and Discovering the Most Detestable Treasons, Which Thei Haue Pretended ... agaynste ... Englande* (Lambrecht, 1556).
3   SLP, Henry VIII (1531) 65.

TASTE

Dining Habits

1   www.hamptoncourt.com
2   Morison, Fynes, *Itinerary* (1617).
3   SLP, Henry VIII (1526).
4   Sim, Alison, *The Tudor Housewife* (Sutton, 1996).
5   Harrison, *The Description of England.*
6   Erasmus, Desiderius, *De Civilitate Morum Puerilium* [*A Handbook of Good Manners for Children*] (1530).
7   *Schoole of Good Vertue and Booke of Nurture for Children* (date unknown)
8   Harrison, *The Description of England.*
9   Morison.
10 SLP, Henry VIII, miscellaneous, 1535.

On the Menu

1   Vives, *Tudor School Boy Life.*
2   *The Book of Kervynge* (1508).
3   *Ibid.*
4   *A Proper New Book of Cookery* (1545).
5   *Ibid.*
6   SLP, Henry VIII (October 1518).
7   *Ibid.*
8   CSP, Venice (June 1520) 94.
9   *Ibid.*
10 *Ibid.*
11 SLP, Henry VIII (July 1520) 919.
12 SLP, Henry VIII, Vol. 6.
13 *The Northumberland Household Book* (1770).
14 *Rutland Papers.*
15 *Calendar of the Cecil Papers*, Vol. 2 (1582).
16 Morison, *Itinerary.*
17 Crosby, *Accounts and Papers Relating to Mary, Queen of Scots* (Camden Old Series, 1867).
18 *Close Rolls*, Henry VII, Vol. 2, 389.
19 SLP, Henry VIII (October 1535) 523.
20 *Ibid.*, 597.
21 *Ibid.*, (December 1535) 934.
22 Tusser, *The Book of Husbandrie.*
23 SLP, Henry VIII (September 1546) 2.

Specific Foods

1   Boorde, *A Compendious Regiment.*
2   Sharpe, 'London Letter Book L'.
3   Hentzner, *Itinerarium.*

4   Boorde, *A Compendious Regimenth*.
5   *Ibid.*
6   *Ibid.*
7   *Ibid.*
8   *Ibid.*
9   *Ibid.*
10   Harrison, *The Description of England*.
11   SLP, Henry VIII (1535); miscellaneous 1149.
12   Sharpe, 'London Letter Book L'.
13   *Ibid.*
14   *Ibid.*
15   *Ibid.*
16   Harrison, *The Description of England*.
17   *Ibid.*
18   *Calendar of the Cecil Papers*, Vol. 2, 1578.

Drink

1   Ross, E. Denison (ed.), *Sir Anthony Shurley and His Persian Adventure* (Psychology Press, 2005).
2   Hart-Davis, Adam, *What the Past Did for Us* (Random House, 2011).
3   Elyot, Thomas, *Castel of Helth* (1534).
4   *Ibid.*
5   Boorde, *A Compendious Regiment*.
6   *Ibid.*
7   Burton, *The Early Tudors at Home*.
8   SLP, Henry VIII (July 1520) 919.
9   Plat, Hugh, *A Jewel House of Art and Nature* (publisher unknown, 1594).
10   SLP, Henry VIII (April 1536) 693.

Taste Buds

1   Pepys, MS 1047, *The Gentyllmanly Cokere*.
2   Anon., Harleian MS 5401.
3   *A Proper New Book of Cookery*.
4   Partridge, *Treasury*.
5   Dawson, Thomas, *The Good Housewife's Jewell* (1596).
6   Holinshed, *Raphael Holinshed's Chronicle* (1577).
7   Cogan, Thomas, *Haven of Health* (1589).
8   SLP, Henry VIII (1527) 2702.
9   CSP, Venice, Vol. 1.
10   Byrne, *The Lisle Letters*.

Sweets

1   Boorde, *A Compendious Regiment*.
2   Partridge, *Treasury*.
3   *Ibid.*
4   *Ibid.*

5   *Ibid.*
6   *Ibid.*
7   Elyot, *Castel of Helth.*
8   Boorde *A Compendious Regiment.*

Eating Out

1   Anon. (previously attributed to Lydgate), 'London Lickpenny'.
2   Anon., *The World and the Child* (1522) (T.C. and E.C. Jack, 1909).
3   Shakespeare, *The Merry Wives of Windsor.*
4   Hazlitt, William Carew, *Ancient Cuisine on the British Isles.*
5   Stow, *Survey of London.*
6   *Ibid.*
7   *Ibid.*
8   Vives, *Tudor School Boy Life.*

Supply

1   SLP, Henry VIII (1535) 122.
2   *Ibid.*, 266.
3   *Calendar of the Cecil Papers*, Vol. 2, 1.
4   *Ibid.*, 183.
5   SLP, Henry VIII (1524) 309.
6   SLP, Henry VIII, 37.
7   SLP, Henry VIII (January 1545) 63.
8   *Calendar of the Cecil Papers*, Vol. 1, 981.
9   *Ibid.*, Vol. 2, 186.
10 SLP, Henry VIII (1545) 532.
11 *Ibid.* (1546) 22.
12 *Ibid.* (1520).
13 *Ibid.* (1529) 5967.
14 Byrne, *The Lisle Letters.*
15 Baldwin, *A New History of London.*
16 *Calendar of the Cecil Papers*, Vol. 2, 1265.
17 Harrison, *The Description of England.*
18 SLP, Henry VIII (1527) 2955.
19 *Ibid.* (August 1535) 43.
20 Nicolas, *Privy Purse Expenses of Elizabeth of York* (William Pickering, 1830).
21 *Ibid.*
22 *Calendar of the Cecil Papers*, Vol. 2, 1578.

Dangerous Foods

1   *Calendar of the Cecil Papers*, Vol. 1, 1184.
2   *Ibid.*, Vol. 2, 357.

TOUCH

The Humours in Balance

1   Elyot, *Castel of Helth*.
2   *Ibid.*
3   *Ibid.*
4   *Ibid.*
5   *Ibid.*
6   *Ibid.*
7   *Ibid.*
8   *Ibid.*
9   *Ibid.*
10   *Ibid.*
11   Partridge, *Treasury*.
12   *Ibid.*
13   SLP, Henry VIII (August 1514).
14   *Ibid.*

Plague and Sweat

1   Hall, *Chronicle*.
2   SLP, Henry VIII (1528).
3   *Ibid.*
4   Nichols, *Diary of Henry Machyn*.
5   *Calendar of the Cecil Papers*, Vol 1.
6   Bush, Henry (ed.), *Bristol Town Duties* (1828).
7   *Customs of Rye and Hereford*.
8   SLP, Henry VIII, Vol. 8, appendix to preface.
9   *Ibid.*

Pain and Suffering

1   Elyot, *Castel of Helth*.
2   *Ibid.*
3   Byrne, *The Lisle Letters*.
4   Leland, *The Itinerary of John Leland*.
5   *Calendar of the Cecil Papers*, Vol. 2, 460.
6   *Ibid.*, 1182.
7   *Ibid.*, Vol. 3, 273.
8   Bayly, Walter, *A Brief Discourse of Certain Baths of Medicinal Virtues* (1587).
9   Bacon, Roger, *Letter on the Secret Workings of Art and Nature and on the Vanity of Magic* (reissued Robert Wyer, 1550).
10   Elyot, *Castel of Helth*.
11   Moulton, *This is the Mirror*.
12   *Ibid.*
13   Sidney, Henry, *A Viceroy's Vindication: Sir Henry Sidney's Memoir of Service in Ireland* (Cork University Press, 2002).

14 *Calendar of the Cecil Papers*, Vol. 1, 1382.
15 *Ibid.*, 1440.
16 *Ibid.*
17 *Ibid.*, 1471.
18 Elyot, *Castel of Helth*.
19 *Ibid.*
20 Bacon.
21 Banister, John, *A Needful, New and Necessary Treatise of Chyrurgerie* (1575).
22 Sharpe, fo. 320.
23 Essex Record Office, 22/½0.
24 Essex Record Office, QJF 25/2/1.

Sex, Pregnancy and Birth

1   Elyot, *Castel of Helth*.
2   *Ibid.*
3   *Ibid.*
4   Barrough, John, *The Method of Physicke* (1590).
5   Anon., *Jacob's Well* (date unknown).
6   Anon., *Book of Vices and Virtues* (date unknown).
7   *Ibid.*
8   Anon., *Sidrak and Bokkus* (date unknown).
9   *Calendar of Foreign Papers*, Elizabeth (January 1559).
10 Essex Record Office, BA 1/¼0/1.
11 More detail in Licence, Amy, *In Bed with the Tudors* (Amberley, 2012).

Violence

1   *Customs of Rye and Hereford*.
2   Essex Record Office, QJF 19/2/28.
3   Ibid., Q/SR 8¼7.
4   *Wriothesley's Chronicle*.
5   Custom of Bristol papers.
6   *Calendar of the Cecil Papers*, Vol. 2, 1185.
7   Essex Record Office, R/QS 100/60.

Imprisonment

1   Hall, *Chronicle*.
2   *Elizabeth I: Collected Works* edited by L.S. Marcus, J. Mueller and M. Rose (University of Chicago Press, 2000).
3   *Ibid.*
4   *Ibid.*
5   SLP, Henry VIII (1533), Vol. 6, miscellaneous.
6   *Calendar of the Cecil Papers*, Vol. 1, 1614.
7   SLP, Henry VIII (1535) 431.
8   *Ibid.*, 772.
9   *Ibid.*, 1115.

10 Essex Record Office, QJF 27/2/48.
11 *Ibid.*, T/A 428/1/52.

Poverty

1 *Reginae Elizabethae Anno 43*, Chapter 2.
2 Harrison, *The Description of England.*
3 Awdelay, John, *The Fraternity of Vagabonds* (1575).
4 CSP, Spain, Vol. 1, 1508.
5 SLP, Henry VIII (1535), 451.
6 *Ibid.* (September 1535), 459.
7 *Ibid.* (August 1535), 36.
8 *Ibid.*
9 *Ibid.*
10 *Worcestershire Quarter Sessions*, edited by Brodie Waddell, QJF 24/2/1.
11 *Ibid.*, 24/3/22.
12 *Ibid.*, BA 1/1/3/59.
13 *Ibid.*, BA 1/1/16/29.
14 *Ibid.*, QJF 29/3/21.

Weather

1 Dee, *Private Diary.*
2 *Documents Illustrating the History of St Paul's Cathedral*, XXVI, 1140–1712 (Camden New Series).
3 *Gawdy Family Papers*, unpublished, British Library. Add Ch 53512-18; Add MSS 27395-99, 36989-90; Egerton MSS 2713-22.
4 SLP, Henry VIII (1535) 384.
5 *Ibid.* (April 1530).
6 *Calendar of the Cecil Papers*, Vol. 1, 566.
7 *Ibid.*, 602.
8 *Ibid.*, 961.
9 *Gawdy Family Papers.*
10 *Customs of Rye and Hereford.*
11 Stow, *Survey of London.*
12 Harrison, *The Description of England.*

The Farmer's Cycle

1 Harrison, *The Description of England.*
2 Tusser, *The Book of Husbandrie.*
3 *Ibid.*
4 *Worcestershire Quarter Sessions*, D/DT T16/2.
5 *Ibid.*, Q/SR 59/6.
6 *Ibid.*, Q/SR 73/72.
7 Vaughan, William, *Golden Grove* (1600).
8 Averell, William, *A Marvellous Combat of Contrarieties Malignantly Striving in the Members of Man's Body* (1588).
9 *Ibid.*
10 *Ibid.*

Sport and Games

1   SLP, Henry VIII (September 1535) 422.
2   Berners, Juliana, *Hunting and Hawking* (1596).
3   Blundeville, Thomas, *The Four Chiefest Offices Belonging to Horsemanship* (1566).
4   Ascham, Roger, *Toxophilus* (1545).
5   *Calendar of the Cecil Papers*, Vol. 2, 225.
6   Barwick, Humfrey, *A Brief Discourse, Concerning the Force and Effect of All Manual Weapons of Fire* (1592).
7   Elyot, *Castel of Helth*.
8   Stubbes, *Anatomy of Abuses*.

SELECT BIBLIOGRAPHY

Anglo, Sydney, *Images of Tudor Kingship* (Seaby, 1992).

Anon., *A Pleasant Dialogue or Disputation between the Cap and the Head* (1565).

Anon., *The Hundred Merry Tales* (1526).

Ashelford, Jane, *The Art of Dress: Clothes Through History, 1500–1914* (National Trust, 1996).

Averell, William, *A Marvellous Combat of Contrarieties Malignantly Striving in the Members of Man's Body* (1588).

Baldwin, R., *A New History of London, Including Westminster and Southwark* (1773).

Banister, John, *A Needful, New and Necessary Treatise of Chyrurgerie* (1575)

Bathe, William, *A Brief Introduction to the Skill of Song* (1596).

Bennett, Judith M., and McSheffrey, Shannon, 'Early, Erotic and Alien: Women Dressed as Men in Late Medieval London', *History Workshop Journal*, Volume 77, Issue 1, Spring 2014, pp. 1–25

Bernard, George W., 'The Dissolution of the Monasteries', *History*, Vol. 96, Issue 324, 2011, p. 390.

Bogaert, Arnold, *A Prognostication for Divers Years ...* (John Cook, 1553).

Boorde, Andrew, *Dietary of Helthe* (1542).

Boorde, Andrew, *Principles of Astronomy* (1547).

Bradford, John, *The Copye of a Letter, Sent by Iohn Bradforth to ... the Erles of Arundel, Darbie, Shrewsburye, and Penbroke, Declaring the Nature of the Spaniardes, and Discovering the Most Detestable Treasons, Which Thei Haue Pretended ... Agaynste ... Englande* (Lambrecht, 1556).

Bruce, John and Crosby, Alan J. (eds), *Accounts and Papers Relating to Mary, Queen of Scots* (Camden Society, 1867).

Bullough, Vern L. and Bullough, Bonnie, *Cross-Dressing, Sex and Gender* (University of Pennsylvania Press, 1993).

Burton, Elizabeth, *The Early Tudors at Home* (Allen Lane, 1976).

Bush, Henry (ed.), *Bristol Town Duties* (1828).

Byrne, Muriel St Clare, *The Lisle Letters* (Penguin, 1981).

Calendar of the Cecil Papers in Hatfield House, Vols 1–3 (HMSO, 1883).

Calendar of Foreign Papers, Edward, Mary and Elizabeth, Vol. 1 (1559), edited by Robert Lemon (HMSO, 1856).

Calendar of State Papers, Spain, Vols 1 and 2, edited by G.A. Bergenroth (HMSO, 1862).

Calendar of State Papers, Venice, Vols 1–6, edited by Rawdon Brown (HMSO, 1873).

Cartwright, Kent, *A Companion to Tudor Literature* (John Wiley, 2010).

Chute, Anthony, *Tabaco* (William Barlowe, 1595).

Close Rolls, Henry VII, Vols 1 and 2.

Collier, John Payne, *The Egerton Papers* (Camden Society, 1840).

Cox, Noel, 'Tudor Sumptuary Laws and Academic Dress: An Act against Wearing of Costly Apparel in 1509 and an Act for Reformation of Excess in Apparel in 1533', *Transactions of the Burgon Society*, Vol, 6 (2006), Article 2 (New Prairie Press, 2016).

Cressy, David, *Agnes Bowker's Cat: Travesties and Transgressions in Tudor and Stuart England* (Oxford University Press, 2001).

Cressy, David, *Literacy and the Social Order: Reading and Writing in Tudor and Stuart England* (Cambridge University Press, 1980).

Customs of Rye and Hereford, 13th Report, Appendix, part IV (HMSO London, 1892).

Dee, Dr John, *The Private Diary of John Dee* edited by J.O. Halliwell (Camden, 1842).

Documents Illustrating the History of St Paul's Cathedral, XXVI, 1140–1712 (Camden New Series).

Egerton Manuscripts (British Museum).

Elizabeth I: Collected Works edited by L.S. Marcus, J. Mueller and M. Rose (University of Chicago Press, 2000).

Elyot, Thomas, *Castel of Helth* (1534).

Emmison, F.G., *Elizabethan Life* (Essex Record Office, 1976).

Erasmus, Desiderius, *De Civilitate Morum Puerilium [A Handbook of Good Manners for Children]* (1530).

Erasmus, Desiderius, *In Praise of Folly* (1511).

Ferris, Lesley (ed.), *Crossing the Stage: Controversies on Cross-Dressing* (Routledge, 2005).

Foister, Susan, *Holbein's Ambassadors: Making and Meaning* (National Gallery, 1998).

Gerard, John, *Gerard's Herbal* (1597).

Goodman, Ruth, *How to Be a Tudor: A Dawn to Dusk Guide to Everyday Life* (Penguin, 2006).

Hakluyt, Richard, *Diverse Voyages Touching the Discoverie of America* (1582).

Hall, Edward, *Chronicle* (J. Johnson, 1809).

Harding, V. and Wright, L. (eds), *London Bridge: Selected Accounts and Rentals 1381–1538* (London Record Society, 1995).

Harrison, William, *The Description of England* (1587).

Hazard, Mary E., *Elizabethan Silent Language* (University of Nebraska Press, 2000).

Hentzner, Paul, *Itinerarium* (1598).

Hervey, Mary Frederica Sophia, *Holbein's Ambassadors: The Picture and the Man* (Nabu, 2010).

Ives, Eric, *Anne Boleyn* (Blackwell, 2005).

Kassell, Lauren, *Medicine and Magic in Elizabethan London: Simon Forman, Astrologer, Alchemist and Physician* (Oxford University Press, 2001).

Keene, D.J. and Harding, Vanessa (eds), *Historical Gazetteer of London before the Great Fire* (Cheapside Centre for Metropolitan History, 1987).

Kipling, Gordon (ed.), *The Receyt of the Ladie Kateryne* (Oxford University Press, 1990).

Leland, John, *The Itinerary of John Leland in or about the Year 1535–45* edited by Lucy Toulmin Smith (George Bell, 1907).

Letters and Papers of Henry VIII, Vols 1–21, edited by J.S. Brewer (1–4), James Gairdner (5–21) R.H. Brodie (14–21).

Levens, Peter, *Pathway to Health* (1582).

Licence, Amy, *In Bed with the Tudors* (Amberley, 2012).

MacMillan, Ken, *Stories of True Crime in Tudor and Stuart England* (Routledge, 2015).

Madden, Frederick (ed.), *Privy Purse Expenses of the Princess Mary* (William Pickering, 1831).

Manchester, William, *A World Lit Only by Fire* (Sterling, 1992).

Memorials of the Guild of Merchant Taylors edited by C.M. Clode (Harrison, 1875).°

Morison, Fynes, *Itinerary*, three vols (1617).

Moulton, Thomas, *This Is the Mirror or Glasse of Health* (1545).

Nashe, Thomas, *Christs Teares over Jerusalem* (1593).

Nichols J.G. (ed.), *A Collection of Ordinances and Regulations for the Government of the Royal Household Made in Divers Reigns...* (Society of Antiquities, 1790).

Nichols, J.G. (ed.), *Chronicle of the Greyfriars* (Camden, 1852).

Nichols, J.G. (ed.), *Inventories of the Wardrobe, Plate, Chapel Stuff Etc of Henry Fitzroy, Duke of Richmond, and of the Stuff at Baynard's Castle of Katherine, Princess Dowager* (Camden Society, 1855).

Nichols, J.G. (ed.), *London Pageants 1: An Account of Sixty Royal Processions and Entertainments in the City of London* (J.B. Nichols and Son, 1831).

Nichols, J.G. (ed.), *The Diary of Henry Machyn* (Camden, 1868).

Nichols, Robert E. Jnr, 'Procreation, Pregnancy and Parturition: Extracts from a Middle English Metrical' in *Medical History Journal*, Vol. 11, Issue 2, April 1967.

Nicolas, Nicholas Harris, *Privy Purse Expenses of Elizabeth of York* (William Pickering, 1830).

Nicolas, Nicholas Harris, *Privy Purse Expenses of Henry VIII 1533* (Camden, 1827).

Niebrzydowski, Sue, *Bonoure and Buxom: A Study of Wives in Late Medieval Literature* (Peter Land, 2006).

Partridge, John, *Treasury of Commodious Conceits and Hidden Secrets* (1573).

Plat, Hugh, *A Jewel House of Art and Nature* (1594).

Rappaport, Stephen, *Worlds within Worlds: Structures of Life in Sixteenth Century London* (Cambridge University Press, 2002).

Riddell, Jessica Erin, *'A Mirror of Men': Sovereignty, Performance and Textuality in Tudor England 1501–1559* (unpublished PhD, Queens University, Canada, 2009).

Riello, Giorgio and Rublack, Ulinka (eds), *The Right to Dress: Sumptuary Law in a Global Perspective* (Cambridge University Press, 2019).

Rutland Papers: Original Documents Illustrative of the Courts and Times of Henry VII and Henry VIII edited by John Manners and William Jerdan (Camden Society, 1842).

Sanders, Nicholas, *De Origine ep Progressu Schismatis Anglicani* (1585).

Scott, A.F., *Everyone a Witness: The Tudor Age* (Scott and Finlay, 1975).

Shapiro, Michael, *Gender in Play on the Shakespearean Stage: Boy Heroines and Female Pages* (University of Michigan Press, 1996).

Sharpe, Reginald (ed.), 'London Letter Book L' in *The Calendar of Letter Books of the City of London* (HMSO, 1912).

Sim, Alison, *The Tudor Housewife* (Sutton, 1996).

Skidmore, Christopher, *Edward VI: The Lost King of England* (Weidenfeld and Nicolson, 2008).

Sneyd, Charlotte Augusta, *A Relation, or Rather a True Account, of the Island of England: With Sundry Particulars of the Customs of These People and of the Royal Revenue under King Henry VII, Around the Year 1500* (Camden Society, 1884).

Stow, John, *The Survey of London* (Everyman, 1912).

Stubbes, Philip, *Anatomy of Abuses* (1583).

Tanner, J.R., *Tudor Constitutional Documents* (Cambridge University Press, 1922).

Tillyard, E.M.W., *The Elizabethan World Picture* (Routledge, 2017).

Trevelyan Family Papers (Camden Society, 1853).

Tusser, Thomas, *The Book of Husbandrie* (1577).

Vergil, Polydore, *History of England* (Camden Society, 1846).

Vives, Juan Luis, *Tudor School Boy Life* (Frank Cass and Company, 1908).

Wagner, Anne and Sherwin, Richard K., *Law, Culture and Visual Studies* (Springer, 2013).

Warnicke, Retha M., *The Marrying of Anne of Cleves: Royal Protocol in Tudor England* (Cambridge University Press, 2000).

Williams, C.H. (ed.), *English Historical Documents 1485–1558* (Routledge, 1997).

Wilson, Derek, *Hans Holbein: Portrait of an Unknown Man* (Pimlico, 2006).

Wriothesley's Chronicle Volume 2 edited by William Douglas Hamilton (Camden, 1877).

Württemberg, F., *The Journal of Frederick, Duke of Württemberg* (1592).

ACKNOWLEDGEMENTS

Many thanks go to Mark Beynon, Jezz Palmer, Martin Latham, Jemma Cox, Jess Gofton and the team at The History Press. Thank you to Rufus and Robin, my two wonderful sons, my mother, Susan, and my godmother, Susan, for their constant support. A huge thank you to my dear friends, Anne Marie, Sharon, Paul, Anna, Kat, Tony, Harry, Georgina and Kristie for keeping me sane.

Thank you to my wonderful online friends, from the history community and beyond, and to everyone who has supported and promoted me. Adrienne, Alec, Alexandra, Andy, Angelina, Caroline, Catherine, Connie, Cynthia, Emily, Erika, Geanine, Gilbert, Gina, Heather, Heidi, Helen, Jacquie, Jane, Jayne, Jenny, Joan, Jo Anne, Judith, Karen, Lisa, Lorna, Lynn, Marcus, Marsha, Meghan, Melanie, Mike, Molly, Morag, Naomi, Nathen, Owen, Paul, Pip, Rachel, Sally, Samantha, Sarah, Sheila, Stuart and Susan; I see your regular likes and comments, and I thank you from the bottom of my heart.

Finally, a huge thank you to all my readers, whose kind words have reached me and provided such comfort and encouragement.

INDEX